QuickBooks® 2012
The Official Guide

For QuickBooks
Pro® Users

About the Author

Leslie Capachietti, MBA, is the founder and Principal of Automated Financial Solutions, a financial systems consulting firm that specializes in helping small businesses get the most from their QuickBooks software. She is a nationally recognized QuickBooks expert, author, and speaker, and has trained thousands of fellow accountants on how to better serve their QuickBooks clients. She received her MBA degree from Boston University.

About the Technical Editor

Thomas E. Barich, QuickBooks expert and author, has been working with QuickBooks for more than a decade. In addition to using it to maintain his own books, he provides QuickBooks consulting services to small business clients. He is the author of *QuickBooks 2010 QuickSteps*.

QuickBooks® 2012
The Official Guide

For QuickBooks Pro® Users

LESLIE CAPACHIETTI

New York Chicago San Francisco
Lisbon London Madrid Mexico City Milan
New Delhi San Juan Seoul Singapore Sydney Toronto

The *McGraw·Hill* Companies

Cataloging-in-Publication Data is on file with the Library of Congress

McGraw-Hill books are available at special quantity discounts to use as premiums and sales promotions, or for use in corporate training programs. To contact a representative, please e-mail us at bulksales@mcgraw-hill.com.

QuickBooks® 2012 The Official Guide for QuickBooks Pro® Users

1 2 3 4 5 6 7 8 9 0   DOC DOC   1 0 9 8 7 6 5 4 3 2 1

ISBN   978-0-07-177621-9
MHID   0-07-177621-4

Sponsoring Editor
Megg Morin

Editorial Supervisor
Patty Mon

Project Editor
LeeAnn Pickrell

Technical Editors
Thomas E. Barich,
Real World Training

Copy Editor
Sally Engelfried

Proofreader
Susie Elkind

Indexer
Rebecca Plunkett

Production Supervisor
George Anderson

Composition
Cenveo Publisher Services

Illustration
Cenveo Publisher Services

Art Director, Cover
Jeff Weeks

To all the small business owners who
I've had the privilege to know.

Contents at a Glance

Part One
Getting Started

1 • Using QuickBooks for the First Time 1
2 • The Chart of Accounts 23
3 • Entering Your Customers 41
4 • Entering Your Vendors 69
5 • Creating Items 87
6 • Setting Up Inventory 103
7 • Creating Other Lists You Need 121
8 • Entering Your Starting Balances 135

Part Two
Daily Operations Using QuickBooks

9 • Invoicing Customers 145
10 • Receiving and Tracking Customer Payments 179
11 • Managing Vendor Bills 221
12 • Paying Vendors 243
13 • Working with Bank and Credit Card Accounts 259
14 • Reconciling Bank Accounts 275

15 • Using Online Banking Services 291
16 • Tracking Time and Mileage 311
17 • Running Payroll 331
18 • Payroll Reports and Liability Payments 363
19 • Journal Entries 383

Part Three
Financial Planning and Reporting

20 • Accountant's Copy 397
21 • Creating Reports and Analyzing Your QuickBooks Information . . . 407
22 • Customizing Reports 423
23 • Budgets and Planning Tools 439
24 • Year-End Procedures 459

Part Four
Managing QuickBooks

25 • Printing, E-mailing, and Managing Documents in QuickBooks . . . 475
26 • Managing Users and Permissions 493
27 • Managing Your QuickBooks Files 505
28 • Customizing QuickBooks 527

Part Five
Appendixes

A • Installing QuickBooks on a Network 561
B • Multiple Currencies 571

• Index 583

Contents

Acknowledgments . . . .   *xxix*

Introduction . . . .   *xxxi*

Part One

Getting Started

Chapter 1 • Using QuickBooks for the First Time   1

What to Do Ahead of Time   2

Deciding on the Start Date   2

Gathering the Information You Need   3

Cash Balances   3

Customer Balances   4

Vendor Balances   4

Asset Balances   4

Liability Balances   4

Payroll Information   5

Inventory Information   5

Other Useful Information to Have Available   5

Installing and Launching the Software   5

Creating Your Company File   7

Using Express Start   8

Using Advanced Setup   9

The QuickBooks Setup Wizard   13

Navigate in QuickBooks 14
    Home Page 14
    QuickBooks Centers 15
Customizing the Icon Bar 18
    Changing the Order of Icons 18
    Changing the Icon Bar Display 19
    Removing an Icon 19
    Adding an Icon 19
The Favorites Menu 21
Closing QuickBooks 21

Chapter 2 • The Chart of Accounts 23
The Accounts that QuickBooks Uses 24
    Assets 24
    Liabilities 24
    Equity 24
    Income 25
    Expenses 25
Using Numbered Accounts 26
    Enabling Account Numbers 26
    Creating a Numbering Scheme 28
    Creating Ranges of Numbers 29
Naming Accounts 30
Creating Accounts 30
    Select From Examples 31
    Optional Fields for Accounts 33
Using Subaccounts 35
    Viewing Subaccounts 35
    Creating Subaccounts 36
    Multiple Levels of Subaccounts 36
    Showing Lowest Subaccounts Only 37
Editing Accounts 37
Deleting Accounts 38
Making Accounts Inactive (Hiding Accounts) 38
Merging Accounts 39

Chapter 3 • Entering Your Customers 41
    Building Your Customer List 42
        Address Info Tab 42
        Additional Info Tab 45
        Payment Info Tab 48
        Job Info Tab 49
        Adding Multiple Customer Records 50
    The Customer Center 52
        Customizing the Customers & Jobs List 53
        Customizing the Customer Information Pane 54
        Editing an Individual Customer Record 55
    Using Jobs 56
        Creating Jobs 57
        Editing Jobs 60
    Deleting Customers & Jobs 60
        Making Customers & Jobs Inactive (Hiding) 60
        Merging Customers or Jobs 62
    Using Custom Fields 62
        Adding a Custom Field for Names 63
        Adding Data to Custom Fields 63
    Securing Customer Credit Card Information 64
        More About QuickBooks Customer
            Credit Card Protection 66
        About Complex Passwords 66
        User Permissions for Viewing Credit Card Information . . . 67
        Viewing the Security Log 68

Chapter 4 • Entering Your Vendors 69
    Creating Your Vendors List 70
        Currency 70
        Vendor Address Info Tab 70
        Establishing Rules for Naming Your Vendors 71
        Vendor Additional Info Tab 72
        Account Prefill Tab 73
        Adding and Editing Multiple Vendor Records 74

The Vendor Center 76
    Customizing the Vendor Center 77
Editing Vendor Information 79
Deleting a Vendor 81
Making a Vendor Inactive (Hiding a Vendor) 82
Merging Vendors 82
Using Custom Fields in Vendor Records 83
    Adding a Custom Field for Vendors 83
    Adding Data to Custom Fields 83
Creating 1099 Vendors 85
    Configuring 1099 Options 85
    Marking Vendors as 1099 Recipients 86

Chapter 5 • Creating Items 87
Understanding How Items Are Used 88
Understanding Item Types 89
Building Your Item List 90
    How to Create a Service Item 90
Creating Custom Fields for Items 92
    Creating the Other Items in Your Item List 93
    Changing Item Prices 96
Collecting Sales Tax Using Sales Tax Items 97
    Sales Tax Items 97
    Sales Tax Codes 99
    Sales Tax Payment Basis 99
    Sales Tax Payment Dates 100
Creating and Using Tax Groups 100
    Assigning Sales Tax Codes and Items to Customers 101

Chapter 6 • Setting Up Inventory 103
What Is an Inventory Item? 104
Setting Up QuickBooks for Inventory Tracking 104
    Accounts Required for Inventory Are
    Automatically Created 106
Creating Inventory Items 106

Using Subitems 108
    Creating the Parent Item for a Subitem 108
    Creating Subitems 109
Counting Inventory 110
    Printing the Physical Inventory Worksheet 110
    Planning the Physical Count 112
    Making Inventory Adjustments 112
    Understanding the Effects of an Adjustment 116
    About the Inventory Adjustment Account 116
    Making Other Adjustments to Inventory 117
Running Inventory Reports 117
    Inventory Valuation Summary Report 117
    Inventory Valuation Detail Report 118
    Inventory Stock Status 118
    Physical Inventory Worksheet 119
    Pending Builds 119
    Inventory QuickReports 119

Chapter 7 • Creating Other Lists You Need 121
Fixed Asset Item List 122
Price Level List 123
    Creating a Price Level 124
    Linking Price Levels to Customers 124
Currency List 125
Class List 126
    Creating a Class 126
Other Names List 127
Customer & Vendor Profile Lists 128
    Sales Rep List 129
    Customer Type List 129
    Vendor Type List 129
    Job Type List 130
    Terms List 130
    Customer Message List 131

Payment Method List 131
Ship Via List 132
Vehicle List 132
Memorized Transaction List 133

Chapter 8 • Entering Your Starting Balances 135
What Is an Opening Trial Balance? 136
Ten Steps to Creating an Accurate Opening Trial Balance 137
    1. Gather All the Information You Need 137
    2. Enter Beginning Balances for Simple
       Balance Sheet Accounts 137
    3. Enter Bank Account Balances 139
    4. Enter Outstanding Checks and Deposits 139
    5. Enter Unpaid Accounts Receivable and
       Accounts Payable Transactions 139
    6. Enter Nonposting Transactions 140
    7. Enter Mid-year Income and Expenses (if Applicable) . . . 140
    8. Adjust Sales Tax Payable 141
    9. Establish Inventory Balances 141
    10. Zero Out the Opening Balance Equity Account 143
Run Your QuickBooks Trial Balance Report as of Your Start Date . . . 143

Part Two
Daily Operations Using QuickBooks

Chapter 9 • Invoicing Customers 145
Creating Invoices 146
    Entering Header Information 147
    Entering Line Items 150
    Applying Price Levels 150
    Entering Discounts 151
    Entering Subtotals 152
    Checking the Footer Section 152
    Saving the Invoice 154
Printing Packing Slips 154
    Printing the Default Packing Slip 154

Batch Invoicing 156

Using Memorized Invoices 158

Editing Invoices 159

Voiding and Deleting Invoices 159

Issuing Credits and Refunds 160

    Creating a Credit Memo Against an Invoice 160

    Creating a Credit Memo Without a Previous Invoice 161

    Applying Credit Memos 162

Using Estimates 164

    Creating an Estimate 164

    Creating Multiple Estimates for a Job 166

    Duplicating Estimates 166

    Memorizing Estimates 166

Creating Progress Billing Invoices 167

    Choosing the Estimated Job 167

    Entering Progress Invoice Line Items 168

    Changing Line Items 168

Invoicing Customers for Reimbursable Expenses 170

    Configuring Reimbursement Settings 171

    Creating a Transaction for Reimbursable Expenses 172

    Adding Reimbursable Costs to the Sales Transaction 173

Chapter 10 • Receiving and Tracking Customer Payments . . . . • 179

Receiving Invoice Payments 180

    Setting Default Options for Receiving
       Customer Payments 180

    Recording Invoice Payments 181

    Calculating the Payment 182

    Applying Payments to Invoices 183

    Handling Underpayments 184

    Applying Credits to Invoices 185

    Applying Discounts for Timely Payments 187

    Applying Discounts for Untimely Payments 189

    Posting Discounts 189

    Turning Payments into Bank Deposits 189

    Printing a Receipt for an Invoice Payment 190

Handling Cash Sales 191
    Entering Cash Sale Data 192
    Printing a Receipt for a Cash Sale 193
    Customizing the Cash Receipts Template 193
    Handling Batches of Cash Sales 193
Tracking Your Cash Drawer in QuickBooks 194
    Handling the Over and Short Problem 195
Making Bank Deposits 196
    Choosing the Payments to Deposit 196
    Working in the Make Deposits Window 199
    Printing Deposit Slips 201
Tracking Accounts Receivable 201
    Getting the Most from the Customer Center 201
    The Collections Center 202
    Other Reports You Can Run from the Customer Center ... 203
Running A/R Aging Reports 203
    A/R Aging Summary Reports 204
    A/R Aging Detail Reports 204
    Customizing Aging Reports 205
    Memorizing Aging Reports 209
    Printing Reports 209
Running Customer and Job Reports 210
    Assessing Finance Charges 210
Sending Statements 215
    Entering Statement Charges 215
    Creating Statements 217
    Previewing the Statements 220
    Printing the Statements 220
    Customizing Statements 220

Chapter 11 • Managing Vendor Bills 221
Recording Vendor Bills 222
    Filling in the Details 224
    Splitting Expenses Among Multiple Accounts 225

Using Purchase Orders 226
  Creating a Purchase Order 226
  Using the Manufacturer's Part Number
    in Purchase Orders 227
Managing Inventory Item Purchases 229
  Receiving Inventory Items Without a Bill 229
  Recording Bills for Items Already Received 232
  Receiving Items and Bills Simultaneously 233
Recording Vendor Credits 233
Entering Recurring Bills 235
  Creating a Memorized Bill 235
  Using a Memorized Bill 236
  Creating Memorized Bill Groups 236
  Adding Memorized Bills to Groups 236
Reimbursable Expenses 237
  Options for Managing Reimbursable Expenses 237
  Configuring Reimbursement Tracking 238
  Recording Reimbursable Expenses 241

Chapter 12 • Paying Vendors 243
Choosing What to Pay 244
  Viewing Your Unpaid Bills 244
  Selecting the Bills to Pay 246
  Paying Bills in Full 248
  Making Partial Payments 248
  Using Discounts and Credits 248
  Applying Credits 250
  Sending the Payments 251
  Check Writing Without Entering a Bill 252
  Manual Checks 252
  Printing Checks in a Batch 254
Remitting Sales Tax 254
  QuickBooks' Manage Sales Tax Feature 255
  Running Sales Tax Reports 255
  Paying the Sales Tax 257
  Adjusting Sales Tax Amounts 258

Chapter 13 • Working with Bank and Credit Card Accounts . . . . • 259
    Depositing Money That Isn't from Customers 260
        Using the Account Register for Deposits 260
        Using the Make Deposits Window 261
        Assigning a Payee to a Noncustomer Deposit 261
        Assigning Accounts to Noncustomer Deposits 263
    Transferring Funds Between Accounts 263
        Using the Transfer Funds Transaction Window 264
    Handling a Bounced Check 265
        Creating an Item NSF Check 265
        Creating an Item for Your NSF Charge to Your Customer . . . 265
        Creating an Invoice to Recover the Amounts Owed 266
        Recording Your Bank's NSF Charge to You 267
    Voiding Disbursements 267
    Tracking Cash Disbursements 268
        Tracking Petty Cash 269
        Recording Petty Cash Disbursements 269
        Tracking Other Cash Withdrawals 270
    Managing Credit Card Transactions 271
        Create a Credit Card Account 271
        Treat the Credit Card as a Bill 273

Chapter 14 • Reconciling Bank Accounts 275
    Reconciling in QuickBooks 276
        The Begin Reconciliation Window 276
        Enter Interest Income and Service Charges 277
        Configuring the Reconcile Window 277
        Clearing Transactions 279
        Adding Transactions During Reconciliation 279
        Adding Undeposited Funds During Reconciliation 280
        Deleting Transactions During Reconciliation 280
        Editing Transactions During Reconciliation 280
        Resolving Missing Check Numbers 281
        Finishing the Reconciliation 282
        Printing the Reconciliation Report 282
        Viewing the Last Reconciliation Report 284

If You Don't Balance 284
    Finding and Correcting Problems 284
    Permitting an Adjusting Entry 285
    Correcting Opening Balance Differences 288
    Undoing the Last Reconciliation 289
    Giving Up the Search for a Reason 290

Chapter 15 • Using Online Banking Services 291
If You Don't Balance
Understanding Online Banking 292
Setting Up Online Banking 293
    Finding Your Bank Online 293
    Enabling Online Access for Direct Connect 296
    Enabling Online Access for Web Connect 298
Using the Online Banking Center 301
    Downloading Transactions 302
    Viewing the Downloaded Transactions 302
Matching Transactions 302
    Adding Transactions to the Bank Register 304
    Deleting Unmatched Transactions 307
Using QuickBooks to Pay Your Bills Online 308
    Using the QuickBooks Bill Pay Service 308
Transferring Money Between Accounts Online 309
    Using the Transfer Funds Function 310
    Using the Bank Register to Transfer Funds 310
Receiving Customer Payments Online 310

Chapter 16 • Tracking Time and Mileage 311
Setting Up Time Tracking 312
    Configuring Timekeepers 313
    Configuring the Tasks 315
Working with Timesheets 316
    Setting the Format for Displaying Time 317
    Tracking a Single Activity 317
    Using the Stopwatch 320
    Using Weekly Timesheets 320
    Copying Previous Timesheets 322

Reporting Timesheet Information 322
    Running Timesheet Reports 322
    Editing Entries in a Report 322
    Editing the Original Timesheets 323
    Printing the Weekly Timesheets 323
Invoicing Customers for Time 324
Tracking Mileage 325
    Entering Mileage Rates 327
    Creating a Mileage Item 327
    Entering Mileage 328
    Creating Mileage Reports 329

Chapter 17 • Running Payroll 331
QuickBooks Payroll Services 332
    Direct Deposit 332
    Signing Up for Payroll Services 333
Setting Up Your Payroll 334
    Accounts 334
    Vendors 335
    Payroll Items 336
Setting Up Employees 339
    Create an Employee Template 339
    Creating Employees 341
    Understanding Employee Types 345
Entering Historical Data 346
    How to Enter Historical Data 347
    Entering Payroll History in Batches 348
Using the QuickBooks Payroll Setup Wizard 349
    Company Setup for Payroll 351
    Setting Up Employees in the Wizard 351
    Setting Up Payroll Taxes in the Wizard 352
    Entering Payroll History in the Wizard 352
    Data Review and Payroll Checkup 352
    Finishing Up 352

Payroll Schedules 353
    Creating a Payroll Schedule 354
    Assigning Payroll Schedules to Employees 354
Running Payroll 355
    Changing Paycheck Data 356
    Reviewing the Payroll Run 357
The Employee Center 359
    Employees Tab 360
    Transactions Tab 360
    Payroll Tab 360
    Customizing the Employee Center 360

Chapter 18 • Payroll Reports and Liability Payments 363
Confirming Payroll Payment Schedules 364
    Using the Scheduled vs. Unscheduled Liabilities Window . . . 365
Remitting Liabilities 365
Sending Federal Tax Payments 367
    941/943 Payments 368
    940 Payments 369
Remitting State and Local Liabilities 369
    Remitting State and Local Income Taxes 369
    Remitting Other State Liabilities 370
Remitting Other Payroll Liabilities 370
    Workers Comp 371
Preparing Your 941/943 Form 371
Creating a 941/943 Form 372
    Checking for Errors 374
    Saving and Reopening an Unfinished Form 374
Printing Form 941/943 375
    Preparing Annual Returns 376
    Preparing State and Local Annual Returns 376
    Preparing the 940 Form 376
    Preparing the 944 Form 377

Preparing W-2 Forms 377

Tax Form Worksheets in Excel 380

Setting Report Options 381

Chapter 19 • Journal Entries 383

The QuickBooks Journal Entry Window 384

Creating Journal Entries for Depreciation 387

Creating Accounts for Tracking Depreciation 387

Using Journal Entries to Post to Outside Payroll Services 389

Transferring Money to the Payroll Account 390

Recording the Payroll 390

Recording Liabilities 391

Creating Your Own Payroll Entry Template 392

Reconciling the Payroll Account 393

Part Three
Financial Planning and Reporting

Chapter 20 • Accountant's Copy 397

Understanding the Accountant's Copy 398

Creating an Accountant's Copy 398

Saving the Accountant's Copy on Removable Media 399

Sending an Accountant's Copy to the QuickBooks Server ... 400

Choosing the Dividing Date 401

Merging the Accountant's Changes into Your File 404

Canceling the Accountant's Copy 405

Chapter 21 • Creating Reports and Analyzing Your QuickBooks Information ... 407

Using the Report Center 408

Drilling Down for Details 410

Standard Financial Reports 410

Profit & Loss Report 410

Balance Sheet 411

Trial Balance 413

Cash Flow Reports 413

Other Useful Reports 415
   Sales Reports 415
   Vendor Reports 416
   Inventory and Purchasing Reports 417
   Employees & Payroll Reports 417
   Banking Reports 417
   Reporting by Class 417
   Accountant & Taxes Reports 418
   Voided and Deleted Transactions Reports 419
Company Snapshot 419
Client Data Review 420
External Accountant 421
   Creating an External Accountant 421
   Converting an Existing User to an External Accountant . . . 422

Chapter 22 • Customizing Reports 423
Customization Starts with a Built-in Report 424
Customizing Report Display Settings 425
   Selecting the Report Basis 426
   Selecting Columns 426
   Advanced Options 426
Filtering Report Data 428
Customizing Report Headers and Footers 430
Customizing Report Fonts and Numbers 431
Memorizing Customized Reports 432
   Using a Memorized Report 433
   Using Memorized Report Groups . . . . •433
   Adding Standard Reports to Memorized Reports Groups . . . 436
Sharing Reports You've Customized 436

Chapter 23 • Budgets and Planning Tools 439
How QuickBooks Handles Budgets 440
   Types of Budgets 440
   Budget Data Is Saved Automatically 440
   Creating Multiple Budgets 441

Deleting a Budget 441
Understanding the Budget Window 441
Tasks to Perform Before You Start Your Budget 442
P&L Budgets 443
Create the Budget and Its Criteria 443
Enter Budget Amounts 444
Using Budget Entry Shortcuts 444
Creating a Budget from Last Year's Data 448
Customer:Job Budgets 448
Class Budgets 450
Budget Reports 451
Budget Overview 451
Budget vs. Actual 453
Profit & Loss Budget Performances 453
Budget vs. Actual Graph 454
Exporting Budgets 454
Exporting Budgets to Delimited Text Files 454
Exporting a Budget Report to Excel 455
Importing Budgets Back into QuickBooks 455
Projecting Cash Flow 455

Chapter 24 • Year-End Procedures 459
The Year-End To Do List 460
Reconciling All Bank, Cash, and Credit Card Accounts . . . 460
Inventory Stock Status 460
Fixed Assets 461
Payroll 461
Running Year-End Financial Reports 462
Profit & Loss Reports 462
Year-End Balance Sheet 462
Issuing 1099 Forms 463
Checking the 1099 Setup 463
Using the 1099 Wizard 465
Choose a Filing Method 469
Making Year-End Journal Entries 470

Getting Ready for Taxes 470
    Check Tax Line Information 471
    Calculate Other Important Tax Information 471
    Using TurboTax 472
Closing Your Books 472
    Understanding Closing in QuickBooks 472
    Closing the Year 473
Creating a Year-End Backup 473

Part Four
Managing QuickBooks

Chapter 25 • Printing, E-mailing, and Managing Documents in QuickBooks . . . 475
Setting Up Printing 476
    Configuring Form Printing 477
    Using QuickBooks to Print Checks 479
    Printer Settings vs. Printer Options 481
Printing Checks 482
    Printing Each Check As You Create It 483
    Printing Checks in Batches 484
    Reprinting Checks After a Problem 485
Printing Transaction Forms 485
    Printing Transactions As You Create Them 485
    Previewing Form Printouts 486
    Printing Transaction Forms in Batches 486
E-mailing Forms and Reports 488
    Setting Up E-mail 488
    Sending E-mail 489
Document Management: Using the Attach Documents Feature 491

Chapter 26 • Managing Users and Permissions 493
Why User Logins Are Important 494
Understanding Passwords 494
    Creating Complex Passwords 495

The QuickBooks Admin 495
    Adding or Changing the Administrator Password 496
    Resetting the Admin Password When You Forget It 497
Adding Users 498
    Deleting a User 499
    Editing User Information 499
    Setting User Permissions 499
    Special Permissions Needed for Customer
       Credit Card Data 501
    Configuring Special Areas of QuickBooks 501
    Configuring Rights for Existing Transactions 502
    Users Can Change Their Own Passwords 503
QuickBooks Login Dialog 503

Chapter 27 • Managing Your QuickBooks Files 505
Deleting Company Files 506
    How QuickBooks Loads Company Files 506
    Deleting the File 506
    Eliminating Deleted Files from the Company File List 507
Backing Up and Restoring Files 507
    Backing Up 508
    Scheduling Backups 512
    Restoring a Backup 516
Using a Portable Company File 517
    Creating a Portable Company File 517
Verifying and Rebuilding a Company File 519
Condensing Your Data 520
    Understanding the Data Removal Procedure 520
    Running the Condense Data Utility 521
    Removing All Transactions 523
Updating QuickBooks 524
    Configuring QuickBooks Update Service 525

Chapter 28 • Customizing QuickBooks 527
Customizing Settings and Options 528
    Accounting Preferences 528
    Bills Preferences 530

Calendar Preferences 530
Checking Preferences 530
Desktop View Preferences 532
Finance Charge Preferences 534
General Preferences 534
Integrated Applications Preferences 539
Items & Inventory Preferences 539
Jobs & Estimates Preferences 540
Multiple Currencies Preferences 540
Payments Preferences 540
Payroll & Employees Preferences 542
Reminders Preferences 542
Reports & Graphs Preferences 543
Sales & Customers Preferences 546
Sales Tax Preferences 547
Search Preferences 547
Send Forms Preferences 547
Service Connection Preferences 548
Spelling Preferences 548
Tax:1099 Preferences 549
Time & Expenses Preferences 549
Customizing Transaction Templates 550
Basic Customization of Templates 551
Additional Customization of Templates 553

Part Five

Appendixes

Appendix A • Installing QuickBooks on a Network 561
License Requirements for a Multi-user Installation 562
Multi-user Installation Options 562
Installing QuickBooks on a Peer-to-Peer Network 562
Installing QuickBooks on a Client-server Network 568

Appendix B • Multiple Currencies 571

Setting Up and Configuring Multiple Currencies 572

Creating a Special Backup 572

Enabling Multiple Currencies 572

Selecting Currencies 574

Tracking Exchange Rates 575

Managing Customers and Vendors with Foreign Currencies 576

Creating Customers and Vendors with
Currency Assignments 576

Changing Currency for Existing Customers and Vendors . . . 577

Managing Existing Open Transactions 577

Currency Data in Customer and Vendor Centers 578

Chart of Accounts for Multicurrency Transactions 579

Creating Transactions in Other Currencies 579

Creating Reports on Multiple Currency Transactions 582

• Index 583

Acknowledgments

Special thanks to the team of dedicated and talented folks who worked hard to deliver this book to you.

Megg Morin at McGraw Hill has championed editions of this book for several years. I'm grateful to her for giving me the opportunity to have my name associated with such a first-class publication. Thanks to Technical Editor Thomas E. Barich, whose terrific attention to detail gave me the freedom to focus on the "big picture."

Project Editor LeeAnn Pickrell and Copy Editor Sally Engelfried ensured that their insightful edits and comments made their way back to me with lighting speed.

For his insights on the features of the software that matter most—a special thanks to fellow QuickBooks guru Brad White.

The Publisher would like to give special thanks to Bryan Ruff and Michael Cobb for their help with beta software as well as Lesley Kew, Evelyn Ma, and Amy Schwartz on the QuickBooks team at Intuit for their help at various stages of the project.

Introduction

How to Get the Most from This Book

The information in this book is organized and presented in a way that can benefit both a QuickBooks novice as well as a more experienced user. If you're brand new to QuickBooks, the eight chapters that make up Part One will be required reading. Following the advice and detailed steps outlined in these chapters will help ensure that your QuickBooks file is set up correctly—from the start. From there, you can move on to the topics covered in Part Two, where you'll learn all about the day-to-day bookkeeping chores you'll be performing in QuickBooks. For those who are more experienced QuickBooks users, you can use the information in Parts Two, Three, and Four to confirm that you're on the right track or to learn how to use some of the more advanced features QuickBooks offers.

When you have an immediate need to know how to do something, both the Contents and the Index are designed to make it easy for you to identify quickly where in the book a specific task or feature is covered.

"Extras" Provided in This Book to Help You

This book contains some extra elements that are my way of sharing with you, from my perspective as a QuickBooks ProAdvisor, an occasional best practice and, in some cases, "lessons learned" from years of supporting QuickBooks users. Specifically,

- **ProAdvisor Tips** Give you some additional insight about a subject or a task. Sometimes they're shortcuts, and sometimes they're workarounds.
- **Cautions** Help you avoid making some common mistakes.
- **ProAdvisor Recommends boxes** Are filled with more detailed insights that may be useful to you. Sometimes they provide information about what happens behind the scenes when you perform a task; others are designed to point out how other QuickBooks users perform a task in the program to run their business.

You and Your Accountant

There are a number of places throughout this book where you'll be reminded to call your accountant before making a decision about the best way to enter a beginning balance or handle a particular transaction in QuickBooks. I encourage you to heed this advice. While QuickBooks gives you the tools you need to manage your business's financial operations, your accountant can play a vital role in helping you maintain a healthy and viable business by providing you with valuable tax and strategic business-planning advice. In addition, to help *your accountant* better assist *you*, throughout the book I identify information that I think you should share with your accountant because it tells him or her how QuickBooks handles certain accounting functions—like payroll and inventory, for example.

If you don't have an accountant and want to connect with one, there are also accountants in your area who are certified by Intuit as QuickBooks experts. They often provide on-site assistance with set up and troubleshooting and are a great resource if you get "stuck" while setting up your QuickBooks file—or just want to have an expert review the information you've entered in your system. To locate a Certified QuickBooks ProAdvisor in your area, select Find A Local QuickBooks Expert from the QuickBooks Help menu.

Part One

Getting Started

So you've decided to use QuickBooks to help you manage your business. If this is a brand-new business, congratulations! If you've been newly charged with keeping the books for a business, your decision to use QuickBooks is a smart one.

You'll soon see that QuickBooks is more than just a bookkeeping program. When set up and maintained properly, it will likely become one of your company's most valuable assets. Not only will you use it to track your bank balances and what your customers owe you, but you'll also refer to it as you make important decisions such as hiring more employees, dropping a product line, or even selling your business.

In Part One of this book, you'll learn how to gather the information you need to get started so you can create and start using your company file. You'll also gain an understanding of what steps are most important, what you can do on your own, and when you may need help to ensure that your file is set up right from the start. Part One also includes chapters containing instructions and hints about putting all the important elements into your QuickBooks system, like customers, vendors, general ledger information, and the other lists that contain data to help you track your finances more accurately.

Using QuickBooks
for the First Time

In *this chapter:*

- What to do ahead of time
- Open QuickBooks
- Create a company file
- Navigate in QuickBooks

The first time you open QuickBooks, the QuickBooks Setup window launches. From here, you can begin the process of either creating a brand-new company file or working with an existing file—more about your options a bit later in this chapter.

What to Do Ahead of Time

If you're new to QuickBooks, before you work in the software you have to do three things:

- Decide on the starting date for your QuickBooks system.
- Find all the detailed records, notes, memos, and other items that you've been using to track your financial numbers.
- Create a list that contains the beginning balances (aka an opening trial balance) of things like your bank account, loans outstanding, and other assets that your business owns so you can tell QuickBooks about them. Refer to Chapter 8 for details about creating an opening trial balance for your new QuickBooks file.

It's definitely worth taking the time now to ensure that the information you're using to create your new company file is as accurate as it can be. It's not that you can't change things in QuickBooks after the fact; it's just that if you start with less than accurate data, you sometimes can't figure out which information was off to start with. And if you can't trace the origin of a problem, you run the risk of the problem becoming permanent. So get out that shoebox, manila envelope, or printout of the spreadsheet you've been using to keep track of your business so far. Following the steps outlined in the next few chapters will help give QuickBooks the right foundation for all the calculations it will need to make and all the reports you'll need it to generate.

Deciding on the Start Date

The *start date* is the date on which you begin entering your bookkeeping records into QuickBooks. Transactions may have occurred before this date (and you'll learn that some of them must be entered into QuickBooks) but, from this date on, your transactions will go through QuickBooks.

Choosing a start date is an important decision, since the date you choose can affect how much work it's going to be to set up your QuickBooks company file. For example, a September start date means that every transaction that occurred in your business prior to that date has to be reflected in your QuickBooks system before you start entering September transactions (although you can enter some numbers in bulk instead of entering each individual transaction). If it's March, this decision is a lot easier because you'll be entering only a few months of transactions.

Here's what to think about as you make your choice.

If your goal is to have your new QuickBooks file reflect every detail of your company as of your start date, then you'll want to have every individual transaction in the system. This includes every invoice you sent to customers and all the payments you've received on them, every check you wrote to vendors every payroll check you gave an employee, and so on.

If you're not so ambitious, the second best way to create your new QuickBooks file is to enter summary totals for each of your company's transaction types up until the day before your QuickBooks start date. After that, every single transaction gets entered into QuickBooks.

If it's the first half of the year when you read this, make your start date the first day of the year and then enter everything you've done so far this year. It sounds like a lot of work, but it really isn't. When you start entering transactions in QuickBooks, such as customer invoices, you just pick the customer, enter a little information, and move on to the next invoice. Of course, you have to enter all your customers, but you'd have to do that even if you weren't entering every transaction for the current year.

If it's the middle of the year, you can choose either option. If you have a lot of transactions every month, you might want to enter summary totals to get you up to date and then enter real transactions as they occur, beginning with the start date.

If it's late in the year as you read this, perhaps October or November or later, and you usually send a lot of invoices to customers, write a lot of checks, and do your own payroll, think about waiting until the new year to start using QuickBooks.

Gathering the Information You Need

It's a good idea to have all the information you'll need to complete the setup of your QuickBooks assembled and in one place rather trying to locate each piece of information during the setup.

Read through this section to learn what facts and figures QuickBooks needs to get started. The work you have to do to actually enter your opening account balances and transactions into your new company file is covered step by step in Chapter 8.

Cash Balances

You have to tell QuickBooks what the balance is for each bank account you use in your business. The balance being referred to here is the *reconciled* balance and not simply the balance from your check register. And it should be a reconciled balance as of your QuickBooks starting date.

If you haven't balanced your checkbooks against the bank statements for a while, now would be a good time to do it. In addition to the reconciled balance and the statement itself, you need to have a list of the dates and the amounts (both deposits in transit and checks) of the transactions that haven't yet cleared.

Customer Balances

If any customer owes you money as of your starting date, you have to tell QuickBooks about it. Enter each unpaid customer invoice, using the real, original dates for each invoice. Those dates must be earlier than your QuickBooks start date. This means you have to assemble all the information about unpaid customer invoices, including such details as how much of each invoice was for services, for items sold, for shipping, and for sales tax. To learn how to set up a customer, refer to Chapter 3. As you enter your open customer balances, QuickBooks will automatically create the accounts receivable balance for you. Refer to Chapter 8 for additional guidance on how to enter these important balances in QuickBooks.

Vendor Balances

The vendor balances (the money you owe as of your start date) are treated much like open customer invoices. You basically have the same chores facing you regarding any unpaid bills you owe to vendors, as they also should be entered into QuickBooks using their original dates. Chapter 4 covers what you need to know about setting up and using vendors.

Asset Balances

Besides your bank accounts, you have to know the balance of all your assets. You'll need to know the current value of your fixed assets (like equipment and furniture) and any accumulated depreciation on those assets (you can likely ask your tax preparer for this information). Refer to the section in Chapter 2 titled "The Accounts that QuickBooks Uses" to learn more about the other assets your business may own.

Liability Balances

Get all the information about your liabilities together. While the open vendor bills you enter determine your accounts payable balance automatically, you'll need to know the current balance of any loans or mortgages. If there are unpaid withholding amounts from payroll, they also must be entered. Refer to the section in Chapter 2 titled "The Accounts that QuickBooks Uses" to learn more about how to identify the other liabilities your business may be responsible for.

Payroll Information

If you do the payroll instead of using a payroll service, you'll need to know everything about each employee: social security number, all the information that goes into determining tax status (federal, state, and local), and which deductions are taken for health or pension. You have all this information, of course; you just have to get it together. If your employees are on salary, you've probably been repeating the check information every payday, with no need to look up these items. Dig up the W-4 forms and all your notes about who's on what deduction plan.

You also need to know which payroll items you have to track: salary, wages, federal deductions, state deductions (tax, SUI, SDI), local income tax deductions, benefits, pension, and any other deductions (garnishments, for example). And that's not all—you also have to know the name of the vendor to whom these withholding amounts are remitted (government tax agencies, insurance companies, and so on). Running payroll in QuickBooks is covered in Chapter 17.

Inventory Information

You need to know the name you want to assign to every inventory item you carry, and, of particular importance, how much you paid for each item and how many of each item you have in stock as of the starting date. QuickBooks needs these last two key pieces of information in order to keep an accurate inventory valuation for you. It is also a good time to be thinking about any other information you want to track for each of the items you carry in inventory. For example, is color an important trait or does your supplier identify the part using a different part number? You'll learn more about setting up your inventory in Chapter 6.

Other Useful Information to Have Available

Find last year's tax return. QuickBooks is going to want to know which tax forms you use. Also, there's usually other information on the tax forms you might need (such as depreciation amounts).

Also, if you have a loan or mortgage, have the amortization schedule handy so you can figure out the year-to-date (the "date" is the QuickBooks starting date) principal and interest amounts. Chapter 8 contains detailed instructions on how to set up all your opening account balances.

You're now ready to set up and configure your QuickBooks company file! Let's get started.

Installing and Launching the Software

Whether you're installing QuickBooks from a CD or using a download link from Intuit, the installation process is quite straightforward. Simply follow the installation wizard to where you'll read and accept the Software License Agreement, select where on your computer you want to install the program, and tell the wizard whether you'll be installing the program for multiple users (who will need access to the company file across a network). Refer to Appendix A to learn more about installing QuickBooks in a networked environment.

Once the installation of the program is complete, QuickBooks places a shortcut to the software on your desktop, and that's the easiest way to open the program. If you have other windows covering the desktop, you can use the Start menu, where you'll find QuickBooks in the Programs menu. Place your pointer on the QuickBooks listing in the Programs menu and choose QuickBooks from the submenu.

ProAdvisor Tip: For even faster access to QuickBooks, copy or move the desktop shortcut to your Quick Launch toolbar, which requires only a single click to open software. Right-drag the shortcut icon onto the Quick Launch toolbar, and then choose Move Here (or Copy Here, if you want a shortcut in both places). If you're a Windows 7 user, you may want to pin QuickBooks to the Start menu (right-click the icon and select Pin To Start Menu).

When QuickBooks launches for the first time, the QuickBooks Setup window opens and provides links to help you get started with creating a new company file, updating an existing file, and other useful information. On subsequent launches, the Login page for the last file that you were working in opens. If you choose to not work in this particular file (maybe you want to work in another file or want to check out the sample company files), click the Cancel button on the QuickBooks Login screen. The No Company Open window opens, giving you the following options:

Create A New Company Select this option to begin the process of creating a company file. All of the steps involved in this task are covered in the next section.

Open Or Restore An Existing Company Select this option if you're upgrading from a previous version of QuickBooks. Go through the windows in the Open Or Restore Company Wizard to select your company file. QuickBooks offers to upgrade the file to your new version. Place a check mark in the I Understand That My Company File Will Be Updated To This New Version Of QuickBooks box to accept the offer. QuickBooks then requires that you make a backup of your file in its current version. When the backup is complete, the file is converted to QuickBooks Pro 2012, and you can begin working.

Caution: If you're working in a network environment and you installed QuickBooks Pro 2012 as an upgrade to a previous version, upgrade QuickBooks on the computer that holds the company data file first. Then upgrade QuickBooks on the other computers.

Open A Sample File Click this option to display a list of sample companies you can explore and play with to get familiar with QuickBooks. One company is designed for product-based businesses, the other for service-based businesses.

ProAdvisor Tip: Many QuickBooks users (especially accountants) maintain more than one QuickBooks company file. As you open and work in different files, they will automatically be listed and available for selection in the No Company File Open window. If you find that you no longer want or need a file to be listed here, use the Edit List link to hide a particular file. This action does not remove the file from your computer or network, it only hides it from the list of company files visible from this particular window. If you work in that file again on a future date, it will reappear on the list again for easy access.

Creating Your Company File

For now, choose Create A New Company, because that's what this chapter is all about. The QuickBooks Setup window opens to begin the process of creating your company file (see Figure 1-1).

Let's get your business set up quickly!

Answer some basic questions and we'll do the rest. You can always make changes later. (Recommended for new users)

Watch how easy it is

Express Start

Advanced Setup — Give us more details and we'll guide you step by step through the available options. (Recommended if you want to fine-tune your setup)

Other Options ▼ — Open or convert your existing files from Quicken, Peachtree, Small Business Accounting, Office Accounting or even Quickbooks.

Need help? Give us a call

FIGURE 1-1 The QuickBooks Setup window gives you three options for creating a company file.

QuickBooks offers three ways to create this file:

- Express Start
- Advanced Setup, a wizard in which you move through the pages, answering questions and providing information to fine-tune your setup.
- Other Options, which allows you to create a new file from an existing Quicken file or from Microsoft Office Accounting, Small Business Accounting, or Peachtree Accounting. Select the Convert Other Accounting Software Data option and follow the onscreen directions.

The first two methods are covered in this chapter, starting with Express Start.

Using Express Start

Express Start is a two-screen wizard designed to get your company file created—albeit with only basic information—in just two steps. In the first window, you'll be required to enter your company name, the industry you're in, and the type of tax return you'll be filing. In the second window, you'll have the option to enter your company's contact information and then go straight to having QuickBooks create your company file. The Preview Your Company Settings window lets you preview the features that will be enabled and the accounts that QuickBooks recommends for you, based on the industry and company type you selected.

It's a good idea to take a look at these settings. You can add or remove the accounts listed on the Chart of Accounts tab and confirm the location that your new company file will be saved to.

Using Advanced Setup

To select this setup path, click Advanced Setup on the QuickBooks Setup window. The Easy Step Interview wizard is launched, providing you with a step-by-step approach to creating your company file. As with all wizards, click Next to move through the windows.

Entering Company Information

To begin, QuickBooks needs basic information about your company (see Figure 1-2). Notice that the information about your company name has two entry fields. The first field is for the real company name, the one you do business as. The second field, for your company's legal name, is optional and is used only if the legal name of your company differs from the company name you use for doing business. For instance, your company may do business as Win Contracting, but your legal or corporate name might be Winchester Contracting, Inc.

FIGURE 1-2 Start by entering basic information about your business.

Enter the company tax ID number. If you have a federal employer ID number (EIN), it's a nine-digit number in the format *XX-YYYYYYY*. If you don't have an EIN, enter your social security number.

You have a tax ID number if you have employees, and you may have one if you have a business bank account (many banks require this, although some banks merely ask for a copy of a fictitious name registration certificate and will accept your social security number instead of a federal ID).

If you are a sole proprietor, using your social security number for business purposes, consider applying for a federal ID number. This can help you separate your business and personal finances by using the EIN for business transactions and maintaining a separate bank account in your business name. As your business grows and you hire subcontractors, consultants, or employees, you'll eventually need an EIN to pay these folks. Get it now and avoid the rush.

Enter the contact information (address, telephone, and so on). This data is used on the transactions you print (such as invoices), so enter this data as you want it to appear on printed documents. Click Next when you've filled in your company data.

Selecting the Type of Business

In the next window, select the industry that matches the type of business you have (see Figure 1-3). If you don't see an exact match for your business type, choose one that comes close.

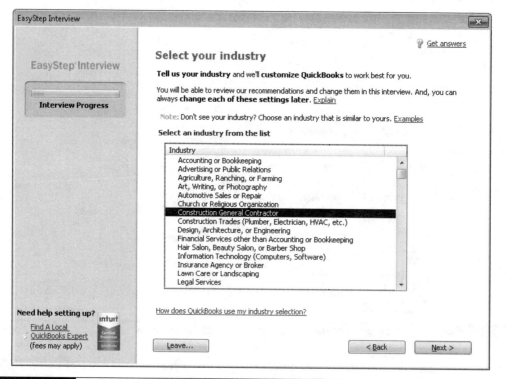

FIGURE 1-3 Find the type of business that matches yours.

Selecting Your Legal Entity Type

The next window displays the various types of legal entities for businesses, such as proprietorship, partnership, corporation, and so on. Select the one that matches the way your business is organized.

If you're not sure, ask your accountant, or find a copy of the business income tax you filed last year (unless this is your first year in business) and match the form number to the list in the window. If you can't find the information, select Other/None. You can change it later in the Company Information dialog accessed from the Company menu. QuickBooks uses this information to attach tax line information to all your accounts that affect your taxes. If you use an Intuit tax preparation program, this information can then be used to prepare a tax return for your business.

Configuring Your Fiscal Year

In the next window, enter the first month of your fiscal year. QuickBooks enters January as the default entry, but if you're not using a calendar year, select the appropriate month from the drop-down list.

Setting Up the Administrator

The next window asks you for an administrator password. It's a good idea to create a password to limit access to your company file and to prevent anyone who gets near your computer from spying on your financial information, especially if you plan on storing customer credit card information. PCI DSS (Payment Card Industry Data Security Standard) compliance standards also require a complex password if you are storing customer credit card information in QuickBooks.

If multiple users will need to work in the file simultaneously (on a network), user names are required (and each should have a password). However, you can wait until after you've finished the EasyStep Interview and implement the feature later, when you can concentrate on the task and make notes about the passwords.

Creating user logins and passwords that let you place restrictions on what users can do and see in QuickBooks is covered in Chapter 26.

Creating Your Company File

The next window explains that you're about to save your company file. Click Next to see the Filename For New Company dialog, which is ready to save the file using a filename based on the company name you've entered. Just click Save to use that filename. Or, if you prefer, you can change the name of the file (especially if your company name is long or complicated). It takes a few seconds for QuickBooks to save the company file and set up all the files for the company. By default, QuickBooks saves your company file in a subfolder under the Documents subfolder.

Most experienced users find it better to create a folder on your hard drive for your QuickBooks data (for instance, C:\QBDataFiles). This makes it easier to find and back up your data.

ProAdvisor Tip: If you run QuickBooks on a network, or another user works in QuickBooks on your computer, make sure the folder you create for your data has permissions set properly. Specifically, the Everyone group must be given Full Control. To learn more about setting up QuickBooks in a multi-user environment, refer to Appendix A.

Customizing Your Company File

The ensuing wizard windows provide a series of choices and options about the way you do business. For example, you're asked what you sell (services, products, or both), whether you charge sales tax, whether you use estimates, and so on. The questions are clearly stated and easy to answer. You don't have to perform any setup tasks if you answer Yes; for example, if you answer Yes when you're asked if you have employees, you don't have to create employee information. You can do all of that later.

Essentially, the wizard is setting configuration options for you, but you can set any of those options for yourself at any time in the future. Information about the options you need to perform certain tasks is found throughout this book, in the appropriate chapters.

Before filling in your answer for your start date, be sure to read the information found earlier in this chapter about this topic.

Creating the Chart of Accounts

The Review Income And Expense Accounts window lets you set up the chart of accounts, which is a list of accounts you'll use to post transactions.

The wizard displays the income and expense accounts it has established for your company, based on the responses you made to the interview question regarding your type of business (see Figure 1-4).

You can select or deselect specific accounts if you know you need or don't need any of the accounts listed. However, it may be easier to go through that process later. You'll likely need additional accounts in your chart of accounts, but it's easier to add them after you've finished this company setup task (setting up your chart of accounts is covered in Chapter 2).

That's it; you're finished with the basics of creating your QuickBooks company file using the Advanced Setup option. You can now continue the work of building out your file by clicking the Go To Setup button and launching the QuickBooks Setup window.

FIGURE 1-4   You can select or deselect accounts now, or wait until you begin using QuickBooks.

The QuickBooks Setup Wizard

The QuickBooks Setup wizard (which launches after either an Advanced or Express Setup) gives you the option of using customized list import options designed to help simplify the task of getting your list information into your new company file. Click the Add button next to the list type that you want to enter. QuickBooks will tell you about any fixes that need to be made to the information prior to importing it. You'll have four options to get your customer and vendor list information into your new company file. You can:

- Import from Outlook
- Import from Yahoo

- Import from Gmail
- Paste from Excel or manually fill in a customized grid

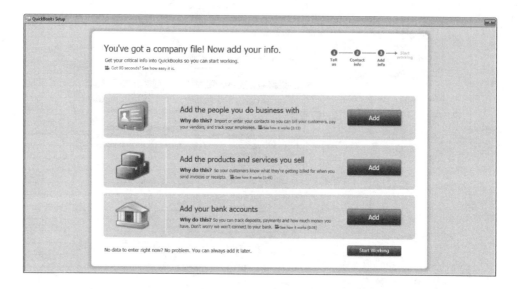

If you prefer to start exploring your file now and work on your lists at a later time, click the Start Working button at the bottom of the window. This will bring you to the Quick Start Center. If you're ready to start working in your new file, close this window to go to the standard QuickBooks Home page. If you're still not ready to dive into the program on your own, you can instead work in the Quick Start Center, which offers a simplified view of the regular QuickBooks Home page. It is also where you can access training videos and other resources that will help prepare you for the important tasks you'll be completing in your QuickBooks file.

Navigate in QuickBooks

With your new file created, let's take a look at how to get around in the software.

The Home page window has the following elements:

- Title bar, which displays the name of your company
- Menu bar, which contains all the commands for working in QuickBooks
- Icon Bar, which contains buttons for quick access to frequently used functions (see the section "Customizing the Icon Bar," later in this chapter).

Home Page

The heart of the Home page has links and icons you use to access the features and functions you need to run your business in QuickBooks. In addition, it's divided into sections to make it easy to find icons and see the workflow those icons represent. Take a moment to review the Home page and identify the Vendor, Customer, Company, and Banking areas on it.

The Home page is dynamic; that is, the icons and workflow arrows it contains change as you enable the various features available in QuickBooks. For example, if you enable inventory tracking, QuickBooks adds icons in the Vendors section for inventory-related tasks.

QuickBooks Centers

QuickBooks centers are windows in which information is displayed about specific areas of your company. Most centers have a dedicated button on the Icon Bar or directly in the middle of the Home page, while others are accessible from the menu bar. You can see current data, analyze that data, and perform tasks. QuickBooks centers include:

- Customer Center
- Vendor Center
- Employee Center
- Report Center
- Online Banking Center
- Doc Center
- App Center
- Lead Center

Customer Center

The Customer Center holds everything you'd ever need to know about your customers. It's where QuickBooks stores your list of customers and all the information about each customer. By changing the options in the available drop-down lists, you can choose the specific information you want to view. You can also perform routine customer-related tasks using the buttons at the top of the Customer Center window. Information about using and customizing the Customer Center is in Chapter 3.

Vendor Center

Like the Customer Center, the Vendor Center makes it easy to view detailed information about your vendors and to enter transactions into QuickBooks related to them. You can learn how to use and customize the Vendor Center in Chapter 4.

Employee Center

If you do your own payroll, open the Employee Center to see detailed information about each employee, your payroll liabilities, and your payroll items. Payroll is covered in Chapter 17.

Report Center

The Report Center, seen in Figure 1-5, is a dynamic version of the Reports menu. There are three views in the Report Center: the Carousel view, the List view, and the Grid view. For each view, the major category of reports is displayed in the left pane. The first time you open the Report Center, you'll open to the Grid view, which allows you to scroll through a visual display of the reports available for each category. The Grid view shows a sample of the actual reports available in each category in a single window and makes it easy to add a report to your Favorites reports list—just click the red heart under the sample report you want to use.

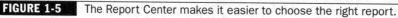

FIGURE 1-5 The Report Center makes it easier to choose the right report.

To change the way you view a category, use the view icons located in the top-right corner of the Report Center window. You can also use the Report Center to access memorized reports as well as a collection of popular reports that other QuickBooks users find useful.

Online Banking Center

This is where you can go to download and enter transactions directly from your credit card and bank accounts into QuickBooks. This is a feature in QuickBooks that's designed to save you from having to manually enter this information into your QuickBooks file. Not every QuickBooks user takes advantage of online banking—but they should.

Doc Center

The Doc Center holds documents and files on your computer that you can then "attach" to a specific transaction or record in QuickBooks. For example, a purchase order a customer sends to you via e-mail or snail mail can be saved or scanned into the Doc Center. Later, with the customer's invoice open, click the attach (paper clip) icon at the top of the Create Invoices window and browse to the document that you've saved on your computer through the Doc Center. A copy of the PO will then be easily retrievable right from their invoice.

App Center

The App Center is where you can learn more about, sign up for, and gain access to the Intuit Workplace Apps. These are web-based applications that are designed to help you further streamline the tasks that are key to the operation of many small businesses. Additional fees may apply.

Lead Center

Unlike the other centers, the Lead Center doesn't have a button of its own on the Icon Bar (although you can add it if you wish by customizing the Icon Bar, as explained in the next section). You access the Lead Center from the Customers menu. You can choose to enter your leads manually, one by one, or copy and paste multiple leads from Excel into a preformatted grid and import them all at once. Regardless of the method you choose, you'll be able to keep track of key contact and sales lead information as well as maintain detailed notes on your progress with each prospect. Tracking your prospects in QuickBooks gives you the advantage of working in one program and makes it easy to turn a lead into a customer once the sale is closed.

Calendar

While not a "center" per se, the QuickBooks Calendar can give you a unique view of all the important transactions and reminders you need to keep track of to keep your business running smoothly. Click the Calendar button on the Icon Bar to open your calendar for the first time. If you haven't yet entered any transactions into your QuickBooks file, your calendar will be empty. Check back in, however, once you've entered some bills or invoices: your calendar will show you the dates that these bills or invoices were created and are due along with any To Do items that you've added.

Customizing the Icon Bar

QuickBooks put icons on the Icon Bar, but the icons QuickBooks chose may not match the features you use most frequently. Putting your own icons on the Icon Bar makes using QuickBooks easier and faster.

To customize the Icon Bar, choose View | Customize Icon Bar to open the Customize Icon Bar dialog, which displays a list of the icons currently occupying your Icon Bar.

ProAdvisor Tip: When you log into QuickBooks with your own login name, the Icon Bar settings you establish are linked to your login name only. You are not changing the Icon Bar for other users.

Changing the Order of Icons

You can change the order in which icons appear on the Icon Bar. The list of icons in the Customize Icon Bar dialog reads top to bottom, representing the left-to-right display on the Icon Bar. Therefore, moving an icon's listing up moves it to the left on the Icon Bar (and vice versa).

To move an icon, click the small diamond to the left of the icon's listing, hold down the left mouse button, and drag the listing to a new position.

Changing the Icon Bar Display

You can change the way the icons display in several ways, which are covered in this section.

Display Icons Without Title Text

By default, icons and text display on the Icon Bar. You can select Show Icons Only to remove the title text under the icons. As a result, the icons are much smaller (and you can fit more icons on the Icon Bar). Positioning your mouse pointer over a small icon displays the icon's description as a Tool Tip.

Change the Icon's Graphic, Text, or Description

To change an individual icon's appearance, select the icon's listing and click Edit. Then choose a different graphic (the currently selected graphic is enclosed in a box), change the Label (the title), or change the Description (the Tool Tip text).

Separate Icons

You can insert a separator between two icons, which is an effective way to create groups of icons (after you move icons into logical groups). The separator is a gray vertical line. In the Customize Icon Bar dialog, select the icon that should appear to the left of the separator bar and click Add Separator. QuickBooks inserts the separator on the Icon Bar and "(space)" in the listing to indicate the location of the separator.

Removing an Icon

If there are any icons you never use or use so infrequently that you'd rather use the space they take up for icons representing features you use a lot, remove them. Select the icon in the Customize Icon Bar dialog and click Delete. QuickBooks does not ask you to confirm the deletion; the icon is just zapped from the Icon Bar.

Adding an Icon

You can add an icon to the Icon Bar in either of two ways:

- Choose Add in the Customize Icon Bar dialog.
- Automatically add an icon for a window (transaction or report) you're currently using.

Using the Customize Icon Bar Dialog to Add an Icon

To add an icon from the Customize Icon Bar dialog, click Add. If you want to position your new icon at a specific place within the existing row of icons (instead of at the right end of the Icon Bar), first select the existing icon that you want to sit to the left of your new icon. Then click Add to display the Add Icon Bar Item dialog.

Scroll through the list to select the task you want to add to the Icon Bar. Then choose a graphic to represent the new icon. If you wish, you can change the label (the title that appears below the icon) or the description (the text that appears in the Tool Tip when you hold your mouse pointer over the icon).

Adding an Icon for the Current Window

If you're currently working in a QuickBooks window and it strikes you that it would be handy to have an icon for fast access to this window, you can accomplish the deed quickly. While the window is active, choose View | Add *Name Of Window* To Icon Bar (substitute the name of the current window for *Name Of Window*). A dialog appears so you can choose a graphic, name, and description for the new icon.

The Favorites Menu

The Favorites menu gives you the flexibility to list up to 30 of the QuickBooks tasks and lists that you use most often, saving you from having to navigate to other areas of the program to complete your most common QuickBooks tasks. To add menu items to your Favorites menu, select Favorites | Customize Favorites from the QuickBooks menu. The Customize Your Menus window opens. Select a menu item, then click the Add button to add it to your Favorites menu. Click OK when finished.

Closing QuickBooks

To exit QuickBooks, click the X in the top-right corner of the QuickBooks window or choose File | Exit from the menu bar. QuickBooks will ask you if you're sure you want to exit. If you choose Yes, the company file open at the time you exit the software is the file that opens the next time you launch QuickBooks.

The Chart of Accounts

In this chapter:

- The accounts that QuickBooks uses

- Decide whether to use numbers for accounts

- Create accounts

- Create subaccounts

- Edit, delete, and merge accounts

Chapter 2

The Accounts that QuickBooks Uses

QuickBooks uses accounts (you can also think of them as categories) to keep track of the many different transactions that occur as you operate your business. The list where all these accounts live is called *the chart of accounts*. For instance, when you deposit money into your bank, there's an account named Bank (which, of course, you can name to match the name of your actual bank), and you post the money to that account. All of your postings to the chart of accounts make up your *general ledger,* which is why you need to put together a list of your accounts, including assets, liabilities, income, and expenses, ahead of time.

Assets

An *asset* is something you own, such as

- Money in your bank accounts (sometimes called *cash on hand*)
- Money owed to you by your customers (called *accounts receivable*)
- Equipment, furniture, and so on (called *fixed assets*)
- The inventory you stock for resale if you are a distributor or manufacturer (called *inventory assets*)

Liabilities

A *liability* is something that you may be holding but does not belong to you. It is something you owe to someone else, such as

- Money you owe your vendors and suppliers (called *accounts payable*)
- Sales tax you have collected and must turn over to the state (called *current liabilities*)
- Money withheld from employees' pay that you must turn over to government agencies (also part of *current liabilities*)
- Outstanding loan balances (called *long-term liabilities*)

Equity

Your *equity* is your net worth and is made up of the following:

- The capital invested in your business (called *capital*)
- The capital you've withdrawn from the business (if your business isn't a corporation)
- The profit (or loss) including accumulated earnings in prior years (called *retained earnings*)

Income

Income, also referred to as *revenue*, is made up of the following:

- Money you collect when you sell products
- Fees you collect for services
- Income derived from interest

Expenses

Expenses are the monies you spend. You use the chart of accounts to divide your expenses by category (account) for the purpose of meeting requirements on tax returns and also for your own analysis. Generally, expenses are divided into two main categories: cost of goods sold (COGS) and general and administrative expenses.

Cost of goods sold is usually tracked for the following categories:

- Cost of raw materials for manufacturing
- Cost of goods you resell in a wholesale or retail business
- Cost of materials consumed/sold in a service business

General and administrative expenses include:

- Overhead (utilities, rent, insurance, and so on)
- Office supplies
- Payroll
- Services you purchase
- Taxes

As you enter transactions in QuickBooks, you don't have to worry about the "behind the scenes" entries that need to be made to the accounts that are affected—QuickBooks takes care of this for you automatically.

For example, if you sell goods or services to a customer and send an invoice and you haven't been paid yet, the Invoice Transaction screen asks you to fill in the name of the customer, the product or service you sold, and the amount you're charging. QuickBooks posts the amount to accounts and to Income and also posts a record of the transaction in the customer's account. Later, when the customer pays the invoice, QuickBooks credits that amount to the accounts receivable account (showing that the invoice is now paid) and increases your bank account for the amount of the payment.

The chart of accounts, also referred to as your general ledger, is where all the financial data you enter in transaction windows lives, categorized and totaled by account. QuickBooks might have created some accounts for you during the initial setup of your company, but you'll likely need additional accounts in order to ensure that your chart of accounts reflects the activities that are unique to your own business. You create the chart of accounts first because some of the other QuickBooks lists you create require you to link the items in those lists to your accounts.

Using Numbered Accounts

By default, QuickBooks uses account names only in the chart of accounts. However, you can change the default so your accounts have numbers in addition to the names.

The advantage of using numbers is that you can arrange each section of the chart of accounts by category and subcategory, because within each type of account QuickBooks displays your chart of accounts in alphanumeric order (without numbers, QuickBooks displays each section of your chart of accounts in alphabetical order).

You can also use numbered subaccounts to provide subtotals for related expenses (or income) right on your QuickBooks reports, without the need to export the report to Excel. See the section "Using Subaccounts" later in this chapter.

One argument for using account numbers is that it gives you the ability to arrange your bank accounts in a logical order, making sure your primary bank account is always at the top of the drop-down list users see when making bank deposits or writing checks. Using account numbers can also be handy if you add another bank account at a different bank, or if you change banks, because it helps you better control the order in which the accounts appear when selecting them in transactions. Even if your old bank was number 10000, and you want your new bank to use that number, it's a simple task to edit the original bank number to 14990 (moving it to the bottom of the list) and give the new bank the 10000 number to keep it at the top of the list.

Enabling Account Numbers

To switch to a number format for your accounts, you have to enable the account number feature. Choose Edit | Preferences from the menu bar to open the Preferences dialog, and select the Accounting icon in the left pane. Click the Company Preferences tab, and select the Use Account Numbers check box (see Figure 2-1).

FIGURE 2-1   Enable numbers for your chart of accounts.

➡ ProAdvisor Recommends

When You Need the Chart of Accounts Displayed in Alphabetical Order

As convenient as it is for you (and your accountant) to have numbered accounts so you can track your finances by category and subcategory, you may have to produce reports for an outside stakeholder (like your bank). They may have certain financial categories that they'll want to look at first, and it's easier for them if your accounts, especially your expenses, are in alphabetical order.

To produce reports without account numbers, putting each account type list back into alphabetical order, turn off the account number feature by deselecting the option in the Preferences dialog. Print the reports, and then turn the feature on again. QuickBooks stores account numbers as part of the account name, so when you re-enable account numbers all your numbers appear exactly as you created them.

If you chose a prebuilt chart of accounts when you set up your company file, those accounts are switched to numbered accounts automatically. However, the QuickBooks numbering scheme is designed to keep accounts in alphabetical order, especially in the Expenses section. This costs you some of the advantages and efficiencies that well-planned numbers bring, but all you have to do is create your own plan and then edit the accounts to change the numbers (see "Editing Accounts" later in this chapter).

Accounts you added yourself (over and above the prebuilt accounts that were automatically brought into your company file) have to be edited to add numbers; QuickBooks doesn't automatically number them.

When you select the option to use account numbers, the option Show Lowest Subaccount Only becomes accessible (it's grayed out if you haven't opted for account numbers). This option tells QuickBooks to display only the subaccount on transaction windows instead of both the parent account and the subaccount, making it easier to see precisely which account is receiving the posting.

If all your accounts aren't numbered and you select Show Lowest Subaccount Only, when you click OK, QuickBooks displays an error message that you cannot enable this option until all your accounts have numbers assigned. After you've edited existing accounts that need numbers (any accounts that QuickBooks didn't automatically number for you), you can return to the Preferences dialog and enable this subaccount option.

Creating a Numbering Scheme

After you've set up numbered accounts, you have a more efficient chart of accounts, so you, your bookkeeper, and your accountant will have an easier time managing your chart of accounts. Numbers give you a quick clue about the type and category of the account you're working with. As you create accounts, be sure to maintain the logic of your numbering system, assigning ranges of numbers to account types. A common approach to account numbering is shown below:

- xxxx Assets
- 2xxxx Liabilities
- 3xxxx Equity
- 4xxxx Income
- 5xxxx Expenses
- 6xxxx Expenses
- 7xxxx Expenses
- 8xxxx Expenses
- 9xxxx Other Income and Expenses

This example uses five digits because QuickBooks uses five-digit account numbers. QuickBooks permits account numbers of up to seven digits, so you're not going to run out of numbers no matter how many accounts you need to run your business efficiently.

Creating Ranges of Numbers

Account types have subtypes, and you need to assign ranges of account numbers to match those subtypes. The starting number of each range has to be the same as the starting number for the account type (for instance, if you use numbers starting with a 1 for assets, all of the number ranges for different subtypes of assets must start with a 1). However, the ranges let you assign specific numbers to specific account types.

So, thinking about the breakdown of assets, you can use 10000 through 10999 for bank accounts, 11000 through 11999 for receivables and other current assets, then use 12000 through 12999 for tracking fixed assets such as equipment, furniture, and so on. Follow the same pattern for liabilities, starting with current liabilities and moving to long term. It's also a good idea to keep all the payroll withholding liabilities accounts (they're current liabilities) together.

You can, if you wish, have a variety of expense types and reserve the starting number for specific types. Some companies, for example, use 5xxxx for sales expenses (they even separate the payroll postings between the salespeople and the rest of the employees), then use 60000 through 79999 for general operating expenses, then use 8xxxx and 9xxxx for other specific expenses that should appear together in reports (such as taxes, penalty fees, and so on). Some companies use one range of expense accounts, such as 70000 through 79999 for expenses that fall into the "overhead" category.

If you have inventory and you track cost of goods, you can reserve a section of the chart of accounts for those account types. Some companies use 43000 through 49999 for cost of goods, and some companies dedicate the numbers in the 5xxxx range to that purpose.

Usually, you should create new accounts by increasing the previous account number by 10 or 20 (or even 100 if you don't have a lot of accounts), so you have room to insert more accounts that belong in the same general area of your chart of accounts when they need to be added later.

➡ ProAdvisor Recommends

Re-sorting Your Chart of Accounts

When you first set up your Chart of Accounts, your accounts are sorted by type and then by number. Because the order of these accounts can be changed manually, you may, over time, find it more difficult to find and work with some accounts in your list. You can fix this by re-sorting the list. Open your Chart of Accounts, click the Account button, and select the Re-Sort List option to return the list to its original order.

Naming Accounts

Whether or not you choose to enable account numbers, you have to give each account a name. What's more, you should take steps to ensure that your account naming convention is consistent and enforced. Why is this important? Because when I visit clients who haven't established and enforced naming conventions, it's not uncommon to find accounts with names such as:

- Telephone Exp
- Exps-Telephone
- Tele Expense
- Telephone
- Tele

The problem here is that every one of those accounts had amounts posted to them. That's because users "guess" at account names when they see a drop-down list, and they point and click on whatever they see that seems remotely related. If they don't find the account the way they would have entered the name, they create a new account (using a name that is logical to them). You can avoid all of those errors by establishing protocols about creating account names, limiting which users have authority to create new accounts, and then making sure your users search the account list before applying an account to a transaction.

Here are a few suggested protocols—you can amend them to fit your own situation or invent different protocols that you're more comfortable with. But the important thing is consistency!

- Avoid apostrophes and quotes.
- Set the number of characters for abbreviations. For example, if you permit four characters, telephone is abbreviated "tele"; a three-character rule produces "tel."
- Decide whether to use the ampersand (&) or a hyphen. For example, is it "Repairs & Maintenance" or "Repairs-Maintenance"?
- Make a rule about whether spaces are allowed. For example, would you have "Repairs & Maintenance" or "Repairs&Maintenance"?

Creating Accounts

After you've done your homework and decided on a naming and numbering scheme, creating accounts is a piece of cake:

1. Press CTRL-A to open the Chart Of Accounts window.
2. Press CTRL-N to enter a new account.

Start by selecting the type of account you want to add.

3. In the Add New Account: Choose Account Type dialog (see Figure 2-2), select the type of account you're creating. If the account type you need doesn't appear in the major category list on the dialog, select Other Account Types and choose an account type from the drop-down list.

4. Click Continue to create the account.

The dialog you see when you fill out account information varies depending on the account type you chose, because different types of accounts require different information. In addition, if you've opted to use numbers for your accounts, there's a field for the account number. Figure 2-3 shows a blank Add New Account dialog for an Expense account.

Select From Examples

If you created your company file in QuickBooks 2012 (instead of updating the file from a previous version of QuickBooks), some account types display a button labeled Select From Examples in the Add New Account dialog. Clicking the button produces a list of accounts that QuickBooks thinks you might want to consider adding to your chart of accounts. As you can see in Figure 2-4, the list of accounts matches the account type you selected when you started the process of adding an account.

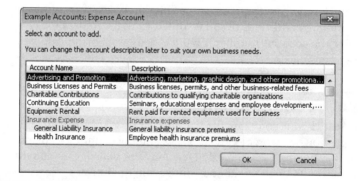

FIGURE 2-3 The only required entry for an account is a name (and number, if you've enabled account numbers in Company Preferences).

FIGURE 2-4 QuickBooks suggests accounts to add to your chart of accounts.

The accounts suggested are those accounts that were available for the industry you selected when you created your company file but were not selected for inclusion in your chart of accounts for one of the following reasons:

- If you add an account from the Select From Examples list, that account is removed from the list. If you delete the account from your chart of accounts, it is put back on the Select From Examples list.
- If you did not select an industry during company file setup (instead, you selected None), the Select From Examples button is grayed out and inaccessible.

The following account types do *not* have the Select From Examples feature:

- Bank
- Credit Card
- Equity
- Account Receivable
- Accounts Payable
- Long Term Liability

Optional Fields for Accounts

The Description field is optional, as is the Note field (which only appears on some account types).

You can assign a Tax-Line Mapping to your accounts (see Figure 2-3), which can be a huge timesaver if you do your own taxes or if your tax preparer is using one of Intuit's tax preparation software programs. QuickBooks exports data for each account to the appropriate tax line if you use Turbo Tax to do your taxes, for example. In order to perform this helpful action, QuickBooks has to know which tax form you use, and you probably provided that information when you set up your company file. If you didn't select a tax form, the Tax-Line Mapping field doesn't appear. You can add tax line information by opening the Company menu, selecting Company Information, and choosing the appropriate income tax form. When you click OK to save the new data, the Tax-Line Mapping field appears on the appropriate account records and you can use the drop-down list to insert the right line number for your tax form. (If you selected a tax form when you set up the company file, QuickBooks automatically inserts the right tax line. If you add the field later and use the drop-down list, you have to know which line each income/expense/ asset account needs to be transferred to on the tax form, which may require some research.)

Some account types (bank, credit card, assets, liabilities, and equity) have a button labeled Enter Opening Balance. Clicking it opens a dialog in which you can enter an opening balance. Do *not* enter opening balances when you're creating accounts, because it causes complications that your accountant won't appreciate. (See the ProAdvisor Recommends: "What You Should Know About Entering Opening Balances for Accounts.")

As you finish creating each account, click Save & New to move to another blank Add New Account dialog. By default, the new dialog is configured for the same account type as the account you just created, but you can change the account type by selecting another type from the drop-down list at the top of the dialog.

When you're finished creating accounts, click Save & Close, and then close the Chart Of Accounts window by clicking the X in the upper-right corner.

➡ ProAdvisor Recommends

What You Should Know About Entering Opening Balances for Accounts

Unless you start your business the day you start using QuickBooks, you haven't yet opened a bank account, and you haven't purchased any equipment for your business, many accounts already have an existing balance. For example, you probably have money in your business bank account, either because your business has been operating for a long time and you're just getting around to using QuickBooks, or you provided startup money for your new business.

It is best not to enter any figures in the Opening Balance field of any account that has this option, because QuickBooks (which is a true double-entry accounting application) needs to make an offsetting entry of the same amount you entered into an offsetting account. Of course, QuickBooks has no way of knowing the source of that money, so the offsetting account it uses is called Opening Bal Equity, which is an account QuickBooks invented for just this purpose. In actuality, the money in your bank account may be the result of a loan you made your business, capital you invested in your business, or sales you made before you started keeping records in QuickBooks.

Your accountant will want to zero out the balance in Opening Bal Equity, and sometimes that's a difficult job because it's hard to tell how the balance was arrived at—was this opening balance the result of transactions in past years? If so, it needs to be moved to the Retained Earnings account. Is it from the current year? If so, what's the real source of the amount (because it has to be moved to the proper account)? Is it a combination of both? If so, you'll have to remember every entry and explain it to your accountant so he or she can move the appropriate amounts to the appropriate accounts.

So it's best to ignore the Opening Balance field when you create an account, and after you've created the account, create a transaction that accurately describes the source of this amount. Chapter 8 details an easy-to-follow process you can use to enter opening balances and historical data correctly and efficiently. Be sure to ask your accountant to help you create the transactions that provide the details behind the opening balances for your accounts.

Using Subaccounts

Subaccounts provide a way to post transactions more precisely by using subcategories for main account categories, while also giving you the ability to view key reports at both the subaccount and parent account level. To create a subaccount, you must first create the parent account.

For example, suppose you have the following parent accounts:

- 60200 Utilities
- 60300 Travel

You can create the following subaccounts:

- 60210 Utilities:Heat
- 60220 Utilities:Electric
- 60310 Travel:Sales
- 60320 Travel:Seminars and Meetings

The colon in the account names listed here is added automatically by QuickBooks to indicate a *parentaccount:subaccount* relationship.

> **ProAdvisor Tip:** To get the most out of using subaccounts when viewing reports, be sure that once you create them you post transactions to the correct subaccount—and not the parent account. Why? Because when you post directly to a parent account (that has subaccounts attached to it), reports that include transactions to this account will appear as if they were posted to a subaccount called "Other."

Viewing Subaccounts

When you have subaccounts, the Chart Of Accounts window displays them indented under their parent accounts (see Figure 2-5), as long as you've configured the window to display accounts in Hierarchical view.

If you know you created subaccounts, but you don't see any indented listings, your Chart Of Accounts window has been configured to display accounts in Flat view (a simple listing of accounts). To remedy this, click the Account button at the bottom of the window and select Hierarchical View.

It's easy to see that the Car/Truck expense account has subaccounts to track expenses more specifically.

Creating Subaccounts

To create a subaccount, you must have already created the parent account. Then take these steps:

1. Open the Chart Of Accounts list.
2. Press CTRL-N to create a new account.
3. Select the appropriate account type.
4. Click Continue.
5. Enter a number (if you're using numbered accounts).
6. Name the account.
7. Click the Subaccount Of check box to place a check mark in it.
8. In the drop-down box next to the check box, select the parent account.
9. Click Save & New to create another account or Save & Close if you're finished creating accounts.

Multiple Levels of Subaccounts

You can have multiple levels of subaccounts. For example, you may want to track income in the following manner:

Income

    Income:Consulting

      Income:Consulting:Engineering

      Income:Consulting:Training Income:Products

    Income:Products:Technical

      Income:Products:Accessories

      Income:Products:Repairs

Creating the sub-subaccounts is as easy as creating the first level subaccounts; just make sure you've already created the first-level subaccounts (which become the parents of the sub-subaccounts; I guess you could call the sub-subaccounts grandchildren). When you fill in the Add New Account dialog, after you check the Subaccount Of check box, select the appropriate subaccount to act as the parent account.

Caution: If you plan on using a third-party, integrated application that shares data with your QuickBooks data file, it is best to avoid using multiple levels of subaccounts because the integrated application may not be able to post to an "imbedded" account. Check with the developer of your integrated application just to be sure.

Showing Lowest Subaccounts Only

When you view accounts in the Chart Of Accounts window, subaccounts appear under their parent accounts, and they're indented. However, when you view a subaccount in the drop-down list of a transaction window, it appears in the format: *ParentAccount:Subaccount.* (If you're using three levels, the list appears as *ParentAccount:Subaccount:Sub-subaccount.*)

For example, if you create a parent account named Income with a subaccount Consulting, the Account field drop-down list in transaction windows shows Income:Consulting. If you've used numbers, remember that the number is part of the account name, so the Account field shows the following:

```
40000-Income:40010-Consulting
```

Because many of the fields or columns in transaction windows are narrow, you may not be able to see the subaccount names without scrolling through each account. This can be annoying, and it's much easier to work if only the subaccount name is displayed. That's the point of enabling the preference Show Lowest Subaccount Only, discussed earlier in this chapter. When you enable that option, you see only the subaccounts in the drop-down list when you're working in a transaction window, which makes it much easier to select the account you need.

Editing Accounts

If you need to make changes to any account information (including adding a number after you enable numbered accounts), select the account's listing in the Chart Of Accounts window and press CTRL-E. The Edit Account dialog appears, which looks like the account card you just filled out. Make your changes and click Save & Close to save them.

Deleting Accounts

It's not uncommon to clean up your chart of accounts to get rid of accounts you'll never use or to remove duplicate accounts. (You can't have two accounts with the same name or number because QuickBooks doesn't permit that, but it's certainly possible to end up with multiple accounts that are similar; for instance, Tele, Telephone.)

To delete an account, select its listing in the Chart Of Accounts window and press CTRL-D. QuickBooks asks you to confirm the fact that you want to delete the account. Click OK to remove the account.

You can delete any account that isn't in use, which means the account has never been used in a transaction, nor linked to a sales or payroll item. You don't have to search all your transactions to find out whether an account has been used in your system; you can just try to delete it and, if it's been assigned to a transaction or item, QuickBooks issues an error message explaining why you can't get rid of this account.

You cannot delete an account that has subaccounts unless you first delete the subaccounts (which can only be accomplished if the subaccounts have never been used or assigned). However, a workaround for saving the subaccounts and getting rid of the parent account is to turn the subaccounts into parent accounts. To accomplish this, either drag the subaccount listing to the left in the Chart Of Accounts window (be sure the window is displaying accounts in Hierarchical view and the list is in its original sort order), or edit the subaccount to remove the check mark in the Subaccount Of check box.

If you can't delete an account but you don't want anyone to use it, you can hide the account (make it inactive). If the account can't be deleted, and it's a duplicate account, you can merge it with the other account (the one you want to continue to use). Those topics are covered next.

Making Accounts Inactive (Hiding Accounts)

When you make an account inactive, you're hiding the account from users. When an account is inactive, it doesn't appear in drop-down lists in transaction windows, so users can't select it. The account continues to exist and its history remains in the system; it just doesn't appear in drop-down lists during transaction entry.

To make an account inactive, right-click its listing in the Chart Of Accounts window and select Make Account Inactive. QuickBooks doesn't ask you to confirm your action. (You can also make an account inactive by selecting it and pressing CTRL-E to open the account record in Edit mode, then select the check box labeled Account Is Inactive to enter a check mark, but that's more work, and I always take the quickest, easiest route for any task.)

By default, inactive accounts aren't displayed in the Chart Of Accounts window, but if you've made any accounts inactive, the Include Inactive check box at the bottom of the window becomes accessible (it's grayed out if no inactive accounts exist). Select the check box to insert a check mark, and you can see your inactive accounts, which are displayed with an "X" to the left of the listing.

To return an inactive account to active status, click the "X" to toggle the account's status to Active (the Chart Of Accounts window must be displaying inactive accounts).

Merging Accounts

Sometimes you have two accounts that should be one. For instance, you may have accidentally created two accounts for the same purpose. As I discussed earlier in this chapter, I've been to client sites that had accounts named Telephone and Tele, with transactions posted to both accounts. Those accounts are definitely candidates for merging. You can only merge accounts when the following conditions exist:

- Both accounts are of the same account type (for example, you cannot merge an Expense account with an Other Expense account).
- Both accounts are at the same level (you cannot merge a subaccount with a parent account).

Take the following steps to merge two accounts:

1. Open the Chart Of Accounts window.
2. Select (highlight) the account that has the name you do not want to use.
3. Press CTRL-E to open the Edit Account dialog.
4. Change the account name or number (or both) to match the account you want to keep.
5. Click Save & Close.
6. QuickBooks displays a dialog telling you that the account number or name you've entered already exists for another account and asks if you want to merge the accounts. Click Yes to confirm that you want to merge the two accounts.

Remember, the way to do this is to start with the "bad" account and rename it to match the "good" account.

Entering Your Customers

n this chapter:

- Build Your Customer List

- The Customer Center

- Create and track customer jobs

- Edit, delete, and merge customers and jobs

- Create custom fields for customers

- Set up security for customer credit card information

QuickBooks handles customers and jobs together. You can create a customer and consider anything and everything you invoice to that customer a single job, or you can create multiple jobs for the same customer.

Some businesses don't worry about jobs; it's just the customer that's tracked. But if you're a building contractor or subcontractor, an interior decorator, a consultant, or some other kind of service provider who usually sends invoices based on a project, you should track jobs.

Jobs don't stand alone as an entity; they are always attached to customers, and you can attach as many jobs to a single customer as you need to.

While you can create a new customer on the fly the first time you invoice them, entering all your existing customers and jobs during your QuickBooks setup is a better idea because you're more likely to end up with more consistent and complete customer records.

Building Your Customer List

You can choose to add customers one by one (the details for using that method are covered in this section), or you can use the Add/Edit Multiple List Entries window, which is covered in this chapter in the section "Adding Multiple Customer Records." Alternatively, you can return to the Quick Start Center to enter these names from another source or program you're currently using. Launch the Quick Start Center by clicking its icon on the top right-hand side of the Home page. With the Quick Start Center open, use the "Return to Add Info" link (located at the top of the window).

To create a new customer manually, first open the Customer Center by clicking the Customers button located on the Icon Bar. Next click the New Customer & Job button at the top of the Customer Center window (navigating the Customer Center is covered in detail later in this chapter) and select New Customer from the submenu. This action opens the New Customer window (see Figure 3-1). Fill in the appropriate information using the guidelines in the following sections.

Address Info Tab

The New Customer window opens with the Address Info tab in the foreground. The first field to enter information in is the Customer Name field. Consider this field an internal code rather than a customer name. The text you enter here doesn't appear on printed invoices or other sales transactions; rather it's the text in the Company Name field that does.

Customer Name Field

You should create a system for how you complete the Customer Name field so that you'll enter every customer in a consistent manner. If you don't, you run the risk of

The customer record holds quite a lot of information.

entering customers multiple times. For example, if your customer is a business, you can simply enter the name of the business, as shown in Figure 3-1. If your customer is an individual, it's a good practice to enter their last name first in the Customer Name field.

Each customer must have a unique entry in this field, so if you have a lot of customers named Johnson, you may want to enter them in a way that makes it easy to determine which Johnson this listing represents. For instance, you could have customer names such as JohnsonJack, JohnsonMary, JohnsonRestaurant, and so on. If you have several Jack Johnsons, you can use JohnsonJackMainSt for the Jack Johnson on Main Street. This field can contain up to 41 characters, so you should be able to invent a customer naming system that works well for you.

Currency

If you've enabled the multiple currencies feature, this field appears so you can select the currencies for this customer (refer to Appendix B if you plan on using the multiple currencies feature).

Opening Balance Field

QuickBooks makes an Opening Balance field available, along with the date for which this balance applies (by default, the current date is inserted). The field is designed to hold the amount this customer currently owes if an open balance exists for the customer.

ProAdvisor Tip: It's best *not* to use the Opening Balance field. Why? If you enter an amount that includes the balance from more than one outstanding invoice, you'll have no detailed records on how this balance was arrived at, which makes it difficult to accept payments against specific invoices. What's more, QuickBooks posts the amount you enter in this field to Accounts Receivable and makes an offsetting entry into an account named Opening Bal Equity. Eventually you or your accountant will need to zero out the balance in Opening Bal Equity, and sometimes that's a difficult job because it's hard to tell how the balance was arrived at—is this an opening balance you entered from past years? Is it from the current year? Is it a combination of both? Entering transactions that represent the way the customer's current status was reached is far more accurate than using the Opening Balance field. That's why it's better to skip this field and then enter an invoice or multiple invoices to post this customer's balance to your books.

Customer Address Info

In the Company and Addresses sections of the window, enter the company name, optionally enter a contact, and enter the billing address. Add any other contact information you want to track for this customer (telephone, e-mail, and so on). Be sure to enter an e-mail address if you want the ability to e-mail this customer invoices or statements in the future.

Ship To Addresses

You can maintain multiple shipping addresses for your customers. Give a name of your own choosing to each Ship To address so you can select it from a drop-down list when you're entering sales transactions. If the shipping address isn't different from the billing address (or if you have a service business and never ship products), you can ignore the shipping address field, or use the Copy button to copy the data from the Bill To field.

To create a shipping address, click the Add New button under the Ship To address block to open the Add Shipping Address Information dialog.

QuickBooks automatically enters the name Ship To 1. Feel free to replace that text with a name that reminds you of the address location (such as Chicago or MainStreet) to make it easier to select this address from a drop-down list when you have to ship goods to this customer. (If you already entered a Ship To address, the default name of the next address is Ship To 2.)

Enter the address information and specify whether this address should be the default Ship To address, then click OK. If needed, enter another Ship To address for this customer.

Additional Info Tab

The information you enter in the Additional Info tab of a customer card (see Figure 3-2) ranges from essential to convenient. Prepopulating the fields with as much information as possible makes your work go faster when you're creating transactions for customers, and it makes it easier to create detailed reports (because you can design reports based on the data entered in the fields).

Keep in mind that the fields you see on the Additional Info tab may not be the same as the fields shown in Figure 3-2. The preferences you configure (for example, whether you track sales tax or have enabled multiple currencies) determine the available fields.

Let's spend a minute going over the fields in this tab. Most of the fields make up various QuickBooks lists (that you can view from the Lists menu), and if you haven't already entered items in those lists, you can do so as you fill out the fields in the customer record.

FIGURE 3-2 Entering additional information makes your work in QuickBooks go faster.

Type

Use the Type field to sort your customers by a type you find important. For example, you may want to use customer types to distinguish between wholesale and retail customers, or to track the source of referrals. QuickBooks maintains this information in a Customer Type List (covered in more detail in Chapter 7).

To use the field, click the arrow to select a type that you already entered, or create a new type.

Terms

Terms, of course, refers to payment terms. Click the arrow to the right of the text box to see the terms that QuickBooks already defined, or choose <Add New> to define a new one.

The terms in the Terms List are for both customers and vendors, and you may need additional terms to meet your customers' and vendors' needs. See Chapter 7 to learn how to create different types of terms.

Rep

This field is the place to track a sales representative, and it's useful whether you pay commissions or you just want to know who is in charge of this customer. Sales reps can be employees, vendors, or "other names" (which means the name is entered in the Other Names list). Select a rep from the list of reps or add a new rep by choosing <Add New>. Chapter 7 has more information on populating this list.

Preferred Send Method

This field stores the default value for the way you want to send invoices, statements, or estimates to this customer (it does not refer to the method you use to send products to the customer). The choices are the following:

- **None** No special features are used to send the documents. You print them and you mail them (the old-fashioned way).
- **E-mail** You e-mail the documents. This feature lets you attach the documents as PDF files to an e-mail message. You can e-mail using Outlook or your Web-based e-mail (such as Yahoo or Gmail, for example). Chapter 9 has the details.
- **Mail** You use a QuickBooks service to mail the invoices. The data is reproduced on a form that has a tear-off your customers enclose with their payment.

Regardless of the method you choose as your default, you can use any send method when you're creating a transaction. Chapter 25 has more information on setting and using these methods.

Sales Tax Information

If you've configured QuickBooks to collect sales tax, there are a few fields you should complete. If the customer is liable for sales tax, select the appropriate sales tax item for this customer, or create a new sales tax item. If the customer does not pay sales tax, select Non (for nontaxable customer) and enter the Resale Number provided by the customer (this is handy to have when the state tax investigators pop in for a surprise audit). See Chapter 5 for a complete discussion of sales tax codes and sales tax items.

Price Level

Price levels are a way for you to customize your prices on a customer level—usually to offer special discounts when that customer makes a purchase. Select an existing price level or create a new one. See Chapter 7 to learn about creating and assigning price levels.

Custom Fields

Custom fields provide an opportunity for you to create fields for tracking special information about your customers (like contract renewal date, for example). Later, you can then sort and arrange your QuickBooks lists and reports using the data from these fields. See the section "Using Custom Fields" later in this chapter.

Payment Info Tab

This tab (see Figure 3-3) puts all the important information about customer finances in one place.

FIGURE 3-3 Use the Payment Info tab to track details needed for this customer's transactions.

Account No.

This is an optional field you can use if you assign account numbers to your customers.

Credit Limit

A credit limit is a way to set a threshold for the amount of money you'll extend to a customer to make "on account" purchases. If a customer places an order, and the new order combined with any unpaid invoices exceeds this threshold, QuickBooks displays a warning. QuickBooks won't prevent you from continuing to sell to and invoice the customer, but you should consider rejecting the order (or shipping it COD).

Caution: Leaving the Credit Limit field blank is not the same as entering a zero. If you want a data entry/sales person to NOT sell to this person, enter a zero in this field.

Preferred Payment Method

This means the customer's preferred method for payments, and a list of payment methods, is offered in the drop-down list. You can select the appropriate item from the list or add a new one by selecting <Add New>. See Chapter 7 for more information on this list.

ProAdvisor Tip: The payment method you select automatically appears on the Receive Payments window when you are using this customer in the transaction. You can change the payment method at that time, if necessary.

Credit Card No.

This field is intended to contain this customer's credit card number, if that's the customer's preferred payment method. If you decide to store this information, be sure to enable QuickBooks Customer Credit Card Protection. For more information on how to turn on this feature, as well as to learn more about important credit card security issues and best practices, see the section "Securing Customer Credit Card Information" later in this chapter.

Job Info Tab

Use the fields on this tab to help you keep track of the status of your work with a customer and to assign a job description and job type. In addition, assigning start and projected end dates will allow you to produce reports that give you feedback on your performance. More information about how this information is used, as well as how to create jobs that are attached to a customer, can be found in the "Using Jobs" section later in this chapter.

ProAdvisor Tip: If you've enabled the multiple currencies feature, select the appropriate currency for this customer. As you can see in Figure 3-4, this customer's currencies is the Euro. See Appendix B for more on the QuickBooks multiple currencies feature.

When you have finished filling out the fields, choose Next to move to another blank customer card so you can enter the next customer. When you have finished entering all of your customers, click OK.

FIGURE 3-4 You can do business with a foreign customer in that customer's currency.

Adding Multiple Customer Records

If you want to add multiple customers at once (or make changes to the information for existing customer records), you can do so quite easily using the Add/Edit Multiple List Entry window. To use this feature, open the Customer Center (by clicking the Customers button located on the Icon Bar), select the New Customer & Job drop-down arrow at the top of the Customer Center window, and then select Add Multiple Customer:Jobs (you can also access this window from the Lists menu).

The Add/Edit Multiple List Entries window opens (see Figure 3-5). From here, you can add new customers and jobs, change customer information, or fill in data you didn't have when you first created the customer record. You can even copy and paste customers from an Excel sheet into the Add/Edit Multiple List Entries window.

Here's a list of some of the important features and functionality that you should be familiar with to get the most benefit from using the Add/Edit Multiple List Entries window:

- **List and View filters** Select the List or View drop-down arrow to display only those records in your list that you want to work with.

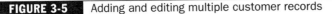

FIGURE 3-5   Adding and editing multiple customer records

- **Find**   Use this field to quickly locate and work with a specific customer record.
- **Customize Columns button**   Use this button to open the Customize Columns window, where you can add columns for the fields within the customer record that you want to modify. For example, if you want to add a job to your Customer list (see the section "Using Jobs" later in this chapter), add the two columns Job Of and Full Customer:Job Name. When you add the Job Of column, it displays a drop-down arrow you can use to associate your new job to its parent customer. The ability to customize the columns also makes it easier to copy and paste from a spreadsheet because you can match the spreadsheet columns to the Add/Edit Multiple List Entry window.

- **Copy Down**   Right-clicking a field in the table allows you to select the Copy Down command, which copies the contents of a selected field to all the remaining records in the list (note, however, that you can't use the Copy Down command with the Name field).
- **Duplicate Row**   Right-clicking with your cursor placed on any row in the table lets you duplicate the selected record in the row below. The new duplicate record name will start with DUP.

The Customer Center

The QuickBooks Customer Center is where all your customers and jobs, and detailed information about those customers and jobs, are kept. It's also where you can go to create, edit, and get reports about customers and jobs.

To open the Customer Center (seen in Figure 3-6), click the Customer Center button located on the Icon Bar or press CTRL-J. You can also open the Customer Center by choosing Customers | Customer Center or by clicking the Customers icon on the Icon Bar.

FIGURE 3-6   The Customer Center is your one-stop location to work with and get information about your customers.

The left pane of the Customer Center has two tabs: Customers & Jobs and Transactions. A customer is always selected in the Customers & Jobs list (by default, the first customer in the list when you first open the Customer Center), and the right pane of the Customer Center displays information about the selected customer or job.

The Transactions tab lists all your sales transactions (invoices, sales receipts, and so on) that are not specific to a particular customer. Selecting a transaction type displays the current transactions of that type in the right pane. The display can be manipulated and filtered by choosing categories and sorting by column.

Customizing the Customers & Jobs List

You can customize the information displayed in the Customers & Jobs list to your own liking. By default, the list has three columns: Name, Balance Total, and Attach (learn about the QuickBooks Attached Documents service in Chapter 25). The Currency column may also be present if you've enabled the multiple currencies feature. You don't even have to select a customer's listing to see the current balance because the balances for all your customers are right in front of you (you may have to scroll down to get to the part of the list that has the customer or job you want to see).

You can add more columns to the Customers & Jobs list. To do so, right-click anywhere in the list and choose Customize Columns to open the Customize Columns dialog seen in Figure 3-7.

FIGURE 3-7 Decide for yourself what you want to see in the Customers & Jobs list.

To add a column, select its label in the left pane and click Add. The information the column describes is displayed for each customer and job in the list. As long as the customer or job you're interested in is displayed on the portion of the list that's visible, the information is available—you don't have to select the listing or open the record.

Some users find it useful to add the Overdue column, so they know which customers have an overdue or almost due invoice. More about this feature and the Customer Collections Center in Chapter 10.

You can rearrange the left-to-right order of the columns by opening the Customize Columns (right-click anywhere in the list and choose Customize Columns) dialog and selecting a column you want to move. Choose Move Up to move a column to the left or Move Down to move it to the right. The order of columns displayed in the Chosen Columns pane of the dialog translates as Top to Bottom = Left to Right.

If you add columns to the Customers & Jobs list, you won't be able to see all the information unless you widen the list's pane and also widen each column. To maximize this pane, click the Show Full List button (an icon with a right-pointing arrow) next to the View field.

Customizing the Customer Information Pane

You can filter the financial information in the right pane by choosing different categories from the drop-down lists in the column headings, and you can sort the information by selecting a column heading to sort by.

In addition, you can add and remove columns by right-clicking anywhere on or below the column headings and choosing Customize Columns. In the Customize Columns dialog (see Figure 3-8), you can add, remove, and change the order of columns.

FIGURE 3-8   Display the information you need for each customer.

Editing an Individual Customer Record

There may be times when you want to edit a customer record individually. You can do this from the Customer Center. Simply locate and double-click the customer's listing in the Customers & Jobs list to open the customer record in Edit mode.

When you open the customer record, you can change any information or fill in data you didn't have when you first created the customer entry.

ProAdvisor Tip: Take care when making changes to the Customer Name field, as it may result in some unintended consequences, such as changing the order in which that name appears in the Customer list and in customer reports and causing a retroactive change to the customer's name on all past transactions. Also, changes in the Customer Name field do not automatically change the name as it appears in the Bill To or Ship To address field—you'll have to remember to update that manually.

Click the Notes button to open a Notepad window that's dedicated to this customer. Use the Date Stamp button to insert the current date automatically when you're adding text to the notepad.

ProAdvisor Tip: If you've entered notes for a customer, when you select a customer in the Customers & Jobs list, some of the text of your notes appears in the top half of the large pane on the right side of the center. For any customer you select, an Edit Notes button appears (as does a To Dos button). You can open the notepad for the selected customer by clicking this icon; you don't have to open the customer record to get to the note. You can also see the notes in the information pane that appears on the right of sales transactions. This is a great way to communicate anything special about a customer among staff members.

Click the New To Do button to compose a reminder specifically for this customer (see Figure 3-9). This is a very useful feature. You get to specify the date on which you want to be reminded (called the Due date) and categorize your new "To Do" as a call or meeting, for example. You can then view your To Do note in the Calendar (discussed in Chapter 1) from the To Do list (accessed through the Customer menu), or directly from the Customer Center. When the task is complete, open the reminder and change its status to Done. This will change its status in the To Do list to closed.

| **FIGURE 3-9** | To Do notes are a useful way to keep track of important customer related tasks. |

Using Jobs

If you plan to track jobs, you can either enter the ones you know about during your QuickBooks setup phase or enter them as you need to. Jobs are attached to customers—they can't stand alone—so the customer to which the job is attached has to exist in your QuickBooks Customers & Jobs list before you can create the job.

Once the job is created, you can track its progress and keep an eye on the promised end date. If you think this will be the only job you perform for this customer, you can do the same thing for a customer without creating a job because the customer record also has a Job Info tab. If you're lucky enough to get another project from the customer, you can always add a new job at a later time.

Creating Jobs

To create a job, open the Customer Center and right-click the listing of the customer for whom you're creating a job. Choose Add Job to open the New Job window, shown in Figure 3-10. Create a name for the job (you can use up to 41 characters) and make it descriptive enough for both you and your customer to understand.

FIGURE 3-10 To create a new job, enter the job name—all the basic information about the customer is already filled in.

If this job requires you to bill the customer at an address that's different from the address you entered for this customer, or to ship goods to a different shipping address, make the appropriate changes in the job's Address Info tab. QuickBooks maintains this information only for this job and won't change the original shipping address in the customer record.

The Additional Info tab and the Payment Info tab are related to the customer rather than the job, so you can skip them.

➡ **ProAdvisor Recommends**

Reps Field

QuickBooks does not have a field on the Additional Info tab for Rep, so if you have different reps assigned to individual jobs for a customer, you may want to consider using one of the following two methods as a workaround:

- Create a custom field for reps.
- Enter the rep's name on the Alt. Contact name on the Address Info tab.

Next, move to the Job Info tab (see Figure 3-11) to fill in the details of this job. All of the information on the Job Info tab is optional.

FIGURE 3-11 Track job details on the Job Info tab.

The Job Status drop-down list offers choices that you can change as the progress of the job moves along. You can change the default text to reflect the way you refer to each progress level, but the changes you make for the text are system wide and affect every job. Here's how to change the text you use to track job status:

1. Choose Edit | Preferences to open the Preferences dialog.
2. Click the Jobs & Estimates icon in the left pane, and then click the Company Preferences tab in the right pane to see the current descriptive text for each status level (see Figure 3-12).
3. Change the text of any status levels if you have a descriptive phrase you like better. For example, you may prefer using the term "Working" instead of "In Progress."

FIGURE 3-12 Customize the text to reflect the way you track a project's progress.

The new text is used on every existing and new job in your system.

The Job Info tab also provides fields to track the start date and the projected end date of the job, as well as a field to enter the real end date (frequently not the same as the projected end date). You can also create job types to categorize jobs and select one of them in the Job Type field (covered in Chapter 7).

When you finish entering all the data about this job, choose Next to create another job for the same customer. Otherwise, click OK to close the New Job window and return to the Customers & Jobs list. The jobs you create for a customer become part of the customer listing.

Editing Jobs

It's common to open a job record to make changes because most people track the current status (and occasionally change the projected end date). In addition, you may want to change some of the basic data you entered for a job.

To edit a job, double-click its listing in the Customers & Jobs list. You can make changes to any of the fields in any tab.

Deleting Customers & Jobs

From time to time you may have the need to delete a customer or a job that you've created. For example, you might create a customer and then realize it's a duplicate record for a customer who already exists in your customer list. Deleting a job is a bit more common than deleting customers because sometimes QuickBooks users add a job when they pitch the client for the work and then delete the job if the customer turns down the offer.

You can only delete a customer or a job if it has never been used in a transaction. I hear from many users who complain that they can't remove a customer that is essentially "dead wood" on their Customers & Jobs list. The customer has a zero balance, and there hasn't been a sale to this customer for a long time (possibly years). Unfortunately, a zero balance doesn't matter; the rule is that you can only delete a customer or a job if it has never been used in a transaction.

In addition, you cannot delete a customer who has at least one job attached to it. Instead, you must first delete the jobs (if they can be deleted), and then delete the customer.

To delete a customer or job (if there are no longer any transactions associated with it), select its listing on the Customers & Jobs list and press CTRL-D. QuickBooks asks you to confirm the fact that you want to delete this customer or job. Click OK to remove the customer or job.

Making Customers & Jobs Inactive (Hiding)

If you have a customer who can't be deleted but is no longer active, you can prevent users from selecting this customer in transaction windows by making the customer inactive (hiding the customer so it doesn't appear in drop-down lists). You can do the same thing for any job.

To make a customer or job inactive, right-click its listing in the Customers & Jobs list and choose Make Customer:Job Inactive.

> **ProAdvisor Tip:** If you make a customer with jobs inactive, all of the jobs are automatically made inactive. You cannot hide a customer without hiding all the jobs associated with that customer.

If your Customers & Jobs list is configured to show Active Customers (the default view), inactive customers and jobs don't appear on the list. To see which customers and jobs are inactive, click the arrow to the right of the View field at the top of the list and select All Customers from the drop-down list. Inactive customers and jobs have an "X" to the left of their listings (see Figure 3-13).

FIGURE 3-13   It's easy to spot inactive customers and jobs.

To make a customer or job active again, select All Customers as the view, and click the "X" next to the hidden customer or job to toggle the setting back to active. If you're reactivating a customer with jobs (which were automatically hidden when you made the customer inactive), QuickBooks asks if you also want to make all the jobs active. (The message actually says, "Do you want to activate the subs as well?") If you click Yes, the customer and all jobs are activated. If you click No, the customer is activated and all the jobs remain inactive; you can activate any of the jobs individually.

> **ProAdvisor Tip:** Historical transactions related to inactive customers and jobs are included in reports, so you can continue to get accurate information about customer activities.

Merging Customers or Jobs

Sometimes you create a customer or job and enter at least one transaction before you realize it's a duplicate of an existing customer or an existing job for the same customer. (Once you enter a transaction, you can't delete the customer or job to correct your error.) The best thing to do in this case is to merge two customers or two jobs and move all the transaction history into one customer record. Use the following steps to do this:

1. Double-click the listing of the customer or job you do *not* want to keep to put its record in Edit mode.
2. Change the customer or job name to match the name of the customer or job you want to keep.
3. Click OK.
4. QuickBooks displays a message telling you that the name is in use and asks if you want to merge the names.
5. Click Yes.

Merging customers only works when one of the following circumstances exists:

- Neither customer has any jobs associated with it.
- The customer name you want to get rid of has no jobs attached (it's OK if the customer name you want to keep has jobs).

Merging jobs only works when both jobs are linked to the same customer.

Using Custom Fields

You can add your own fields to the Customer, Vendor, and Employee records (these are custom fields for names, and there are also custom fields you can create for items).

Custom fields for names are added to all names lists, but you can configure each custom field you create to limit its appearance to specific names lists. For example, you might create a custom field that you want to use in only the Customer & Jobs list or in both the Customer & Jobs and Vendors lists.

Custom fields are useful if there's information you want to track but QuickBooks doesn't provide a field for it. For example, if you want to track customer birthdays or annual renewals for a contract, you can add fields to track that information.

Adding a Custom Field for Names

To add one or more custom fields to names, follow these steps:

1. Open one of the names lists (Customers & Jobs, Vendor, or Employee).
2. Double-click any name on the list to put the record in Edit mode.
3. Move to the Additional Info tab.
4. Click the Define Fields button to open the Set Up Custom Fields For Names dialog, where you can name the field and indicate the list(s) in which you want to use the new field (see Figure 3-14).

FIGURE 3-14 Custom fields appear on all the records of the list(s) you select.

That's all there is to it, except you must click OK to save the information. When you do, QuickBooks displays a message reminding you that if you customize your templates (forms for transactions, such as invoices or sales receipts), you can add these fields. Instructions for adding fields to transaction templates are found in Chapter 28.

The Additional Info tab for every name in the list(s) you selected now shows those fields.

Adding Data to Custom Fields

To add data to the custom fields for each name on the list, select the name and press CTRL-E to put the record into Edit mode. Move to the Additional Info tab where the custom field you created appears (see Figure 3-15).

FIGURE 3-15 Add data to the custom field for each customer to which this custom field is relevant.

Be sure you enter data in a consistent manner for each customer, or you won't be able to get the information when you customize a report to include this information. For example, one of the custom fields shown in Figure 3-15 holds a date. In this case, the date is entered in the format: Year-Month, using a four-digit year and a three-character month.

If you use that format for all customers who have contract renewal dates (such as 2012-Jun or 2013-Jan), you can filter a customer list report to show all customers with contracts that are renewing 2012-Sep. If, however, you use Sept for some data entry, and Sep for other data entry, or if you forget to enter a dash and used a space, you won't see all the customers with September renewal dates.

Securing Customer Credit Card Information

QuickBooks provides security features for companies that store customer credit card data in their company files. These features are designed to help you meet the requirements set by the payment card industry that are known as the *Payment Card Industry Data Security Standard* (PCI DSS).

If you log in to your company file as Admin, you may see a reminder about enabling credit card protection when you open the file.

You should enable the credit card protection feature as soon as possible, but if you don't respond to the reminder by selecting Enable Protection, you can perform the task by choosing Company | Customer Credit Card Protection and selecting Enable Protection.

Caution: You must be logged in as the user named Admin to configure credit card protection.

In the explanatory window that opens, select Enable Protection to begin setting up this feature. The first chore you face is changing your own Admin password so it matches the standards for complex passwords required by the credit card protection feature (see Figure 3-16).

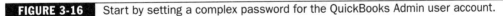

FIGURE 3-16 Start by setting a complex password for the QuickBooks Admin user account.

The Challenge Question section is mandatory. If you forget your password, you can click the Reset Password button on the Login dialog. When you answer the challenge question correctly, QuickBooks lets you change your password to a new complex password. When you complete the dialog and click OK, QuickBooks confirms the fact that you've changed your password and informs you that you'll have to repeat this task every 90 days.

QuickBooks also displays a message to inform you that customer credit card protection has been enabled.

> **ProAdvisor Tip:** Although not recommended, you can disable the customer credit card protection feature: reopen the Customer Credit Card Protection window, leave the password information blank, and then click Cancel.

More About QuickBooks Customer Credit Card Protection

- All users who have permission to view full credit card detail in the customer record must set up a *complex password* (see the next section, "About Complex Passwords").
- The password must be changed every 90 days. Users who don't change their password cannot open the file. If the Admin fails to change his or her password, the credit card protection feature is disabled (and you see messages about your failure to comply with the rules set for businesses that accept credit cards).
- You cannot reuse any of the last four passwords.
- If a user enters an incorrect password three times (users sometimes guess different passwords when they can't remember their password), the company file closes for that user.
- Only the user named Admin can configure the functions in this feature.
- The QuickBooks credit card security audit log tracks all actions that involve credit cards (including viewing customer credit card information).

About Complex Passwords

Complex passwords (sometimes called *strong passwords*) are passwords that can't easily be discovered by hacker software that uses permutations and combinations of letters and numbers to break into password-protected files.

The more complex a password is, the higher the odds are against breaking in. For example, a password that contains seven characters and includes one uppercase letter and six lowercase letters is harder to break than a password that is entirely uppercase or lowercase (the odds are somewhere in the range of one in many millions). When you mix numbers with letters, and at least one letter is in a different case than the others, the odds grow even greater. If you add characters and at least two of those characters are numbers, and at least two of the letters are in a different case than the other letters, the odds of breaking in grow to pretty astronomical levels.

User Permissions for Viewing Credit Card Information

With credit card protection enabled, when you set up users and give them Full Access to the Sales and Accounts Receivable area, those users are not given permission to view customer credit card information unless you specifically select that option.

Users who do not have permission to view credit card information see only the last four numbers of the credit card when they open the Payment Info tab of a customer's record (see Figure 3-17).

FIGURE 3-17   Users without the proper permissions can't see credit card numbers.

Users who have permission to view customer information are forced to create a complex password during their next login (see Figure 3-18).

When you set up new users and give them permission to access customer information, it's not necessary to set up a complex password for them. Provide a regular, easy to enter password, and QuickBooks will force a password change during the first login. (See Chapter 26 to learn more about setting up users and permissions.)

Any user with permission to view customer information must create a complex password.

Viewing the Security Log

When credit card protection is enabled, QuickBooks maintains a security log called the Customer Credit Card Audit Trail. This log can be viewed only by the Admin. To open the log, choose Reports | Accountant & Taxes | Customer Credit Card Audit Trail.

The log tracks logins, logouts, and any activity related to customer credit card data, with the most recent event listed at the top of the log.

Entering Your Vendors

n this chapter:

- Build your vendor list

- The Vendor Center

- Editing vendors

- Deleting vendors

- Merging vendors

- Creating custom fields for vendor records

QuickBooks refers to the businesses or individuals that you purchase goods and services from as vendors, and the names of these vendors have to be entered into your QuickBooks system before you can enter bills or otherwise pay them. In most cases, it's easier to enter their information before you start entering transactions. Otherwise, you'll have to go through the process of establishing the vendor and entering all the detailed information about that vendor at the moment you need to enter a bill or write a check to them.

Creating Your Vendors List

As with your Customers List, you have a few options when building your list of vendors in QuickBooks. You can choose to add them one by one (the details for using that method are covered in this section), you can use the Add/Edit Multiple List Entries window (which is covered later in this chapter), or you can return to the Quick Start Center to enter or import these names from another source or program you currently use. See Chapter 1 for details on how to launch and use the tools in the Quick Start Center.

To create a vendor, you'll first need to open the Vendor Center. From the Vendors menu, select Vendor Center. Now click the New Vendor icon above the Vendors list and select New Vendor (more about the Vendor Center later in this chapter). The New Vendor dialog, as seen in Figure 4-1, opens.

Start by filling in the Vendor Name field at the top of the dialog. (You may not want to use the real vendor name; to learn why, see the section "Establishing Rules for Naming Your Vendors" later in this chapter.)

It's best *not* to enter anything in the Opening Balance field. Instead, separately enter the existing open vendor bills that represent the current open (unpaid) balances. See Chapter 8 to learn how get vendor history into your company file.

Currency

If you've enabled multiple currencies, select the appropriate currency for this vendor if the vendor is in another country (refer to Appendix B for more information on the QuickBooks multiple currencies feature).

Vendor Address Info Tab

Fill in as much information about vendor names, contacts, telephone numbers, and so on, as you think you'll need. The Billed From address block is important if you're planning to print checks and the vendor doesn't enclose a return envelope. It's where you'll likely send your payment to, while the Shipped From Address is used if your

FIGURE 4-1 Vendor records are less complicated than customer records.

vendor requires that you send a purchase order to a different address and the orders you receive from them are also from that address. You can purchase window envelopes, and when you insert the check in the envelope, the vendor name and address block is in the right place.

Establishing Rules for Naming Your Vendors

It's a good idea to think through how you want to enter information in the Vendor Name field. While this field doesn't appear on checks or purchase orders, it's used to sort and select vendors when you need to select a vendor from a drop-down list or when you want to create a report about vendor activity.

Think of the Vendor Name field as an internal company code. Take your phone bill as an example. You can use your telephone number as the Vendor Name, but in the Company Name field use the name of the telephone company.

Note that when you enter the phone company's name in the Company Name field, QuickBooks duplicates that data in the Print On Check As field. In addition, by using codes in the Vendor Name field, you can create as many vendor records as you have phone numbers and then can generate individual checks to pay each phone bill.

The need for consistent naming rules such as this becomes even more important (and more apparent) when you're dealing with government and tax agencies. Think of how many checks you send to your state or local governments for different reasons. There may be checks for remitting sales tax, employee payroll withholding, corporate income tax, to name a few. To avoid confusion, especially when multiple payments are made the same day (but the addresses on the enclosed envelopes or coupons are different for each type of payment), consider using Vendor Name entries that contain the name of the form number or type of tax you are remitting. Every one of those vendor records can have your own state Department of Revenue as the data for the Print On Check As field.

Vendor Additional Info Tab

The Additional Info tab for vendors (see Figure 4-2) has several important categories:

- **Account No.** Enter your account number with this vendor (to the vendor, it's your customer number), and the number will appear in the memo field of printed checks.
- **Type** Optionally, select a vendor type or create one. The Type field is handy if you want to sort vendors by type, which makes reports more efficient. For example, you can create vendor types for inventory suppliers, tax authorities, and so on.
- **Terms** Enter the terms for payment this vendor has assigned to you.
- **Credit Limit** Enter the credit limit this vendor has given you.
- **Tax ID** Use this field to enter the social security number or EIN if this vendor receives a Form 1099.
- **1099 status** If appropriate, select the check box for Vendor Eligible For 1099 (learn how to turn on the 1099 tracking feature later in this chapter).
- **Custom Fields** You can create custom fields for vendors (see the section "Using Custom Fields in Vendor Records" later in this chapter).

FIGURE 4-2 Add data to this tab to make it easier to print checks and produce detailed reports.

Account Prefill Tab

You'll definitely want to use this feature as it's a great way to save time and ensure accuracy when filling out vendor bills or writing checks. You can prefill an account for this vendor (see Figure 4-3) and have the right account(s) appear automatically in the transaction window.

When you're using the vendor in a transaction, you can replace the prefilled account, if necessary.

You can prefill up to three accounts for a vendor. This feature can be very useful for your Internet service provider, for example, where you may want to split out Internet service and telephone. Another good use is for making loan payments (which require postings to principal and interest) and other multi-account payments.

FIGURE 4-3 Prefill the usual posting account for a vendor to save time and avoid errors.

ProAdvisor Tip: If you have a vendor that needs only one account, but you often split the amount due in order to assign parts of the bill to customers, enter the same account in all three fields of the Account Prefill tab. QuickBooks will list all the accounts in the transaction window. For example, parts of your telephone bill (usually long distance charges) may be charged to multiple clients as reimbursable expenses.

After you fill in the information on all the New Vendor tabs, choose Next to move to the next blank card and enter the next vendor. When you're finished, click OK.

Adding and Editing Multiple Vendor Records

Suppose you want to add additional information to many or all of your vendor records at once, or you want to find an easy way to enter new vendors in a more streamlined way? You can use the Add/Edit Multiple List Entries window to do just that.

From the Vendor Center, select New Vendor | Add Multiple Vendors (you can also access this window by selecting Lists | Add/Edit Multiple List Entries and selecting Vendors as the list type). The Add/Edit Multiple List Entries window opens, as shown in Figure 4-4.

FIGURE 4-4   Adding and editing multiple vendor records

From here you can add new vendors, change or update key information, or fill in data you perhaps didn't have when you first created the vendor. You can even copy and paste vendors from an Excel worksheet into the Add/Edit Multiple List Entries window to quickly create a new vendor record.

Here's a list of some of the important features and functionality that you should be familiar with to get the most benefit from using the Add/Edit Multiple List Entries window:

- **List and View filters**   Select the List or View drop-down arrow to display only those records in your list that you want to work with.
- **Customize Columns button**   Use this button to open the Customize Columns window. Here you can add the columns to the vendor record that you want to modify or to match the columns to a spreadsheet that you want to copy and paste from into QuickBooks.

- **Copy Down** By right-clicking a field in the table, you can select the Copy Down command, which copies the contents of a selected field to all the remaining records in the list (however, you can't use the Copy Down command with the Name field).
- **Duplicate Row** By right-clicking any row in the table, you can duplicate the selected record in the row below. The new duplicate record name will start with DUP.

The Vendor Center

The Vendor Center is where your Vendors list is stored, along with all the information about each vendor's transactions. To open the vendor center, choose Vendors | Vendor Center from the menu bar (or click the Vendors icon on the Icon Bar). The Vendor Center displays your Vendors list, gives you quick access to key reports and makes it easy to enter vendor transactions (see Figure 4-5).

FIGURE 4-5 The Vendor Center is where the key information about your vendors lives.

The left pane of the Vendor Center has two tabs: Vendors (which is your Vendors list) and Transactions. A vendor is always selected in the list (by default, the first vendor in the list when you first open the Vendor Center), and the right pane of the Vendor Center displays the details that you'll want to track for the selected vendor as well as any transactions related to them.

The transaction information in the bottom of the right pane can be filtered by choosing different categories from the drop-down lists and can be sorted by selecting a column heading. The Transactions tab lists all vendor transaction types. Selecting a transaction type displays the current transactions of that type in the right pane. The display can be manipulated and filtered by choosing categories and sorting by column.

Customizing the Vendor Center

You can customize the information displayed in the Vendors list (the Vendors tab in the left pane of the window), as well as the Vendor Information pane on the right side of the window.

Customize the Vendors List

By default, the Vendors list has three columns: Name, Balance Total, and Attach. The Attach column displays a paper clip icon next to the vendor name if you've attached a scanned or other document to that record using the Document Center. Use the scroll bar to get to the part of the list that has the vendor you want to see.

You can use the View drop-down list at the top of the Vendors tab to display your vendors in any of following ways:

- All Vendors
- Active Vendors
- Vendors With Open Balances
- Custom Filter

Use the Custom Filter to display only vendors that match the criteria you set in the Custom Filter dialog. The options in the dialog are easy to understand and use.

You can add more columns to the list by right-clicking anywhere in the list and choosing Customize Columns to open the Customize Columns dialog seen in Figure 4-6.

FIGURE 4-6 Decide for yourself what you want to see in the Vendors list.

To add a column, select its label in the left pane and click Add. The information the column describes is displayed for each vendor in the list. As long as the vendor you're interested in is displayed on the portion of the list that's visible, the information is available—you don't have to select the listing or open the record.

You can rearrange the left-to-right order of the columns by opening the Customize Columns dialog and selecting a column you want to move. Choose Move Up to move a column to the left or Move Down to move it to the right. The order of columns displayed in the Chosen Columns pane of the dialog translates as Top to Bottom = Left to Right.

If you add columns to the Vendors list, you won't be able to see all the information unless you widen the list's pane and also adjust the width of each column. To maximize this pane, click the Show Full List Only button (shown in Figure 4-5).

Customize the Vendor Information Pane

You can filter the information that's displayed for each vendor by choosing different criteria for the three filters displayed above the columns. In addition, you can add and remove columns by clicking anywhere on or below the column headings and choosing Customize Columns. In the Customize Columns dialog (see Figure 4-7), add, remove, and change the order of columns. Note that if you use the Memo field in vendor transactions, it's useful to add that field to the columns.

FIGURE 4-7 Change the information that appears for each vendor in the vendor information pane.

Editing Vendor Information

You can edit a vendor's information by double-clicking the vendor's listing in the Vendors list. The vendor's record opens in Edit mode, as seen in Figure 4-8.

You can fill in data details you didn't enter when you first created the vendor. (Many QuickBooks users prefer to enter just the vendor name and company name when they set up vendors, so they can start entering historical transactions immediately. Later, when they have some time, they edit the record to fill in the missing data.)

You can change any data you've previously entered, but change the data in the Vendor Name field with caution, since doing so will change the way it appears in your Vendors list and key vendor reports. Changing the Vendor Name field can also change the name associated with past transactions that you have cleared in QuickBooks. For example, if your phone company changes from AT&T to Verizon, and you change the vendor name, all past checks and bill payments written to AT&T will show as written to Verizon.

You can also keep miscellaneous notes about a vendor for your own records. Click the Notes button to open a Notepad window that's dedicated to this vendor. You can

FIGURE 4-8   You can edit and update vendor information easily and at any time.

enter information or remarks about an order. Click the Date Stamp button to auto-insert the current date in front of any note you enter.

Click the New To Do button to compose a reminder specifically for this vendor. This is a very useful feature. You can specify the date on which you want to be reminded (called the due date) and categorize your new "To Do" as a call or meeting, for example. You can then view your To Do note in the calendar (discussed in Chapter 1), or directly from the Vendor Center. When the task is complete, open the reminder and change its status to Done. This will change its status in the To Do list to closed.

Deleting a Vendor

You can only remove a vendor from the list if that vendor has never been involved in a transaction. It doesn't matter if there's no open balance, or the last transaction was a long time ago; the fact that a vendor is in your transaction history means you cannot delete the vendor.

To delete a vendor, select its listing in the Vendors tab of the Vendor Center and press CTRL-D. QuickBooks asks you to confirm the fact that you want to delete the vendor; just click OK to finish the task. If the vendor has ever been involved in a transaction, QuickBooks issues an error message saying you can't delete this vendor.

If you can't delete a vendor but you don't want this vendor used in transactions, you can hide the vendor's listing (covered next).

Making a Vendor Inactive (Hiding a Vendor)

If you have a vendor who can't be deleted, but you don't want to use the vendor anymore, you can prevent users from selecting this vendor in transaction windows by making the vendor inactive (hiding the vendor name so it doesn't appear in drop-down lists).

To make a vendor inactive, right-click its listing in the Vendors list and choose Make Vendor Inactive.

If your Vendors list is configured to show Active Vendors (the default view), inactive vendors don't appear on the list. To see which vendors are inactive, click the arrow to the right of the View field at the top of the list and select All Vendors from the drop-down list. Inactive vendors have an "X" to the left of their listings. To make a vendor active again, select All Vendors as the view, and click the "X" next to the hidden vendor or job to toggle the setting back to active. Inactive vendors are included in reports, so you can continue to get accurate reports on purchases and other vendor activity.

Merging Vendors

Sometimes you create a vendor and enter transactions for them before you realize it's a duplicate of an existing vendor. This can happen if you haven't established a naming convention for entering data in the Vendor Name field when creating a vendor.

You'll need to merge the two vendors and move all the transaction history into one vendor record. Here are the steps:

1. Double-click the listing of the vendor you do *not* want to keep, which opens its record in Edit mode.
2. Change the data in the Vendor Name field to match the name of the vendor you want to keep.
3. Click OK.
4. QuickBooks displays a message telling you that the name is in use and asks if you want to merge the names.
5. Click Yes.

Remember, the trick to merging is to start with the vendor name you *don't* want and merge into the vendor name you *do* want.

Using Custom Fields in Vendor Records

You can add your own fields to the Vendor, Customer, and Employee records. QuickBooks provides the ability to create custom fields for Names lists (and also offers custom fields for Items).

Custom fields for Names lists are added to all Names lists, but you can configure each custom field you create to limit its appearance to specific Names lists. For example, you might create a custom field that you want to use in only the Vendors list, or in both the Customers & Jobs and Vendors lists.

Custom fields are useful if there's information you want to track but QuickBooks doesn't provide a field for it. For example, if you have vendors with whom you've signed contracts, you might want to add a field that will let you track contract renewal dates.

Adding a Custom Field for Vendors

To add one or more custom fields to the vendor list, follow these steps:

1. Open the Vendor Center.
2. Select any name on the Vendor list and press CTRL-E to put the record in Edit mode.
3. Move to the Additional Info tab.
4. Click the Define Fields button to open the Set Up Custom Fields For Names dialog, where you can name the field and indicate the list(s) in which you want to use the new field (see Figure 4-9).

That's all there is to it, except you must click OK to save the information. When you do, QuickBooks flashes a message reminding you that if you customize your templates (forms for transactions, such as bills or checks), you can add these fields. The Additional Info tab for every name in the list(s) you selected now shows those fields, and you can add data to any name for which these fields have relevance.

Adding Data to Custom Fields

To add data to the custom fields for each name on the list that needs the data, select the name and press CTRL-E to put the record into Edit mode. Move to the Additional Info tab where the custom field you created appears (see Figure 4-10).

Be sure that you enter data in a consistent manner for each vendor, or you won't be able to get the information when you customize a report to include this information. For example, consider the data entered in the custom field "Last Review Date" shown in Figure 4-10. If you enter **Dec 31, 2011** for some vendors and **12/31/2011** for others, and then customize a report looking for 12/31/2011, all the Dec 31, 2011 vendors will be missing from the report.

FIGURE 4-9 Design custom fields that you can use for one list or multiple lists.

FIGURE 4-10 Add data to the custom field for each vendor to which this custom field is relevant.

Creating 1099 Vendors

QuickBooks supports only the 1099-MISC form. If any vendors are eligible for 1099 reporting, you need to enter additional information about them when setting them up. The focus of this chapter is on accomplishing this task before you begin making payments to a 1099 vendor. The process of verifying and filing 1099 forms in QuickBooks is covered in detail in Chapter 24.

Configuring 1099 Options

First, make sure your file is set up to track and process 1099 forms: choose Edit | Preferences, click the Tax: 1099 icon, and move to the Company Preferences tab to see your settings (see Figure 4-11). Be sure you've clicked Yes next to the Do You File 1099-MISC Forms? question.

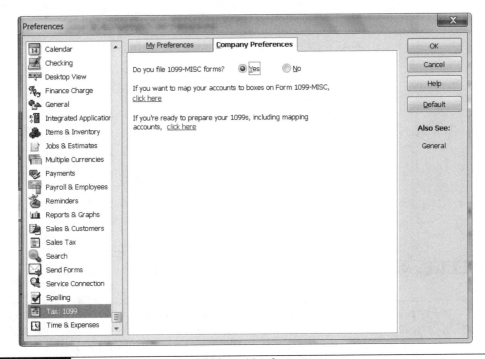

FIGURE 4-11   Be sure to turn on the 1099 tracking feature.

Marking Vendors as 1099 Recipients

Generally speaking, you are required to issue Form 1099-MISC at the end of the calendar year to a vendor who operates as a business, unless the vendor is a corporation.

To issue Form 1099, you must have the vendor's federal Tax Identification Number (TIN), which can be a social security number or an Employer Identification Number (EIN). Open each appropriate vendor listing and move to the Additional Info tab. Select the option labeled Vendor Eligible For 1099, and fill in the Tax ID Number as shown in Figure 4-12.

FIGURE 4-12 Mark each eligible vendor for 1099 reporting and fill in the Tax ID number.

ProAdvisor Tip: 1099 reporting rules are becoming more complex each year. It's a very good idea to check in with your accountant about the latest IRS rules regarding which vendors should receive a 1099 from you. Be sure to also ask your accountant if there are any other guidelines that you should be aware of.

Creating Items

In this chapter:

- Understand how items are used

- Learn about different types of items

- Create an item

- Set up sales tax items

In QuickBooks, *items* are what you use to list the things you sell on an invoice (and in other sales-related transactions). You can also use items on a bill to tell QuickBooks about the things you're buying from a vendor. An item can be a product (that you may or may not be tracking as inventory), a service, or another necessary entry on a sales or purchase transaction.

What other necessary entries could there be besides products and services? If you think about it and picture an invoice, there are more items required than might occur to you. Are you required to charge sales tax? If you do, that's an item. Do you accept prepayments or give discounts? Those are items. Do you subtotal sections of your invoices to apply discounts or taxes? That subtotal is also an item. Do you charge for shipping or restocking fees? Those are items.

In this chapter, the different types of items you can use in QuickBooks are covered in detail, with the exception of inventory items (which are covered in Chapter 6) and payroll items (covered in Chapter 17).

Understanding How Items Are Used

Items are most often used in sales-related transactions where each line in the document (an invoice or sales receipt, for example) is populated with an item that you've created and configured. What's more, every item you create is linked to an account in your chart of accounts, so that when you're creating a transaction you don't have to worry about the account to which any individual line item on an invoice or sales receipt is posted—your item takes care of all that behind-the-scenes accounting for you.

Most items are linked to an income account, because most of the items that appear on a sales transaction are things you're selling to the customer. You can link all of your items to one income account (called "Income" or "Sales"), or you can track different types of items by linking them to different income accounts. For example, you might want to link all product sales to an income account named "Product Sales" and link the services you sell to an income account named "Service Sales." The advantage of linking certain types of items to certain income accounts is that when you look at a standard Profit & Loss report, you can tell at a glance what your sales totals are for each group of item types. You can also create reports on your items themselves. QuickBooks offers several item reports that give you insight into details like your best sellers and your most profitable and least profitable items, to name a few.

Some items, however, are not linked to income accounts, because they're not income. For example, sales tax isn't income to you, it's money you collect for someone else (your state or local government) and have to turn over to the proper tax authority. Because you're holding someone else's money, sales tax items are linked to a liability account.

Discounts you give your customers are items too, and you should link them to accounts specifically designed for that purpose. That way, you can easily see in your reports the savings and incentives that you've passed on to your customers.

As you can see, items are a bit more complicated than you may have thought, but creating and configuring them is not so complicated if you follow the steps outlined in this chapter.

Understanding Item Types

QuickBooks needs to categorize the items that you add to your item list, and it does this by using item types. It isn't always clear how and when some of the item types are used, or for that matter why you must define an item in a particular way. Use the following definitions as a guide when you plan the building of your item list:

Service This is a service you provide to a customer. You can create services that are charged by the job or by the hour and are performed by an employee or an outside contractor.

Inventory Part This is a product you buy for the purpose of reselling. Inventory parts are treated differently in accounting; you post their cost as you sell them (*not* when you write the check to purchase them). This item type isn't available if you haven't turned on the inventory tracking feature in the Items & Inventory section of the Preferences dialog. Setting up and managing inventory requires that you understand the ground rules and valuation method that QuickBooks uses. Be sure to refer to Chapter 6 if you plan on tracking inventory, as it covers this topic in great detail.

Non-inventory Part This item type is a product you buy and sell but don't track as inventory (such as merchandise that is always drop shipped to a customer), as well as products you buy but don't sell (such as boxes and bubble wrap).

Other Charge You'll use this item type for things like shipping charges or other line items that don't fit into a service or product item.

Subtotal This item type automatically adds up the line items that come immediately before it on a sales transaction. It provides a subtotal before you add other charges or subtract discounts.

Group This item type can be a big time saver because it's used to enter a group of individual items all at once, instead of entering each individual item on the sales transaction (each item must first exist on its own in your Item List).

For example, if you always have a shipping charge accompanying the sale of a particular item, you can create a group item that includes those two items.

Discount When entered on a sales transaction, this item allows you to apply either a percentage or dollar discount to the item immediately above it (including subtotal items). You may want to create more than one item that falls within this item type—for example, a discount for wholesale customers and a discount for a volume purchase. When you create a discount item, you can indicate a flat dollar value or percentage of the original price.

Payment   If you receive a prepayment (either a total payment or a partial payment as a deposit), you indicate it as a line item using this item type.

Sales Tax Item   Create one of these item types for each sales tax authority for which you collect (available only if sales tax is enabled).

Sales Tax Group   This is for multiple sales taxes (state and local) that apply to the customer.

Building Your Item List

Regardless of the type of item you want to create, the process of building your item starts by choosing Lists | Item List from the menu bar. The information that QuickBooks needs to create an item depends on the type of item you're creating. While service items are relatively simple to create, Inventory items require a bit more planning (which is why they are covered separately in Chapter 6). Let's start by learning how to create a service item.

How to Create a Service Item

With the Item List open (as described in the previous section), press CTRL-N. The New Item window opens, displaying a list of item types, as described in the previous paragraphs. Select Service as the type. Note the many fields displayed in the blank New Item window (see Figure 5-1).

FIGURE 5-1   The fields in the New Item dialog hold the information you need to use the item in transactions, post it correctly to your general ledger, and produce accurate reports.

The Item Name/Number field is the place to insert a unique identifying code for the item. In this case, the Item Name/Number can simply be the service that's being offered—in our example, it's Design Services. Later, when you are filling out invoices (or purchase orders), this is the identifier you see in the drop-down list.

Next you see the Subitem Of check box. If you wanted to make Design Services a subitem of another item called Architectural Services, for example, you would check this box. Why would you want to use subitems? First, it gives you the ability to track the sales (and purchases) of categories of that item at a more granular level. Second, it allows you to organize a complex Item List in a way that makes sense to you and others in your company.

Next you see the option to tell QuickBooks if this service is used in assemblies (only QuickBooks Premier and Enterprise Editions offer the assembly feature) or is performed by a subcontractor or partner. When you check this box, the item record expands to include fields that allow you to link both the expense side of this item as well as the income side to the appropriate account in your chart of accounts. Use the drop-down arrow to select an appropriate expense account. You can fill in the Cost field here or leave it at zero if you pay more than one rate for that service to different subcontractors. Later, when you pay the vendor you've hired as a subcontractor for this service, you'll select this item (using the Item tab on either the Write Checks or Enter Bills windows) and fill in a cost.

In the Rate field, enter the amount or hourly rate you charge for this service. You can leave this field at zero if your business doesn't have a standard rate for this service and it makes more sense for you to fill it in when you create an invoice or sales receipt. Next, be sure to use the Tax Code drop-down arrow to indicate whether or not this service is taxable, then carefully choose which income account you want QuickBooks to link this item to. Use the Notes button to open a notepad to record and store any special information that you want to keep track of about this item.

When you're done, click OK to return to the Item List or Next to create another new item.

Creating Custom Fields for Items

With custom fields, you can capture and use unique information about the products and services you sell. For example, you may want to add information about the size or color of an item that you carry in stock or identify the location in your warehouse where a particular part is stored. You can create up to five fields by following these steps:

1. Open the Item List and select an item.
2. Press CTRL-E to edit the item.
3. Click the Custom Fields button. (The first time you create a custom field, a message appears telling you that there are no custom fields yet defined; click OK.)
4. When the Custom Fields dialog appears, click Define Fields.
5. When the Set Up Custom Fields For Items dialog opens, enter a name for each field you want to add.

6. Place a check mark in the Use column to use the field.
7. Click OK.

As you create your fields, keep in mind that all fields are shared among all the items in your Item List (with the exception of subtotals, sale tax items, and sales tax groups), whether they're inventory, non-inventory, or service items, and the maximum number of fields available to you is five. Refer to Chapter 28 to learn more about how to add these fields to your invoices and other QuickBooks templates.

Creating the Other Items in Your Item List

While many of the fields in the New Item window are pretty much the same regardless of the type of item you're creating, there are some fields that are particular to the type of item you're creating. The following section covers these other item types while also pointing out any unique fields you should be aware of.

Non-inventory Items

As with service items, you have the option of making a non-inventory item "two-sided," meaning when you check the This Item Is Used In Assemblies Or Is Purchased For A Specific Customer:Job box, you can designate both an income and expense account at the same time (see Figure 5-2). This makes item and other detailed reports much more valuable. In addition, if your vendor references this non-inventory part using their own unique number, you can store that number/reference in the Manufacturer's Part Number field. This information then becomes available to you for purchasing activities.

FIGURE 5-2 Create a non-inventory part when you don't need to track on-hand quantities.

▶▶ ProAdvisor Recommends

The Importance of Items for Job Costing

Because items are most often associated with sales transactions, many QuickBooks users who are service-based are not accustomed to using them in purchase transactions (bills and checks). Be sure that when you're entering a bill (covered in Chapter 11) or check that relates to a purchase you've made for a specific customer job, you click the Items tab (instead of the Expenses tab) and select the service or non-inventory part item that you used on the sales transaction for that customer job (see Figure 5-3). In addition, be sure that this item is "two-sided" (see the "Non-inventory Items" section). Following this logic gives you the ability to take full advantage of the many job-related reports that come with QuickBooks Pro. For example, from the Reports menu, select Jobs, Time & Mileage. You'll see several reports designed to give you insight into precisely where you're making (or losing) money on a job and how your original estimate for a job compares to the actual costs and revenues you've realized as of a particular date.

FIGURE 5-3 Using the Items tab on a bill or check helps you get the most from job costing reports.

Other Charge Items

Other charge items are generally used to list amounts for things like shipping and handling or any other miscellaneous charges that you want to appear on a sales transaction. A key feature of this item type is that it can also be set up as a percentage of another item or as a subtotal by listing it directly below the line item that you want it to refer to.

Subtotal Items

This is a very useful item type because it allows you to add and total groups of items within the body of an invoice or sales receipt. It's very easy to use: simply list the subtotal item immediately after the list of items that you want to display a subtotal for.

Group Items

A group item is an efficient way to list items that you typically sell together on an Invoice or Sales Receipt. For example, you may run a promotion where you bundle discounted installation services with the purchase of a high-end lighting fixture. In this case, you would create a group item that includes the fixture and the installation as a single item (see Figure 5-4).

FIGURE 5-4 When you use a group item, you can choose to show all the items on a sales transaction or show only one description line.

Before you attempt to create a group item, be sure that the individual items have already been entered into your item list. Then follow these steps:

1. From the Item List, press CTRL-N to open the New Item window.
2. Select Group from the Type drop-down list.
3. Create a name for the new group in the Group Name/Number field.
4. Optionally, enter a description. Note that whether or not you select the Print Items In Group option (which ensures that individual items in the group will appear in the transaction), your entry in the Description field is what will appear on the sales transaction—unless you decide to change it, of course.
5. Select each item that is to be part of this group, and enter the quantity (if applicable) for each item.
6. Click OK.

Discount Items

Discount items work by affecting the line item immediately preceding it. When you create the item, you can indicate either a flat rate or a percentage.

Payment Items

Payment items are used to record the receipt of a partial payment on a sale. When listed on an invoice, it reduces the balance due.

Subitems are a convenient way to list your items in your Item List in a logical order. For example, if you're a distributor of lighting fixtures, you might create a parent inventory item called Bath/Vanity fixtures and list the individual items that you sell under that category as the subitems. Creating and using subitems is covered in more detail in Chapter 6.

Changing Item Prices

If you want to implement a price increase (or decrease) for one or more of the services or products you sell, use the Change Item Prices window.

1. From the Customers menu, select Change Item Prices.
2. In the Change Item Prices window, use the Item Type filter to list only those items of a particular type (service, inventory part, inventory assembly, non-inventory part, or other charge).
3. Place a check mark next to the items subject to a price change and tell QuickBooks whether the price should be adjusted from the unit cost of that item or from the current price.
4. Click the Adjust button to effect the change, then click OK.

Collecting Sales Tax Using Sales Tax Items

If you collect and remit sales tax, you need to configure your sales tax preferences in QuickBooks. You must set up tax codes to link to your customers so you know whether a customer is liable for sales tax, and you must set up tax items so you can set a percentage rate and link the item to a taxing authority.

Start your sales tax setup by choosing Edit | Preferences from the menu bar. Click the Sales Tax icon in the left pane and select the Company Preferences tab to see the window shown in Figure 5-5.

If you used Advanced Setup and you didn't enable the sales tax feature, you can do it now by selecting the Yes option in the section labeled Do You Charge Sales Tax? The following sections cover the other options in this dialog.

Sales Tax Items

A sales tax item is a collection of data about a sales tax, including the rate and the agency to which the sales tax is remitted. QuickBooks uses sales tax items to calculate the Tax field at the bottom of sales forms and to prepare reports for tax authorities. You can create your first sales tax item here in the Sales Tax Preferences or in the Item List (see the section "Creating Sales Tax Items in the Item List").

FIGURE 5-5 Set your sales tax preferences.

Most Common Sales Tax

The Sales Tax Preferences dialog (as shown in Figure 5-5) has a field named Your Most Common Sales Tax Item, and you must enter a sales tax item in that field. Of course, to do that, you must first create at least one sales tax item. This item becomes the default sales tax item for any customers you create hereafter, but you can change any customer's default sales tax item any time.

Creating Sales Tax Items in the Item List

You can create a sales tax item while in your Item List by following these steps:

1. Select Lists | Item List from the main menu to open the Item List.
2. PRESS CTRL-N to open the New Item dialog.
3. Select Sales Tax Item as the item type.
4. Enter a name for the item (use the state's code for the specific sales tax rate and taxing authority) and optionally enter a description.
5. Enter the tax rate.
6. Select the tax agency (a vendor) to which you pay the tax from the drop-down list, or add a new vendor by choosing <Add New>.
7. Click OK.

Sales Tax Codes

Sales tax codes are used by QuickBooks to designate an item as taxable or nontaxable when that item is listed on a sales transaction. However, it's not difficult to create codes to track sales tax status in a manner more detailed than taxable and nontaxable: you just add new sales tax codes to fit your needs.

Follow these steps to add a new sales tax code:

1. Select Lists | Sales Tax Code List.
2. Press CTRL-N to open the New Sales Tax Code window.
3. Enter the name of the new code (up to three characters in length).
4. Enter a description.
5. Select Taxable if you're entering a code to track taxable sales.
6. Select Non-taxable if you're entering a code to track nontaxable sales.
7. Click Next to set up another tax code.
8. Click OK when you've finished adding tax codes.

While you can always use the default nontaxable code that QuickBooks provides called "Non," you may be required (depending on your state sales tax agency) to provide further definition of your nontaxable sales to identify nonprofit organizations, government agencies, sales to resellers, or out-of-state customers, for example. The same logic may apply to taxable customers as well; some state agencies will require that you provide a breakdown of your company's taxable sales.

C a u t i o n : It's always a good idea to check in with your local taxing authority prior to setting up your sales tax codes and items.

Sales Tax Payment Basis

There are two ways to remit sales tax to the taxing authorities, and they're listed in the When Do You Owe Sales Tax section of the Sales Tax Preferences dialog:

- As Of Invoice Date, which is accrual-based tax reporting.
- Upon Receipt Of Payment, which is cash-based tax reporting.

Check with your accountant (and the taxing authority) to determine the method you need to select. Each state has its own reporting rules.

Sales Tax Payment Dates

You must indicate the frequency of your remittance to the taxing authority in the When Do You Pay Sales Tax section of the Preferences dialog. Your sales tax licensing agency indicates the schedule you must use.

Creating and Using Tax Groups

A tax group is a collection of two or more individual tax items that are displayed as one tax to a customer on a sales transaction. For example, you might be required to collect 6.25 percent state sales tax in addition to 5 percent county sales tax because of the county your business operates from. This is especially important in some states where city, county/parish, and state portions are paid to different tax entities. When you use a sales tax group, QuickBooks keeps track, behind the scenes, of which taxing authority the tax collected is due to, but the customer sees only a 11.25 percent sales tax rate (see Figure 5-6). To create a tax group, you must first create the individual tax items and then add those items to the group item.

FIGURE 5-6 A sales tax group is made up of sales tax items.

Follow these steps to create a tax group:

1. Open the Item List by choosing Lists | Item List.
2. Press CTRL-N to open the New Item dialog.
3. Select Sales Tax Group as the Type.
4. Enter a name for the group.
5. Enter a description (which appears on your sales forms).
6. In the Tax Item column, choose the individual tax code items you need to create this group (QuickBooks fills in the rate, tax agency, and description of each tax you already selected). Note that the calculated total (the group rate) appears at the bottom of the dialog.
7. When all the required tax code items have been added, click OK.

Assigning Sales Tax Codes and Items to Customers

When you turn on the Sales Tax preference and create your first sales tax item, QuickBooks asks if you want to make all of your customers as well as your inventory and non-inventory parts taxable.

If you do not de-select either of these options, QuickBooks will apply the "taxable" tax code to all customers and to your inventory parts as well. You can modify this setting at the customer level in the Additional Info tab of a customer's record.

If your customer list is large, opening each record to make this change to several records can be quite tedious and time consuming. Instead, you can use the Add/Edit Multiple List Entries window to assign or change the tax items or codes for multiple customers in a single view. To utilize this feature, from within the Customer Center, point your mouse anywhere on the Customer:Job list and right-click.

Select Add/Edit Multiple Customers:Jobs to open the Add/Edit Multiple List Entries window. You may have to customize the columns in this window to bring these fields into view.

ProAdvisor Tip: You can use the Add/Edit Multiple List Entries window to modify the tax code setting for your items as well. With your Item List open, right-click anywhere in the list and select Add/Edit Multiple Items to open the Add/Edit Multiple List Entries window.

Setting Up Inventory

In *this chapter:*

- Create inventory items

- Deal with physical inventory counts

- Adjust inventory numbers

- Run inventory reports

Accurately keeping track of the inventory items that you sell is no easy task. In fact, for many businesses, the warehouse can be a source of frustration and erroneous information. The term "warehouse" is used generically here to indicate the place where you store inventory, but it may be your basement or garage instead of a real warehouse. This chapter covers how to set up your inventory; Chapter 11 covers what you need to know to purchase, receive, and manage your inventory.

What Is an Inventory Item?

An inventory item is a product you manufacture, assemble, or purchase for the purpose of selling to a customer.

Items that you store to use in the normal course of business that are resold to customers as part of other services being involved are also inventory. But if you're a plumber and you store valves, pipes, and other plumbing parts to use when you perform a job, you may choose to track those items as non-inventory items (especially if they are low-value items). If you're a consultant who uses consumables or supplies in the course of your consulting work and you keep those products on hand to sell to customers, you can also choose not to track those supplies as inventory.

> **ProAdvisor Tip:** QuickBooks provides an item type called a non-inventory part that you can use to indicate products you used when you invoice customers. You can create reports on those items to track quantity and revenue amounts. These item types don't require you to attend to the kinds of details and tax reports that inventory items do.

The hallmark of an item that is configured as an inventory part is that it is made or purchased solely for the purpose of resale; the trade your business engages in is the sale of products. The types of businesses that typically track inventory are manufacturers (who may use inventory parts to create other inventory parts), wholesale distributors, and retailers.

Setting Up QuickBooks for Inventory Tracking

To track inventory, you must first enable the inventory feature. Choose Edit | Preferences and select the Items & Inventory category in the left pane. Move to the Company Preferences tab (see Figure 6-1) to see the inventory options.

FIGURE 6-1 Enable inventory and set the features to use for inventory tracking.

When you turn on the inventory feature, you also turn on the purchase order feature (although you don't have to use purchase orders to use the inventory feature). In addition, the dialog offers two options that help you keep your inventory records accurately:

- **Warn About Duplicate Purchase Order Numbers** When enabled, if you use a PO number that's already in use, QuickBooks will display a message warning you of that fact. (The system doesn't prevent you from using the duplicate number, but it's a good idea to heed the warning to avoid problems.)

- **Warn If Not Enough Inventory Quantity On Hand (QOH) To Sell** When enabled, QuickBooks flashes a warning if you fill out a sales transaction that has a quantity greater than the current available units of that product. You can continue the sale if you wish and track the unfilled quantity as a backorder (covered later in this chapter).

ProAdvisor Tip: The Company Preferences tab of the Items & Inventory Preferences dialog contains an Advanced Inventory Settings button. This feature, available only in QuickBooks Enterprise Solutions, allows you to track inventory across multiple locations. Click the "Learn about serial #/lots, FIFO and multi-location inventory" link to see if it's a fit for your business and learn how to upgrade to QuickBooks Enterprise Solutions.

Accounts Required for Inventory Are Automatically Created

After you've enabled inventory tracking and created your first inventory item, QuickBooks adds the following accounts to your chart of accounts:

- An Other Current Asset account named Inventory Asset
- A cost of goods sold account named Cost Of Goods Sold

You'll learn how QuickBooks posts amounts to these accounts during the discussions in this chapter.

Creating Inventory Items

Now you're ready to create your first inventory item. Open the Item List (choose Lists | Item List from the menu bar) to open the Item List window. Then press CTRL-N to open the New Item dialog and select Inventory Part from the drop-down list as the item type.

Fill in the information using the guidelines that follow (Figure 6-2 is an example of a blank inventory item record):

- The Item Name/Number is the way you will reference the item in the software—which is not necessarily the same way you'll want to describe this item to your customers in sales transactions. This field must be unique in your Item List.
- The Manufacturer's Part Number (useful if you're a distributor or retailer) lets you include the manufacturer's part number on your purchase orders. If you purchase from a distributor instead of a manufacturer, enter the distributor's part number. This makes creating an accurate purchase order much easier.
- The text you enter in the Description On Purchase Transactions field automatically appears when you create a purchase order. The text you enter in the Description On Sales Transactions field automatically appears in sales transaction forms, such as invoices, estimates, and sales receipts.

FIGURE 6-2 An inventory item record contains all the information you need to use it in transactions.

- You can enter a cost, but it's really a convenience for creating purchase orders (the cost appears automatically in the PO, which is useful if the cost doesn't change often). QuickBooks does not use this figure for posting cost of goods sold; instead, it uses the average cost of this item based on your item receipt and inventory adjustment transactions (all covered later in this chapter).

- If you enter a Sales Price, that amount is automatically entered when you create sales transactions (but you can change the price on an individual sales transaction).

- Choose the Tax Code for this item, which indicates whether the item is taxable to customers.

- Select the appropriate posting accounts for Cost Of Goods Sold and Income.

- Enter a number in the Reorder Point field that reflects the minimum quantity you want to have in stock. When this quantity is reached, QuickBooks will issue a reminder about reordering if you've enabled the Reminders feature. To turn on the Reminders feature, choose Edit | Preferences and click the Reminders category. On the My Preferences tab, check the Show Reminders List When Opening A Company File check box. On the Company Preferences tab, choose either Show Summary or Show List for the Inventory To Reorder option.

- *Do not* enter anything in the On Hand or Total Value fields. Instead, let QuickBooks track these values as you receive items into inventory and/or use the inventory adjustment feature. Inventory adjustments are covered later in this chapter.

Chapter 5 covers the Notes and Custom Fields buttons found on the New and Edit Item windows.

Using Subitems

Subitems are useful when there are choices for items and you want all the choices to be part of a larger hierarchy so you can sell them easily and track them efficiently. For instance, if you sell widgets in a variety of colors, you may want to create a subitem for each color: red widget, green widget, and so on. Or perhaps you sell shoes and want to separate your products by type, such as sandals, sneakers, loafers, dress shoes, and so on.

Creating the Parent Item for a Subitem

In order to have a subitem, you must have a parent item. Figure 6-3 shows the record of an item that has been specifically created as a parent item, using the Inventory Part type in the Type drop-down list.

FIGURE 6-3 This item isn't sold to customers—it exists only as a parent item to define a category of items that you sell.

Here are some guidelines for creating an inventory item that's designed to be a parent item:

- Use a generic name for the item; the details are in the subitem names.
- Don't enter a description; save that for the subitems.
- Don't enter the cost.
- Don't enter the price.
- Don't enter a reorder point.
- Don't enter the quantity on hand.
- Enter the Inventory Asset, COG, and Income accounts because they are required fields for all inventory items.

Creating Subitems

Having created the parent item, subitems are easy to create. Open a blank New Item window (press CTRL-N) and follow these steps:

1. In the Item Name/Number field, enter the code for this item. It can be a color, a size, a manufacturer name, or any other code that makes this subitem unique when compared to other subitems under the same parent item (see Figure 6-4).

FIGURE 6-4 Creating inventory subitems makes it easier to identify items in your item list.

2. Check the Subitem Of box, and then select the parent item from the drop-down list that appears when you click the arrow to the right of the field.

3. Enter the Manufacturer's Part Number (for creating purchase orders).

4. Optionally, enter any descriptions you want to appear on purchase orders and sales transactions.

5. Optionally, enter the cost that you expect to pay for this item and a preferred vendor.

6. Optionally, enter the sales price.

7. Enter the general ledger account information (Inventory Asset, Cost Of Goods, and Income accounts).

8. Enter the reorder point if you're using that feature.

9. Click Next to enter another inventory item, or click OK if you're finished.

Counting Inventory

For some business owners, there's nothing more dreaded than doing a physical inventory. However, no matter how careful you are with QuickBooks transactions, no matter how strict your internal controls are for making sure everything that comes and goes is accounted for, you'll often find that your physical inventory does not match your QuickBooks figures. Don't worry; you're not alone.

Printing the Physical Inventory Worksheet

It's time to count your inventory! Start by printing a Physical Inventory Worksheet (see Figure 6-5). To open a worksheet, select Reports | Inventory | Physical Inventory Worksheet. This report lists your inventory items and subitems in alphabetical order, along with the current quantity on hand, which is calculated from your QuickBooks transactions. In addition, there's a column that's set up to record the actual count as you walk around your warehouse with this printout (and a pen) in hand. Click the Print button in the worksheet window to bring up the Print Reports window. In the Number Of Copies box, enter as many copies as you need.

Physical Inventory Worksheet

| Customize Report | Share Template | Memorize | Print | E-mail ▼ | Excel ▼ | Hide Header | Refresh | Sort By | Default ▼ |

Winchester Distributors

Physical Inventory Worksheet

All Transactions

Item	Description	Preferred Vendor	Quantity On Hand	Physical Count
Indoor Electri...	100' 12-2 NM-B with Gr...		600	_____ ◀
Bath/Vanity F...			0	_____
Bath/Vanity F...	Brushed Nickel with Op...	Foster Lighting	102	_____
Bath/Vanity F...	Solid Brass with Etched...	Foster Lighting	0	_____
Bath/Vanity F...	Solid Brass with Etched...	Foster Lighting	120	_____
Bath/Vanity F...	White with Satin White G...	Foster Lighting	26	_____
Bath/Vanity F...	Pearl Nickel, 5 Light	Paulsen's Lighting	58	_____
Bath/Vanity F...	Polished Chrome, 4 Light	Paulsen's Lighting	73	_____
Bath/Vanity F...	Polished Brass, 6 Light	Paulsen's Lighting	33	_____
Bath/Vanity F...	Beveled Mirror with Etc...	Hall Lighting & Acc...	13	_____
Ceiling fixtures			0	_____
Ceiling fixture...	Brass Pendant with Rib...	Foster Lighting	90	_____
Ceiling fixture...	Desert Stone Finish	Foster Lighting	84	_____
Ceiling fixture...	Brushed Nickel Pendant...	Foster Lighting	60	_____
Ceiling fixture...	Tapestry with Etched G...	Foster Lighting	127	_____
Ceiling fixture...	Brushed Nickel with Rib...	Foster Lighting	67	_____
Ceiling fixture...	Steel Colonial with Opal...	Hall Lighting & Acc...	111	_____
Ceiling fixture...	Gold Colonial	Hall Lighting & Acc...	83	_____
Ceiling fixture...	Millstone Finish, 1 light	Paulsen's Lighting	20	_____
Ceiling fixture...	Copper Verde, Seeded ...	Paulsen's Lighting	12	_____
Ceiling fixture...	Textured White Pendant	Paulsen's Lighting	104	_____
Ceiling fixture...	Cobblestone Pendant w...	Paulsen's Lighting	66	_____
Ceiling fixture...	Flat Glass, Polished Bra...	Paulsen's Lighting	44	_____
Ceiling fixture...	White Dome	Paulsen's Lighting	41	_____
Ceiling fixture...	Polished Brass with Wh...	Paulsen's Lighting	95	_____
Ceiling fixture...	Cobblestone Pendant Bar	Paulsen's Lighting	10	_____
Ceiling fixture...	Textured White Pendan...	Paulsen's Lighting	9	_____
Chandeliers			0	_____
Chandeliers:2...	Tapestry with Faux Ala...	Foster Lighting	21	_____

FIGURE 6-5 The most important column is the one with blank lines, which is where you enter the physical count.

ProAdvisor Tip: By default, the Physical Inventory Worksheet displays only the inventory items that have an active status. If you made any inventory items inactive and you think (or know) there are units in stock of that item, consider filtering the report to show the inactive items so you can identify any on-hand quantities for these items. If any items are obsolete or discontinued, be sure to adjust their quantities (or value) to zero. If you think they may have a resale value, consider making them active again.

Planning the Physical Count

While QuickBooks lacks an automatic "freeze" feature, you can perform this action manually. After you print the worksheet (which you don't do until you're ready to start counting), be sure that all sales transactions will be handled differently until after the inventory count is adjusted. There are a number of ways to do this.

- Print an extra copy of each invoice and save the copies in a folder. Don't pick and pack the inventory for the invoices until after the count.
- Prepare a form for salespeople to fill out the name and quantity of inventory items sold during the freeze, and delay picking and packing the inventory until after the count.
- Delay entering invoices until after the count is over. (This is not a good idea if counting takes a couple of days.)
- Don't receive inventory in QuickBooks (don't fill out a Receive Items or Enter Bill for Received Items form) until after the count.
- If inventory arrives in the warehouse during the count, don't unpack the boxes until after the count.

When you start counting the inventory, be sure there's a good system in place. The most important element of the system is *having somebody in charge*. One person, with a master inventory worksheet in hand, must know who is counting what. When each counter is finished, his or her sheet should be handed to the person in charge and the numbers should be copied onto the master inventory worksheet. (This is why you print multiple copies of the worksheet.) Note the date and time the count was reported.

After the count, bring in any inventory that's arrived during the count. Then start picking and packing your orders so you can generate income again.

Making Inventory Adjustments

After you've finished counting the inventory, you may find that the numbers on the worksheet don't match the physical count. In fact, it's almost a sure bet that the numbers won't match.

Most of the time, the physical count is lower than the QuickBooks figures. This is called *shrinkage*. Shrinkage is a way of describing unexplained missing inventory. Unfortunately, most of the time the reason is employee theft—a well-documented fact. Another reason for shrinkage is breakage, but most of the time that's reported by employees, and you can adjust your inventory because you know about it.

Adjusting the Count

Now you have to tell QuickBooks about the results of the physical count, and you accomplish that by choosing Vendors | Inventory Activities | Adjust Quantity/Value On Hand. The Adjust Quantity/Value On Hand window opens, which is shown in Figure 6-6. Inactive items also appear on the Adjust Quantity/Value On Hand window.

Here are guidelines for filling out this window:

- Select Quantity from the Adjustment Type drop-down menu.
- Enter the date (usually inventory adjustments are made at the end of the month, quarter, or year, but there's no rule about that).
- Click the Find & Select Items button to open the Find & Select Items window. Here you tell QuickBooks which items you want to adjust. Click the Add Selected Items button to add the items you've selected to the adjustment window.

- Use an optional reference number to track the adjustment.
- In the Adjustment Account field, enter the inventory adjustment account in your chart of accounts. (See the section "About the Inventory Adjustment Account" for important information about which account you should use).

FIGURE 6-6 The Adjust Quantity/Value On Hand window

- The Customer:Job field is there in case you're sending stuff to a customer but didn't include the items on any invoices for that customer or job. This is a way to effect a transfer of the inventory; the inventory count is changed and the cost is posted to the customer or job.
- If you've enabled the class tracking feature, a Class field appears if the adjustment can be assigned to a class.
- Use either the New Quantity column or the Qty Difference column to enter the count (depending on how you filled out the worksheet and calculated it). Whichever column you use, QuickBooks fills in the other column automatically.
- Anything you enter in the Memo field appears on your Profit & Loss Detail report, which prevents the question, "What's this figure?" from your accountant.

When you complete the entries, the total value of the adjustment you made is displayed below the Qty Difference column. That value is calculated by using the average cost of your inventory. For example, if you received ten widgets into inventory at a cost of $10.00 each and later received ten more at a cost of $12.00 each, your average cost for widgets is $11.00 each. If your adjustment is for minus one widget, your inventory asset value is decreased by $11.00.

Adjusting the Value

You can be more precise about your inventory valuation; in fact, you can override the average cost calculation and enter a true value when you fill out this transaction window.

Select Total Value from the Adjustment Type drop-down menu. Two new columns named Total Value and New Value appear in the window (see Figure 6-7).

The value of the total adjusted count is displayed for each item, and you can change the value to eliminate the effects of averaging costs up to this point (although as you continue to receive inventory items, QuickBooks continues to use average costing). You can change the current value of any item.

FIGURE 6-7 Adjust the costs of inventory to reflect actual value.

Return to the Adjust Quantity window and enter the data. When you've finished making your changes, click Save & Close to save your new inventory numbers.

ProAdvisor Tip: To adjust both quantity and value at the same time, select Quantity And Total Value from the Adjustment Type drop-down list.

Understanding the Effects of an Adjustment

When you adjust the inventory count, you're also changing the value of your inventory asset. After you save the adjustment, the inventory asset account register reflects the differences for each item.

But this is double-entry bookkeeping, which means there has to be an equal and opposite entry somewhere else. For example, when you sell items via customer invoices, your inventory asset decreases while at the same time your cost of goods sold increases. When you're adjusting inventory, however, there is no sale involved (nor is there a purchase involved). In this case, the balancing entry is made to an inventory adjustment account (discussed in the following section), which must exist in order to adjust your inventory.

If your inventory adjustment lowers the value of your inventory, the inventory asset account is credited and the adjustment account receives a debit in the same amount. If your adjustment raises the value of your inventory, the postings are opposite.

About the Inventory Adjustment Account

Before you can make adjustments to your inventory, you should first create an account to receive that adjustment. Most users name it the Inventory Adjustment account, and it can either be a Cost Of Goods Sold or an Expense account. Check with your accountant on what account type works best for your situation.

If you use a COGS account when you use the Adjust Quantity/Value On Hand window, QuickBooks issues a warning message when you enter your adjustment account in the Adjustment Account field.

If your accountant wants you to use a cost of goods account, be sure to select the option to stop showing this message before you click OK to continue working in this window.

Making Other Adjustments to Inventory

You can use the Adjust Quantity/Value On Hand window to make adjustments to inventory at any time and for a variety of reasons unconnected to the periodic physical count.

- Breakage or other damage
- Customer demo/sample units
- Gifts or bonuses for customers or employees
- Removal of inventory parts in order to create built or preassembled inventory items

The important thing to remember is that tracking inventory isn't just to make sure that you have sufficient items on hand to sell to customers (although that's certainly an important point). Equally important is the fact that inventory is a significant asset, just like your cash, equipment, and other assets. It affects your company's worth in a substantial way.

Running Inventory Reports

You'll probably find that you run reports on your inventory status quite often. For many inventory-based businesses, tracking the state of the inventory is the second most important set of reports (right behind reports about the current accounts receivable balances).

QuickBooks provides several useful, significant inventory reports, which you can access by choosing Reports | Inventory. The available reports are discussed in this section.

Inventory Valuation Summary Report

This report gives you a quick assessment of the value of your inventory. By default, the date range is the current month to date, but you can change that to suit your needs. Each item is listed with the following information displayed in columns.

Item Description   The description of the item, if you entered a description for purchase transactions.

On Hand The current quantity on hand, which is the net number of received items and sold items. Because QuickBooks permits you to sell items you don't have in stock (a very bad idea, which can wreak havoc with your financials), it's possible to have a negative number in this column.

Avg Cost QuickBooks uses the totals from each transaction for receipt of inventory to calculate this figure.

Asset Value The value posted to your Inventory account in the general ledger. The value is calculated by multiplying the number on hand by the average cost.

% Of Tot Asset The percentage of your total inventory assets that this item represents.

Sales Price The price you've set for this item. This figure is obtained by looking at the item's configuration window. If you entered a price when you set up the item, that price is displayed. If you didn't enter a price (because you chose to determine the price at the time of sale), $0.00 displays. QuickBooks does not check the sales records for this item to determine this number, so if you routinely change the price when you're filling out a customer invoice, those changes aren't reflected in this report.

Retail Value The current retail value of the item, which is calculated by multiplying the number on hand by the retail price (if the retail price is set).

% Of Tot Retail The percentage of the total retail value of your inventory that this item represents.

Inventory Valuation Detail Report

This report lists each transaction that involved each inventory item. The report shows no financial information about the price charged to customers because your inventory value is based on cost. You can double-click any transaction line to see the details of that transaction (including the amount you charged for the item).

Inventory Stock Status

There are two Stock Status reports: Inventory Stock Status By Item and Inventory Stock Status By Vendor. The information is the same in both reports, but the order in which information is arranged and subtotaled is different. You can use these Stock Status reports to get quick numbers about inventory items, including the following information:

- The preferred vendor
- The reorder point
- The number currently on hand

- A reminder (a check mark) for ordering items that are below the reorder point
- The number currently on order (a purchase order exists but the order has not yet been received)
- The next delivery date (according to the data in the purchase orders)
- The average number of units sold per week

Physical Inventory Worksheet

This is the report you print when it's time to take an inventory count. See the section "Counting Inventory," earlier in this chapter, for more information.

Pending Builds

If you happen to be using one of the Premier or Enterprise editions of QuickBooks and you build and track *assemblies*, this report details the current state of items you assemble from existing inventory items (called *builds*). If you find that you need this feature, you can upgrade to either one of these editions quite easily.

Inventory QuickReports

QuickBooks provides a reporting feature called QuickReports that provides detailed sales and purchase information about an individual item. QuickReports are available from the Item List window and are the fastest way to take a look at all the transactions for an item.

In the Item List window, select an item and click the Reports button (at the bottom of the list) to open a drop-down menu from which you can select the QuickReport for that item. You can change the date range for the report, and you can double-click any transaction line to drill down to the transaction details.

Creating Other Lists
You Need

n this chapter:

- Fixed Asset Item list

- Price Level list

- Currency list

- Class list

- Other Names list

- Customer & Vendor Profile lists

- Memorized Transaction List

In Chapters 2 through 6 you learned how to set up the key lists that QuickBooks uses in nearly every transaction you enter and how important these lists are. There are other lists, however, that you'll find in the Lists menu that not only help make your work in QuickBooks more efficient, but also make it easier to create customized reports that contain details you find helpful.

These lists don't require extensive amounts of data, and you may not use all of them. Some of these items are in the Lists menu, and some of them are in a submenu of the Lists menu called Customer & Vendor Profile Lists.

Fixed Asset Item List

Use the Fixed Asset Item list to store information about the fixed assets your business owns. Choose Lists | Fixed Asset Item List to open the list which provides you a way to track data about the assets you purchase and depreciate. As you can see in Figure 7-1, you can record many details about each asset.

FIGURE 7-1 Store information about your businesses assets in the Fixed Asset Item list.

Keep in mind that this is an inert list, meaning that it doesn't provide any links to any financial data in your QuickBooks company file. It does not interact with the chart of accounts, so any values you enter in this list have to be entered in your Fixed Asset accounts separately.

This list does not add any financial information to your company file, nor does it perform any calculations. It's merely a way to use QuickBooks to catalog your fixed assets instead of whatever list you're keeping in Microsoft Word, Microsoft Excel, a legal pad, or a shoebox full of index cards.

C a u t i o n : Be aware that items added to the Fixed Asset Item list will be visible in the drop-down list you see when you create a transaction that involves your regular items (the "regular" items you create to transact business, which are discussed in Chapters 5 and 6), such as an invoice, a cash sale, or a purchase order. If you accidentally select a fixed asset item while creating a sales transaction, for example, your financial records can become confusing. If you use the Fixed Asset Item list, consider making all the items in the list inactive to suppress their display in drop-down lists. To make an item inactive, highlight it while in list view, then right-click and select Make Item Inactive.

P r o A d v i s o r   T i p : Using the Fixed Asset Item list to track your businesses assets can assist your accountant in the year-end tax related chores they perform for you. If your accountant is using the Premier Accountant Edition version of QuickBooks, they can open your company file and read from your Fixed Asset Item list using a program call the Fixed Asset Manager (FAM). FAM works by pulling the information it needs from your QuickBooks company file to calculate the depreciation for a given period and then posting a journal entry back to your company file.

Price Level List

The Price Level list is an easy way to apply special pricing to customers and jobs. This list is only available if price levels are enabled in the Sales & Customers section of your Preferences. To turn on this feature, use the following steps:

1. Choose Edit | Preferences and select the Sales & Customers category in the left pane.
2. Move to the Company Preferences tab.
3. Select the option labeled Use Price Levels.
4. Click OK.

Creating a Price Level

To create a price level, open the Price Level list from the Lists menu and press CTRL-N to open the New Price Level dialog.

Each price level has two components: a name and a formula. The name can be anything you wish, and the formula is a percentage of the price you entered for the items in your Item List (the formula increases or reduces the price by the percentage you specify).

For example, you may want to give your favorite customers a deep discount. Name the price level something like "PreferredCustomer." Then enter a healthy percentage by which to reduce the price of items purchased by this customer. Or you may want to create a discount price level for customers that are nonprofit organizations.

On the other hand, you may want to keep your regular prices steady and increase them for certain customers (perhaps customers who don't pay in a timely manner).

You can also use numbers for the price-level names, perhaps making the highest numbers the highest prices.

Linking Price Levels to Customers

After you create price levels, you can apply a price level to customers. Open the Customers & Jobs list in the Customer Center and double-click the customer's listing. Select or create a new price level from the Price Level drop-down list on the Additional Info tab.

Once a price level is linked to a customer, sales transactions for that customer reflect the price level automatically. See Chapter 9 to learn how to create sales transactions with price levels.

Currency List

Available only if you've enabled the QuickBooks multiple currencies feature, the Currency list specifies the currencies you want to work with (see Figure 7-2). Multiple currencies can be turned on in the Company Preferences area. From the Edit menu, select Preferences | Multiple Currencies. By default, the majority of currencies are marked Inactive; open this list to activate the currencies you need so they appear in drop-down lists. Refer to Appendix B for more information on the QuickBooks multiple currencies feature.

FIGURE 7-2 Activate the currency you need for your customers and vendors.

C a u t i o n : Be sure to make a backup copy of your company file before turning the multiple currencies feature on in your company file. Once it is enabled it cannot be turned off.

Class List

Classes provide a method of organizing your company's transactions by division, allowing you to produce comprehensive Profit & Loss reports by class. Some of the common reasons to configure classes include:

- Tracking account balances and reporting by location if you have more than one office
- Financial reporting by business type (perhaps you manage both a retail and wholesale division)

The Class list appears in the Lists menu only if you've enabled the Use Class Tracking feature. From the Edit menu, select Preferences | Accounting | Company Preferences | Use Class Tracking.

You should use classes for a single purpose; otherwise, the feature won't work properly. For example, you can use classes to separate your business into locations or by type of business, but don't try to do both. If you need to further define a class or narrow its definition, you can use subclasses.

When you enable classes, QuickBooks adds a Class field to transaction forms. Optionally, you can require that QuickBooks prompt you to assign a class to when you enter transactions. For each transaction or each line of any transaction, you can assign one of the classes you created.

Creating a Class

To create a class, choose Lists | Class List from the QuickBooks menu bar to display the Class List window. Press CTRL-N to open the New Class dialog.

Fill in the name of the class. and then click Next to add another class, or click OK if you are finished.

> **ProAdvisor Tip:** If you decide to use classes, it's a good idea to create a class for general overhead expenses. You can then allocate the amounts accumulated in this overhead class to other classes with a journal entry at a later time if you wish. Using journal entries in QuickBooks is covered in Chapter 19.

Creating a Subclass

Subclasses let you post transactions to specific subcategories of classes, and they work similarly to subaccounts in your chart of accounts. If you set up a subclass, you must post transactions only to the subclass, never to the parent class. However, unlike the chart of accounts, classes have no option to force the display of only the subclass when you're working in a transaction window. As a result, if you're using subclasses you should keep the name of the parent class short, to lessen the need to scroll through the field to see the entire class name.

You create a subclass using the same steps required to create a class. After you enter a name for the subclass in the Class Name field, click the check box next to the option Subclass Of to insert a check mark. Then select the appropriate parent class from the drop-down list.

Other Names List

QuickBooks provides a list called Other Names, which is the list of people whose names are used when you write checks, but they don't fit the definition of vendor because you don't need to track payables and transactions the way you do for a vendor.

The names in the Other Names list appear in the drop-down list when you write checks but are unavailable when you're entering vendor bills, vendor credits, bill payments, purchase orders, or sales transactions.

One of the most common reasons to add a name to the Other Names list is to write checks to owners and partners. Strictly speaking, these people aren't vendors of your company, and they aren't employees. You can also use the Other Names list for Cash and use that name when you write checks for cash to fill your petty cash box (covered in Chapter 13).

> **ProAdvisor Tip:** If you reimburse employees for expenses they incur, and you don't want to manage the reimbursement through their paychecks, create an Other Name listing for those employees and use that name for reimbursements. QuickBooks does not allow duplicate names, so you'll have to change the name you use in the Employee list slightly to create the Other Name listing (for instance, add an "RE" for "reimbursable expenses" to the end of their name).

To open the Other Names list, choose Lists | Other Names List. To create a new name for the list, press CTRL-N to open a New Name window.

The New Name window provides fields for the address (handy for printing checks you're going to place into window envelopes), telephone numbers, and other contact information.

C a u t i o n : Only use the Other Names list for check payees you don't have to track as vendors. Otherwise, you could end up having to move these names to the Vendor List if you find you need to track their activities as a vendor or issue them a Form 1099.

Customer & Vendor Profile Lists

The Profile lists are those lists that appear in the submenu you see when you choose Customer & Vendor Profile Lists. Most of the lists in the submenu are designed to help you categorize and refine the information you keep about your customers and vendors. Other lists can contain data that is available when you create transactions.

Sales Rep List

By definition, a *sales rep* is a person who is connected to a customer, usually because he or she receives a commission on sales to that customer. However, it's quite common to track sales reps who are not necessarily paid commissions as a way to determine who is the primary contact for a customer (some people call this a *service rep*).

To create a sales rep, the rep's name has to exist in your QuickBooks system as a vendor, employee, or a member of the Other Names list.

To create a new sales rep from an existing name, open the Sales Rep list and press CTRL-N to open a New Sales Rep form. Select the person's name from the drop-down list. QuickBooks automatically fills in the Sales Rep Initials field (which is the data used in reports and transaction windows that have a Sales Rep field) and the Sales Rep Type (the list that contains this sales rep). You can modify the Sales Rep Initials field if you wish.

Customer Type List

When you create your customer list, you may decide to use the Customer Type field as a way to categorize your customers. This gives you the opportunity to sort and select customers in reports, so you can view the total income from specific types of customers.

For example, you may use the Customer Type list to track the source of referrals, or to separate wholesale and retail customers.

Vendor Type List

When you create your Vendors list, you may decide to use the Vendor Type field as a way to categorize your vendors and suppliers. This will allow you to sort and select vendors in reports so you can view the total expenses from specific types of vendors.

Job Type List

Use the Job Type list to set up categories for jobs. For example, if you're a plumber, you may want to separate new construction from repair work.

Terms List

QuickBooks keeps both customer and vendor payment terms in one list, so the terms you need are all available whether you're creating an invoice, entering a vendor bill, or creating a purchase order. To create a terms listing, open the Terms List window and press CTRL-N to open the New Terms window seen in Figure 7-3.

FIGURE 7-3   Set up the terms you need for both customers and vendors.

Use the Standard section to create terms that are due at some elapsed time after the invoice date:

- Net Due In is the number of days allowed for payment after the invoice date.
- To create a discount for early payment, enter the discount percentage and the number of days after the invoice date that the discount is in effect. For example, if 30 days are allowed for payment, enter a discount percentage that is in effect for 10 days after the invoice date (such terms are usually referred to as "*X* percent 10, net 30," substituting the amount of the discount for *X*).

ProAdvisor Tip: Discounts for early payment are commonly found only in the manufacturing and wholesale distribution industries and are applied to product sales. It would be unusual to receive (or give) such discounts for ordinary business expenses, such as utilities, rent, services rendered, and so on.

Use the Date Driven section to describe terms that are due on a particular date, regardless of the invoice date:

- Enter the day of the month the invoice payment is due.
- Enter the number of days before the due date that invoices are considered payable on the following month.
- To create a discount for early payment, enter the discount percentage and the day of the month at which the discount period ends. For example, if the standard due date is the 15th of the month, you may want to extend a discount to any customer who pays by the 8th of the month.

Customer Message List

If you like to write messages to your customers when you're creating a sales transaction (an invoice or a cash sales receipt), you can enter a bunch of appropriate messages ahead of time and then just select the one you want to use. For example, you may want to insert the message "Thanks for doing business with us" or "Happy Holidays!"

Press CTRL-N to enter a new message to add to the list. You just have to type out the text (which can't be longer than 101 characters, counting spaces)—this is one of the easier lists to create. Keep in mind, however, that once a message is used in a transaction, you can't delete it. However, if it becomes obsolete you can make it inactive to remove it from your message choices.

Payment Method List

You can accept and track payments from customers in multiple ways. QuickBooks prepopulates the Payment Methods List with the most common payment types (like credit card, check, and cash). If you have a payment method that isn't listed, you can add that method to the list. To do so, select Lists | Customer & Vendor Profile Lists | Payment Method List, then press CTRL-N to open the New Payment Method window. Name the payment method and select the appropriate payment type.

Maintaining this list not only provides some detail about the payments you receive (in case you're having a conversation with a customer about invoices and payments), but also allows you to print reports on payments that are subtotaled by the method of payment, such as credit card, check, cash, and so on. In addition, your bank may use the same subtotaling method on your monthly statement, which makes it easier to reconcile the bank account.

Ship Via List

Use the Ship Via list to add a description of your shipping method to your invoices (in the field named Via), which many customers appreciate. QuickBooks prepopulates the list with a variety of shipment methods, but you may need to add a shipping method. To do so, select Lists | Customer & Vendor Profile Lists | Ship Via List, then press CTRL-N to add a new Shipping Method entry to the list. All you need to do is enter the name, for example, Our Truck or Sam's Delivery Service.

If you use one shipping method more than any other, you can select a default Ship Via entry, which appears automatically on your invoices (you can change it on any invoice if the shipping method is different). The default entry is in the Sales & Customers category of the Preferences dialog, where you can select the Usual Shipping Method entry you want to appear by default on your sales transactions. You can also enter the FOB site you want to appear on invoices, if you wish to display this information.

FOB (Free or Freight On Board) is the site from which an order is shipped and is also the point at which transportation and other costs are the buyer's responsibility.

Vehicle List

The Vehicle list lets you create vehicle records in which you track mileage for vehicles used in your business. You can use the mileage information for tax deductions for your vehicles and to bill customers for mileage expenses. However, even if you don't bill customers for mileage or your accountant uses a formula for tax deductions, the Vehicle list is a handy way to track information about the vehicles you use for business purposes. (You can learn how to track mileage and bill customers for mileage in Chapter 16.)

To add a vehicle to the list, select Lists | Customer& Vendor Profile Lists | Vehicle List, then press CTRL-N to open a New Vehicle dialog. The record has two fields:

- Vehicle, in which you enter a name or code for a specific vehicle. For example, you could enter BlueTruck, 2012 Toyota, Ford Mustang Convertible, or any other recognizable name.
- Description, in which you enter descriptive information about the vehicle.

While the Description field is handy for standard description terms (such as black or blue/white truck), take advantage of the field by entering information you really need. For example, the VIN, the license plate number, the expiration date for the plate, the insurance policy number, or other "official" pieces of information are good candidates for inclusion. You can enter up to 256 characters in the Description field.

The Templates list is covered in Chapter 28, "Customizing QuickBooks."

Memorized Transaction List

The Memorize Transaction feature in QuickBooks saves you from having to enter the same transaction multiple times. With few exceptions, the transactions that you enter in QuickBooks can be memorized and set to automatically post on the day and with the frequency you need. "Memorizing" your monthly rent check, for example, can help ensure that this important obligation gets posted and sent out in a timely manner each month. And because the memorized transaction already includes the name of your landlord, the rent amount, and the rent expense account assignment, you only have to enter this information once for it to appear on each monthly check.

The transactions that you memorize (such as invoices, checks, bills, general journal entries, etc.) are all stored in the Memorized Transaction List. Chapter 9 provides a step-by-step example of how to memorize an invoice; follow these same steps to memorize all other transactions.

To view or edit a memorized transaction, choose Lists | Memorized Transaction List to open the list (see Figure 7-4). Highlight a transaction name and click the Memorized Transaction button at the bottom of the window, then choose Edit Memorized Transaction. You can also use the Memorized Transaction List to enter a memorized transaction manually.

Transaction Name	Type	Source Account	Am...	Frequency	Auto	Next Date
◆Overhead	General Journal	13100 · Pre-paid Insurance	675....	Never		
◆Recurring Depr Entry - Mo...	General Journal	54000 · Job Expenses:54599 · Less Discounts Taken	19.60	Monthly	✓	12/31/2012
◆Reyes Properties	Check	10100 · Checking	1,20...	Monthly	✓	01/01/2013
◆Sergeant Insurance	Check	10100 · Checking	675....	Monthly		01/15/2013

FIGURE 7-4 Use the Memorized Transaction List to edit or post a memorized transaction.

Entering Your Starting Balances

n this chapter:

- What is an opening trial balance?

- Ten steps to creating an accurate opening trial balance

If you've created your company file, created your lists, and completed all the other setup-related activities covered in the first seven chapters of this book, then you've built about 80 percent of your new QuickBooks file. If these key tasks have not yet been completed, you should return to this chapter when they are.

The last 20 percent of the setup process involves entering your beginning balances and the historical transactions (if any) needed to ensure that your data file accurately reflects your business's financial position on the day you start using your QuickBooks software. Entering accurate beginning balances and the detail behind these balances is perhaps the most important part of the setup process. Why? Because if you start with inaccurate or incomplete starting balances, you'll compromise your ability to rely on the key reports that QuickBooks offers to manage your business. In addition, you'll likely spend more time and money (mostly payable to your accountant) fixing these balances at year end. So it's definitely worth your time and effort to get the numbers right from the start.

What Is an Opening Trial Balance?

Your opening trial balance is simply a detailed listing of the value of your company's assets, liabilities, and equity. If your QuickBooks start date is the beginning of the year (which is the most common start date), your opening trial balance for the first day of the year has no income or expenses to report. It will, however, contain the balances that have accumulated in your Asset, Liability, and Equity accounts since you've been in business. With the help of your accountant, you should prepare what I call a pre-QuickBooks opening trial balance. Your accountant knows that much of the information needed for the pre-QuickBooks trial balance will come directly from the balance sheet they prepared for you the previous year end. The pre-QuickBooks opening trial balance doesn't have to be fancy—it can be created in Excel or on a piece of paper—but, of course, it must be accurate. A typical pre-QuickBooks opening trial balance for a business with a QuickBooks start date of January 1, 2013 might look something like this:

Account Type	Account	Debit	Credit
Assets	Bank	$25,000	
Asset	Accounts Receivable	$15,000	
Asset	Inventory	$30,000	
	Fixed Assets	$15,000	
	Accumulated Depreciation		$2,500
Liabilities	Loan from Bank		$20,000
Liabilities	Accounts Payable		$7,500
Equity	Equity (Capital, Prior Retained Earnings, and so on)		$55,000

Your mission is to get these beginning balances into your QuickBooks file. You might want to bookmark this page, as I'll be referring to the numbers in the preceding table throughout the rest of the chapter.

Ten Steps to Creating an Accurate Opening Trial Balance

While there's certainly more than one way to get your beginning balances into your new QuickBooks data file, I have found that the majority of my clients (and their accountants) have had the most success—and the least stress—when they follow the ten simple steps outlined here.

1. Gather All the Information You Need

In Chapter 1, a detailed list of the information and "other useful bits of paper" that you should have at your fingertips prior to entering your beginning balances was provided. If you haven't already organized these essential records and numbers, or if you don't remember exactly what you need to compile, return to Chapter 1 to refresh your memory.

2. Enter Beginning Balances for Simple Balance Sheet Accounts

For this second step, you'll use a journal entry to enter the beginning balances for accounts *except* bank accounts, accounts receivable, accounts payable, inventory, and sales tax payable. Those balances will be created later when you enter outstanding individual transactions and other adjustments. So what accounts are left to enter? Your fixed assets (including any accumulated depreciation) such as vehicles, furniture, and equipment, as well as any loans payable. You'll want to check in with your accountant for other balances that should also be entered as part of this first step, such as prepaid expenses, unpaid payroll taxes, or employee advances. Your journal entry should be dated as of the closing date of the prior fiscal year. In this example, the fiscal and calendar year are the same.

From the Company menu, select Make General Journal Entries to open the Make General Journal Entries window. Using the trial balance figures in the table shown earlier in this chapter, your journal entry should look like the one shown in Figure 8-1.

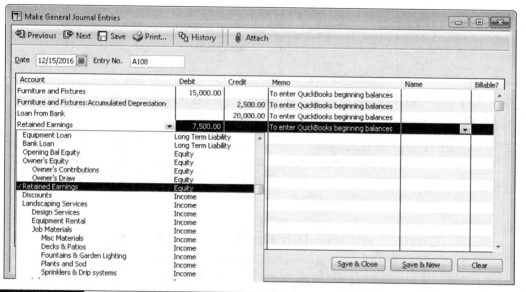

FIGURE 8-1 Use a journal entry to establish some of your beginning balances.

You'll see that after the balances for Fixed Assets (in this case Furniture and Fixtures), Accumulated Depreciation, and the Bank Loan have been entered, there's a debit balance of $7,500.00 that needs to be assigned to an account in order for the entry to be in balance. QuickBooks has a special account that's reserved just for that purpose called Opening Balance Equity. Using this account to balance the entry will require you (or your accountant) to zero this balance out (and any other balances posted to this account during the setup) to a retained earnings account in order to complete the setup. That adds another, often overlooked, journal entry requirement in the setup process. Alternatively, you can post this offsetting balance directly to a retained earnings or owner's equity account (as shown in Figure 8-1). Check with your accountant on the method that works best in your situation.

If you choose this alternate method, QuickBooks warns you that you're posting to an account that's intended to track profits from earlier periods. Clicking OK allows you to continue with the posting. Select Save & Close to save this entry.

3. Enter Bank Account Balances

The next step is to establish the bank balance. Use the bank register to do this. Select Banking | Use Register to open the register for your bank account. Enter the ending balance as it appears on the bank statement from the last month of the previous year in the Deposit side of the register. Be sure to put a note in the memo field (as shown in Figure 8-2) that will help remind you what this entry was for later on. Again, you can choose to post the offsetting balance to the Opening Balance Equity Account or directly to a retained earnings account (see Figure 8-2). Click the Record button to save your entry.

FIGURE 8-2 Post the offsetting balance to a Balance Equity Account or a retained earnings account.

4. Enter Outstanding Checks and Deposits

With your register still open, enter all outstanding transactions—checks and deposits—that occurred prior to the QuickBooks start date (see Figure 8-3). This step ensures that these items will appear in the first bank reconciliation you perform in QuickBooks. In the example, there are two checks outstanding from November 2012. Be sure to use the *original* transaction date to post these outstanding transactions.

5. Enter Unpaid Accounts Receivable and Accounts Payable Transactions

To establish your accounts receivable balance, create an invoice for each customer invoice that was still open as of the end of the previous fiscal year using the original transaction date and all other invoice details (customer name, item(s) purchased,

Date	Number	Payee		Payment	✓	Deposit	Balance
	Type	Account	Memo				
11/24/2012	2368	Accounting Firm		1,000.00			-1,000.00
	CHK	Professional Fees	Check outstanding as of 12/31/				
11/30/2012	2370	My Health Insurance Co.		1,000.00			-2,000.00
	CHK	Insurance					
12/31/2012						27,000.00	25,000.00
	TRANSFR	Retained Earnings	Balance per 12/31/2012 Bank S				
12/31/2012	Number	Payee		Payment		Deposit	
		Account	Memo				

Ending balance   25,000.00

FIGURE 8-3   Use the bank register to enter outstanding checks and deposits.

terms, etc.). Don't forget to enter any unused customer credits as well. In the example, there are two outstanding customer invoices that total $15,000.00. For more information on how create an invoice, refer to Chapter 9.

Likewise, to establish your accounts payable balance, create a bill for each unpaid vendor bill as well as any unused vendor credits. Use the original transaction data and all other bill details. In my example, I entered two unpaid bills totaling $7,500.00. For more information on how to enter vendor bills and credits, refer to Chapter 11.

6. Enter Nonposting Transactions

You should record all open purchase orders and estimates, again with their original dates and details. While this step is optional because these "nonposting" transactions have no effect on your opening balances, you'll then be able to, in the case of a PO, for example, receive these items through QuickBooks or, in the case of an estimate, generate an invoice when you're awarded the job. Estimates are covered in Chapter 9 and purchase orders in Chapter 6.

7. Enter Mid-year Income and Expenses (if Applicable)

If your QuickBooks start date is a mid-year date, enter a journal entry that summarizes the year-to-date balances in all income and expense accounts as of the QuickBooks start date. You may also want to enter monthly totals rather than one lump sum to give yourself the ability to run monthly Profit and Loss Statements for your entire fiscal year. Post the difference in debits and credits either to the Opening Balance Equity Account or directly to a retained earnings/equity account.

8. Adjust Sales Tax Payable

If you collect sales tax, you may need to adjust the Sales Tax Payable account to be sure that it is in sync with the amount (if any) listed on your pre-QuickBooks opening trial balance. This adjustment should be made after all open invoices are entered, since recording open invoices can affect the Sales Tax Payable account in QuickBooks. Use the Sales Tax Adjustment window to do this: select Vendors | Sales Tax | Adjust Sales Tax Due. For more information on how to use the Sales Tax Adjustment window, refer to Chapter 12.

9. Establish Inventory Balances

If your business carries inventory, you have to tell QuickBooks about the on-hand quantities of each of your inventory items as of your QuickBooks start date. This step assumes that you've already entered your Item List (minus any on-hand quantity information) and that each item has a cost associated with it. If this is not the case, you'll want to update your inventory list with that information prior to completing this step. Chapter 6 covers the details of how to set up an inventory item.

On-hand quantities are added using the Adjust Quantity/Value On Hand window. Select Vendors | Inventory Activities | Adjust Quantity/Value On Hand. Be sure that Quantity appears in the Adjustment Type drop-down menu field. In my simple example, this business carries only a single inventory item that has a cost of $300.00. As of December 31, 2012, I had 100 units in inventory (see Figure 8-4), so I added that quantity in the New Quantity column. The Qty Difference column populates automatically.

Note that QuickBooks requires you to select an offsetting Adjustment Account in order to add the on-hand quantities to inventory. Like the other beginning balance entries, you can choose to post the offsetting balance that the software requires to either Opening Balance Equity or directly to a retained earnings/equity account. You'll see a message telling you that QuickBooks is expecting you to use an expense account as the adjustment account.

FIGURE 8-4 Use the Adjust Quantity/Value On Hand window to establish your opening inventory balance.

This statement is true for most of your future adjustments—when you'll be using the Adjust Quantity/Value On Hand window to record obsolescence and shrinkage, for example. But in this instance, go ahead and post to one of your equity accounts.

Caution: Using the Adjust Quantity/Value On Hand (aka Inventory Adjustment) window to establish beginning on-hand inventory quantities is an acceptable method for an existing business with an existing inventory as of their QuickBooks start date. For all other situations, you should "receive" items as normal into your inventory using the steps outlined in Chapter 11.

10. Zero Out the Opening Balance Equity Account

If you've elected to use the Opening Balance Equity account to establish your opening balances, you'll need to zero out this account in order to complete your setup.

Use a journal entry dated with the QuickBooks start date and an offsetting entry to a retained earnings account (or another account of your accountant's choosing).

Run Your QuickBooks Trial Balance Report as of Your Start Date

You'll want to run your QuickBooks Opening trial balance to be sure that it's in sync with your pre-QuickBooks opening trial balance. Figure 8-5 shows my Trial Balance report in QuickBooks of January 1, 2013, my QuickBooks start date (note that you can run this report as of 12/31/12). Also note that it exactly matches the figures and totals shown in the table at the beginning of this chapter.

If you follow the steps outlined in this chapter and work closely with your accountant, establishing accurate opening balances can be a surprisingly straightforward and angst-free process.

Good luck!

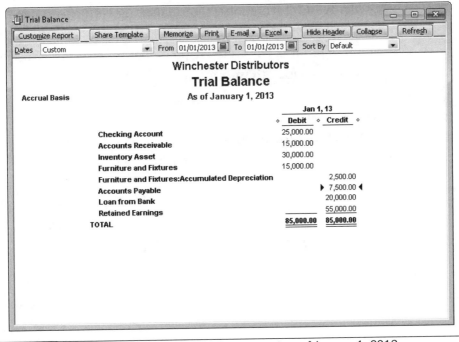

FIGURE 8-5   Drum roll please...the Trial Balance report as of January 1, 2013

Part Two

Daily Operations Using QuickBooks

The chapters in Part Two cover the most common day-to-day bookkeeping chores you'll be performing in QuickBooks. These chapters contain the instructions and tips that will help you complete these routine tasks efficiently and accurately. From time to time there will also be information that you can pass along to your accountant, who may want to know how QuickBooks is handling the tasks you're performing.

Part Two covers what you need to know about sending invoices to your customers and recording the payments you receive from them. You'll learn how to track and pay the bills you receive from vendors. There's plenty of information about managing your inventory— buying it, selling it, and counting it—and keeping QuickBooks up to date on those figures. There are chapters that cover payroll, discussing the ways to manage both in-house payroll systems and outside services.

You'll also learn how to manage your bank accounts, create transactions that provide job-costing data, and make adjustments to account balances by creating journal entries.

Invoicing Customers

In this chapter:

- Create invoices

- Use price levels, discounts, and subtotals

- Edit and memorize invoices

- Issue credit memos

- Create and work with estimates and progress billing

- Invoice customers for reimbursable expenses

For many businesses, the only way to get money in is to send an invoice to a customer (the exception is retail, of course). Creating an invoice in QuickBooks is easy once you understand what all the parts of the invoice do and how to modify these parts to reflect the way you do business.

In addition to invoices, you may have to issue credits, print packing slips, and create estimates. In this chapter, these and other sales-related transactions are covered.

Creating Invoices

QuickBooks gives you multiple ways to open a blank Create Invoices window, which is a blank invoice form that includes a History pane on the right side (see Figure 9-1). You can select Customers | Create Invoices from the menu bar or press CTRL-I, or click the Create Invoices icon in the Customers section of the Home page.

FIGURE 9-1 The Create Invoices window has all the fields you need to track sales and manage all the particulars that relate to a sale.

Several invoice templates are built into QuickBooks, and you can use any of them as well as create your own (covered in Chapter 28). The first thing to do is decide whether the displayed template suits you. You should probably look at the other templates before settling on the one you want to use. To do that, click the arrow below the Template field (located in the upper right-hand corner of the window) and select another invoice template from the drop-down list:

- The Finance Charge template appears if you enable finance charges in the Finance Charge category of the Preferences dialog. Information about finance charges is in Chapter 10.
- The Packing Slip template is discussed in the section "Printing Packing Slips," later in this chapter.
- The Product template has more fields and different columns because it's designed for product sales, including inventory items.
- The Professional and Service templates are almost identical. There's a difference in the order of the columns, and the Service template has a field for a purchase order number.
- The Progress template, which is covered later in this chapter in the "Creating Progress Billing Invoices" section, is designed specifically for progress billing against a job estimate. It doesn't appear in the Template list unless you have specified Progress Invoicing in the Company Preferences tab of the Jobs & Estimates category of the Preferences dialog.

For this discussion, we'll use the Product template. If you're using any other template, you'll still be able to follow along, even though your invoice form may lack some of the fields related to products.

The top portion of the invoice is for the basic information and is called the *invoice header*. The middle section, where the billing items are placed, is called the *line item* section. The bottom section, called the *footer*, holds the totals and other details (such as customer messages). Each section of the invoice has fields into which you enter data.

Entering Header Information

To create an invoice, start with the customer or the job. Click the arrow to the right of the Customer:Job field to see a list of all your customers. If you've attached jobs to any customers, those jobs are listed under the customer name. Select the customer or job for this invoice. You'll notice that if you've selected an existing customer or job, the pane to the right of the invoice form will display their most recent transactions, including the current balance if one exists. To close this pane, simply click the little blue arrowhead immediately above the customer's name.

If the customer isn't in the system, choose <Add New> to open a new customer window and enter all the data required for setting up a customer. Read Chapter 3 for information on creating customers and jobs.

If you've charged reimbursable expenses or assigned time to this customer, QuickBooks displays a message reminding you to add those charges to this invoice. You'll learn how to charge customers for reimbursable expenses in Chapter 11.

In the Date field, the current date is showing, but if you want to change the date, you can either type in a new date or click the calendar icon at the right side of the field to select a date. If you change the date, the new date appears automatically in each invoice you create during this session of QuickBooks (the current date returns after you close and then reopen the software). You can change that behavior by changing its configuration option in the My Preferences tab of the General category of the Preferences dialog (choose Edit | Preferences to open the dialog). Select the option Use Today's Date As Default instead of the default option Use The Last Entered Date As Default.

The first time you enter an invoice, fill in the invoice number you want to use as a starting point. Hereafter, QuickBooks will increment that number for each ensuing invoice.

▶▶ ProAdvisor Recommends:

Multiple Invoice Numbering Schemes

QuickBooks is smart enough to work with alphanumeric invoice numbers. This means if the previously saved invoice number was R-0001, the next invoice number will be R-0002. But suppose you run a contracting business and you'd like your residential invoices to have the numbering scheme "R-0001" and your commercial invoices to use "C-0001," and you don't want to manually change the numbering scheme each time? Consider creating another A/R account (refer to Chapter 2 lo learn how to create a new account). This will allow you to easily maintain the different numbering schemes when creating an invoice.

If you do decide to use more than one Accounts Receivable account, the top of the Invoice window has a field to select the A/R account you want to use to post this transaction. Keep in mind that you must select the same A/R account when it comes time to receive payment for the invoice.

The Bill To address is taken from the customer record, as is the Ship To address that's available on the Product Invoice template (using the Ship To address you configured to be the default Ship To address). You can select another Ship To address from the drop-down list or add a new Ship To address by choosing <Add New> from the list. Learn more about defining a default Ship To address for a customer in Chapter 3.

If you have a purchase order from this customer, enter the PO number in the P.O. Number field. Optionally, you can click the Attach icon, located at the top of the Invoice window, to scan and store an online copy of the customer's PO (or any other document that you'd like to associate with this transaction) that relates to this sale so you can easily retrieve it at a later date if the need arises. The ability to attach documents in QuickBooks is an additional service for which fees may apply.

The Terms field is filled in automatically with the terms you entered for this customer when you created it. You can change the terms for this invoice if you wish. If terms don't automatically appear, it means you didn't enter that information in the customer record. If you enter it now, when you save the invoice QuickBooks offers to make the entry the new default for this customer by adding it to the customer record.

ProAdvisor Tip: If you enter or change any information about the customer while you're creating an invoice, QuickBooks offers to add the information to the customer record when you save the invoice. If the change is permanent, click the Yes button in the dialog that displays the offer. This saves you the trouble of going back to the customer record to make the changes. If the change is only for this invoice, click the No button. If you never make permanent changes, you can tell QuickBooks to turn off this feature by changing the option in the Company Preferences tab in the General category of the Preferences dialog. Select the option Never Update Name Information When Saving Transactions.

The Rep field (available by default in the Product template, but it can be added to any template) will automatically fill in the salesperson attached to this customer. If you didn't link a salesperson when you filled out the customer record, you can click the arrow next to the field and choose a name from the drop-down list. If the Rep you want to use doesn't exist, you can select <Add New> to add the rep on the fly. See Chapter 7 to learn how to add reps to your system.

The Ship field (only available in the Product and Packing Slip templates) is for the ship date, and the date defaults to the invoice date. You can change the date if you're not shipping until a later date.

The Via field (only available in the Product and Packing Slip templates) is for the method of shipping. Click the arrow next to the field to see the available shipping choices or select <Add New>. (See Chapter 7 for information about adding to this list.)

The F.O.B. field (only available in the Product and Packing Slip templates) is used by some companies to indicate the point at which the shipping costs are transferred to the buyer and the assumption of a completed sale takes place. If you use Free on Board (FOB), you can enter the applicable data in the field; it has no impact on your QuickBooks financial records and is there for your convenience only.

Entering Line Items

You can now begin to enter the items for which you are billing this customer. Click in the first column of the line item section.

If you're using the Product invoice template, that column is Quantity. (If you're using the Professional or Service invoice template, the first column is Item.) Enter the quantity of the first item you're invoicing.

An arrow appears on the right edge of the Item Code column. Click it to see a list of the items you sell (see Chapter 5 to learn how to enter items), and select the item you need. The description and price are filled in automatically, using the information you provided when you created the item. If you didn't include description and/or price information when you created the item, you can enter it manually now.

QuickBooks does the math, and the Amount column displays the total of the quantity times the price. If the item and the customer are both liable for tax, the Tax column displays "Tax."

Repeat this process to add all the items that should be on this invoice. You can add as many rows of items as you need; if you run out of room, QuickBooks automatically adds pages to your invoice.

For line items that are inventory items, QuickBooks checks the Quantity on Hand (QOH) and warns you if you don't have enough inventory to fill the sale. It's a warning only; QuickBooks lets you complete the sale anyway, but it's never a good idea to sell into negative QOH, as it can inadvertently affect the average cost of that item.

Applying Price Levels

If you've enabled price levels in QuickBooks Preferences and created entries in your Price Level List (explained in Chapter 7), you can change the amount of any line item by applying a price level. Most of the time, your price levels are a percentage by which to lower (discount) the price, but you may also have created price levels that increase the price.

If you have already assigned a price level to this customer, the appropriate price shows up automatically. If not, to assign a price level, click within the Price Each column to display an arrow. Click the arrow to see a drop-down list of price level items, and select the one you want to apply to this item. As you can see in Figure 9-2, QuickBooks has already performed the math, so you not only see the name of your price level, you also see the resulting item price for each price level. After you select a price level, QuickBooks changes the amount you're charging the customer for the item and adjusts the amount of the total for this item.

FIGURE 9-2 Assign a predefined price level to the price of any item.

The customer sees only the price on the invoice; there's no indication that you've adjusted the price. This is different from applying a discount to a price (covered in the next section), where a discrete line item exists to identify the discount.

Entering Discounts

You can also adjust the invoice by applying discounts. Discounts are entered as line items, so the discount item has to exist in your Item List.

When you enter a discount, its amount (usually a percentage) is applied based on the line item *immediately* above it. For example, suppose you have already entered the following line items:

- Qty of 1 for Some Item with a price of $100.00 for a total line item price of $100.00
- Qty of 2 for Some Other Item with a price of $40.00 for a total line item price of $80.00

Now you want to give the customer a 10 percent discount, so you've created a 10 percent discount item in your Item List (if you're not sure how to do this, refer to Chapter 5). If you enter the discount item on the line immediately after it, QuickBooks will calculate the discount value as 10 percent of the *last* line you entered—an $8.00 discount.

Entering Subtotals

If you want to apply the discount against multiple (or all) line items, you must first enter a line item that subtotals those lines. To do this, use a subtotal item type that you've created in your Item List. Then enter the discount item as the next line item, and when the discount is applied to the previous amount, that previous amount is the amount of the subtotal. The discount is based on the subtotal.

Subtotals work by adding up all the line items that have been entered after the last subtotal item. (The first subtotal item adds up all line items starting at the first line item on the invoice.) This gives you the ability to discount some line items but not others and to apply a different discount rate to each group (subtotaled) of items.

Because discounts are displayed on the invoice, your discount policies are made clear to the customer.

Checking the Footer Section

When you're finished entering all the line items and any discounts, you'll see that QuickBooks has kept a running total, including taxes, in the footer section of the invoice (see Figure 9-3).

FIGURE 9-3 The invoice is complete, and all the items and discounts are accounted for in the Balance Due field.

Adding a Message

If you want to add a message, click the arrow in the Customer Message field to see the messages you created in the Customer Message list (described in Chapter 7). You can create a new message if you don't want to use any of the existing text by choosing <Add New> from the message drop-down list and entering your text in the New Customer Message window. Click OK to enter the message in the invoice. QuickBooks automatically saves the message in the Customer Message list so you can use it again. You can also type the message directly in the Customer Message field, which opens a Customer Message Not Found dialog that offers you the chance to do a QuickAdd to put your new message in the Customer Message list.

Adding a Memo

You can add text to the Memo field at the bottom of the invoice. This text doesn't print on the invoice—it appears only on the screen (you'll see it if you reopen this invoice to view or edit it). However, the memo text *does* appear on statements next to the listing for this invoice. Therefore, be careful about the text you use—don't enter anything you wouldn't want the customer to see (unless you never send statements).

Choosing the Method of Sending the Invoice

Note at the bottom of the invoice template there are two standard options for sending the invoice: To Be Printed and To Be E-mailed. Select the appropriate method if you're going to print or e-mail all your invoices after you finish entering them. If you select the e-mail option, you have to provide more information, all of which is covered in Chapter 25. If you're interested in learning more about accepting online payments for invoices, click the "Learn More" link next to the Show Online Payment Link On Invoices check box. Additional fees may apply.

ProAdvisor Tip: In the General section of the Preferences window, there's a default setting that automatically saves a transaction (like an invoice or check) before printing. I recommend that you (or another QuickBooks user) don't turn off this default setting—it's not only a good business practice to save a transaction before you print it, but it's also a way to protect your business from dishonest users.

Saving the Invoice

Choose Save & New to save this invoice and move on to the next blank invoice form. If this is the last invoice you're creating, click Save & Close to save this invoice and close the Create Invoices window.

Printing Packing Slips

QuickBooks provides a template for a packing slip, which is basically an invoice that doesn't display prices. The theory behind packing slips is that product prices are not necessarily something that warehouse personnel who manage, pack, and unpack products need to know.

Printing the Default Packing Slip

To print the default packing slip, complete the invoice. Then click the arrow next to the Print icon at the top of the Create Invoices window and select Print Packing Slip from the drop-down list. The Print Packing Slip dialog opens so you can select your printing options (see Figure 9-4).

FIGURE 9-4 Select the appropriate options for printing the packing slip.

Changing the Default Packing Slip

If you create your own customized packing slip template, you can select it each time you print a packing slip, or you can make that new form the default packing slip by choosing Edit | Preferences to open the Preferences dialog.

Go to the Sales & Customers category and click the Company Preferences tab. In the Choose Template For Invoice Packing Slip field, select your new packing slip form from the drop-down list and click OK. If you have multiple packing slips, you can choose any of them for printing. Instead of selecting Print Packing Slip from the Print button's drop-down list in the Create Invoices window, select a packing slip template from the drop-down list in the Template field. The Create Invoices window changes to display the packing slip, as shown in Figure 9-5.

I know I just told you that a packing slip doesn't display any amounts, and there they are! Confused? Don't be! The packing slip in Figure 9-5 is the Intuit Packing Slip, which has one set of configuration options for the screen and another set of configuration options for the printed version. In this case, the amounts are visible on the screen but will not appear on the printed version. This is true for any packing slip template you create as a customized template. It's a handy feature, as you'll learn when you read the section on customizing templates in Chapter 28.

To see what the printed version of the packing slip looks like, click the arrow next to the Print icon on the Create Invoices window toolbar, and choose Preview. Satisfied? Close the Preview window and return to the Create Invoices window. Now you can print the packing slip.

FIGURE 9-5 View a packing slip before you print it.

Batch Invoicing

Suppose you manage a landscaping company and you charge the same maintenance fee to several of your customers. Batch invoicing gives you an easy way to create and send the same invoice to these customers. You can also choose to create a billing group and add customer names to that group if those customers will need to be invoiced for a similar service in the future.

1. From the Customers menu, select Create Batch Invoices. You'll see a reminder about updating your customer information. Review and click OK.
2. From the Batch Invoice window (refer to Figure 9-6), individually select the names of customers for whom you want to create an invoice, and click the Add button to include them in this batch. Alternatively, you can create a billing group (by selecting <Add New> from the Billing Group drop-down arrow) to which you can add customers in the same manner. Click Next.
3. Select the items for your batch invoice and update the invoice date and template if necessary. Click Next.

4. Review the list of batch invoices to be created. You can deselect a customer to prevent them from receiving an invoice in this batch by clicking the check mark next to their name in the Select column. Click the Create Invoices button.

5. Review the Batch Invoice Summary window to confirm and execute the send methods (either Print or E-mail) of the invoices in the batch. Click Close when finished or to send any unmarked (meaning there's no send method in the customer record) invoices later.

FIGURE 9-6 Choose the customers to invoice in this batch or create a new billing group.

ProAdvisor Tip: This invoicing method relies on the details you've entered for your customers (like mailing address, terms, and send method), so to get the full benefit from using this feature you'll want to be sure that this information is up to date and complete.

Using Memorized Invoices

If you have a recurring invoice (common if you collect rent from tenants, for example), you can automate the process of creating it. Recurring invoices are those that are posted to QuickBooks at regular intervals, usually for the same amount.

Create the first invoice, filling out all the fields. If there are any fields that will change, leave those fields blank and fill them out each time you send the invoice. Then press CTRL-M to open the Memorize Transaction dialog.

Fill in the fields using the following guidelines:

- Change the title in the Name box to reflect what you've done. It's easiest to add a word or phrase to the default title (which is the customer or job name), such as Retainer. You can use up to 31 characters, including spaces.

- Choose Add To My Reminders List. Then specify how and when you want to be reminded in the How Often and Next Date fields. The reminder will appear in the automatic QuickBooks Reminder window.

- Choose Do Not Remind Me if you have a great memory, or if you only use this memorized invoice for special occasions.

- Choose Automate Transaction Entry if you want QuickBooks to issue this invoice automatically. If you opt for automatic issuing of this invoice, you must fill in the fields so that QuickBooks performs the task accurately, as follows:

  - The How Often field is where you specify the interval for this invoice, such as monthly, weekly, or so on. Click the arrow to see the drop-down list and choose the option you need.

  - The Next Date field is the place to note the next instance of this invoice.

  - The Number Remaining field is a place to start a countdown for a specified number of invoices. This is useful if you're billing a customer for a finite number of months because you only have a one-year contract, for example.

  - The Days In Advance To Enter field is for specifying the number of days in advance of the next date you want QuickBooks to create the invoice.

Click OK when you have finished filling out the dialog. Then click Save & Close in the Invoice window to save the transaction. Later, if you want to view, edit, or remove the transaction, you can select it from the Memorized Transaction List, which you open by pressing CTRL-T.

Editing Invoices

If you want to correct an invoice (perhaps you charged the wrong amount or forgot you'd promised a different amount to a particular customer), you can do so quite easily.

You can open the Create Invoices window and click the Previous button to move back through all the invoices in your system. However, if you have a great many invoices, it's faster to open the Customer Center, select the customer or job, and double-click the appropriate invoice in the right pane.

Use the following guidelines when you're editing a previously entered invoice:

- If a previously entered invoice has been paid, don't change anything, unless you want to edit the text in the memo field.
- If a previously entered invoice has not been paid but has been mailed, you shouldn't edit anything, although it's probably safe to enter or modify text in the memo field if necessary.
- If the previously entered invoice has not yet been sent to the customer, you can make any changes you wish.

When you click Save & Close, QuickBooks displays a message dialog asking whether you want to save the changes you made. Click Yes.

Voiding and Deleting Invoices

There's an enormous difference between voiding and deleting an invoice. Voiding an invoice makes the invoice nonexistent to your accounting and customer balances. However, the invoice number continues to exist (it's marked "VOID") so you can account for it—missing invoice numbers are just as frustrating as missing check numbers. To void an invoice, open it and right-click a blank spot in the header or footer section. Choose Void Invoice from the context menu and close the Invoice window. When QuickBooks asks if you want to record your change, click Yes.

Deleting an invoice, on the other hand, removes all traces of it from your transaction registers and most reports. To do this, open the invoice, right-click a blank spot in the header or footer section, and choose Delete Invoice. QuickBooks asks you to confirm your action.

ProAdvisor Tip: QuickBooks tracks transactions that you void, unvoid (a voided transaction that you decide to re-enter into QuickBooks), or delete, and it displays them in two reports: the Voided and Deleted Transactions Summary report and the Voided and Deleted Transactions Detail reports. Both reports show transactions that have been voided, unvoided, or deleted in the date range selected for the report. These reports can be accessed by selecting Reports | Accountant & Taxes | Voided/Deleted Transactions Summary (or Detail).

Issuing Credits and Refunds

Sometimes you have to give money back to a customer. You can do this in the form of a credit against current or future balances, or you can write a check and refund money you received from the customer. Neither is a lot of fun, but it's a fact of business life.

Creating a credit memo is similar to creating an invoice. You can use the credit memo to either reduce a customer's balance or issue a cash refund to them. What's more, QuickBooks makes it easy for you to issue a credit against a particular invoice or retain it as an available credit to be used on a future date. (Information about applying the credit memo against the customer's account when you're entering customer payments is in Chapter 10.)

Creating a Credit Memo Against an Invoice

Suppose you've sold merchandise to a customer on an invoice and later they return some or all of the items. You can issue a credit memo directly from the original invoice, saving you the time of having to research the particulars of the original sale (such as price and quantity sold). This feature also saves you from having to re-enter the item information a second time on the credit memo.

To issue a credit memo, locate and open the original invoice. Click the Create icon (see Figure 9-7) and select Credit Memo For This Invoice. All items from the invoice are automatically listed on the newly created credit memo. From here you can edit the line items as needed to account for what is being returned. When you save the credit memo, QuickBooks asks you to specify the way you want to apply the credit amount. See the section "Applying Credit Memos" for information on how to do this.

FIGURE 9-7 Creating a credit memo from the original invoice will save you time and ensure accuracy.

Creating a Credit Memo Without a Previous Invoice

To create a credit memo that is not attached to a particular invoice, choose Customers | Create Credit Memos/Refunds from the menu bar to open a blank Create Credit Memos/Refunds window.

Select the appropriate customer or job, and then fill out the rest of the heading. Move to the line item section and enter the item, the quantity, and the rate for the items in this credit memo. Do *not* use a minus sign—QuickBooks knows what a credit is.

Click Save & Close to save the credit memo (unless you have more credit memos to create—in which case, click Save & New). When you save the credit memo, QuickBooks asks you to specify the way you want to apply the credit amount. See the next section, "Applying Credit Memos."

Applying Credit Memos

When you save the credit memo, QuickBooks displays a dialog where you can choose the way to apply this credit.

Retaining the Credit

Choose Retain As An Available Credit to let the credit amount stay with the customer. You can apply the credit to a future invoice, or apply it to a current open invoice later if the customer sends a payment that deducts the credit. When you create new invoices or apply customer payments to existing invoices, the credit is available.

If the credit is for a job and the job doesn't have any outstanding invoices, you should retain the credit, because you can re-assign and then apply it against a different job for the same customer.

Giving a Refund for the Credit

Choose Give A Refund to give money back to the customer. When you click OK, the Issue A Refund window opens (see Figure 9-8). Use the following guidelines to configure the Issue A Refund window:

- In the Issue This Refund Via field, select the method for the refund from the drop-down list (cash, check, or credit card).
- If you choose Cash, QuickBooks assumes you're taking the money out of a cash drawer or petty cash box and deducts the amount from the bank account you set up to track your cash. (Be sure to select the appropriate bank account in the Account field.)
- If you choose Check, the dialog adds an option labeled To Be Printed, which is selected by default.

Issue a Refund

A refund is due to	Cruz, Albert:Kitchen Remodel
Refund Amount	$ 1,200.00
Date	12/15/2012 ☐ Ref/Check No. To Print
Address	Albert Cruz 852 Ocean View Rd. Bayshore, CA 94326
Memo	

Issue this refund via Check

Account Company Checking Accc

Ending Balance 99,761.85

Class

☑ To be printed   [OK] [Cancel]

FIGURE 9-8   Tell QuickBooks how to manage the refund you want to send to the customer.

- If you print checks, leave the check mark in the check box, and click OK. The check is added to the list of checks to be printed when you choose File | Print Forms | Checks. (The check also appears in the bank account register with the notation "To Print.")
- If you write checks manually, deselect the check mark in the To Be Printed check box, and click OK. The check is added to your bank account register, using the next available check number. Don't forget to create and send the check.
- If you choose Credit Card, follow the usual procedure for creating a credit card transaction.

Applying the Credit to an Invoice

Choose Apply To An Invoice to apply the credit to a current invoice. When you click OK, QuickBooks displays a list of open invoices for this customer (or this job, if the credit is for a job) and automatically applies the credit against the oldest invoice (see Figure 9-9).

If the credit is larger than the oldest invoice, QuickBooks applies the remaining amount of the credit to the next oldest invoice. If there are no additional invoices, the remaining amount of the credit is held in the customer's record and is treated as a retained credit. Click Done to save the transaction.

	Date	Job	Number	Orig. Amt.	Amt. Due	Amt. Applied
✓	12/15/2012	Cottage - New Construction	01-1051	99,412.50	99,412.50	1,200.00
	12/31/2012	Cottage - New Construction	01-1046	30,150.00	30,150.00	0.00
			Totals	129,562.50	0.00	1,200.00

Apply Credit to Invoices
Credit Memo
Customer:Job   Cruz, Albert:Cottage - New Construction
Ref. No.   01-1056   Original Amt.   1,200.00
Date   12/15/2012   Remaining Credit   0.00

Clear Selections

Done   Cancel

FIGURE 9-9 Select the invoice against which you want to apply the credit.

Using Estimates

Certain customers or certain types of jobs may require you to create an estimate. An estimate isn't an invoice, but it can be used as the basis of an invoice (or multiple invoices if you choose to send invoices as the job progresses). Estimates are also a great way for you to create a "budget" for the job on which you're bidding, since there are some key job reports in QuickBooks that help you keep track of actual job income and costs versus what was initially estimated.

ProAdvisor Tip: Estimates are available only if you enable them in the Jobs & Estimates section of the Preferences dialog (Edit I Preferences).

Creating an Estimate

The first (and most important) thing to understand is that creating an estimate doesn't affect your financial records. No amounts in the estimate post to income, accounts receivable, or any other general ledger account.

To create an estimate, choose Customers | Create Estimates from the menu bar. As you can see in Figure 9-10, the Create Estimates transaction window looks very much like an invoice and also contains a customer History pane to the right. You'll notice that once you've selected an existing customer or job, the History pane will display their most recent transactions, including the current balance if one exists. To close the History pane, simply click the little blue arrowhead immediately to the left of the customer's name as it appears in the pane. Fill out the fields in the same manner you use for invoices.

FIGURE 9-10 Estimates provide a way to bid for a job and then track your progress on it.

Some estimate templates permit you to invoice customers with a markup over cost (such as the built-in Custom Estimate template). This is often the approach used for time and materials on bids. Just enter the cost and indicate the markup in dollars or percentage. If you decide to change the total of the item, QuickBooks will change the markup to make sure the math is correct.

If the item you use has been configured for both a cost and price, the estimate uses the cost. If the item you use is only configured for a price, the estimate uses the price as the cost.

The Markup field is displayed only on the screen version of the estimate—this column doesn't appear on the printed version. And if you've created price levels, they'll appear in the Markup field for easy selection.

Creating Multiple Estimates for a Job

You can create multiple estimates for a customer or a job, which is an extremely handy feature. You can create an estimate for each phase of the job or create multiple estimates with different prices. Of course, that means each estimate has different contents.

When you create multiple estimates for the same job, the Estimate Active option is selected by default. If a customer rejects any estimates, you can either delete them or deselect the Estimate Active option—effectively closing the estimate.

Duplicating Estimates

You can duplicate an estimate, which provides a quick way to create multiple estimates with slightly different contents. Choose Edit | Duplicate Estimate while the estimate is displayed in your QuickBooks window (or right-click in the estimate header or footer and choose Duplicate Estimate from the shortcut menu). The Estimate # field changes to the next number, while everything else remains the same. Make the required changes, and then click Save & Close.

Memorizing Estimates

If you frequently present the same estimated items to multiple customers, you can use the Memorize Estimate feature to create boilerplate estimates for future use. QuickBooks removes the name when memorizing the document so you can easily use it for other jobs.

First, create an estimate, filling in the items that belong on it. Don't fill in amounts that usually change (such as quantities, or even prices). Then press CTRL-M (or from the Edit menu, select Memorize Estimate) to memorize the estimate. Use the following guidelines to fill out the Memorize Transaction dialog:

- Give the estimate a name that reminds you of its contents.
- Select the option Don't Remind Me.
- Click OK.

To use this boilerplate estimate, press CTRL-T or choose Lists | Memorized Transaction List to open the Memorized Transaction List. Double-click the estimate, fill in the Customer:Job information and any pricing information that's not automatically included, and then save it. The memorized estimate isn't changed; only the new estimate is saved.

Creating Progress Billing Invoices

If you've enabled estimates and progress billing in the Jobs & Estimates category of the Preferences dialog (reached by choosing Edit | Preferences), you can use the Progress Invoice template to invoice your customers as each invoicing milestone arrives.

Choosing the Estimated Job

Progress invoices are invoices that are connected to an estimate for a customer or job. Open the Create Invoices window, select Progress Invoice from the Template drop-down list, and choose the customer or job for which you're creating the progress invoice. Because you've enabled estimates in your QuickBooks Preferences, the system always checks the customer record to see if you've recorded any estimates for this customer or job, and if so, presents them.

Select the estimate you're invoicing against and click OK. QuickBooks then asks you to specify what to include on the invoice.

Fill out the dialog using the following guidelines:

- You can bill for the whole job, 100 percent of the estimate. When the line items appear, you can edit individual items.
- You can create an invoice for a specific percentage of the estimate. The percentage usually depends upon the agreement you have with your customer. For example, you could have an agreement that you'll invoice the job in a certain number of equal installments, or you could invoice a percentage that's equal to the percentage of the work that's been finished.
- You can create an invoice that covers only certain items on the estimate, or you can create an invoice that has a different percentage for each item on the estimate. This is the approach to use if you're billing for completed work on a job that has a number of distinct tasks. Some of the work listed on the estimate may be finished and other work not started, and the various items listed on the estimate may be at different points of completion.

After you've created the first progress billing invoice for an estimate, a new option is available for subsequent invoices. That option is to bill for all remaining amounts in the estimate (it replaces the 100 percent option). This is generally reserved for your last invoice, and it saves you the trouble of figuring out which percentages of which items have been invoiced previously.

As far as QuickBooks is concerned, the items and prices in the estimate are not etched in stone; you can change any amounts or quantities you wish while you're creating the invoice. Ultimately, however, your ability to invoice for amounts that differ from the estimate depends on your agreement with the customer.

Entering Progress Invoice Line Items

After you choose your progress billing method and click OK, QuickBooks automatically fills in the line item section of the invoice based on the approach you selected. For example, in Figure 9-11, I opted to create a progress bill for 50 percent of the estimate because half the work was done.

Changing Line Items

If you chose to invoice a percentage of the estimate's total, the amount of every line item on the estimate reflects that percentage. This doesn't work terribly well for those lines that have products (it's hard to sell a percentage of a physical product). You can leave the invoice as is, because the customer will probably understand that this is a progress invoice, or you can make changes to the invoice.

FIGURE 9-11 Progress invoices are automatically filled in using the information in the estimate.

In addition, the line items for services rendered may not be totally accurate. For example, some of the line items may contain service categories that aren't at the same percentage of completion as others.

To change the invoice and keep a history of the changes against the estimate, don't just make changes to the line items on the invoice. Instead, click the Progress icon on the toolbar of the Create Invoices window. This opens a dialog (see Figure 9-12) that allows reconfiguration of the line items. You can change the quantity, rate, or percentage of completion for any individual line item.

If you select Show Quantity And Rate, the columns in the dialog display the columns from the estimate, and you can make changes to any of them. Click the Qty column for any line item to highlight the number that's been used to calculate the invoice. Replace the number with the amount you want to use for the invoice. You can also change the rate as agreed to by you and the customer.

If you select Show Percentage, the dialog displays the Curr % column, which shows the percentage of completion for this and previous billings. The percentages compare the dollar amounts for invoices against the estimated total. You can change the percentage for any line item.

You can make changes to the data that QuickBooks automatically inserted in the invoice.

Select both options if you need to make changes to one type of progress on one line item and another type of progress on another line item. All the columns (and all the previous billings, if any exist) appear in the window.

Click OK when you have finished making your adjustments. You return to the invoice form, where the amounts on the line items have changed to match the adjustments you made. Click Save & New to save this invoice and move on to the next invoice, or click Save & Close to save this invoice and close the Create Invoices window.

Using this method to change a line item keeps the history of your estimate and invoices intact, as opposed to making changes in the amounts directly on the invoice form, which does not create a good audit trail.

Invoicing Customers for Reimbursable Expenses

When you pay vendors, some purchases may be made on behalf of a customer, or they may be purchases needed to complete a job. When you create a vendor bill or write a check to a vendor, you can specify expenses as reimbursable and link those expenses to a specific customer or job (covered in Chapter 11).

You can automatically invoice customers for those expenses. In addition, you can link mileage costs and time costs (for employees or subcontractors) to customers and automatically invoice customers for those expenses. (Chapter 16 has information on tracking mileage and time.)

Any amounts you link to a customer are saved in the customer record, and you can collect the money by adding those amounts to the next invoice you create for that customer. In fact, you could create an invoice specifically for the purpose of collecting reimbursable expenses, with no other services or products included on the invoice.

Configuring Reimbursement Settings

In addition to enabling the option to track reimbursable costs when entering transactions for vendors (vendor bills are covered in Chapter 11 and writing checks to vendors is covered in Chapter 12), QuickBooks offers configuration options for the way you invoice customers when you want to recover your reimbursable expenses. To establish your own preference, choose Edit | Preferences and select the Sales & Customers category in the left pane. In the My Preferences tab, select one of the available options.

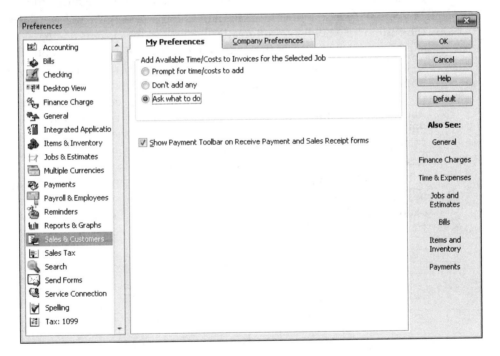

Prompt For Time/Costs To Add   Choosing this option tells QuickBooks to open the Choose Billable Time And Costs dialog, which displays the current reimbursable expenses whenever you create an invoice or sales receipt for a customer with outstanding reimbursable costs. This is the option to select if you always (or almost always) collect reimbursable costs from customers.

Don't Add Any Selecting this option prevents the automatic display of the Choose Billable Time And Costs dialog. Choose this option if you collect reimbursable expenses periodically on separate invoices. When you're ready to create an invoice for these expenses, click the Add Time/Costs button on the sales transaction form.

Ask What To Do Select this option to tell QuickBooks to ask you what you want to do whenever you create a sales transaction for a customer with outstanding reimbursable costs. Depending on your selection in that dialog (discussed in the next section), you can add the costs to the sales transaction or omit them.

Creating a Transaction for Reimbursable Expenses

When you're creating a sales transaction (an invoice or a sales receipt) for a customer that has outstanding reimbursable costs, QuickBooks uses the preference you set (as described in the previous section) to determine how to manage those costs.

If you selected the preference Prompt For Time/Costs To Add, when you select the customer, QuickBooks automatically displays the current reimbursable expenses so you can select those you want to include in the current transaction.

If you selected the preference Don't Add Any, the invoice or sales receipt transaction window opens as usual. If you want to check for reimbursable costs for this customer and then decide whether you want to recover any of them, click the Add Time/Costs button at the bottom of the transaction form. When the Choose Billable Time And Costs dialog opens, you can see if there are any reimbursable expenses you want to collect. If so, follow the instructions presented in the next section, "Adding Reimbursable Costs to the Sales Transaction."

If you selected the preference Ask What To Do, when you select a customer that has unpaid reimbursable costs in the transaction window, QuickBooks displays a dialog asking how you want to handle those amounts. Your response determines whether the Choose Billable Time And Costs dialog opens automatically.

Adding Reimbursable Costs to the Sales Transaction

To collect reimbursable costs from a customer, select those costs from the Choose Billable Time And Costs dialog. Each type of expense is displayed in its own tab, and you must examine each tab to see if any amounts exist. Unfortunately, the amount displayed on each tab doesn't help you head for the appropriate tab—all the amounts are set at $0.00 because those numbers represent the amount you selected to add to the sales transaction, not the amount accumulated in reimbursable expenses. So start clicking each tab to find reimbursable expenses to transfer to the transaction.

When you find a tab that has contents, click in the leftmost column to place a check mark next to the expense(s) you want to include (see Figure 9-13).

FIGURE 9-13 Select the reimbursable time, expenses, mileage, or items you want to add to the transaction you're preparing.

Click OK to move the item(s) to the transaction window to join any other items you're entering in that transaction. You may find reimbursable expenses on more than one tab; for example, you may have expenses on the Expenses tab and items on the Items tab. You have to check each tab.

QuickBooks automatically transfers the selected reimbursable costs to the invoice. The description of reimbursable expenses on the invoice is taken from the text you entered in the Memo column when you entered the vendor's bill. If you didn't use that Memo column, you'll have to enter text manually in the Description column of the invoice (which is a real test of your memory). Otherwise, the customer sees only an amount and no explanation of what it's for. (The description of mileage or item costs is taken from the Description field of the item you configured.)

Adding Taxes to Reimbursable Expenses

If an expense is taxable and the customer is not tax exempt, choose the option Selected Expenses Are Taxable. When the expenses are passed to the invoice, the appropriate taxes are applied. If you select the taxable option and the customer is tax exempt, QuickBooks won't add the sales tax to the invoice.

If some expenses are taxable and others aren't, you have to separate the process of moving items to the invoice. First, deselect each nontaxable expense by clicking its check mark to remove it (it's a toggle). Click OK to put those expenses on the invoice. Then return to the Choose Billable Time And Costs window, put a check mark next to each nontaxable expense, deselect the Selected Expenses Are Taxable option, and click OK.

Omitting the Details on the Invoice

Each of the tabs has the option Print Selected Time And Costs As One Invoice Item. When you click OK and view the results in the invoice, you still see each individual item. Don't panic—you're not just seeing things. The screen version of the invoice continues to display the individual items. However, when you print the invoice, you'll see a single line item with the correct total in the Amount column.

QuickBooks changes the format of the printed invoice to eliminate the details but doesn't change the data in the onscreen version of the invoice. This means you can open the invoice later and see the detailed items, which is handy when the customer calls to ask, "What's this reimbursable expense item on my bill?"

Excluding a Reimbursable Expense

If you have some reason to exclude one or more expenses from the current invoice, just avoid putting a check mark in the column. The item remains in the system and shows up on the Choose Billable Time And Costs window the next time you open it. You can add the item to the customer's invoice in the future.

Removing a Reimbursable Expense from the List

Suppose when it's time to invoice the customer, you decide that you don't want to ask the customer to pay an expense you marked as reimbursable; you've changed your mind. The Choose Billable Time And Costs window has no Delete button and no method of selecting an item and choosing a delete function. You could deselect the check mark that tells QuickBooks to move the item to the sales transaction, but afterwards, every time you open the window, the item is still there—it's like a haunting.

The solution lies in the Hide column. If you place a check mark in the Hide column, the item is effectively deleted from the list of reimbursable expenses that you see when you're preparing invoices but the amount is still in your system. This means you won't accidentally invoice the customer for the item, but the link to this expense for this customer continues to appear in reports about this customer's activity, which is helpful for job costing. In effect, by selecting the Hide option, you've marked the expense as "nonbillable," and it's not available in the future.

Changing the Amount of a Reimbursable Expense

You're free to change the amount of a reimbursable expense. To accomplish this, select the amount in the Amount column of the Billable Time And Costs window on the Expenses tab, and enter the new figure.

If you reduce the amount, QuickBooks does not keep the remaining amount on the Billable Time And Costs window. You won't see it again because QuickBooks makes the assumption you're not planning to pass the remaining amount to your customer in the future.

You may want to increase the charge for some reason (perhaps to cover overhead), but if you're increasing all the charges, it's easier to apply a markup (covered next) than to change each individual item.

Marking Up Reimbursable Expenses

You can mark up any expenses you're invoicing, which many companies do to cover any additional costs incurred, such as handling, time, or general aggravation. To apply a markup, select the items you want to mark up by placing a check mark in the Use column in the Expenses tab of the Choose Billable Time And Costs window. Then enter a markup in the Markup Amount Or % field in either of the following ways:

- Enter an amount.
- Enter a percentage (a number followed by the percent sign).

Specify the account to which you're posting markups. You can create an account specifically for markups (which is what I do because I'm slightly obsessive about analyzing the source of all income) or use an existing income account.

When you click OK to transfer the reimbursable expenses to the customer's invoice, you'll see the reimbursable expenses and the markup as separate items.

Although it would be unusual for you to be marking up items without having discussed this with your customer, if you don't want your customer to see the markup amounts, select the Print Selected Time And Costs As One Invoice Item option. You'll see the breakdown on the screen version of the invoice, but the printed invoice will contain only the grand total.

One big difference between using the markup function and just changing the amount of the reimbursable expense in the Amount column is the way the amounts are posted to your general ledger. If you use the markup function, the difference between the actual expense and the charge to your customer is posted to the markup account. If you change the amount of the expense, the entire amount is posted to the income account you linked to the reimbursable expense account.

ProAdvisor Tip: If you void or delete a saved sales transaction that contains reimbursable expenses, these expenses are not automatically made "billable" again. You'll need to go to the original expense transaction and click the Invoice icon in the Billable column to make it available to invoice again.

Receiving and Tracking Customer Payments

n this chapter:

- Apply customer payments

- Apply credits and discounts to invoices

- Handle cash sales

- Deposit customer payments into your bank account

- Track receivables

- Impose finance charges

- Send statements to customers

For most businesses, the most rewarding accounts receivable chore is receiving a payment from a customer. You need to make sure, however, that you apply customer payments correctly so that you and your customers have the same information in your records.

Receiving Invoice Payments

As you create invoices and send them to your customers, there's an expectation that money will eventually arrive to pay off those invoices. There are two standard ways to apply the payments that pay off invoices:

Balance Forward This is a system in which you consider the total of all the outstanding invoices as the amount due from the customer, and you apply payments against that total. It doesn't matter which particular invoice is being paid because it's a running total of payments against a running total of invoices.

Open Item This is a system in which payments you receive are applied to specific invoices. Most of the time, the customer either sends a copy of the invoice along with the check or notes the invoice number that is being paid in the Memo field of the check, or on a check stub, to make sure your records agree with the customer's records.

Setting Default Options for Receiving Customer Payments

In QuickBooks, payments are applied to specific invoices, not to a general balance forward. You can change how QuickBooks applies payments with just a matter of a mouse click or two, using the following steps:

1. Choose Edit | Preferences and click the Payments icon in the left pane.
2. Move to the Company Preferences tab.
3. In the Receive Payments section, select or deselect options to match your needs:
   - Automatically Apply Payments means that when you enter the amount you've received from the customer, QuickBooks will automatically pay off matching invoices, first by amount, then by the oldest due date.
   - Automatically Calculate Payments tells QuickBooks to let you omit the amount of the customer's payment in the transaction window and select invoices to pay off. QuickBooks adds up the invoice amounts and applies the total as the customer's payment. (This assumes the customer has sent a payment that matches the total.)
   - Use Undeposited Funds As A Default Deposit To Account automatically posts the payments you receive to the Undeposited Funds account, and you deposit the funds into a bank account.

Recording Invoice Payments

When a payment arrives from a customer, choose Customers | Receive Payments to open a blank Receive Payments window, as shown in Figure 10-1. If you have multiple A/R accounts, a field exists at the top of the window so you can select the A/R account to which this customer's invoices were posted.

FIGURE 10-1 The Receive Payments window has all the fields needed to apply payments accurately and to choose QuickBooks customer payment options.

Click the arrow to the right of the Received From field and select the customer or job from the drop-down list using the following guidelines:

- Select the customer. The current balance for this customer automatically appears in the Customer Balance field.
- If the payment is for a job, select the job. The current balance for this job automatically appears in the Customer Balance field.
- If the payment covers multiple jobs, select the main customer name to see all invoices for all jobs. The current balance for this customer automatically appears in the Customer Balance field.

In the Amount field, enter the amount of this payment. (You can omit this step and let QuickBooks calculate the amount of the payment—see the section "Calculating the Payment").

Click the arrow to the right of the Pmt. Method field and select the payment method:

- If the payment method is a check, enter the check number in the Check # field that appears.
- If the payment method is a credit card, complete the Card No. and Exp. Date fields. (If you have a merchant account with the QuickBooks Merchant Account Service, click the option Process <credit card name> Payment When Saving.)

The Memo field is optional, and you can use it if you have a note you want to link to this payment record.

In the Deposit To field (if it exists), select the bank account for depositing the payment, or select Undeposited Funds if you're using that account to receive payments (see the section "Turning Payments into Bank Deposits," later in this chapter). If the Deposit To field doesn't exist, your Payments Preferences are configured to deposit payments to the Undeposited Funds account automatically (a good idea).

ProAdvisor Tip: You can add any additional payment methods you need by choosing <Add New> in the Pmt. Method drop-down list (see Chapter 7 to learn about adding items to QuickBooks lists).

Calculating the Payment

If you've enabled the Automatically Calculate Payments option in the Payments category of the Preferences dialog (the default setting), you can skip the Amount field and move directly to the list of invoices in the Receive Payments window. As you select each invoice for payment, QuickBooks calculates the total and places it in the Amount field.

If you haven't enabled the option to calculate payments automatically and you select an invoice listing without entering the amount of the payment first, QuickBooks issues an error message, telling you that the amount of the payment you're applying is higher than the amount you entered in the header section (the amount you received from the customer). In that case, enter the amount of the payment in the Amount field at the top of window.

Applying Payments to Invoices

By default, QuickBooks automatically applies the payment to the oldest invoice(s), unless the amount of the payment exactly matches the amount of another invoice, as seen in Figure 10-2.

FIGURE 10-2 QuickBooks has applied the payment to an invoice that exactly matches the payment.

You could face any of several scenarios when receiving customer payments:

- The customer has one unpaid invoice, and the payment is for the same amount as that invoice.
- The customer has several unpaid invoices, and the payment is for the amount of one of those invoices.
- The customer has several unpaid invoices, and the payment equals the total of multiple invoices.
- The customer has one or more unpaid invoices, and the payment is for an amount lower than any single invoice.

- The customer has several unpaid invoices, and the payment is for an amount greater than any one invoice but not large enough to cover two invoices.
- The customer has one or more unpaid invoices, and the payment is for a lesser amount than the current balance. However, the customer has a credit equal to the difference between the payment and the customer balance.

You have a variety of choices for handling any of these scenarios, but for situations where the customer's intention isn't clear, the smart thing to do is to just call and ask how the payment should be applied. You must, of course, apply the entire amount of the customer's check. If you are not tracking invoices and are instead using a balance forward system, just let QuickBooks continue to apply payments against the oldest invoices.

If the customer payment doesn't match the amount of any invoice, check to see whether the customer indicated a specific invoice number for the payment. If so, apply the payment against that invoice; if not, let the automatic selection of the oldest invoice stand.

Handling Underpayments

After you apply the customer's payment, if it isn't sufficient to pay off an existing invoice, the lower-left corner of the Receive Payments window displays a message that asks whether you want to leave the underpaid amount as an underpayment or write it off.

If you want to ask the customer about the reason for the underpayment, click the button labeled View Customer Contact Information to open the customer record and view their contact information.

If you opt to retain the underpayment, the invoice you selected for payment remains as a receivable, with a new balance (the original balance less the payment you applied). When you click Save & Close (or Save & New if you're entering more customer payments), QuickBooks makes the appropriate postings.

If you select the option to write off the underpayment, when you click Save & Close or Save & New, QuickBooks opens the Write Off Amount dialog so you can choose the posting account, and, if applicable, apply a class to the transaction.

Discuss the account to use for a write off with your accountant. You can create an Income or Expense account for this purpose, depending on the way your accountant wants to track receivables you've decided to forgive.

Applying Credits to Invoices

You can apply any existing credits to an open invoice, in addition to applying the payment that arrived. If credits exist, customers usually let you know how they want credits applied, and it's not unusual to find a note written on the copy of the invoice that the customer sent along with the check (a check that probably represents the net due when the credit is applied).

When credits exist for the customer or job you select in the Receive Payments transaction window, QuickBooks displays a note to that effect in the window (see Figure 10-3).

FIGURE 10-3 This customer has a credit balance that can be applied to the invoice along with the payment the customer sent.

To apply a credit balance to an invoice, click the Discount & Credits button on the Receive Payments window, which opens the Discount And Credits dialog.

Select the credit(s) you want to apply and click Done. Depending on the circumstances, here's how QuickBooks handles the credits:

The Credit Total Is Equal to or Less Than the Unpaid Amount of the Oldest Invoice
This reduces the balance due on that invoice. If the customer sent a payment that reflects their net balance due (balance minus unused credits), the invoice has no remaining balance.

If applying the existing credit along with the payment doesn't pay off the invoice, the balance due on the invoice is reduced by the total of the payment and the credit.

The amount of the credit is added to the postings for the invoice. Don't worry—this change only affects the invoice balance and the accounts receivable posting; it doesn't change the amount of the payment that's posted to your bank account.

The Credit Total Is Larger Than the Amount Required to Pay Off an Invoice
If the customer payment is smaller than the amount of the invoice, but the amount of credit is larger than the amount needed to pay off the invoice, the balance of the credit remains available for posting to another invoice.

To apply the unapplied credit balance to another invoice, click Done and select the next invoice in the Receive Payments window. Then click the Discount &

Credits button and apply the credit balance (or as much of it as you need) against the invoice. Any unused credits remain for the future.

You should send a statement to the customer to reflect the current, new invoice balances as a result of applying the payments and the credits to make sure your records and your customer's records match.

Applying Credits to a Different Job

You may have a situation in which a customer has already paid the invoices for a job when the credit is created, or has paid for part of the job, exceeding the amount of the credit. If the customer tells you to apply the entire credit balance to another job or to float the credit and apply it against the next job, open the credit transaction and change the job. Then apply the credit to an invoice for the job you specified, or tell QuickBooks to retain it as an available credit that you'll apply when payment arrives.

Applying Discounts for Timely Payments

If you offer your customers terms that include a discount if they pay their bills promptly (for instance, 2%10 Net30), you must apply the discount to the payment if it's applicable.

Figure 10-4 shows the Receive Payments window for a customer who has an invoice that is eligible for a discount for timely payment. QuickBooks has displayed

FIGURE 10-4 A discount date appears for invoices that are eligible for a discount.

a message that discounts are available. However, if there are multiple invoices listed in the transaction window, the only clue you have to recognize an invoice with such a discount is the fact that the Disc. Date column shows the date by which the invoice must be paid to receive the discount. For invoices without discount terms, that column is blank in the Receive Payments window—in fact, if there are no invoices with available discounts for a customer, the Disc Date column does not appear at all.

QuickBooks doesn't apply the discount automatically, for instance, by offering a column with the discount amount and selecting that amount as part of the payment. Instead, you must select the invoice (unless QuickBooks automatically selected it in order to apply the payment) and click the Discount & Credits button to see the Discount And Credits dialog connected to this invoice.

If the payment arrived by the discount date, QuickBooks inserts the amount of the discount to use. Accept the amount of discount and enter a Discount Account (see "Posting Discounts" later in this section). If the payment did not arrive by the discount date, QuickBooks displays 0.00 as the discount amount—see the next section, "Applying Discounts for Untimely Payments," for the solution.

You can change the amount of the discount, which you may want to do if the customer only made a partial payment (less than is required to pay off the invoice after the discount is applied) and you want to give a proportionately smaller discount.

Click Done to return to the Receive Payments window. You'll see that QuickBooks has added a discount column and displayed the discount amount in that column. If the net amount and the customer payment amount are the same, the invoice is now paid off.

Applying Discounts for Untimely Payments

Sometimes customers take the discount even if the payment arrives after the discount date. You can apply the payment to the invoice and leave a balance due for the discount amount that was deducted by the customer, if you wish. However, most companies give the customer the discount even if the payment is late, as part of "good will."

When you click the Discount & Credits button in that case, QuickBooks does not automatically fill in the discount amount because the discount period has now passed. To preserve your goodwill with that customer, simply enter the amount of the discount manually, select the posting account, and then click Done to apply the discount to the invoice.

Posting Discounts

To track the amount of money you've given away with discounts, you should create a specific account in your chart of accounts. You could post discounts to your standard income account(s), which would be reduced every time you apply a discount. However, it's better to create an Income account (such as "Discounts Given") so you can easily track the discounts you're allowing your customers to take over time.

C a u t i o n : If there's an account named Discounts in the part of your chart of accounts that's devoted to expenses or cost of goods, don't use that account for your customer discounts, because it's there to track the discounts you take with your vendors.

Turning Payments into Bank Deposits

Use the Deposit To field in the Receive Payments window to select an account for depositing the payments. You can select a bank account or select the Undeposited Funds account.

If you don't see the Deposit To field, it means your Payments Preference setting is set to post payments automatically to the Undeposited Funds account. (To confirm, on the Company Preferences tab, select Edit | Preferences | Payments.)

Using the Undeposited Funds account is almost always the best way to handle money you receive.

Depositing Cash Receipts into the Undeposited Funds Account

When you enable automatic use of the Undeposited Funds account (or manually select that account in the transaction window), each payment you receive is entered into the account named Undeposited Funds (QuickBooks establishes this account automatically). It's an account type of Other Current Asset.

When you finish applying customer payments in QuickBooks, and you're ready to make your bank deposit, you move the money from the Undeposited Funds account into a bank account by choosing Banking | Make Deposits from the menu bar. (See the section "Making Bank Deposits" later in this chapter for the rest of the details.)

While the Undeposited Funds account shows each individual payment you received, the bank account shows only the total amount of each bank deposit (the payments you selected for transfer to the bank from the Undeposited Funds account). This matches the bank statement that shows up each month, making it easier to reconcile the account.

Depositing Cash Receipts into a Bank Account

Depositing each payment directly to the bank means you don't have to take the extra step involved in moving cash receipts from the Undeposited Funds account into the bank account. However, each payment you receive appears as a separate entry when you reconcile your bank account.

If you receive six payments totaling $10,450.25 and take the checks to the bank that day, your bank statement shows that amount as one deposit. When you reconcile the bank statement, each deposit you made (for each individual payment you received) is listed in your bank register. You'll have to select each payment individually, mark it as cleared, and make sure it matches the day's deposits on the bank statement. (See Chapter 14 for detailed instructions on reconciling bank accounts.)

Printing a Receipt for an Invoice Payment

You can print a receipt for an invoice payment by clicking the Print icon at the top of the Receive Payments window. Most customers don't expect printed receipts for invoice payments, but you may have a customer who requests one.

Handling Cash Sales

In QuickBooks, a *cash sale* is handled via a transaction called a Sales Receipt. It's a sale for which you haven't created an invoice, because the exchange of product or services and the payment from the customer occurred simultaneously (and that payment can be in the form of a check or credit card, not just cash). This means you have no accounts receivable as a result of the transaction. While you can have a cash sale for either a service or a product, it's far more common to sell products for cash. In my experience, most service companies use invoices, and most retail companies deal with cash.

> **ProAdvisor Tip:** If you're running a retail store, the Sales Receipt feature in QuickBooks isn't necessarily the most efficient way to handle your transactions and manage your inventory. You should consider using specialized retail software, like QuickBooks Point of Sale, which takes care of opening the cash register drawer automatically at the end of a sale, tracks your inventory, and helps you better manage your cash. If you want to learn more about the QuickBooks Point of Sale product, visit the QuickBooks website: quickbooks.intuit.com.

There are two methods for handling cash sales in QuickBooks:

- Record each cash sale as a separate record. This is useful for tracking sales of products or services to customers. It provides a way to maintain historical records about those customers in addition to tracking income and inventory.
- Record sales in batches (usually one batch for each business day). This method tracks income and inventory when you have no desire to maintain historical information about each customer that pays cash.

To record a cash sale, choose Customers | Enter Sales Receipts from the menu bar, which opens the Enter Sales Receipts window shown in Figure 10-5. You'll notice there's a pane to the right of the form that displays a customer's history, which includes the most recent transactions including current balance, if one exists. To close this pane, simply click the little blue arrowhead to the left of the name tab.

FIGURE 10-5 A Sales Receipt form is like an invoice, a receive payment form, and a printable customer receipt, all rolled into one transaction window.

Entering Cash Sale Data

If you want to track customer information, enter a name in the Customer:Job field or select the name from the drop-down list. If the customer doesn't exist, you can add a new customer by choosing <Add New>.

If you're not tracking customers, create a customer for cash sales, such as "Cash Sale."

Even if you use a generic "cash sale" customer name, you can still type in the customer's name and address in the Ship To field. (You'll have to add this field to the default Sales Receipt template—see Chapter 28, "Customizing QuickBooks," to learn more about customizing transaction templates.) In the future, you can run the Sales by Ship To Address Report (Reports | Sales | Sales by Ship To Address) to view a report that shows the transactions for this generic "cash sale" customer that includes the information you've entered in the "Ship To" field.

Every field in the Enter Sales Receipts window works exactly the way it works for invoices and payments—just fill in the information. To save the record, click the Save button on the Enter Sales Receipts tool bar. You can also select Save & New to bring up a new blank record or click Save & Close if you're finished.

Printing a Receipt for a Cash Sale

Some cash customers want a receipt. Click the Print button in the Enter Sales Receipts window to open the Print One Sales Receipt dialog. If you're not printing to a dot-matrix printer with multipart paper and you want a copy of the receipt for your files, be sure to change the specification in the Number Of Copies box to 2.

Customizing the Cash Receipts Template

There are some fields missing from the default QuickBooks cash receipts template (which is named Custom Sales Receipt). For example, there's no place for a sales rep, which is needed if you're paying commissions on cash sales, or you just want to track the person who made the sale. As I just mentioned, there's no Ship To address if the customer pays cash and wants delivery, nor is there a Ship Via field.

The solution is to customize the Custom Sales Receipts form. Specific instructions on customizing templates are in Chapter 28, so I won't go over all those steps here; instead, use the guidelines in the following sections to change the Custom Sales Receipt template.

Change the Options in the Header Tab

Depending on your needs, you should consider one or more of the following suggestions for making changes in the Header tab of the Additional Customization dialog box:

- If you ever ship products to cash customers, select the Ship To field for both the Screen and the Print forms.
- If you're tracking salespersons (either for commission or just to know who made the sale), add the Rep field. You can add the field to the screen version and omit it from the print version.
- If you ship products to cash customers, add the Ship Date and Ship Via fields to the screen and print versions.

Change the Options in the Columns Tab

Use the Columns tab to add or remove columns in the line item section of the form. You can also change the order in which the columns appear. (For instance, perhaps you'd rather have Qty in the first column instead of the Item number.)

Handling Batches of Cash Sales

If you operate a restaurant, you might want to consider batching your cash transactions on a daily basis. This works only if you don't care about maintaining information about the customers and no customer expects a printed receipt from QuickBooks. This technique also works if you have a business in which sales and service personnel return to the office each day with customer payments in hand.

Create a customized template using the steps described in Chapter 28, with the following guidelines:

- Name the form appropriately (for example, "Batch Sales" or "Sales Batch").
- On the Header tab, keep only the Date and Sale Number fields in the header part of the template.
- On the Columns tab, deselect all the optional fields, leaving only the Item, Description, and Amount columns selected.
- On the Footer tab, remove the Message field.

To batch-process cash sales, use the new template with the following procedures:

- Use a customer named "Cash" or "DailySale."
- In the line item section, use a new line for each sale, regardless of whether the same customer is purchasing each item, each item is purchased by a different customer, or there's a combination of both events.
- Use the Save & Close button at the end of the day. If you need to close the window during the day (perhaps you'd like to get some other work done in QuickBooks), open the Sales Receipt window and click the Previous button to find your previous record.

Tracking Your Cash Drawer in QuickBooks

If you deal in real cash, have a cash register, and are not using QuickBooks Point of Sale (see the ProAdvisor Tip in the previous section), consider these suggested steps for keeping track of your cash drawer that are intended to help make your bookkeeping chores easier.

There are two basic ways to track receipts from cash sales separate from customer payments; pick the one that best suits your needs:

- Post the cash receipts to the Undeposited Funds account but deposit those funds separately from noncash payments when you work in the QuickBooks Payments To Deposit window.
- Post the cash receipts directly to a new bank account called "Cash in Drawer" (or something similar). Then, when you empty the drawer and deposit the cash into your bank account, you can record it in QuickBooks by making a Transfer (Banking | Transfer Funds) from the Cash Drawer account into the appropriate bank account.

The advantage of having a "Cash in Drawer" account is that you can match the contents of the physical till of your cash register to an account in QuickBooks. In a perfect world, you'll open the register for the Cash in Drawer account in QuickBooks and see that it matches your actual drawer count. The world isn't perfect, however, and sometimes the two amounts will not be equal. To resolve this, refer to the following section, "Handling the Over and Short Problem."

Handling the Over and Short Problem

If you literally take cash for cash sales, when you count the money in the till at the end of the day, you may find that the recorded income doesn't match the cash you expected to find in the till. Or you may find that the money you posted to deposit to the bank doesn't match the amount of money you put into the little brown bag you took to the bank.

One of the problems you face is how to handle this in QuickBooks. If you post $100.00 in cash sales but only have $99.50 in cash to take to the bank, how do you handle the missing 50 cents? You can't just post $100.00 to your bank account (well, you could, but your bank account won't reconcile).

The solution to the over/short dilemma is to address it in your bookkeeping procedures. Track it. In many cases, the Overs and Shorts balance out—short one day, over another.

Creating Over and Short Accounts

To track over/short, you need to have some place to post the discrepancies, which means you have to create some new accounts in your chart of accounts, as follows:

- Create an account named Over, using the account type Income.
- Create an account named Short, using the account type Income.

If you're using numbered accounts, use sequential numbers on the next level from your regular Income accounts. For example, use 49000 if your regular Income accounts are 40000, 40100, 40300, and so on.

If you want to see a net number for over/short (a good idea), create three accounts. Create the parent account first and name it Over-Short (or Over&Short), and then make the Over and Short accounts subaccounts of the parent account. If you use account numbers, make the three numbers sequential, for instance:

- 49000 Over/Short (parent account)
- 49010 Over (subaccount)
- 49020 Short (subaccount)

Creating Over and Short Items

If you track cash sales by tracking batches of sales in a Sales Receipt transaction, you need items for your overages and shortages (in QuickBooks, you need items for everything that's connected with entering sales data in a transaction window). Create items for overages and shortages as follows:

- Create two Other Charge items, one named Overage, the other named Shortage.
- Don't assign a price.
- Make the item nontaxable.
- Link each item to the appropriate account (or subaccount) that you just created for Over/Short.

Now that you have the necessary accounts and items, use the Over and Short items right in the Enter Sales Receipts window to adjust the difference between the amount of money you've accumulated in the cash-sale transactions and the amount of money you're actually depositing to the bank. It's your last transaction of the day. Remember to use a minus sign before the figure when you use the Short item.

Making Bank Deposits

By default, when you receive a customer payment or save a Sales Receipt, QuickBooks posts the total on that receipt to the Undeposited Funds account. When it's time to go to the bank, you have to tell QuickBooks about your bank deposit.

Choosing the Payments to Deposit

As you've been completing the receive payment and cash sales forms, QuickBooks has been keeping a list of these transactions in the Undeposited Funds account. These transactions remain in Undeposited Funds until you clear them by depositing them into your bank account. (If you've been depositing every payment and cash receipt to a specific bank account, this section doesn't apply to you.)

To tell QuickBooks about the details of your bank deposit, choose Banking | Make Deposits from the menu bar, which brings up the Payments To Deposit window, shown in Figure 10-6.

FIGURE 10-6 All the income you've collected since the last bank deposit is waiting to be deposited.

ProAdvisor Tip: You may have other deposits to make, perhaps refunds, loan proceeds, capital infusion, or some other type of deposit. Don't worry—you can tell QuickBooks about them in the next transaction window. This window is only displaying the payments you've entered into QuickBooks through customer-based transaction windows.

Notice the following about the Payments To Deposit window:

- The Type column displays information about the payment type for each transaction—PMT for payment of an invoice (as shown in Figure 10-6) and RCPT for a cash sale.
- The Payment Method column displays the specific payment method for each transaction, such as cash, check, a specific credit card, and so on.

This information is important because you should match it to the way your bank records deposits; otherwise, bank reconciliation becomes much more complicated.

For example, your bank probably lists credit card deposits separately from a deposit total for cash and checks, even if all the money was deposited the same day. That's because your credit card deposits are probably made directly to your bank account by your merchant account bank.

Select Deposit Items

If you only have a few transactions to deposit, select those you just deposited (when you went to the bank) by clicking their listings to place a check mark in the left column. Click Select All if you took all the payments to the bank for deposit.

Separate Deposit Items by Payment Method

If you have to separate deposits by type, select a payment method from the drop-down list at the top of the Payments To Deposit window. Choose Selected Types to open the Select Payment Types list and choose either individual or multiple payment types to include in the same deposit.

For example, you may use the Other category to signify a money order or a traveler's check, and you're listing those items on the same deposit slip in which you listed checks. The listings on the Payments To Deposit window change to include only the deposits that match the selected payment method.

Separate Deposits by Bank Account

If you're depositing money into multiple bank accounts, select only the transactions that go into the first account. After you complete the deposit, start this process again and deposit the remaining transactions into the other account(s).

Credit Card Deposits

You shouldn't deposit credit card payments until your merchant bank notifies you that the funds have been placed in your account.

- If you have QuickBooks online banking, the deposit shows up in the downloaded report from your bank (see Chapter 15 to learn about managing online banking transactions).
- If you have online access to your merchant card account, the transfer will appear on the activities report on the website.
- If you don't have any form of online access, you'll have to wait for the monthly statement to arrive (or contact the bank periodically to see if anything showed up in your account).

If your merchant bank deducts fees before transferring funds, learn how to deposit the net amount in the section "Calculating Merchant Card Fees," later in this chapter.

Working in the Make Deposits Window

After you select the appropriate payment method (or select all payments), click OK in the Payments To Deposit window to bring up the Make Deposits window shown in Figure 10-7.

FIGURE 10-7 The Make Deposits form is a virtual bank deposit slip.

Select the bank account you're using for this deposit. Then make sure the date matches the day you physically deposit the money.

Adding Items to the Deposit

If you want to add deposit items that weren't in the Payments To Deposit window, click anywhere in the Received From column to make it accessible and select an existing name by clicking the arrow, or click <Add New> to enter a name that isn't in your system. If the source of the check is any entity that isn't a customer or vendor (perhaps you're depositing your own check to put additional capital into the company, or you have a check representing a bank loan), you can either skip the Received From column or add the name to the Other Names List. (If you don't need to track the entity as a customer or vendor, it's fine to skip the name.)

Press TAB to move to the From Account column and enter the account to which you're posting this transaction. Following are some common scenarios:

- If the check you're depositing represents a bank loan, use the liability account for that bank loan (you can create it here by choosing <Add New> if you didn't think to set up the account earlier). The bank should be in your Vendor List because you have to write checks to repay the loan.
- If the check you're depositing represents an infusion of capital from you, use the owner's capital account in the Equity section of your chart of accounts.
- If the check is a refund for an expense (perhaps you overpaid someone, and they're returning money to you), use the vendor's name and post the deposit to the same expense account you used for the original transaction.
- If the check is a rebate from a manufacturer instead of the vendor, skip the Received From column and post the amount to the original expense account you used when you purchased the item.

Use the TAB key to move through the rest of the columns, which are self-explanatory.

Calculating Merchant Card Fees

If your merchant card bank deposits the gross amount of each transaction and charges your bank account for the total fees due at the end of the month, you don't have to do anything special to deposit credit card payments. You can deal with the fees when your bank statement arrives by entering the fee directly in the bank account register, posting the amount to the merchant card fee expense account.

If your merchant card bank deducts fees from transactions and deposits the net proceeds to your account, it takes a few extra steps to track credit card transactions and deposit the correct amount.

Select the credit card transactions in the Payments To Deposit window. These are gross amounts, representing the sales price you charged (and the customer paid). Then click OK to move the deposits to the Make Deposits window.

In the first empty line below the transactions that were transferred to the Make Deposits window, click the Account column and select the account to which you post merchant card fees.

Move to the Amount column and enter the fee as a negative number. Now, the net matches the amount that the merchant card company deposited in your bank account, and your merchant card expense has been posted to the general ledger.

ProAdvisor Tip: Using the QuickBooks Merchant Service can make it easier to track and account for customer credit card payments. With this service, your customer's credit card charges are processed directly through QuickBooks and you can download the fees directly into your check register. They appear the way they do in your bank statement, which can prevent data entry errors and reduce the time it takes to reconcile your bank account. QuickBooks Merchant Service is an add-on service and additional fees apply.

Getting Cash Back from Deposits

If you're getting cash back from your deposit, you can tell QuickBooks about it right on the Make Deposits window, instead of making a journal entry to adjust the total of collected payments against the total of the bank deposit.

Enter the account to which you're posting the cash (usually a petty cash or Draw account), and enter the amount of cash you want back from this deposit. Even though you can put the cash in your pocket, you should account for it. As you spend the cash for business expenses, you can post the expense directly in the same petty cash account register.

Printing Deposit Slips

If you want to print a deposit slip or a deposit summary, click the Print button in the Make Deposits window. QuickBooks asks whether you want to print a deposit slip and summary or just a deposit summary.

If you want to print a deposit slip that your bank will accept, you must order printable deposit slips from QuickBooks. The QuickBooks deposit slips are guaranteed to be acceptable to your bank. You must have a laser printer or inkjet printer to use them. When you print the deposit slip, there's a tear-off section at the bottom of the page that has a deposit summary. Keep that section for your own records and take the rest of the page to the bank along with your money.

If you don't have QuickBooks deposit slips, select Deposit Summary Only and fill out your bank deposit slip manually. Be sure to fill out the payment method field (cash or check), or QuickBooks won't print the deposit slip. A Print Lists dialog appears so you can change printers, adjust margins, or even print in color. Choose Print to send the deposit information to the printer. When you return to the Make Deposits window, click Save & Close to save the deposit.

Tracking Accounts Receivable

Collecting the money owed to you can be one of the biggest headaches in running a business. You have to track what's owed and who owes it, and then expend time and effort to collect it. All of the effort you spend on the money your customers owe you is called *tracking accounts receivable* (or, more commonly, *tracking A/R*). QuickBooks offers several tools and reports that simplify this necessary chore.

Getting the Most from the Customer Center

In Chapter 3, you were introduced to the Customer Center, the place where you access and work with your customers and jobs as well as view all the transactions associated with them. The Customer Center also contains links that give you quick access to key reports and the Collections Center, a tool that will help you keep your client balances in check.

The Collections Center

The Collections Center is located within the Customer Center. Its purpose is to help you keep track of past due and almost past due customer balances while also giving you an easy way to send e-mail reminders to the customers that are listed there.

1. Open the Customer Center by choosing Customers | Customer Center or by clicking the Customers icon on the Icon Bar.
2. Click the Collections Center button located at the top of the window. The Collections Center opens to the Overdue tab.

From this list, you can review the details of individual invoices in question by double-clicking that invoice. The list can also be sorted by balance or days overdue by clicking the appropriate column heading. If you've entered an e-mail address in the customer's record, you can also send a reminder e-mail to one or all of the customers on this list. Just click Select And Send E-mail at the top of the Overdue tab window. You'll see a yellow alert icon in the Notes/Warnings column if an e-mail address is missing. Clicking this icon allows you to add an e-mail address to the customer's record if you choose.

The Notes icon next to the customer name lets you document your collections activities or view previous entries. To see a list of customers that have upcoming invoices due, select the Almost Due tab.

Other Reports You Can Run from the Customer Center

You can run some key reports on individual customers right from the Customer Center. Simply highlight the customer or job and click the Reports links located in the upper right-hand corner of the customer information pane. The reports available are

- **Quick Report**   Displays all transactions related to that customer within a specified date range.
- **Open Balance**   Displays the transaction (invoices, payments, and credit memos) that make up a customer's current balance.
- **Show Estimates**   Displays all estimates created for the customer within a specified date range.
- **Customer Snapshot**   Displays a dashboard-like view of a customer's relationship with you (including what they buy, how they pay, and how long they've been doing business with you).

Running A/R Aging Reports

A/R aging reports are lists of the money owed you by your customers, and they're available in quite a few formats. They're designed for you, not for your customers. You run them whenever you need to know the extent of your receivables. Many companies run an aging report every morning, just to keep an eye on the amount of money due them on a particular day.

➡ **ProAdvisor Recommends**

Accounts Receivable (A/R) Totals

The total amount of A/R is the value of your A/R asset. It can be an important asset and, in fact, banks give lines of credit and loans using the A/R balance as part of the collateral.

When you look at your balance sheet, the general ledger A/R balance and the total on the A/R aging report should be the same (for the same date)—not close, not almost, but exactly the same.

If your A/R account balance doesn't match your A/R report for the same date, it likely means that the A/R account balance was changed using a journal entry (versus via a transaction like an invoice or a customer payment).

The quickest way to find a journal entry (or entries) posted directly to the A/R account is to run a Quick Report for this account. With the Chart of Accounts open, highlight your A/R account. Click the Reports button at the bottom of the window and select Quick Report. By default, this report will show every transaction ever posted to this account. Your job is to find journal transactions in this report, and you can do that either by sorting the report by transaction type or filtering it to show only the "journal" transactions (Chapter 22 covers Customizing Reports).

If you find journal transactions, they should be reviewed and either replaced with a transactional document or removed altogether. Consult with your accountant if you're not sure how to handle a particular transaction.

A couple of aging reports are available in QuickBooks, and you can also customize any built-in reports so they report data exactly the way you want it. To see an aging report, choose Reports | Customers & Receivables, and then choose either A/R Aging Summary or A/R Aging Detail (these reports are explained in the upcoming sections).

A/R Aging Summary Reports

The quickest way to see how much money is owed to you is to select A/R Aging Summary, which produces a listing of customer balances (see Figure 10-8).

A/R Aging Detail Reports

If you choose Aging Detail from the Accounts Receivable reports menu, you see a much more comprehensive report, such as the one seen in Figure 10-9. The report is sorted by aging interval, showing individual transactions, including finance charges, for each aging period.

FIGURE 10-8 A summary report provides totals for each customer, broken down by aging periods.

Customizing Aging Reports

If you don't use (or care about) all of the columns in the A/R Aging Detail report, or you'd prefer to see the information displayed in a different manner, you can customize the report. Start by clicking the Customize Report button on the report to see the Modify Report window shown in Figure 10-10.

Customizing the Columns

The most common customization is to get rid of any column you don't care about. For example, if you use the Classes feature but don't care about that information in your aging report, get rid of the column. Or you might want to get rid of the Terms column since it doesn't impact the totals. To remove a column, scroll through the Columns list and click to remove the check mark, then click OK to accept your changes. The column disappears from the report.

FIGURE 10-9 Detail reports display information about every transaction that's involved in each customer's A/R balance.

While you're looking at the list of column names, you may find a column heading that's not currently selected but that contains information you'd like to include in your report. If so, click that column listing to place a check mark next to it. The column appears on the report and the data linked to it is displayed.

Filtering Information

If you want to produce an aging report for a special purpose, you can easily filter the information so it meets criteria important to you. To filter your aging report, click the Filters tab (see Figure 10-11).

Select a filter and then set the conditions for it. (Each filter has its own specific type of criteria.) For example, you can use this feature if you want to see only those customers with receivables higher than a certain figure or older than a certain aging period.

FIGURE 10-10   Customize the A/R Aging Detail report to get exactly the information you need.

FIGURE 10-11   Filters let you specify criteria for displaying data.

CAUTION: If you filter the report in a way that affects the amounts, your report total will not match your A/R account balance. Use this type of filter only to get certain types of information for yourself, not for an "official" aging report.

Configuring Header/Footer Data

You can customize the text that appears in the header and footer of the report by making changes in the Header/Footer tab shown in Figure 10-12.

FIGURE 10-12 Specify the text you want to display on the top and bottom of the report.

You'll probably find that your decisions about the contents of the header and footer depend on whether you're viewing the report or printing it. And, if you're printing it, some stuff is more important if an outsider (a banker or your accountant) will be the recipient of the report, rather than your credit manager.

For example, the date and time of preparation is more important for outsiders than for you. Incidentally, on the Header/Footer tab, the Date Prepared field has a meaningless date—don't panic, your computer hasn't lost track of the date. That date is a format, not today's date. Click the arrow to the right of the field to see the other formats for inserting the date. The Page Number field also has a variety of formats to choose from.

You can eliminate a Header/Footer field by removing the check mark from the field's check box. For fields you want to print, you can change the text. You can also change the layout by choosing a different Alignment option from the drop-down list.

Customizing the Appearance

Click the Fonts & Numbers tab to change the format of the report. You can change the way negative numbers are displayed, and you can change the fonts for any or all of the individual elements in the report.

When you close the report window, QuickBooks may ask if you want to memorize the report with the changes you made (if you told QuickBooks to stop asking, you won't see the message). Click Yes so you don't have to go through all the modifications again. If QuickBooks doesn't ask, memorize the report using the instructions in the next section.

Memorizing Aging Reports

If you've customized a report and have the columns, data, and formatting you need, there's no reason to reinvent the wheel the next time you need the same information. Instead of going through the customization process again next month, memorize the report as you designed it. Then you can fetch it whenever you need it.

Click the Memorize button in the report window. When the Memorize Report dialog appears, enter a new name for the report, optionally save it within a report group, and click OK.

From now on, this report name will be on the list of memorized reports you can select from when you choose Reports | Memorized Reports from the menu bar.

ProAdvisor Tip: When you use a memorized report, only the criteria and formatting is memorized. Each time you open the report, the data is generated from the QuickBooks transaction records, so you get current, accurate information.

Printing Reports

Whether you're using the standard format or one you've customized, you'll probably want to print the report. When you're in a report window, click the Print button at the top of the window to bring up the Print Reports dialog. If the report is wide, use the Margins tab to set new margins, and use the options on the Settings tab to customize other printing options.

Running Customer and Job Reports

Customer and job reports are designed to give you information about the selected customers/jobs instead of providing information on the totals for your business. There are plenty of customer reports available from the menu that appears when you choose Reports | Customers & Receivables, including but not limited to:

- **Customer Balance Summary Report** Lists current total balance owed for each customer.
- **Customer Balance Detail Report** Lists every transaction for each customer with a net subtotal for each customer and job.
- **Open Invoices Report** Lists all unpaid invoices, sorted and subtotaled by customer and job.
- **Collections Report** Includes the contact name and telephone number, along with details about invoices with balances due. With this report in hand, you're all set to call the customer and have a conversation, and you can answer any questions about invoice details.
- **Accounts Receivable Graph** Shows a graphic representation of the accounts receivable. For a quick overview, there's nothing like a graph.
- **Unbilled Costs By Job** Tracks job expenses that were linked to customers or jobs that you haven't yet invoiced.
- **Transaction List By Customer** Displays individual transactions of all types for each customer.
- **Customer Contact List** Displays an alphabetical list of customers along with the contact, telephone numbers, billing address, and current open balance for each. Give this list to the person in charge of collections.
- **Item Price List** Lists all your items with their prices and preferred vendors.

Assessing Finance Charges

You can impose finance charges on overdue amounts as an incentive to get your customers to pay on time. Incidentally, this isn't "found money"; it probably doesn't cover its own cost. The amount of time spent tracking, analyzing, and chasing receivables is substantial, so imposing finance charges can be a way to help offset the time and resources needed to collect past due balances.

Configuring Finance Charges

To use finance charges, you have to establish the rate and circumstances under which they're assessed. Your company's finance charges are configured as part of your company preferences. Choose Edit | Preferences to open the Preferences dialog. Then click the Finance Charge icon in the left pane and select the Company Preferences tab (see Figure 10-13).

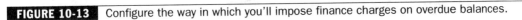

FIGURE 10-13 Configure the way in which you'll impose finance charges on overdue balances.

Here are some guidelines for filling out this dialog:

- In the Annual Interest Rate field, replacing the default data (0.00%) with any positive number automatically enables the Finance Charges feature (the dialog has no Yes/No check box to enable or disable finance charges).
- Notice that the interest rate is annual. If you want to charge 1.5 percent a month, enter **18%** in the Annual Interest Rate field.
- You can assess a minimum finance charge for overdue balances. QuickBooks will calculate the finance charge, and if it's less than the minimum, the amount will be rolled up to the minimum charge you specify here.
- Use the Grace Period field to enter the number of days of lateness you permit before finance charges are assessed.
- During setup, QuickBooks probably created an account for finance charges. If so, select it. If not, enter (or create) the account you want to use to post finance charges (it's an income account).
- The issue of assessing finance charges on overdue finance charges is a sticky one. In fact, this calculation method may be illegal in your state, so check with the appropriate agency before implementing. Selecting this option means that a customer who owed $100.00 last month and had a finance charge assessed of

$2.00 now owes $102.00. As a result, the next finance charge is assessed on a balance of $102.00 (instead of on the original overdue balance of $100.00).

- Specify whether to calculate the finance charge from the due date or the invoice date (it's common to use the due date).

- QuickBooks creates an invoice automatically when finance charges are assessed in order to have a permanent record of the transaction. By default, these invoices aren't printed; they're just accumulated along with the overdue invoices so they'll print as a line item on a monthly statement. You can opt to have the finance charge invoices printed, which you should do only if you're planning to mail them to nudge your customers for payment.

Click OK to save your settings after you've filled out the window.

Assessing Finance Charges

You should assess finance charges just before you create customer statements, which is commonly a monthly chore. Choose Customers | Assess Finance Charges from the menu bar. The Assess Finance Charges window opens (see Figure 10-14) with a list of all the customers with overdue balances.

FIGURE 10-14 QuickBooks automatically assesses finance charges as of the assessment date you specify.

If you have any customers that have made payments that you haven't yet applied to an invoice, or if any customers have credits that you haven't yet applied to an invoice, an asterisk (*) appears to the left of the customer or job name. Close the Assess Finance Charges window and correct the situation, then return to this window.

Choosing the Assessment Date

Change the Assessment Date field (which displays the current date) to the date on which you actually want to impose the charge—this date appears on customer statements. It's common to assess finance charges on the last day of the month. When you press TAB to move out of the date field, the finance charges are recalculated to reflect the new date.

Selecting the Customers

You can eliminate a customer from the process by clicking in the Assess column to remove the check mark. QuickBooks does not have a finance charge assessment option on each customer record, so all customers with overdue balances are included when you assess finance charges. This means you have to know off the top of your head which customers are liable for finances charges and which aren't—or you have to keep a list near your desk.

It can be time consuming to deselect each customer, so if you have only a few customers for whom you reserve this process, choose Unmark All, then reselect the customers you want to include.

Changing the Amounts

You can change the calculated total if you wish (a good idea if there are credit memos floating around that you're not ready to apply against any invoices). Just click the amount displayed in the Finance Charge column to activate that column for that customer. Then enter a new finance charge amount. If you need to calculate the new figure (perhaps you're giving credit for a floating credit memo), press the equal sign (=) on your keyboard to use the QuickBooks built-in calculator.

Checking the History

To make sure you don't assess a charge that isn't really due (or fair), you can double-check by viewing a customer's history from the Assess Finance Charges window. Highlight a customer listing and click the Collection History button to see a Collections Report for the selected customer (see Figure 10-15). Your mouse pointer turns into a magnifying glass with the letter "z" (for "zoom") in it when you position it over a line item. Double-click any line item to display the original transaction window if you need to examine the details.

FIGURE 10-15 You can check a customer's history to make sure the finance charges are legitimate.

Saving the Finance Charge Invoices

If you're sure all the calculations and figures are correct, click Assess Charges in the Assess Finance Charges window. When you create your customer statements, the finance charges will appear. If you've opted to skip printing the finance charge assessments as invoices, there's nothing more to do. If you're printing the finance charges, see the next paragraph.

Selecting Printing Options

If you want to print the finance charge invoices (they really are invoices because they add charges to the customer balance), be sure to select the Mark Invoices "To Be Printed" check box on the Assess Finance Charges window. You can send the printed copies to your customers as a nagging reminder. If you only care about having the finance charge on the monthly statement (the common method for most businesses), deselect the printing option.

To print the finance charge invoices, choose File | Print Forms | Invoices. The list of unprinted invoices appears, and unless you have regular invoices you didn't print yet, the list includes only the finance charge invoices. If the list is correct, click OK to continue on to the printing process.

Sending Statements

On a periodic basis, you should send statements to your customers. (Most businesses send statements monthly.) They serve a couple of purposes: they remind customers of outstanding balances, and they provide detailed documentation of your records, which your customers can match against their own records.

If you're coming to QuickBooks from a manual system or a system in which you tracked invoices and payments in a spreadsheet, statements will seem like a miraculous tool. Creating statements from customer cards maintained manually in a word processing document or in a spreadsheet is a nightmare. As a result, companies without real accounting software generally don't even bother to try.

Entering Statement Charges

Before creating statements, you should create any transactions that should appear on the statements. Invoices and payments appear automatically, but you may want to add statement charges. A *statement charge* is a charge you want to pass to a customer for which you don't create an invoice. You can use statement charges for special charges for certain customers, such as a general overhead charge, or a charge you apply for your own out-of-pocket expenses (instead of using the reimbursable expenses feature for expenses incurred on behalf of the customer). Some companies use statement charges instead of invoices for invoicing regular retainer payments.

You must add statement charges before you create the statements (or else the charges won't show up on the statements). Statement charges use items from your Item List, but you cannot use any of the following types of items:

- Items that are taxable, because the statement charge can't apply the tax
- Items that have percentage discounts (instead of discounts with specific amounts), because the statement charge can't look up the discount percentage (and therefore can't apply it)
- Items that represent a payment transaction, because those are negative charges, which a statement charge doesn't understand

Statement charges are recorded directly in a customer's register or in the register for a specific job. To create a statement charge, choose Customers | Enter Statement Charges from the menu bar to open the customer register, which looks like Figure 10-16. By default, QuickBooks opens the register for the first customer in your Customers & Jobs List; you can use the drop-down list at the top of the

FIGURE 10-16 Statement charges are entered directly in a customer or job register.

window to select a different customer. Then use the following steps to add statement charges (use the TAB key to move through the register's fields):

1. Select the appropriate customer or job from the drop-down list in the Customer:Job field at the top of the register.
2. Enter the date on which the statement charge is being assessed.
3. In the Item field, select the item for the statement charge from the drop-down list.
4. Enter a quantity in the Qty field if the item is invoiced by quantity.
5. Enter a rate (or accept the default rate if one exists) if you're using the Qty field.
6. Enter the amount charged if the Qty and Rate fields aren't used (if they are, the total amount is entered automatically).
7. Optionally, edit the item description.
8. Optionally enter the billed date, which does not have to match the transaction date in the first column of the register. Postdating or predating this field determines which statement it appears on.
9. Optionally enter the due date, which affects your aging reports and your finance charge calculations.
10. When all the fields you want to use are filled in, click Record to save the transaction.

Continue to select customers and/or jobs to enter additional statement charges.

Creating Statements

Before you start creating your statements, be sure that all the transactions that should be included on the statements have been entered into the system. Did you forget anything? Applying credit memos? Applying payments? Assessing finance charges? Entering statement charges?

When all customer accounts are up to date, choose Customers | Create Statements to open the Create Statements dialog, shown in Figure 10-17.

FIGURE 10-17 Configure the specifications for selecting customers who receive statements.

Selecting the Date Range

The statement date range determines which transactions appear on the statement. The printed statement displays the previous balance (the total due before the "From" date) and includes all transactions that were created within the date range. The starting date should be the day after the last date of your last statement run. If you do monthly statements, choose the first and last days of the current month; if you send statements quarterly, enter the first and last dates of the current quarter—and so on.

If you choose All Open Transactions As Of Statement Date, the printed statement just shows unpaid invoices and charges and unapplied credits. You can narrow the criteria by selecting the option to include only transactions overdue by a certain number of days (which you specify). However, this makes the printed statement more like a list than a standard statement.

Selecting the Customers

It's normal procedure to send statements to all customers, but if that's not the plan, you can change the default selection.

If you want to send statements to a group of customers, click the Multiple Customers option to display a Choose button next to the option. Click the Choose button to bring up a list of customers and select each customer you want to include. You can manually select each customer, or select Automatic and then enter text to tell QuickBooks to match that text against all customer names and select the matching customers. (The automatic match option isn't efficient for multiple customers because it only matches exact text, not partial text, and therefore only matches one customer at a time.) Click OK when all the appropriate customers are selected.

If you're sending a statement to one customer only, select One Customer, and then click the arrow next to the text box to scroll through the list of your customers and select the one you want.

To send statements to customers who are designated with a specific customer type, select the Customers Of Type option, and then select the customer type you want to include from the drop-down list. This works, of course, only if you created customer types as part of your QuickBooks setup.

> **ProAdvisor Tip:** If you want to send statements to certain customers only, create a customer type for statement recipients, like "Statements." Refer to Chapter 7 to learn how to create a new customer type.

Filtering for Send Methods

If your customers vary in the way you send them statements (the option selected in the Preferred Send Method field of the customer record), you can opt to handle your statement delivery in batches, using one delivery method per batch. To do this, select the Preferred Send Method option, and then select the send method for this batch from the drop-down list that appears:

- **E-mail**   Sends the statements by e-mail using a compatible e-mail application.
- **Mail**   Sends the statements to QuickBooks Billing Solutions, where the invoice is created with a tear-off slip that the customer can use to pay the invoice. QuickBooks mails the invoice. (This is a fee-based service.)
- **None**   Means no special handling. You print the statements, put them in envelopes, and mail them.

Specifying the Printing Options

You can specify the way you want the statements to print using the following criteria and options in the Select Additional Options section:

- You can print one statement for each customer, which lists all transactions for all that customer's jobs, or you can print a separate statement for each job.
- You can opt to show invoice item details instead of just listing the invoice on the statement. If your invoices have a lot of line items, this could make your statements very long (possibly too many pages to get away with a single postage stamp). However, this option can speed up collections since the customer won't have to call you with questions like, "What makes up this balance?" or "What was that charge for again?" So, if customers often call you after you send less detailed statements, consider this alternative.
- Printing statements in order by ZIP code is handy if you're printing labels that are sorted by ZIP code. This option is also important if you have a bulk mail permit, because the post office requires bulk mail to be sorted by ZIP code.
- By default, the original due date for each transaction listed on the statement is displayed on the statement. If you have some reason to hide this information from your customers (I can't think of a good reason), QuickBooks offers the opportunity to deselect the option.

Specifying the Statements to Skip

You may want to skip statement creation for customers who meet the criteria you set in the Do Not Create Statements section of the dialog. If statements are the only documents you send to customers (you don't send the individual invoices and credits you create), selecting any of these options makes sense.

If, however, you use statements to make sure you and your customers have matching accounting records, you should create statements for all customers except inactive customers.

Last Call for Finance Charges

If you haven't assessed finance charges and you want them to appear on the statements, click the Assess Finance Charges button. The Assess Finance Charges window opens, showing customers who have been selected for finance charges.

If you've already assessed finance charges, QuickBooks will warn you (when you click the Assess Charges button) that finance charges have already been assessed as of the selected date. If you ignore the message, another round of finance charges is imposed (and you'll have a lot of angry and distrustful customers). Therefore, this window is useful only if you don't assess finance charges as described earlier in this chapter.

Previewing the Statements

Before you commit the statements to paper, you can click the Preview button to get an advance look. This is not just to see what the printed output will look like; it's also a way to look at the customer records and to make sure that all the customers you selected are included.

Use the Zoom In button to see the statement and its contents close up. Click the Next Page button to move through all the statements. Click Close to return to the Create Statements window.

Printing the Statements

When everything is just the way it should be, print the statements by clicking the Print button in either the Print Preview window or the Create Statements window. If you click Close in the Preview window, you return to the Create Statements window—click Print to open the Print Statement(s) window, where you can choose the Preview button again if you need to take another look at what will be sent to the printer. Clicking the Print button from the Preview window will send the entire statement print job to the default printer (with no additional opportunities to change the print settings).

Customizing Statements

You don't have to use the standard statement form—you can design your own. The instructions for creating a template with customized fields and columns are in Chapter 28. If you want to create a customized template for statements, think about adding the Terms field to the statement (which is not selected by default). It doesn't seem fair to tell a customer of amounts past due without reminding the customer of the terms.

Managing Vendor Bills

In *this chapter:*

- Enter vendor bills

- Using purchase orders

- Receive inventory purchases

- Enter vendor credit memos

- Enter recurring bills

- Track reimbursable expenses

There are two ways to pay vendors in QuickBooks: You can enter the bill you received into QuickBooks and then pay it later, or you can simply write a check without entering a bill. This chapter covers the process of entering bills and also shows you how to link expenses on those bills to customers, so you can later send an invoice to the customer in order to be reimbursed for the vendor expense (that topic is covered in Chapter 9).

Chapter 12 covers paying vendors, either by paying the bills you entered into QuickBooks, or writing a check without entering a bill first.

Entering your bills into QuickBooks and then paying them in a separate transaction is accrual accounting. That means an expense is posted to your Profit & Loss statement when you enter the bill, not when you actually pay the bill. Your Accounts Payable account should always equal the total of unpaid bills in your company file.

However, if your taxes are filed on a cash basis (which means an expense isn't posted until you actually pay the bill), be assured (and assure your accountant) that QuickBooks understands how to report your financial figures on a cash basis. (See Chapter 21 for information on preparing financial reports.)

Recording Vendor Bills

When the mail arrives, after you open all the envelopes that contain checks from customers (which most business owners do first), you should tell QuickBooks about the bills that arrived.

To enter your bills, choose Vendors | Enter Bills from the menu bar. When the Enter Bills window opens (see Figure 11-1), you can fill out the information from the bill you received.

> **ProAdvisor Tip:** If you're using multiple currencies, the Amount Due field uses the currency of the vendor you select, along with the appropriate amount in your currency (the multiple currencies feature covered in Appendix B).

The window has three sections: the heading section, which contains information about the vendor and the bill, the details section, in which you record the data related to your general ledger accounts, and the history section on the right-hand side of the form. When you create a new bill for a vendor that you've done business with before, this pane will become filled with information about them, including their most recent transactions. To close this pane, simply click the little blue arrowhead on the top left-hand side of the History pane.

FIGURE 11-1 The Enter Bills window has a heading section and a details section.

The details section has two tabs: Expenses and Items. In this section, bills that are posted to Expenses are covered; entering items is covered later in this chapter with the discussion of handling the purchase of inventory items.

ProAdvisor Tip: An A/P Account field (and accompanying drop-down list) appears at the top of the Enter Bills window only if you have multiple Accounts Payable accounts. For example, some manufacturers and distributors separate payables for overhead expenses from payables to suppliers of inventory parts (usually called Accounts Payable—Trade).

Depending on the bill, you may be able to assign the entire bill to one expense account (the easiest task), or you may have to split the bill among multiple expense accounts. For example, your utility bills are usually posted to the appropriate utility account (electric, heat, and so on). However, credit card bills may be split among numerous expenses, and loan payments are split between interest (an expense account) and principal (a liability account).

Filling in the Details

In the Vendor field, click the arrow to choose this vendor from the list that appears. If the vendor isn't on the list, choose <Add New> to add this vendor to your QuickBooks vendor list. Then fill out the rest of the bill window as follows:

1. Enter the bill date. The due date then fills in automatically, depending on the terms you have with this vendor.

2. Enter the vendor's invoice number in the Ref. No. field.

3. Enter the amount of the bill in the Amount Due field.

4. In the Terms field, if the displayed data doesn't reflect your terms with this vendor, click the arrow to display a list of terms, and select the one you need. If the terms you have with this vendor aren't available, choose <Add New> to create a new Terms entry. The due date changes to reflect the terms.

5. To enter the accounts information, click in the Account column on the Expenses tab, and then click the arrow to display your chart of accounts. Select the account to which this bill should be posted. QuickBooks automatically assigns the amount you entered in the Amount Due field to the Amount column. (See Chapter 4 to learn how to configure vendors so the posting account is automatically filled in.)

6. If you wish, enter a note in the Memo column.

7. In the Customer:Job column, enter a customer or job if you're paying a bill that you want to track for job costing, or if this bill is a reimbursable expense. See the discussions on tracking and charging customers for reimbursable expenses a bit later in this chapter and in Chapter 9.

8. If you're tracking classes, a Class column appears; enter the appropriate class.

9. When you're finished, click Save & New to save this bill and bring up another blank Enter Bills window. When you've entered all your bills, click Save & Close.

ProAdvisor Tip: If you don't set up terms for a vendor, the due date is automatically filled out using the default number of days for paying bills. QuickBooks sets this default at ten days, but you can change the default by choosing Edit | Preferences and going to the Company Preferences tab of the Bills category.

Splitting Expenses Among Multiple Accounts

Some bills aren't neatly assigned to one account in your general ledger; instead, they're split among multiple accounts. The most common examples are a loan repayment where you post the interest to your Interest expense account and the principal to the liability account for the loan, or a credit card bill that covers multiple categories of expenses (if you're treating those bills as vendor bills and not managing your credit card as a liability, as discussed in Chapter 13).

Entering a vendor bill with split expenses is the same as entering a vendor bill that's assigned to one expense (as described in the previous section), until you begin assigning the expense accounts and amounts in the details section of the Enter Bills window.

When you enter the first account in the Account column, QuickBooks automatically applies the entire amount of the bill in the Amount column. Replace that data with the amount you want to assign to the account you selected.

Then, on the next row, select the next account. As you add each additional account to the column, QuickBooks assumes that the unallocated amount is assigned to that account (see Figure 11-2). Repeat the process of changing the amount and adding another account until the total amount assigned to accounts equals the amount of the vendor bill.

FIGURE 11-2 QuickBooks keeps recalculating, so the last account posting entry automatically has the correct amount.

ProAdvisor Tip: If you don't fill in an amount for the bill in the header section, or you make a typo and the amounts in the line items don't match the total, click the Recalculate button to have QuickBooks add the line items and insert the total in the Amount Due field.

Using Purchase Orders

You can use purchase orders to order inventory items or manufacturing parts from your suppliers.

If you want to order services or other non-inventory items, such as office supplies or professional services, and the vendor requires a purchase order, you can create non-inventory or service items in QuickBooks and link them to an expense account (rather than an income account) for use on a PO.

Creating a purchase order has no effect on your financial records. No amounts are posted because purchase orders exist only to help you track what you've ordered against what you've received. You create the financial transactions when the items and the vendor's bill are received.

When you enable the Inventory and Purchase Order features, QuickBooks creates a nonposting account named Purchase Orders. You can double-click the account's listing to view and drill down into the purchase orders you've entered, but the data in the register has no effect on your finances and doesn't appear in financial reports.

Creating a Purchase Order

Use the following steps to create a purchase order:

1. Choose Vendors | Create Purchase Orders from the menu bar to open a blank Create Purchase Orders window.
2. Fill in the purchase order fields, which are easy and self-explanatory (see Figure 11-3).
3. Click Save & New to save the purchase order and move on to the next blank purchase order form, or click Save & Close if you have created all the purchase orders you need right now.

FIGURE 11-3 A purchase order looks similar to an invoice, but it has no effect on your financial records.

You can print the purchase orders as you create them by clicking the Print icon at the top of the window as soon as each purchase order is completed. If you'd prefer, you can print them all in a batch by clicking the arrow to the right of the Print button on the last purchase order window and selecting Print Batch. If you want to print them later, be sure the option To Be Printed is selected on each PO. When you're ready to print, choose File | Print Forms | Purchase Orders.

You can also e-mail the purchase orders as you create them, or e-mail them as a batch by selecting Send Batch from the drop-down list next to the E-mail icon on the transaction window's toolbar.

When the inventory items and the bill for them are received, you can use the purchase order to automate the receiving of inventory into your warehouse as well as the entry of the vendor's bill.

Using the Manufacturer's Part Number in Purchase Orders

If the item you're ordering has a manufacturer's part number (MPN) in the item record, you should use that data in your purchase order to avoid any confusion. However, you have to customize the purchase order template to display the MPN data.

Choose Vendors | Create Purchase Orders to open a PO transaction window. Then use the following steps to customize the PO template:

1. Click the arrow to the right of the Customize icon on the PO window's toolbar, and select Manage Templates.

2. Click the Copy button to make a copy of the default template that you can then modify—which you should rename so it's easily identifiable later. Click OK to open the Basic Customization window.

3. At the bottom of the Basic Customization window, click the Additional Customization button.

4. Move to the Columns tab to see the dialog shown in Figure 11-4.

5. Add the Man. Part Num field to the screen, printed copy, or both by clicking in the appropriate boxes to add a check mark (adding the field to both the screen and print versions is best).

FIGURE 11-4 Add a column for the Manufacturer's Part Number to your PO template.

6. Enter the number for this column, working from left to right across the columns. For example, entering 3 puts the MPN in the third column. When you press TAB, QuickBooks automatically renumbers the column order to accommodate your selection.

7. Optionally, change the text that appears as the column title. By default, the title is MPN, but you might want to change it to something like Part # or Part No.

Check the Print Preview pane on the right side of the dialog to make sure the layout works. QuickBooks will also prompt you if the template needs additional adjustments to the layout. Adding this column doesn't overcrowd the template, but if you previously customized the template to add columns or fields, you may have to rework your changes (see Chapter 28 to learn everything about customizing templates). If the layout looks presentable, click OK to save your changes.

Hereafter, when you create a PO for an item that has the MPN stored in its record, the data appears automatically in the MPN column.

Managing Inventory Item Purchases

If the vendor bill you're recording is for inventory items, you need to take a different approach, because the accounting issues (the way you post amounts) are different. Frequently, two transactions are involved when you buy items for inventory:

- You receive the inventory products.
- You receive the bill for the inventory products.

Sometimes the bill comes before the products, sometimes the products arrive first, and sometimes both events occur at the same time (the bill is in an envelope pasted to the carton or included inside the carton). If you created a purchase order for these items, you can use it to automate the receiving and vendor bill entry processes when they and the bill for them arrive.

Receiving Inventory Items Without a Bill

If the inventory items arrive before you receive a bill from the vendor, you must use the Create Items Receipts window to tell QuickBooks about the new inventory. This form brings the items into inventory so they become available for resale. Use the following steps to receive inventory in this scenario:

1. Choose Vendors | Receive Items from the menu bar to open a blank Create Item Receipts window (see Figure 11-5).

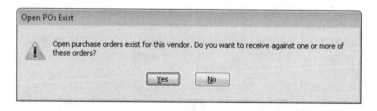

FIGURE 11-5 Receive items into inventory without a bill using Item Receipts.

2. Select the vendor name, and if open purchase orders exist for this vendor, QuickBooks notifies you:

3. If you know there isn't a purchase order for this particular shipment, click No, and just fill out the Create Item Receipts window manually.

4. If you know a purchase order exists for this shipment, or if you're not sure, click Yes. QuickBooks displays all the open purchase orders for this vendor so you can put a check mark next to the appropriate PO (or multiple POs if the shipment that arrived covers more than one PO). If no PO matching this shipment is listed on the Open Purchase Orders list for this vendor, click Cancel on the Open Purchase Orders window to return to the receipts window and fill in the data manually.

5. If a PO exists, QuickBooks fills out the Create Item Receipts window using the information in the PO. Check the shipment against the PO and change any quantities that don't match.

6. Click Save & New to receive the next shipment into inventory, or click Save & Close if this takes care of all the receipts of goods.

QuickBooks posts the amounts in the purchase order to your Accounts Payable account as an Item Receipt type. When the bill arrives with the actual costs, the Accounts Payable account will be updated accordingly and the transaction type changed to Bill. (See the "ProAdvisor Recommends: "How QuickBooks Posts Inventory Receipts and Bills.")

➡➡ ProAdvisor Recommends

How QuickBooks Posts Inventory Receipts and Bills

Technically, an accounts payable liability should only be connected to a bill and not an Item Receipt. In most cases, the bill you eventually receive for the goods you've received will have the same unit cost as the Item Receipt. Sometimes, however, the cost per item listed on the Item Receipt may not be the same as the cost per item on the final bill. Whatever the reason, the bill that arrives will presumably have the correct costs, and those costs are the amounts that should be posted to the A/P account.

If this situation occurs, QuickBooks allows you to adjust the initial posting you made to A/P when you received the items, so that the new amounts match the bill. This means that on one date your A/P total and inventory valuation may have one amount, and a few days later, the amount may have changed even though no additional transactions are displayed in reports. If the interval between those days crosses the month, or even worse, the year, your accountant might have a problem trying to figure out what happened. But now that you understand what happens, you can explain the logic behind the change.

Recording Bills for Items Already Received

After you receive the items, eventually the bill comes from the vendor. To enter the bill, do *not* use the regular Enter Bills window, which would cause another posting to Accounts Payable. Instead, do the following:

1. Choose Vendors | Enter Bill For Received Items to open the Select Item Receipt dialog.
2. Select the vendor, and you'll see the current items receipt information for that vendor.

3. Select the appropriate listing and click OK to open an Enter Bills window. The information from the items receipt is used to fill in the bill information.
4. Change anything in the Items tab that needs to be changed, such as a different cost per unit.
5. To add any shipping or handling charges, move to the Expenses tab and enter the appropriate accounts and amounts.
6. If you made any changes, you must click the Recalculate button so QuickBooks can match the total in the Amount Due field to the changed line item data.
7. Click Save & Close.

Even if you didn't make any changes, and the bill matches the Receipts transaction, QuickBooks displays a message asking if you're sure you want to save the changes. Say Yes. The message appears because you've changed the transaction from a receipt of goods transaction to a vendor bill transaction and QuickBooks overwrites the original postings that were made when you received the items. If you look at the Accounts Payable register (or the Inventory Assets register) after you receive the items, the transaction type is ITEM RCPT. When you save this transaction, QuickBooks overwrites the entire transaction, changing the transaction type to BILL (and also uses the new amounts if you made changes).

Receiving Items and Bills Simultaneously

If the items and the bill arrive at the same time (sometimes the bill is in the shipping carton), you must tell QuickBooks about those events simultaneously. To do this, choose Vendors | Receive Items And Enter Bill. The standard Enter Bills window opens, and when you enter the vendor's name you may see a message telling you an open PO exists for the vendor. The message dialog asks if you want to receive these goods (and the bill) against an open PO.

Click Yes to see the open POs for this vendor and select the appropriate PO. The line items on the bill are filled in automatically, and you can correct any quantity or price difference between your original PO and the actuals. When you save the transaction, QuickBooks receives the items into inventory in addition to posting the bill to A/P.

If no PO exists, enter the item quantities and amounts. When you save the transaction, QuickBooks receives the items into inventory in addition to posting the bill to A/P.

Recording Vendor Credits

If you receive a credit from a vendor, you must record it in QuickBooks. Then you can apply it against an open vendor bill or let it float until your next order from the vendor. (See Chapter 12 for information about paying bills, which includes applying vendor credits to bills.)

QuickBooks doesn't provide a discrete credit form for accounts payable; instead, you can change a vendor bill form to a credit form with a click of the mouse. Follow these steps to create a vendor credit:

1. Choose Vendors | Enter Bills to open a blank Enter Bills window.
2. Select the Credit option at the top of the window, which automatically deselects Bill and changes the fields on the form (see Figure 11-6).
3. Choose the vendor from the drop-down list that appears when you click the arrow in the Vendor field.
4. Enter the date of the credit memo.
5. In the Ref. No. field, enter the vendor's credit memo number.

FIGURE 11-6 When you select the Credit option, the Enter Bills transaction window changes— the fields for terms and due date disappear.

6. Enter the amount of the credit memo.

7. If the credit is not for inventory items, use the Expenses tab to assign an account and amount to this credit.

8. If the credit is for inventory items, use the Items tab to enter the items, along with the quantity and cost, for which you are receiving this credit.

9. Click Save & Close to save the credit (unless you have more credits to enter— in which case, click Save & New).

ProAdvisor Tip: You can temporarily use an RA (Return Authorization) number you received on the telephone as the Ref. No. of your credit. This can help you keep track of when (or if) the actual credit memo is issued by the vendor. When the credit memo arrives, you can replace the QuickBooks Ref. No. with the actual credit memo number. Enter the original RA number in the Memo field for future reference in case there are any disputes.

Entering Recurring Bills

You probably have quite a few bills that you must pay every month. Commonly, the list includes your rent or mortgage payment, loan payments, or a retainer fee (for an attorney, accountant, or subcontractor).

You can make it easy to pay those bills every month without entering a bill each time. QuickBooks provides a feature called *memorized transactions,* and you can put it to work to make sure your recurring bills are covered.

Creating a Memorized Bill

To create a memorized transaction for a recurring bill, first open the Enter Bills window and fill out the information as you normally would. If the amount of a recurring bill isn't always exactly the same, it's okay to leave the Amount Due field blank. You can fill in the amount each time you use the memorized bill.

Before you save the transaction, memorize it. To accomplish this, press CTRL-M to open the Memorize Transaction dialog. Use these guidelines to fill out the Memorize Transaction dialog:

- Use the Name field to enter a name for the transaction. QuickBooks automatically enters the vendor name, but you can change it. Use a name that describes the transaction so you don't have to rely on your memory.
- Select Add To My Reminders List (the default) to tell QuickBooks to issue a reminder that this bill must be put into the system to be paid.
- Select Do Not Remind Me if you want to forego getting a reminder and enter the bill yourself.
- Select Automate Transaction Entry to have QuickBooks enter this bill as a payable automatically, without reminders. Specify the number of Days In Advance To Enter this bill into the system. At the appropriate time, the bill appears in the Select Bills To Pay List you use to pay your bills (covered in Chapter 12).
- Select the interval for this bill from the drop-down list in the How Often field.
- Enter the Next Date this bill is due.
- If this payment is finite, such as a loan that has a specific number of payments, use the Number Remaining field to specify how many times this bill must be paid.

Click OK in the Memorize Transaction window to save it, and then click Save & Close in the Enter Bills window to save the bill.

C a u t i o n : When you select the reminder options for the memorized bill, the reminders appear only if you're using reminders in QuickBooks. Choose Edit I Preferences and click the Reminders category icon to view or change reminders options.

Using a Memorized Bill

If you've opted to enter the memorized bill yourself instead of having it automatically added to the Select Bills To Pay List, you must open it to make it a current payable. To open a memorized bill, use the following steps:

1. Press CTRL-T to open the Memorized Transaction List window.
2. Double-click the appropriate listing to open the bill in the usual Enter Bills window with the next due date showing.
3. If the Amount Due field is blank, fill it in.
4. Click Save & Close to save this bill so it becomes a current payable and is listed as a bill that must be paid when you write checks to pay your bills. (See Chapter 12 for information about paying bills.)

Creating Memorized Bill Groups

If you have a whole bunch of memorized transactions to cover all the bills that are due the first of the month (rent, mortgage, utilities, car payments, whatever), you don't have to select them for payment one at a time. You can create a group and then invoke actions on the group (automatically performing the action on every bill in the group). To accomplish this, use the following steps:

1. Press CTRL-T to display the Memorized Transaction List.
2. Right-click any blank spot in the Memorized Transaction window and choose New Group from the shortcut menu.
3. In the New Memorized Transaction Group window, give this group a name (such as 1st Of Month or 15th Of Month).
4. Fill out the fields to specify the way you want the bills in this group to be handled.
5. Click OK to save this group.

Adding Memorized Bills to Groups

After you create the group, you can add memorized transactions to it as follows:

1. In the Memorized Transaction List window, select the first memorized transaction you want to add to the group.
2. Right-click and choose Edit Memorized Transaction from the shortcut menu.
3. When the Schedule Memorized Transaction window opens with this transaction displayed, select the option named Add To Group.
4. Select the group from the list that appears when you click the arrow next to the Group Name field and click OK.

Repeat this process for each bill you want to add to the group. As you create future memorized bills, just select the Add To Group option to add the bills to the appropriate group straightaway.

If you have other recurring bills with different criteria (perhaps they're due on a different day of the month, or they're due annually), create groups for them and add the individual transactions to the group.

Reimbursable Expenses

A reimbursable expense is one that you incurred on behalf of a customer. Even though you pay the vendor bill, there's an agreement with your customer that you'll send an invoice to recover your costs. There are two common types of reimbursable expenses:

- General expenses, such as long-distance telephone charges, parking and tolls, and other incidental expenses, might be incurred on behalf of a client. Those portions of the vendor bill that apply to customer agreements for reimbursement are split out when you enter the bill.
- Specific goods or services that are purchased on behalf of the customer.

Options for Managing Reimbursable Expenses

You have two ways to manage reimbursable expenses:

- Pay the bill, post it to an expense, and then let QuickBooks automatically post the customer's reimbursement to the same expense account. This cancels the original expense and reduces the expense total in your Profit & Loss statements, so that the expense amount reflects the net between what you paid and what you collected for reimbursement.
- Pay the bill, post it to an expense, and then let QuickBooks automatically post the customer's reimbursement to an income account that's created for tracking reimbursements. This lets you track totals for both expenses and reimbursements.

You may want to discuss these choices with your accountant. Many businesses prefer the second option—tracking the expenses and reimbursements separately—just because it's more apparent when you're analyzing your expenses and income. The steps for this second approach are detailed in the following section. If you prefer to reduce your expense totals by posting reimbursements to the expense account you used when you entered the vendor's bill, these instructions don't apply to you.

Configuring Reimbursement Tracking

To track reimbursed costs from customers, you need to enable reimbursement tracking in QuickBooks, and you must also create income accounts that are used for collecting reimbursements.

Enabling Reimbursement Tracking

To tell QuickBooks that you want to track reimbursable costs, you must enable the feature in the Preferences dialog box, using the following steps:

1. Choose Edit | Preferences to open the Preferences dialog.
2. Select the Time & Expenses icon in the left pane.
3. Click the Company Preferences tab.
4. In the Invoicing Options section of the dialog, click the check box next to the option labeled Track Reimbursed Expenses As Income to put a check mark in the box.
5. Click OK.

Applying Automatic Markups

The Time & Expenses Preferences window has an option for setting a default markup percentage. You can use this feature to have QuickBooks automatically mark up expenses you're linking to a customer for reimbursement. Be sure to select (or create new) the default account that you want to use to track the income generated by the markup. Most businesses use something like "markup income."

The default markup percentage is unrelated to the option to track reimbursed expenses as income. You can apply this markup whether you're tracking reimbursed expenses as income or posting the reimbursements to the original expense account.

You can also override any automatic markup that QuickBooks applies, so filling in a percentage in this field doesn't prevent you from setting up your own pricing formula for any individual item.

ProAdvisor Tip: The markup percentage that you designate in the Time & Expenses Preference can also be applied to the product and services that you sell. Specifically, when you enter an amount in the Cost field when you're creating a new item or editing an existing one, QuickBooks will automatically fill in the item's Price field by marking up the cost with this percentage.

Setting Up Income Accounts for Reimbursement

When you enable the reimbursement tracking option, QuickBooks adds a new field to the dialog you use when you create or edit an expense account. As you can see in Figure 11-7, you can configure an expense account so that reimbursements for the expense are posted to an income account. Whenever you post a vendor expense to this account and also indicate that the expense is reimbursable, the amount you charge to the customer when you create an invoice for that customer is automatically posted to the income account that's linked to this expense account.

FIGURE 11-7 Configure expense accounts to post reimbursements to an income account.

You may have numerous expense accounts that you want to use for reimbursable expenses; in fact, that's the common scenario. Portions of telephone bills, travel expenses, subcontractor expenses, and so on are frequently passed on to customers for reimbursement.

The easiest way to manage all of this is to enable those expense accounts to track reimbursements and post the income from customers to one account named Reimbursed Expenses. However, QuickBooks requires a one-to-one relationship between a reimbursable expense and the reimbursement income from that expense. As a result, if you have multiple expense accounts for which you may receive reimbursement (which is pretty common), you must also create multiple income accounts for accepting reimbursed expenses.

This is a one-time chore, however, so when you've finished setting up the accounts, you can just enter transactions, knowing QuickBooks will automatically post reimbursed expenses to your new income accounts.

The best way to set up the income accounts you'll need for reimbursement is to use subaccounts. That way, your reports will show the total amount of income due to reimbursed expenses, and you have individual account totals if you have some reason to audit a total.

◆ Name	⚡	Type ▲	Balance Total	Attach
◆40400 · Reimbursable Expenses		Income		
◆40402 · Reimbursable Telephone		Income		
◆40401 · Reimbursable Travel		Income		
◆40500 · Discounts on Sales		Income		
◆49900 · Uncategorized Income		Income		
◆4100 · Revenue		Income		
◆4800 · Vendor Refunds		Income		
◆5100 · Direct Labor		Cost of Goods Sold		
◆5130 · Wages - Sales-Inside		Cost of Goods Sold		

Depending on the company type you selected when you created your company file, QuickBooks may have already created a Reimbursed Expenses account in the Income section of your chart of accounts. If so, you already have a parent account, and you only have to set up subaccounts.

If you don't already have an income account named Reimbursed Expenses, follow these steps to create the parent account:

1. Open the chart of accounts by pressing CTRL-A or by clicking the Chart of Accounts icon on the Home page.
2. Press CTRL-N to open the Add New Account: Choose Account Type dialog.
3. Select Income as the account type and click Continue.
4. In the Add New Account dialog, enter an account number (if you use numbers) and name the account Reimbursed Expenses (or something similar).
5. Click Save & New.

Now that you've created the parent account, you can create all the subaccounts you need, using the same steps you used to create the parent account, with the following changes:

- If you're using numbered accounts, use the next sequential number after the number you used for the parent account.
- Name the account for the type of expense you're tracking, such as Telephone Reimbursements.
- Select the Subaccount Of check box and link it to the parent account you created.

Repeat this process as many times as necessary. Your reports show the individual account postings as well as a total for all postings for the parent account.

Don't forget to edit any of your existing expense accounts that you'll use to invoice customers for reimbursements. Select the account and press CTRL-E to open the account record in Edit mode. Then select the check box to track reimbursed expenses and enter the appropriate income account.

Recording Reimbursable Expenses

If you want to be reimbursed by customers for expenses you incurred on their behalf, you must enter the appropriate data while you're filling out the vendor's bill (or writing a direct disbursement check to a vendor for which you don't enter bills). After you enter the account and the amount, click the arrow in the Customer:Job column and select the appropriate customer or job from the drop-down list.

Entering data in the Customer:Job column automatically places a check box with a check mark inserted in the Billable? column. The expense is charged to the customer, and you can pass the charge along to the customer when you create an invoice (covered in Chapter 9).

ProAdvisor Tip: You can click the check box to remove the check mark if you don't want to bill the customer for the expense but you still want to track what you're spending for the customer or the job. This disables the reimbursement feature, but the expense is still associated with the customer/job so that you can track job costs.

Sometimes, a vendor's bill is for an amount that's not entirely chargeable to a customer. Some of the amount may be your own responsibility, and it may also be that multiple customers owe you reimbursement for the amount. (This is often the case with telephone expenses when your customers reimburse you for long-distance charges.)

Follow these steps to create a vendor bill (or a direct disbursement check if you're not entering vendor bills) that splits expenses between you and a customer or multiple customers:

1. Select the vendor and enter the amount and other data needed in the header section.
2. Select the expense account, and then enter the portion of the bill that is your own responsibility.
3. In the next line, select the same account, and then enter the portion of the bill you are charging back to a customer.
4. Enter an explanation of the charge in the Memo column. (When you create the invoice, the text in the Memo column is the only description the customer sees.)
5. In the Customer:Job column, choose the appropriate customer or job (be sure that the Billable box next to the customer or job name is checked).
6. Optionally, assign the expense to a class.
7. Repeat steps 3 through 6 to include any additional customers for this expense account.

When you're finished, the total amount entered should match the amount on the vendor's bill (see Figure 11-8).

FIGURE 11-8   Charge portions of an expense to one or more customers by splitting the total expense among customers when you enter the vendor bill.

Paying Vendors

In *this chapter:*

- Choose bills to pay

- Apply discounts and credits

- Use the Write Checks window

- Remit sales tax

Periodically, you have to pay your vendors, and in QuickBooks you have some choices about the way you perform that task:

- You can enter vendor bills into QuickBooks when they arrive (covered in Chapter 11) and then pay them.
- You can save the bills in a large envelope or box and just write checks when you're ready to pay them, skipping the step of recording the bills in QuickBooks.

Some companies do both. They enter vendor bills into QuickBooks and go straight to writing checks for vendors that don't send bills (such as the landlord, the mortgage company, the bank loan, and so on).

ProAdvisor Tip: If you're using the multiple currencies feature, amounts are displayed in the vendor's currency as well as your own currency.

Choosing What to Pay

When it comes time to pay your bills, you may find that you don't have the cash or credit available to pay every bill that's entered, or even to pay the entire amount due for each bill.

There are many opinions out there about how to decide what to pay when money is tight, and the term "essential vendors" is used quite often. "Essential" can be a very subjective term, since having electricity can be just as important as buying inventory items. Having worked with hundreds of clients over the years, however, I can pass on to you two key "lessons learned" that are based on those clients' experiences:

- The government (taxes) comes first. Never, never use payroll withholding money to pay bills.
- It's better to send lots of vendors small checks than to send gobs of money to a couple of vendors who have been applying pressure. Vendors hate being ignored much more than they dislike small payments on account.

Viewing Your Unpaid Bills

Start by examining the bills you entered in QuickBooks that are due. The best way to see that list is in detailed form instead of a summary total for each vendor. To accomplish this, choose Reports | Vendors & Payables | Unpaid Bills Detail to see a list of your outstanding vendor bills (see Figure 12-1).

FIGURE 12-1 Check the details for your current unpaid bills.

By default, the report is sorted by vendor name, and you may find that choosing Date from the drop-down list in the Sort By field is helpful in deciding which bills need urgent attention.

Double-click any entry if you want to see the original bill you entered, including all line items and notes you made in the Memo column.

You can filter the report to display only certain bills by clicking Customize Report and selecting the Filters tab in the Modify Report dialog. Use the filters to change what's displayed in the report. For example, you might want to filter for bills that are more than a certain number of days overdue for "essential" vendors only. If you're short on cash, this type of information can help you decide who gets paid and work out a payment plan that will maintain good relationships with your vendors.

Selecting the Bills to Pay

When you're ready to tell QuickBooks which bills you want to pay, choose Vendors | Pay Bills. The Pay Bills window appears (see Figure 12-2), and you can make your selections by placing a check mark next to the bills you want to pay. You can also choose which open bills to work with in this window by using the filters, as described next.

FIGURE 12-2 Paying bills starts in the Pay Bills window.

Due On Or Before Selecting this option displays all the bills due on or before the date displayed. Note that the default date that's automatically inserted in this field is ten days from the current date, but you can change the date to display more or fewer bills. If you have discounts for timely payments with any vendors, this selection is more important than it seems. The due date isn't the same as the discount date. Therefore, if you have terms of 2% 10 Net 30, a bill that arrived on April 2 is due on May 2 and won't appear on the list if the due date filter you select is April 30.

Unfortunately, the discount date is April 12, but you won't know because the bill won't appear. If you want to use a due date filter, go out at least 30 days. (See "ProAdvisor Recommends: Applying Discounts for Timely Payments" later in this chapter.)

Show All Bills   Shows all the bills in your system, regardless of when they're due. This is the safest option (and it's selected by default), because you won't accidentally miss a discount date. On the other hand, the list can be rather long.

A/P Account   If you have multiple A/P accounts, select the account in the drop-down account menu at the top of the window to which the bills you want to pay were originally posted. If you don't have multiple A/P accounts, this field doesn't appear in the window. If you do have multiple A/P accounts, you have to repeat this process for each of them.

Filter By   This filter lets you choose to see open bills for a particular vendor or all vendors (the default filter).

Sort By   Determines the manner in which your bills are displayed in the Pay Bills window. The choices are

- Due Date (the default)
- Discount Date
- Vendor
- Amount Due

Payment Date   This is the date that appears on your checks. By default, the current date appears in the field, but if you want to predate or postdate your checks, you can change that date. You can also tell QuickBooks to date checks on the day of printing by changing the Checking Preferences. If you merely select the bills today and wait until tomorrow (or later) to print the checks, the payment date set here still appears on the checks.

Payment Method   The Method drop-down list displays the available methods of payment: Check and Credit Card are listed by default, but if you've signed up for QuickBooks online bill payment services, that payment method also appears in the list (see Chapter 15 to learn about using QuickBooks for online banking, including online bill payments).

If you are paying by check and QuickBooks prints your checks, be sure the To Be Printed option is selected. When you finish selecting payments, click the Pay Selected Bills button, and QuickBooks opens the Payment Summary dialog where you can choose to print the checks now or wait until later. (See Chapter 25 to learn how to set up and configure check printing.)

If you prepare checks manually, select Assign Check Number, and when you click the Pay Selected Bills button, QuickBooks opens the Assign Check Numbers dialog so you can specify the starting check number for this bill-paying session.

Payment Account   The Account drop-down list displays the checking or credit card account you want to use for these payments. If you made changes to the selection fields (perhaps you changed the Sort By option to Due Date), your list of bills to be paid may change. If all the bills displayed are to be paid either in full or in part, you're ready to move to the next step. If there are still some bills on the list that you're not going to pay, you can just select the ones you do want to pay. Selecting a bill is simple—just click the leftmost column to place a check mark in it. You can also click Select All Bills to select all of them (and click the leftmost column to toggle off the check mark of any bills you don't want to pay in this bill-paying session).

Paying Bills in Full

The easiest bills to pay (if you have enough cash in the bank or credit on your credit cards) are those you want to pay in full, when none of them have credits or discounts to worry about. Select the bills, and then click Pay Selected Bills.

Making Partial Payments

If you don't want to pay a bill in full, you can easily adjust the amount by clicking the check mark column on the bill's listing to select the bill for payment. Then move to the Amt. To Pay column and replace the amount that's displayed with the amount you want to pay. When you press TAB, the total at the bottom of the column is recalculated (and QuickBooks reserves the unpaid balance for your next bill payment session).

Using Discounts and Credits

QuickBooks has a configuration option you can set to determine whether you make the decision about applying discounts and credits at the time you select the bill for payment, or let QuickBooks apply the amounts automatically to bills that you select for payment.

To set your default options, choose Edit | Preferences and select the Bills category in the left pane. In the Company Preferences tab, select either or both of the options Automatically Use Credits or Automatically Use Discounts and enter the account to which you want to post the discounts.

The account for the discounts you take (sometimes called *earned discounts*) can be either an income or expense account. While there's no absolute right and wrong here, my vote would be to recognize it as a reduction in an expense—and if that expense account is a Cost Of Goods Sold account, it means you'll show a higher gross margin as a result of paying your bills promptly. So if you think of the discount as income (money you've brought into your system by paying your bills promptly), make the account an income account. If you think of the discount as a reverse expense (money you've saved by paying your bills promptly), make the account an expense account (it posts as a minus amount, which means it reduces total expenses).

▶▶ ProAdvisor Recommends

Applying Discounts for Timely Payments

In many cases, early payment discounts are offered by those vendors from whom you buy inventory items. Consider putting the discount account in the section of your chart of accounts that holds the Cost Of Goods Sold accounts. In fact, the most efficient way to do this is to have a parent account called Cost Of Goods Sold and then create two subaccounts:

- Cost Of Goods Purchased
- Discounts Taken

Only post to the subaccounts (make sure your inventory items are linked to the Cost Of Goods Purchased subaccount). You'll be able to see the individual amounts on your financial reports, and the parent account will report the net COGS.

QuickBooks may have created a Cost Of Goods Sold account automatically during your company setup. If not, create one and then create the subaccounts.

Applying Discounts

Bills that have terms for discounts for timely payment display the Discount Date (in the Disc. Date column). Bills that have no data in that column do not have discount terms.

If you enabled automatic application of discounts and credits, when you select the bill by clicking the check mark column, the discount is automatically applied. You can see the amount in the Disc. Used column, and the Amt. To Pay column adjusts accordingly.

If the discount isn't applied automatically, it's probably because today's date is later than the discount cutoff date. Don't worry, you can take the discount anyway—see the next section, "Taking Discounts After the Discount Date."

If you're making a partial payment and want to adjust the discount, click the Set Discount button to open the Discount And Credits window and enter the amount of the discount you want to take. Click Done, and when you return to the Pay Bills window, the discount is applied and the Amt. To Pay column has the correct amount.

Taking Discounts After the Discount Date

Many businesses deduct the discount amount even if the discount period has expired. The resulting payment, with the discount applied, is frequently accepted by the vendor if the payment is received within a few business days of the discount period. You'll quickly learn which vendors will accept a discounted payment and which won't. Seeing that the discount you took has been added back in the next statement you receive is a pretty good hint that you're not going to get away with it the next time.

To take a discount after the discount date, select the bill for payment, and then click the Set Discount button to open the Discount And Credits window. The amount showing for the discount is zero. Enter the discount you would be entitled to if you paid the bill in a timely fashion and click Done.

Applying Credits

If you configured QuickBooks to take credits automatically, when you select a bill for payment, if credits exist for the vendor, the amount of the credit appears in the Credits Used column, and the Amt. To Pay column is adjusted.

If you didn't enable automatic credit application, when you select the bill, the amount of existing credits appears below the list of bills. Click Set Credits to open the Discount And Credits window. Make the appropriate selections of credit amounts, and click Done to change the Amt. To Pay column to reflect your adjustments.

If credits are applied automatically and you don't want to take the credit against this bill (perhaps you want to save it for another bill), click Set Credits to open the Discount And Credits window. Deselect the credit and click Done.

If your total credits with the vendor are equal to or exceed the bill you select, QuickBooks does not create a check, because the bill is paid in its entirety with credits (the Payment Summary window that displays indicates an Amount Paid of $0.00).

Sending the Payments

When you finish selecting the bills to pay, click Pay Selected Bills. QuickBooks transfers all the information to the general ledger and fills out your checkbook account register with the payments.

If you chose the option to print checks, QuickBooks displays a Payment Summary dialog (see Figure 12-3) that offers several choices for your next step:

- Choose Pay More Bills to return to the Pay Bills window and select other bills to pay (you'll print these checks later). Use this choice to pay bills without printing checks, such as sending payments to vendors you've configured for online payments.
- Choose Print Checks to print your checks now.
- Click Done to close the Payment Summary dialog and close the Pay Bills window, and print your checks later.

When you defer printing, the checks are posted to the bank account register with the notation To Print. Choose File | Print Forms | Checks to print your checks.

FIGURE 12-3   You can print checks now, or wait until later.

If you selected the Assign Check Number option because you manually write checks, QuickBooks displays the Assign Check Numbers dialog.

- If you select the option Let QuickBooks Assign Check Numbers, QuickBooks looks at the last check number used in the bank register and begins numbering with the next available number.
- If you select the option Let Me Assign The Check Numbers Below, enter the check numbers in the dialog.

When you click OK, QuickBooks opens the Payment Summary dialog that displays the payments. Click Pay More Bills if you want to return to the Pay Bills window, or click Done if you're finished paying bills.

If you're paying bills online, select the Online Payment option when you select those bills. QuickBooks retains the information until you go online. (See Chapter 15 to learn about online banking.)

Check Writing Without Entering a Bill

You can record and print a check in QuickBooks without ever having first entered a bill. In fact, if you've decided not to enter vendor bills, this is how you'll always pay your vendors. However, even if you are entering vendor bills on a regular basis, you sometimes need to write a quick check without going through the process of first entering the bill, selecting it, paying it, and printing the check—for example, when a delivery person is standing in front of you waiting for a COD check and doesn't have time for you to go through all those steps.

Manual Checks

If you use manual checks, you can write your checks and then tell QuickBooks about it later, or you can bring your checkbook to your computer and enter the checks in QuickBooks as you write them. You have two ways to enter your checks in QuickBooks: in the bank register or in the Write Checks window.

Writing Checks in the Bank Register

To use the bank register, open the bank account register and enter the check directly in a transaction line, as follows:

1. Enter the date.
2. Press TAB to move to the Number field. QuickBooks automatically fills in the next available check number.
3. Press TAB to move through the rest of the fields, filling in the name of the payee, the amount of the payment, and the expense account you're assigning to the transaction.
4. Click the Record button to save the transaction.

Repeat the steps for the next check and continue until all the manual checks you've written are entered into the register.

Caution: You can't use the check register to purchase items: you must use the Write Checks transaction window. There, you can use the Items tab to tell QuickBooks exactly which items you're purchasing.

Using the Write Checks Window

You can also use the Write Checks window to tell QuickBooks about a check you manually prepared. To get there, press CTRL-W. When the Write Checks transaction window opens (see Figure 12-4), select the bank account you're using to write the checks.

FIGURE 12-4 Fill out the onscreen check the same way you'd fill out a paper check—they look the same.

The next available check number is already filled in unless the To Be Printed option box is checked (if it is, click it to toggle the check mark off and put the check number in the window). QuickBooks warns you if you enter a check number that's already been used. It's worth noting that the warning doesn't appear until you fill in all the data and attempt to save the check.

Fill out the check, posting amounts to the appropriate accounts. If the check is for inventory items, use the Items tab to make sure the items are placed into inventory. When you finish, click Save & New to open a new blank check. When you're through writing checks, click Save & Close to close the Write Checks transaction window. All the checks you wrote are recorded in the bank account register.

Printing Checks in a Batch

If you pay your bills by printing checks from the Write Checks window, by default QuickBooks saves the checks you prepare and then prints them in a batch instead of one at a time.

Open the Write Checks window and make sure the To Be Printed option is selected. Fill out all the fields for the first check and click Save & New to move to the next blank Write Checks window. Continue to fill out checks, until every check you need to print is ready. Then print the checks using one of the following methods:

- Click Save & Close when you are finished filling out all the checks, and then choose File | Print Forms | Checks from the menu bar.
- In the last Write Checks window, click the arrow to the right of the Print button at the top of the Write Checks window and choose Print Batch.

Remitting Sales Tax

If you collect sales tax from your customers, you have to turn that money over to the state taxing authorities. Instead of using the Pay Bills feature to do this, QuickBooks uses a special system to track and pay sales taxes.

Many states have county, city, or parish tax authorities, each with its own rate. Businesses in those states may have to remit the sales tax they collect to both the state and the local sales tax authority, and the sales tax a customer pays is the total of all the taxes from these various tax authorities. As a result, tracking sales tax properly can be a complicated process.

This discussion assumes you've created the sales tax items you need (covered in Chapter 5), and each item is linked to the right tax authority as a vendor.

QuickBooks' Manage Sales Tax Feature

QuickBooks provides a feature called Manage Sales Tax that acts as a "home page" for information and help, as well as links to reports and payment forms covered in this section. You can open the Manage Sales Tax window (see Figure 12-5) by choosing Vendors | Sales Tax | Manage Sales Tax.

FIGURE 12-5 The Manage Sales Tax window has links to sales tax functions.

The menu commands needed to access features and functions are provided in the following sections, but you can also use the links on the Manage Sales Tax window for some of those chores.

Running Sales Tax Reports

At some interval determined by your taxing authority, you need to report your total sales, your nontaxable sales, and your taxable sales, along with any other required breakdowns. Oh, yes, you also have to write a sales tax payment check (or multiple checks) to remit the taxes.

Sales Tax Liability Report

QuickBooks has reports to help you fill out your sales tax forms. Choose Vendors | Sales Tax | Sales Tax Liability. Use the Dates drop-down list to select an interval that matches the way you report to the taxing authorities. By default, QuickBooks chooses the interval you configured in the Preferences dialog, but that interval may only apply to your primary sales tax. If you collect multiple taxes due at different intervals, you must create a separate report with the appropriate interval to display those figures. Figure 12-6 shows a Sales Tax Liability report for a monthly filer.

FIGURE 12-6   The Sales Tax Liability report displays taxable and nontaxable sales for each tax code.

Tax Code Reports

If you have to report specific types of taxable or nontaxable sales, you can obtain that information by creating a report on the tax code you created to track that information. Choose Lists | Sales Tax Code List and select (highlight) the tax code for which you need a report. Press CTRL-Q to see a report on the sales activity with this tax code. Change the date range to match your reporting interval with the sales tax authority (this isn't a sales tax report, so QuickBooks doesn't automatically match the settings in the Sales Tax Preferences dialog).

You don't have to create these reports one sales tax code at a time; you can modify the report so it reports all of your sales tax codes or just those you need for a specific tax authority's report. In fact, you can modify the report so it reports totals instead of every sales transaction.

Click the Customize Report button on the report window. In the Display tab, use the Columns list to deselect any items you don't require for the report (for example, the Type, Date, and Number of an invoice/sales receipt, and the contents of the Memo field).

In the Filters tab, choose Sales Tax Code from the Filter list. Click the arrow to the right of the Sales Tax Code field and select the appropriate option from the drop-down list, choosing one of the following options:

- All Sales Tax Codes, which displays total activity for the period for every code
- Multiple Sales Tax Codes, which opens the Select Sales Tax Code window, listing all codes, so you can select the specific codes you want to report on
- All Taxable Codes, which displays total activity for the period for each taxable code
- All Non-Taxable Codes, which displays total activity for the period for each nontaxable code

Click OK to return to the report window, where your selections are reflected. Unless you want to take all these steps again when you need this report, click the Memorize button to memorize the report.

Paying the Sales Tax

After you check the figures (or calculate them, if you have multiple reports with different standards of calculation), it's time to pay the tax, using the following steps:

Caution: Don't use the bank account register or Write Checks window to pay sales taxes. Such payments won't be applied to your sales tax reports correctly. Instead, use the Pay Sales Tax method shown in this section.

1. Choose Vendors | Sales Tax | Pay Sales Tax to open the Pay Sales Tax dialog.

2. Select the bank account to use.

3. Check the date that's displayed in the field named Show Sales Tax Due Through. It must match the end date of your current reporting period (for instance, monthly or quarterly).

4. Click in the Pay column to insert a check mark next to those you're paying now. If you're lucky enough to have the same reporting interval for all taxing authorities, just click the Pay All Tax button (the label changes to Clear Selections).

5. If you're going to print the check, be sure to select the To Be Printed check box at the bottom of the dialog. If you write the check manually, or if you remit sales tax online using an electronic transfer from your bank, deselect the To Be Printed check box. Then, if you're writing a manual check, insert the check number, and if you're remitting online, either remove the check number entirely or enter EFT (for electronic payment) in the No. field.

6. Click OK when you've completed filling out the information.

The next time you print or write checks, the sales tax check is in the group waiting to be completed.

Adjusting Sales Tax Amounts

If you need to adjust the amount of sales tax due (most states offer a discount for timely payment), select the appropriate sales tax item in the Pay Sales Tax window and click the Adjust button to open the Sales Tax Adjustment dialog.

Specify the amount by which to reduce the tax amount for timely payment or to increase the amount, if you're late and paying a penalty. Specify an Adjustment Account and click OK to return to the Pay Sales Tax window, where the amount has been changed to reflect your adjustment.

Working with Bank and Credit Card Accounts

*I*n this chapter:

- Make deposits that aren't customer payments

- Transfer funds between accounts

- Manage petty cash

- Maintain and track credit card balances

To ensure that QuickBooks is accurately keeping track of all your business activity, every penny that goes through your bank accounts should be entered in QuickBooks. Most deposits and withdrawals are easy to enter in bank accounts because the transaction windows you use take care of adding or removing funds automatically.

But there are times when money is deposited or withdrawn outside of the usual transaction windows, and this chapter covers what you need to know to handle these situations.

Depositing Money That Isn't from Customers

Even though QuickBooks takes care of recording the deposits into your bank account when you receive money from customers (covered in Chapter 10), there are times when you receive money that's unconnected to a customer payment. Some of the common reasons for such deposits are

- Rebate checks from manufacturers or stores
- Checks from vendors with whom you have a credit balance and requested a check
- Infusion of capital from an owner or partner
- Loan from an owner, partner, officer, or bank

Entering a noncustomer deposit into a bank account is easy. If the deposit is the only deposit you're making and it will appear on your statement as an individual deposit, you can work directly in the account register. If you're going to deposit the check along with other checks, use the Make Deposits window.

Using the Account Register for Deposits

To work directly in the bank account register, open the register by choosing Banking | Use Register, and then selecting the appropriate bank account. When the account register window opens, the next available transaction line is highlighted and the current date is displayed. Use the following steps to record the deposit directly into the bank account register.

1. Change the date if necessary, and then press TAB to move to the Number field.
2. Delete the check number if one automatically appears (or wait until you enter the amount in the Deposit column, at which point QuickBooks deletes the check number).

3. Press TAB to move past the next three columns to get to the Deposit column, or click in the Deposit column to move there immediately. (See "Assigning a Payee to a Noncustomer Deposit" later in this section to learn about your options when tracking a payee for this type of deposit.)

4. Enter the amount of the deposit.

5. Move to the next field (Account) and assign the deposit to the appropriate account. (See "Assigning Accounts to Noncustomer Deposits" later in this section for guidelines.)

6. Use the Memo field to enter an explanation in case your accountant asks you about the deposit.

7. Click the Record button.

Using the Make Deposits Window

Sometimes it's better to use the Make Deposits window for an unusual deposit, because you're planning to deposit the check along with other checks, and you want your deposit records to match the bank statement. Use the following steps to accomplish this:

1. Choose Banking | Make Deposits to open the Payments To Deposit window.

2. In the Payments To Deposit window, select the deposits you're taking to the bank (the check you want to deposit at the same time is not listed because the window only shows the money you've received through customer transactions).

3. Click OK to move to the Make Deposits window.

4. Click in the From Account column of the blank line under the last entry (or in the Received From column if you need to track the payee).

5. Select the appropriate account for this deposit.

6. Optionally, enter data in the Memo, Chk No., and Pmt Meth. fields (and don't forget the Class field if you're tracking classes).

7. Enter the amount.

Your check is added to the total of the deposit you're making (see Figure 13-1).

Assigning a Payee to a Noncustomer Deposit

You can, if necessary, enter a payee name in the Received From column, but QuickBooks doesn't require that. Most of the time, a payee isn't needed. For example, if you're depositing a rebate on a purchase you made, there's a good chance the company that wrote the check doesn't exist in your QuickBooks system, and there's no point in adding a name you don't need to produce reports about.

FIGURE 13-1 Recording the deposit of a rebate check, along with a customer payment.

If the money is from an owner or partner, the name should exist in your system in the Other Names list. If the money is from a corporate officer, that officer probably exists as an employee, but you cannot use the employee name for this transaction. Instead, create the name in the Other Names list to track this deposit. Use a different name (most users append an extra letter or symbol to the new name because you can't have duplicate names).

If you're depositing the proceeds of a bank loan, you need a vendor because you'll be writing checks to pay back the principal and interest.

If you type a payee name that doesn't exist in any of your name lists, QuickBooks displays a Name Not Found message offering you the following selections:

- **Quick Add**   Lets you enter a name without any additional information
- **Set Up**   Lets you create a new name using the regular New Name window
- **Cancel**   Returns you to the original window you were working in so you can either choose another name or delete the name of the nonexistent payee

If you select Quick Add or Set Up, you're asked which type of name you're adding: Vendor, Customer, Employee, or Other. Unless this payee will become a vendor or customer, choose Other.

Assigning Accounts to Noncustomer Deposits

If you're depositing your own money into the business and the business is a proprietorship or partnership, that's capital and you should post the deposit from a capital account (it's an equity account). If you're depositing the proceeds of a loan (from yourself as a corporate officer or from a bank), post the deposit from the liability account for the loan (you may have to create the liability account). If you're making a deposit that's a refund from a vendor, you can post the amount to the expense account that was used for the original expense.

When in doubt, post the amount to the most logical place and ask your accountant for verification (or post the amount to the Ask My Accountant account if you have one). You can always edit the transaction later or make a journal entry to post the amount to the right account.

Transferring Funds Between Accounts

Moving money between bank accounts is a common procedure in business. If you have a bank account for payroll, you have to move money out of your operating account into your payroll account every payday. Some people deposit all the customer payments into a money market or savings account (which pays interest) and then transfer the necessary funds to an operating account when it's time to pay bills. Others do it the other way around, moving money not immediately needed from the business operating account to a money market account. Lawyers, agents, real estate brokers, and other professionals have to maintain escrow accounts and move money between them and the operating account. You can use either of two methods to transfer funds between bank accounts:

- Use the QuickBooks Transfer Funds transaction window.
- Post a check from the sending bank to a transfer account and then bring the funds into the receiving account from the funds transfer account.

Both methods are quite easy, and I'll go over them in this section.

Using the Transfer Funds Transaction Window

QuickBooks offers a Transfer Funds feature, which is the best solution to record a "noncheck" transfer of funds between bank accounts that are held either by the same or different banks (you call the bank or use their online website to move the funds).

The Transfer Funds feature also works if you write a check (either because the bank accounts are in separate banks or because you prefer to have a check as a record of the transfer), but adding the check number to the transaction involves an extra step, and QuickBooks will insert the same check number in both bank accounts (which can mess up your check numbering system in the receiving bank account). If you don't mind the fact that a check number from one bank account appears in the other bank account, then the Transfer Funds feature remains an easy method for transferring funds.

To transfer money between accounts using the Transfer Funds transaction window, follow these steps:

1. Choose Banking | Transfer Funds from the menu bar to open the Transfer Funds Between Accounts dialog.
2. Fill out the fields.

3. Click Save & Close (or Save & New if you have another transfer to make).

QuickBooks posts the transaction (you'll see it marked as TRANSFR in both bank accounts if you open their registers) without affecting any totals in your financial reports. All the work is done on the balance sheet, but the bottom line of your balance sheet doesn't change because money was neither added nor removed from your company.

If you wrote a check from one account and took it to the bank to effect the transfer, open the register of the sending bank, select the transaction line, enter the check number in the Number field, and click Record. QuickBooks displays a dialog asking you to confirm the fact that you're changing the transaction (click Yes). That number is also recorded on the transaction line in the receiving bank register, and you cannot remove it.

Handling a Bounced Check

When you receive and deposit a check from a customer for payment on an open invoice, QuickBooks is performing two tasks for you. First, it's reducing your Accounts Receivable account (on the day you posted that check), and second, it's increasing your bank account in the same amount. A week later, when your bank notifies you that your customer's check has bounced, you need to perform the following four actions in QuickBooks.

First, reduce your bank account by the amount of the bounced check. Second, increase your Accounts Receivable account by the amount of the bounced check (because your customer still owes you for this invoice). Third, invoice your customer for the nonsufficient funds (NSF) fee, and fourth, post your bank's NSF charge to you in your bank register.

While this may seem like a lot of work for one bounced check, by using special items, you can make it easier to reflect this activity in QuickBooks and recoup your money.

Creating an Item NSF Check

Create an Other Charge Item to capture the amount of the check that bounced. Leave the Amount or % field blank, select Non for the Tax Code, and link this item to your bank account (whichever account you deposit your checks into).

Creating an Item for Your NSF Charge to Your Customer

Again using the Other Charge type, create a nontaxable item to charge your customer an NSF fee. You can fill in a value for the amount if you wish (or you can enter it when you list it on an invoice). This item can be linked to your bank service charge expense account.

Creating an Invoice to Recover the Amounts Owed

Create an invoice that includes the special items you just created to handle bounced checks (see Figure 13-2). When (or if) the payment arrives, you use Receive Payments to record the customer's payment.

FIGURE 13-2 Use special items on an invoice to take care of all the entries you need to adjust your accounting totals for a bounced check.

When you enter the NSF item on the invoice, it credits the bank account, which, in effect, reverses the amount of the original deposit of the check. It also provides both transactions in the Reconcile window when your statement arrives so you can reconcile each entry.

The amount you enter for the service charge item can be larger than the amount your bank charged you (you'll want to check your state's laws on this matter). In fact, if you have a lot of customers who bounce checks, you could end up with a negative expense total for the bank service charge account.

Recording Your Bank's NSF Charge to You

As a final step, don't forget to record the fee that your bank is charging you for your customer's bounced check. The easiest way to record this fee is directly in your bank account register. Simply enter the date and the amount of the fee in the Payment column with a note about the NSF charge in the Memo field. And while you don't need to designate a check number or payee, you'll want to be sure you attribute this fee to your customer. To do this while in the register, click the Splits button to open additional fields for the transaction.

Then in the Customer:Job column, use the drop-down arrow to select the customer to whom the NSF fee applies.

Voiding Disbursements

Sometimes you have to void a check that you've written. Perhaps you decided not to send it for some reason, or perhaps it was lost in the mail. Whatever the reason, if a check isn't going to clear your bank, you should void it. Deleting (versus voiding) a check removes all history of the transaction from your register. This is not a good way to keep financial records—especially in the event of an audit. Voiding a check keeps the check number but sets the amount to zero.

The way QuickBooks completes the process of voiding a check can differ based on whether the check was used to record an expense or whether it was used to record the purchase of an asset, like new furniture for your office or inventory.

The process starts the same way, however, by opening the bank account register and selecting the disbursement that you want to void. Next, right-click to open the shortcut menu and choose Void Check. In the first case—when you record the voiding of an expense-related check—QuickBooks will give you the option of allowing the program to automatically create two journal entries for you. Selecting Yes will ensure that the voiding of this check does not affect any of your prior accounting periods.

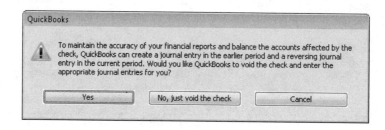

Selecting No keeps the check number along with its current date and then simply sets the amount of the check to zero without making any adjustments to a prior period.

In the second case—when you're voiding a check that is posted to an asset or liability account—the offer for the automatic journal entries is not made. The check is simply adjusted to zero along with the amounts posted to the other balance sheet accounts. Click Record to save the transaction.

Tracking Cash Disbursements

Many businesses maintain a petty cash box to dispense cash to employees (or owners) who need cash to recover money they've spent for the company or as an advance against future expenditures. This box functions like a cash register till and requires similar accounting processes to make sure QuickBooks has the correct balance for the till.

Some businesses have debit cards for the business account, which they use to withdraw money from an ATM machine or use at the cash register to pay for a business purchase.

When you use cash, whether it's cash from the petty cash box or a withdrawal via an ATM machine, you have to account for it. The following section contains some suggested procedures you can use to manage and record these cash transactions.

Tracking Petty Cash

If you keep a cash box for business expenses, your chart of accounts should have a petty cash account. This account functions like a cash register till: You put money in it, and then you account for the money that's spent from it, leaving the rest in the till until it, too, is spent. Then you put more money into the till. The petty cash account doesn't represent a real bank account; it just represents that portion of the money in the real bank account that moved into the till. If you don't have a petty cash account in your chart of accounts, create one using the following guidelines:

- The account type is Bank.
- If you number your accounts, use a number that places your new petty cash account near the other (real) bank accounts in your chart of accounts.
- Leave the opening balance at zero.

Tracking What You Put Into Petty Cash

You have to put money into your petty cash till, both literally and figuratively (in this requires recording a withdrawal from your bank account and putting the money into your petty cash account). Most of the time you'll write a check for petty cash from your bank account. Consider using the following guidelines:

- Create a name in the Other Names list for the payee (usually the name is "Cash").
- Write the check from your bank account and post it to the petty cash account. You can use the Write Checks window to accomplish the task, or enter the transaction directly in the bank account register. Don't use the Transfer Funds feature if you actually wrote a check and stood in line at the bank to cash it, and you have to account for the check number.

You don't post a petty cash deposit to an expense. Those postings are recorded when you account for the spent funds, not for the moment at which you deposit the cash.

Recording Petty Cash Disbursements

As you take cash out of the petty cash box in the office (which was put into the box after you cashed a check), you must record those expenditures in the petty cash register.

It's easiest to use the Write Checks window to record petty cash expenses, because you can record the customer or job when necessary (either for reimbursement or for job costing) and also assign a class.

Open the Write Checks window and select the petty cash bank account. You can delete the check number QuickBooks automatically inserts in the Number field, or you can leave the number there (you'll never get a statement that you have to reconcile, so it doesn't matter). You can either skip the Payee field or use a payee named Cash or PettyCash (in the Other Names list).

You can create the check when the first expense occurs, and then open the same check and continue to add to it until the next time you put cash into the till; you can wait until you're running out of cash and need to replenish the till; or you can create a weekly or monthly transaction.

The disbursements you enter track what was spent, not what was taken out of the till. If you spent less than the amount of cash you withdrew from the till, the balance should go back into the till. You'll probably spend it later, and at that point you'll repeat this task to account for that spending.

> **ProAdvisor Tip:** When you open the Write Checks window, QuickBooks uses the same bank account that you worked in the last time you wrote a check. A common mistake is not noticing that when you are trying to write a real check you're using the petty cash account instead of your actual checking account. To help prevent you or a member of your staff from inadvertently posting a check to the wrong bank account, consider changing the onscreen account color of the petty cash account so it has a different color than your regular checking account. To do this, with your petty cash account check register open, choose Edit | Change Account Color. Choose a standard color or create one of your own.

Replacing the Cash Spent

As you dispense cash from the till, you need to replace it. The usual method is to bring the cash till back to its original balance (the amount of the first check you wrote to petty cash). Use the same steps you used to write the first check to petty cash, and use the total amount of funds disbursed as the amount of the check.

Tracking Other Cash Withdrawals

Many businesses use ATM and debit cards in their day-to-day transactions. Recording these transactions is essentially the same as recording a check. However, ATM/debit card transactions can differ from checks in that often the amount withdrawn doesn't have a specific expense attached to it at the time it's withdrawn. To track these amounts, use your Petty Cash account (bank account type) to post to when recording the withdrawal from your bank account. Then as the person who made the withdrawal begins handing in receipts, you can debit the appropriate expense account directly from this account's register.

Managing Credit Card Transactions

When you use a credit card to make purchases for your business, you have two choices about the way you can enter and manage those transactions in QuickBooks: create a credit card account or treat the credit card as a bill.

Create a Credit Card Account

With this option, you create a credit card account on your balance sheet that has its own register and to which you'll post individual transactions. The advantage of this method is that, as with your bank account, you can perform a reconciliation of this account (refer to Chapter 14 for details on how to reconcile a bank account) and use online banking to download transactions from your credit card company. To create a credit card account, follow these steps:

1. With the Chart of Accounts List open, select CTRL-N to open the Add New Account window.
2. Select Credit Card as the account type and click Continue.
3. Enter the name of the credit card (usually the issuer's name).
4. Optionally, enter a credit card number (this is required if you'll be using online banking, which is covered in Chapter 15).
5. Click Save & Close.

You can now enter individual transactions into your account in one of two ways: select Banking | Enter Credit Card Charges to enter your transactions in the Enter Credit Card Charges window (see Figure 13-3), or enter them directly into the credit card account register.

There are several fields to fill out when you use the Enter Credit Card Charges window.

1. Use the drop-down menu in the Credit Card field to select the credit card you want to post transactions to.
2. Select either the Purchase/Charge or Refund/Credit option.
3. In the Purchased From field, you can enter the name of the establishment where the card was used. If it's not important for you to track that information, you can leave that field blank (this helps keep your vendor list from growing too large).

FIGURE 13-3 Use the Enter Credit Card Charges window to track individual credit card charges.

4. Enter the date of the transaction.

5. Optionally, fill in the Ref No. field (you can find the reference number on the credit card statement).

6. Fill in the amount of the charge.

7. Use the Expenses tab for general expenses, or use the Items tab if the transaction was for the purchase of an item for inventory or a customer.

8. If you track classes, assign the transaction to the appropriate class.

When it's time to make a payment on this card, you'll use the Write Checks window and fill in the Pay To The Order Of field with the credit card company name. In the Account section (on the Expenses tab), select the credit card account from your chart of accounts.

Treat the Credit Card as a Bill

The second way to manage your credit card is to enter the charges on the statement just as you would a bill from a vendor. Select Vendors | Enter Bills and then list each transaction that appears on the statement (including any finance charges) in the Expenses tab for general expenses (see Figure 13-4), or use the Items tab if the transaction was for the purchase of an inventory item. The advantage of this method is that in addition to your charges being posted to the appropriate expense account as you enter the bill, any amount outstanding on the card is included as part of your accounts payable and listed on your reports as such. The drawback of this method, however, is that if you wait for your credit card bill to come in the mail, you could be posting these individual credit card charges a month or even two months after they were actually incurred. This may become an issue if the charges you made were in December, for example, and your statement arrives in January, the start of a new tax year. Be aware of the timing of when these expenses show on your Profit & Loss statement, and be sure to consult with your accountant if you choose to employ this method.

FIGURE 13-4 You can enter your credit card statement just as you would any other vendor bill.

Reconciling Bank Accounts

n this chapter:

- Work in the QuickBooks reconciliation windows
- Troubleshoot differences in the beginning balance

Reconciling a bank account is one of the most important tasks connected with financial record keeping—but ironically, it's also one of the most avoided tasks. When you use QuickBooks, however, the job of reconciling your accounts becomes a very manageable one.

Reconciling in QuickBooks

Most of the time, performing a bank reconciliation in QuickBooks is easy and straightforward. If you've been keeping your QuickBooks up to date you shouldn't have to make a lot of "catch up" entries because most of the data you need is already in your bank register.

The following sections explain the steps involved in reconciliation in the order that you'll be performing them. By the way, these same steps apply to reconciling a credit card account.

The Begin Reconciliation Window

Reconciling your bank account starts with the Begin Reconciliation window, which you open by choosing Banking | Reconcile (see Figure 14-1). If you have more than one bank account, or you have credit card accounts you reconcile in addition to bank accounts, select the account you want to reconcile from the drop-down list in the Account field.

FIGURE 14-1 The first window summarizes bank activity.

Enter the statement date from your bank statement and then check the Beginning Balance field in the window against the beginning balance on the bank statement. (Your bank may call it the *starting balance*.) If your beginning balances match, enter the ending balance from your statement in the Ending Balance field. If this is the *first* time you're reconciling the bank account in QuickBooks, your Beginning Balance field in QuickBooks will automatically be zero. Enter the ending balance from your statement in the Ending Balance field in QuickBooks.

If the beginning balances don't match and this is not the first time you're reconciling the bank account in QuickBooks, read "ProAdvisor Recommends: Troubleshooting Differences in the Beginning Balance" later in this chapter, and then return to this section of the chapter to perform the reconciliation.

Enter Interest Income and Service Charges

Your bank statement lists interest earned and bank service charges if either or both are applicable to your account. Enter those numbers in the Begin Reconciliation window and choose the appropriate account for posting.

If you use online banking (covered in Chapter 15) and the interest payments and bank charges have already been entered into your register as a result of downloading transactions, do *not* enter them again in the Begin Reconciliation window—they'll be in the register list you see in the next window and you can clear them the way you clear checks and deposits.

Use the Service Charges field to enter a standard monthly charge (including charges that may be assessed for failure to maintain a minimum balance). Standard bank charges typically do not include special charges for bounced checks, fees for electronic bank transfers, or any purchases you made that are charged to your account (such as the purchase of checks or deposit slips). Those should be entered in your bank register as discrete transactions using the Memo field to explain the transaction. This will make them easier to find in case you have to talk to the bank about your account.

Configuring the Reconcile Window

After you've filled out the information in the Begin Reconciliation dialog, click Continue to open the Reconcile window, shown in Figure 14-2.

You can configure the way transactions are displayed to make it easier to work in the window.

FIGURE 14-2 Uncleared transactions appear in the Reconcile window.

Sorting the Data

By default, QuickBooks sorts transactions first by date, then by transaction number. For example, in the Checks And Payments pane, if multiple checks have the same date, those checks are sorted in numerical order.

Reconciling is easier if you sort the data to match the way your bank arranges the statement. For instance, if you have a lot of electronic payments in addition to checks, and your bank lists the electronic payments separately from checks, click the Chk # column to list withdrawals without check numbers separately from checks.

Eliminating Future Transactions

If the list is long, you can shorten it by selecting the option Hide Transactions After The Statement's End Date. Theoretically, transactions that weren't created before the ending date couldn't have cleared the bank. Removing them from the window leaves only those transactions likely to have cleared. If you select this option and your reconciliation doesn't balance, deselect the option so you can clear the transactions in case one of the following scenarios applies:

- You issued a postdated check and the recipient cashed it early. Since occasionally a bank won't enforce the date, this is a real possibility.

- You made a mistake when you entered the date of the original transaction. You may have entered a wrong month or even a wrong year, which resulted in moving the transaction date into the future.

Clearing Transactions

Now you must tell QuickBooks which transactions have cleared. If this is your first bank reconciliation in QuickBooks, on the Deposits And Other Credits side of the Reconcile window you'll see a deposit transaction that represents the beginning bank balance you (or your accountant) entered either via a journal entry (read Chapter 19 to learn more about journal entries) or directly in the check register when you set up your QuickBooks data file. You'll need to "clear" this transaction during your first reconciliation. When you clear a transaction in the Reconcile window, a check mark appears in the leftmost (Cleared) column to indicate that the transaction has cleared the bank. If you clear a transaction in error, click again to remove the check mark—it's a toggle.

Use the following shortcuts to speed your work:

- If all, or almost all, of the transactions have cleared, click Mark All. Then deselect the transactions that didn't clear.
- Mark multiple, contiguous transactions by dragging down the Cleared column.
- Click the Highlight Marked box so that the items you mark as cleared have a shaded background, making them easier to distinguish from those that haven't cleared.
- If the account you're reconciling is enabled for online access, click Matched to automatically clear all transactions that were matched in the QuickStatements you've downloaded over the month. QuickBooks asks for the ending date on the statement and clears each previously matched transaction up to that date.

As you check each cleared transaction, the Difference amount in the lower-right corner of the Reconcile window changes. The goal is to get that figure to 0.00.

Adding Transactions During Reconciliation

While you're working in the Reconcile window, if you find a transaction on the statement that you haven't entered into your QuickBooks software (probably one of those ATM transactions you forgot to enter), you don't have to shut down the reconciliation process to remedy the situation. You can just enter the transaction into your register.

To open the bank account register, right-click anywhere in the Reconcile window and choose Use Register from the shortcut menu. When the account register opens, record the transaction. Return to the Reconcile window, where that transaction is now conveniently waiting for you to check off as cleared.

You can switch between the Reconcile window and the register for the account you're reconciling all through this process. Use the Window menu on the QuickBooks Menu bar to move between them, or have QuickBooks display the Open Windows List by selecting View | Open Window List.

Adding Undeposited Funds During Reconciliation

If the statement shows a deposit that doesn't appear in your reconcile window, don't add the deposit to your register until you check the Payments To Deposit window (choose Banking | Make Deposits). Most of the time you'll find the payments listed there, still awaiting deposit, even though you obviously went to the bank and deposited those checks. Select the payments that match the total shown on the bank statement and go through the Make Deposits function. When you're finished, the deposit appears in the Reconcile window. If the deposit isn't in the Payments To Deposit window, then you forgot to enter a transaction. Enter the transaction now, using the appropriate transaction window. Make sure you deposit it into the bank account to have it appear in the Reconcile window.

Deleting Transactions During Reconciliation

Sometimes you find that a transaction that was transferred from your account register to this Reconcile window shouldn't be there. This commonly occurs if you entered an ATM withdrawal twice. Or perhaps you forgot that you'd entered a deposit, and a couple of days later you entered it again. Whatever the reason, occasionally there are transactions that should be deleted.

To delete a transaction, double-click its listing in the window to open the original transaction. Then, right-click and select Delete (QuickBooks asks you to confirm the deletion). The transaction disappears from the Reconcile window and the bank register.

Editing Transactions During Reconciliation

Sometimes you'll want to change some of the information in a transaction. For example, when you see the real check, you realize the amount you entered in QuickBooks is wrong. You might even have the wrong date on a check.

Whatever the problem, you can correct it by editing the transaction. Double-click the transaction's listing in the Reconcile window to open the original transaction window. Enter the necessary changes and close the window. Answer Yes when QuickBooks asks if you want to record the changes, and you're returned to the Reconcile window where the changes are reflected.

Resolving Missing Check Numbers

Most banks list your checks in order and indicate a missing number with an asterisk on the bank statement. For instance, you may see check number 5003 followed by check number *5007 or 5007*. When a check number is missing, it means one of three things:

- The check is still outstanding.
- The check number is unused and is probably literally missing.
- The check cleared in a previous reconciliation.

If a missing check number on your bank statement is puzzling, you can check its status. To see if the check cleared in the last reconciliation, open the Previous Reconciliation report (discussed later in this chapter) by choosing Reports | Banking | Previous Reconciliation.

To investigate further, right-click anywhere in the Reconcile window and choose Missing Checks Report from the shortcut menu. When the Missing Checks dialog opens, select the appropriate account (if you have multiple bank accounts). You'll see asterisks indicating missing check numbers, as seen in Figure 14-3.

Winchester Distributors
Missing Checks
All Transactions

Type	Date	Num	Name	Memo	Account	Split	Amount
Check	01/01/2012	5000	Online Accounting	Set up Quick...	1110 · Company C...	6277 · Accou...	-225.00
Check	01/01/2012	5001	Kuver Property	Janaury Rent	1110 · Company C...	6295 · Rent	-583.75
Check	01/05/2012	5002	Deborah Wood (O...	Petty Cash	1110 · Company C...	1140 · Petty C...	-500.00
Check	01/08/2012	5003	Gas & Electic Com...	ACCT# 0987...	1110 · Company C...	6970 · Utilities	-65.08
*** Missing numbers here ***							
Check	01/15/2012	5007	Automobile Loan C...	Car lease	1110 · Company C...	6131 · Car Le...	-563.00
Check	01/22/2012	5008	Cell Phone Company	Cell	1110 · Company C...	6320 · Teleph...	-101.18
Check	01/22/2012	5009	Fisse Fast Packag...	ACCT# 2560...	1110 · Company C...	6255 · Postag...	-78.00
Check	01/22/2012	5010	Local Phone Comp...	6503221414	1110 · Company C...	6320 · Teleph...	-253.00
Check	01/22/2012	5011	Office Supply Store	Acct# 27804	1110 · Company C...	6310 · Supplies	-634.21
Check	01/25/2012	5012	King, Vicki		1110 · Company C...	6240 · Meals...	-55.00
Check	01/25/2012	5013	Gretton Insurance...	WC Policy #...	1110 · Company C...	-SPLIT-	-231.84
Check	01/25/2012	5014	Payroll Service Co.	Payroll	1110 · Company C...	6278 · Payro...	-127.08
Check	01/25/2012	5015	Pace Shipping Sup...	Acct# 45980	1110 · Company C...	6250 · Office...	-25.00
Check	01/25/2012	5016	Deborah Wood (O...	13103 Exp R...	1110 · Company C...	6330 · Travel	-55.23
Check	01/25/2012	5017	Health Insurance Co.	Employee He...	1110 · Company C...	-SPLIT-	-543.83
Check	01/25/2012	5018	Novello Lights Mag...	Q1 07 Ad	1110 · Company C...	6100 · Adver...	-500.00
Check	01/26/2012	5019	Deborah Wood (O...	Owners Draw	1110 · Company C...	3120 · Debor...	-10,500.00
Check	01/29/2012	5020	Credit Card	ACCT# 3786...	1110 · Company C...	2050 · QuickB...	-95.71
Check	01/29/2012	5021	Gretton Insurance	Liability Ins	1110 · Company C...	1255 · Prepa...	-6,875.00

FIGURE 14-3 A few checks are missing from the QuickBooks bank register.

If a check number is listed in your Missing Checks Report, it's truly missing; it doesn't exist in the register. Investigate the following possible causes:

- You deleted the check that was assigned that number.
- The check is physically missing (usually because somebody grabbed one or more checks to carry around).
- Checks jammed while printing, and you restarted the print run with the number of the first available check (QuickBooks doesn't mark checks as void in that case, it just omits the numbers in the register so they show up in the Missing Checks Report).

Finishing the Reconciliation

If this isn't the first reconciliation you're performing, there's a good chance that the Difference figure at the bottom of the Reconcile window displays 0.00. If there is a difference, refer to "ProAdvisor Recommends: Troubleshooting Differences in the Beginning Balance" later in this chapter.

Click Reconcile Now and print either a summary or detail (or both) Reconciliation Report.

Printing the Reconciliation Report

When you have a balanced reconciliation (even if it results from an adjusting entry), QuickBooks offers congratulations and also offers to print a reconciliation report. (The dialog has a Close button to skip the report, but you should keep a copy of all your reconciliation reports.)

QuickBooks saves the report whether you print it, view it, or cancel it. You can view it in the future by choosing Reports | Banking | Previous Reconciliation.

Deciding on the Type of Report

QuickBooks offers two reconciliation report types: Detail and Summary. Here are the differences between them:

- The Detail Report shows all the transactions that are cleared and all the transactions that haven't cleared (called *in transit* transactions) as of the statement closing date. Any transactions dated after the statement closing date are listed as *new transactions*.
- The Summary Report breaks down your transactions in the same way, but it doesn't list the individual transactions; it shows only the totals for each category: Cleared, Uncleared (in transit), and New.

Selecting the Detail Report makes it easier to resolve problems in the future. You have a list of every check and deposit and when it cleared.

Print vs. Display

You also have to decide whether to print or to display the report. Make your decision according to how you think you might use the report.

Printing a Reconciliation Report

If you opt to print both reports, the Print Reports dialog opens so you can select the printer. If you select either the Summary or Detail Report, the Print Reports dialog offers options, as follows:

- Print the report to the selected printer. You can file the printout in case you ever need to refer to it.
- Print the report to a file. The file option offers several formats in a drop-down list, so you can load the resulting file into the software of your choice. This gives you the opportunity to store multiple reports in one application (or even one file) and sort the data as you wish. The following file options are available:
  - **ASCII text**   Is straight, unformatted text.
  - **Comma delimited**   Automatically puts a comma between each field (column). Select this option if you want to use the file in a spreadsheet or database program capable of importing comma-delimited files. Most spreadsheet software can handle comma-delimited files.
  - **Tab delimited**   Is the same as comma delimited, but the field delimiter is a tab marker instead of a comma. All spreadsheet and database software can handle tab-delimited files.

When you print a report to a disk file, QuickBooks opens a Create Disk File window with the folder that holds your QuickBooks software as the target folder. The file extension matches the file type you selected. You can change the container to any other folder in the system—you might want to create a subfolder in your My Documents folder to hold these files.

Displaying the Reconciliation Report

If you choose to display a report (or both reports), you see the usual QuickBooks report format. You can modify the report to change the font, the columns, and so on. In addition, you can click the Export icon at the top of the report window and send the report to Excel, where you can manipulate the data to match your needs.

Viewing the Last Reconciliation Report

Even if you don't display or print a reconciliation report after you reconcile an account, QuickBooks saves the report. If you're trying to track down a discrepancy in the beginning balance, viewing the last reconciliation report may be helpful.

Click Reports | Banking | Previous Reconciliation to open the Select Previous Reconciliation Report dialog, and select the options for the type and format of the report you want to see.

If You Don't Balance

If the account doesn't reconcile (the Difference figure isn't 0.00), and you don't have the time, energy, or emotional fortitude to track down the problem at the moment, you can stop the reconciliation process without losing all the transactions you cleared.

Click the Leave button in the Reconcile window and do something else for a while. Have dinner, play with the cat, go to the movies, clear your mind. When you restart the reconciliation process, all the entries you made are still there.

Finding and Correcting Problems

When you're ready to investigate the cause of a difference between the ending balance and the cleared balance, follow the guidelines presented here to find the problem.

Count the number of transactions on the bank statement. Then look in the lower-left corner of the Reconcile window, where the number of items you have marked cleared is displayed. Mentally add another item to that number for each of the following:

- A service charge you entered in the Begin Reconciliation box
- An interest amount you entered in the Begin Reconciliation box

If the numbers differ, the problem is in your QuickBooks records; there's a transaction you should have cleared but didn't or a transaction you cleared that you shouldn't have.

If you're sure you didn't make any mistakes clearing transactions, do the following:

- Check the amount of each transaction against the amount in the bank statement.
- Check your transactions and make sure a deposit wasn't inadvertently entered as a payment (or vice versa). A clue for this is a transaction that's half the difference. For example, if the difference is $220.00, find a transaction that has an amount of $110.00 and make sure it's a deduction if it's supposed to be a deduction (or the other way around).
- Check for transposed figures. Perhaps you entered a figure incorrectly in the register, such as $549.00 when the bank clears the transaction as $594.00. A clue that a transposed number is the problem is that the reconciliation difference can be divided by nine.

If you find the problem, correct it. When the Difference figure is 0.00, click Reconcile Now.

> **ProAdvisor Tip:** You might want to let somebody else check over the statement and the register, because sometimes you can't see your own mistakes.

Permitting an Adjusting Entry

If you cannot find the problem, you can tell QuickBooks to make an adjusting entry to force the reconciliation to balance. The adjusting entry is placed in the bank account register and is offset in an expense account named Reconciliation Discrepancies (the account is created automatically the first time you encounter this problem). If you ever figure out what the problem is, you can make the proper adjustment transaction and delete the adjusting entry.

To force a reconciliation, click Reconcile Now, even though there's a difference. A message appears to offer the opportunity to make an adjusting entry. Click Enter Adjustment.

➡ **ProAdvisor Recommends**

Troubleshooting Differences in the Beginning Balance

If this isn't the first time you've reconciled the bank account, the beginning balance that's displayed on the Begin Reconciliation window should match the beginning balance on the bank statement. That beginning balance is simply the ending balance arrived at from the last reconciliation you did.

If the beginning balance doesn't match the statement, it means that you or someone else working in your QuickBooks file did one (or more) of the following:

- You changed the amount on a transaction that had previously cleared.
- You voided a transaction that had previously cleared.
- You deleted a transaction that had previously cleared.
- You removed the cleared check mark from a transaction that had previously cleared.
- You manually entered a cleared check mark on a transaction that had not cleared.

You have to figure out which one of those actions you took after you last reconciled the account, and luckily, QuickBooks has a tool to help you. Click the Locate Discrepancies button on the Begin Reconciliation window to open the Locate Discrepancies dialog seen in Figure 14-4.

FIGURE 14-4   You have tools to help you track down the reason for an incorrect starting balance.

Viewing the Discrepancy Report

Click Discrepancy Report to see if any transactions that were cleared during a past reconciliation were later changed or deleted (see Figure 14-5).

FIGURE 14-5 Someone uncleared a transaction that was cleared during a previous reconciliation.

This report shows you the details of the transactions that cleared during a previous reconciliation if any changes were made to those transactions since that reconciliation. If the Reconciled Amount column shows a positive number, the original cleared transaction was a deposit; a negative number indicates a disbursement.

The Type Of Change column provides a clue about the action you must take to correct the unmatched beginning balances.

- **Uncleared**   Means the check mark was removed in the Cleared column of the register.
- **Deleted**   Means you deleted the transaction.
- **Amount**   Means you changed the amount of the transaction. The difference between the amount in the Reconciled Amount column and the amount in the Effect Of Change column is the amount of the change.

This report doesn't offer a Type Of Change named "Void," so a voided transaction is merely marked as changed, and the text in the Type Of Change column is Amount. A transaction with a changed amount equal to and opposite of the original amount was almost certainly a transaction you voided after it cleared.

Correcting Opening Balance Differences

Use the information in the Discrepancy Report to correct the problems you created by changing previously cleared transactions.

Correcting Changed Transactions

If you cleared or uncleared a transaction manually, open the bank register and undo this action by clicking in the Cleared column (designated by a check mark) until a check mark appears next to the transaction. If you changed the amount of a transaction that had cleared and the transaction still exists in the register with an amount (it's not marked VOID), change the amount back to the original amount for that transaction.

Replacing Voided or Deleted Cleared Transactions

If the beginning balance is incorrect because you removed a transaction that had cleared (either by voiding or deleting it), you have to put the transaction back into your register. You can get the information you need from the Discrepancy Report.

- If a transaction is there but marked VOID, re-enter it, using the data in the reconciliation report. That transaction wasn't void when you performed the last reconciliation; it had cleared. Therefore, it doesn't meet any of the reasons to void a transaction.

- If a transaction appears in the reconciliation report but is not in the register, it was deleted. If it cleared, it can't be deleted. Re-enter it, using the data in the reconciliation report.

- Check the amounts on the printed check reconciliation report against the data in the register to see if any amount was changed after the account was reconciled. If so, restore the original amount.

If you re-enter a transaction that was voided or deleted after it cleared, and you put a check mark into the Cleared Column (the column with a check mark as the column title), QuickBooks adds it to your reconcile window with a check mark already in place. This action doesn't adjust your opening balance on the Begin Reconciliation window, but it does readjust the math so the current reconciliation works and next month's opening balance will be correct.

ProAdvisor Tip: You don't have to be in the Begin Reconciliation window to see a Discrepancy Report. You can view the contents at any time by choosing Reports | Banking | Reconciliation Discrepancy.

Undoing the Last Reconciliation

QuickBooks lets you undo the last reconciliation, which means that all transactions cleared during the reconciliation are uncleared. This is a good way to start over if you're mired in difficulties and confusion during the current reconciliation, and the problems seem to stem from the previous reconciliation (especially if you forced reconciliation by having QuickBooks make an adjusting entry).

Click the Undo Last Reconciliation button on the Begin Reconciliation dialog. QuickBooks suggests you click Cancel and back up your company file before continuing, which is an excellent idea (so you can restore the data in its reconciled state in case this process doesn't work properly). Then, begin reconciling again, click Undo Last Reconciliation, and click Continue.

QuickBooks performs the following actions:

- Removes the cleared status of all transactions you cleared during the last reconciliation.
- Leaves the amounts you entered for interest and bank charges (so don't re-enter them).

When the process completes, QuickBooks displays a message to describe those actions and tell you they were performed. Click OK to clear the message and return to the Begin Reconciliation dialog.

If QuickBooks made an adjustment entry during the last reconciliation, click Cancel to close the Begin Reconciliation dialog. Open the account's register and delete the adjustment entry—it's the entry posted to the Reconciliation Adjustment account. Hopefully, this time the reconciliation will work and you won't need another adjusting entry.

Start the reconciliation process again for the same month you just "undid." When the Begin Reconciliation window opens, the data that appears is the same data that appeared when you started the last reconciliation—the last reconciliation date, the statement date, and the beginning balance are back.

Enter the ending balance from the bank statement. Do *not* enter the interest and bank charges again; they were *not* removed when QuickBooks undid the last reconciliation. Instead, find them in the Reconcile window and clear them (they're not labeled, so you have to look for the appropriate date and amount).

Good luck!

Giving Up the Search for a Reason

You may not be able to find a reason for the difference in the beginning balances. If you've reached the point where it isn't worth your time to keep looking, go ahead and click the Reconcile Now button. QuickBooks will make an adjusting transaction at the end of the reconciliation process that will post to an expense account that is automatically created for you called Reconciliation Discrepancies. If you ever learn the reason for the difference, you can remove the adjustment and post the correct transaction.

Using Online Banking Services

In this chapter:

- Online banking options

- Set up online accounts

- Download account activity into QuickBooks

- Use renaming rules to match payee names

- Create online payments to vendors

- Transfer funds between banks electronically

You can use your Internet connection to access a wide range of online services offered by financial institutions to QuickBooks users, including the following:

- Transaction download, which means you can view the current balances of your bank and credit card accounts, see which transactions have cleared, and control how those transactions get posted into your QuickBooks file.
- Online payments, which means you send vendor checks through your bank, directly from QuickBooks, instead of writing checks.

The QuickBooks Online Banking Center is what you'll use to access to your bank and credit card accounts online, so you can download transactions and enter them into their respective registers.

ProAdvisor Tip: To take advantage of online credit card tracking, you must first set up your credit cards as credit card accounts (account type) in your chart of accounts. If you're not sure how to do this, refer to Chapter 13. You can then follow the steps outlined in this chapter to configure these accounts for online banking.

Understanding Online Banking

With QuickBooks' online banking features, you use the Internet to connect to your financial institution (remember, the term "financial institution" also applies to your credit card companies) and access information about your accounts. QuickBooks supports two methods for online banking services, as listed next. Many financial institutions offer one method, while some offer both.

- **Web Connect** This is the method you use when your financial institution doesn't provide a way to connect your QuickBooks data directly to the data on their own server. Instead, there's a page on the bank's website that lets you view and download your transactions or statement and import the downloaded file into QuickBooks.
- **Direct Connect** With this method, your financial institution exchanges data interactively with QuickBooks. This allows you to take advantage of all types of additional online banking services, such as transaction data downloads directly into your QuickBooks bank register, transfers between bank accounts, electronic messages between you and the financial institution, and online bill payments (optional at some financial institutions). Some financial institutions charge a fee for some or all of the services available through Direct Connect.

Setting Up Online Banking

To use online banking, your bank must support at least one QuickBooks online access feature. There are three online banking services available:

- Transaction download
- Online credit card services
- Online bill paying

You can sign up for any or all of these services. If your bank supports only online account access and doesn't support online bill paying or online credit card services, you can still work directly with the QuickBooks online banking services to automate your bill payment process. See "Using QuickBooks to Pay Your Bills Online" later in this chapter.

The process of enabling online banking has three steps:

1. Apply for online services with your bank.
2. Receive a personal identification number (PIN) or password from your bank to make sure your online account is secure. This may or may not be the same password you currently use for online account access.
3. Enable a QuickBooks account (or multiple accounts) for online services.

Once a QuickBooks bank account is enabled for online banking, you can download transaction information from your bank and match it to your bank register. To get started, choose Banking | Online Banking from the menu bar. The submenu has the following commands related to online banking services:

- Online Banking Center
- Set Up Account For Online Services
- Participating Financial Institutions
- Import Web Connect File
- Create Online Banking Message (to your financial institution)
- Change Online Banking Mode
- Inquire About Online Bill Payment

Finding Your Bank Online

If you haven't signed up for (or discussed) online services with your bank, and you're not sure if your bank has online services, choose Participating Financial Institutions to see if your bank participates. QuickBooks may display a dialog telling you it has to open an Internet browser. Click OK, and when you're connected to the Internet, you see the Financial Institutions Directory website (see Figure 15-1).

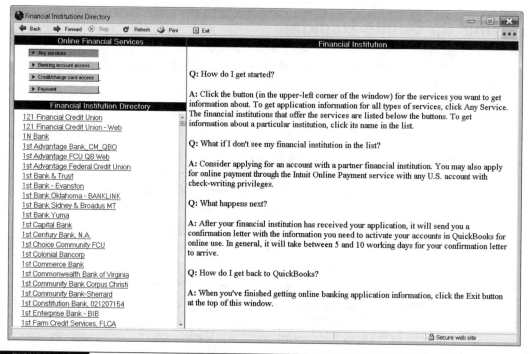

FIGURE 15-1 Select the type of online service you want, and then scroll through the list to see if your bank is included.

The four choices at the top of the left pane determine the contents of the Financial Institutions Directory list that QuickBooks displays. The window opens with the choice labeled Any Services preselected, and all the banks listed provide some type of online service.

If you're interested in a particular online service (for example, you only care about bank account access to download transactions), select that option, and the list of banks changes to those banks that offer the selected service.

Scroll through the list to find your bank and click its listing. The right pane of the Financial Institutions Directory window displays information about your bank's online services (see Figure 15-2). If your bank isn't listed, you cannot set up any QuickBooks online banking services.

Click the Apply Now button if you want to start the application process here and now. If no Apply Now button exists, follow the instructions for setting up online services at the bank—usually the bank displays a phone number. If online applications

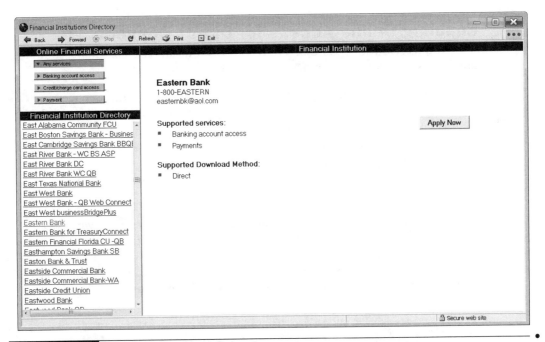

FIGURE 15-2   This bank has Direct Connect.

are available, fill out the form and submit the information. Your bank will send you information about using its online service, a login name (sometimes called a company ID), and a PIN or a password. This is the information you need to enable the bank account for online access.

After you've completed the paperwork at your bank and received your login ID and a PIN or a password, QuickBooks walks you through the process of enabling your bank account for online banking in QuickBooks.

Those steps differ depending on whether your bank uses Direct Connect or Web Connect. The following sections cover both scenarios.

> **ProAdvisor Tip:** Accounts that are enabled for online access have a symbol that looks like a lightning bolt in the Online Access column of your chart of accounts—the column heading doesn't say "Online Access," it just has the lightning bolt symbol.

Enabling Online Access for Direct Connect

After you receive your ID and PIN or password, you can enable a bank account for online access with Direct Connect in any of the following ways:

- Choose Banking | Online Banking | Setup Account For Online Services and select the bank account you want to configure for online services in the Set Up Account For Online Services dialog.
- Open an existing bank account (select the account in the Chart of Accounts List and press CTRL-E) and click Set Up Online Services.
- Click Yes in the Set Up Online Services dialog that appears when you create a new bank account.

QuickBooks opens the Set Up Account For Online Services For *<Name you used for your bank account in the chart of accounts>* dialog seen in Figure 15-3. Select your bank from the drop-down list of participating financial institutions and click Next. (You don't have to scroll through the list; instead, as you type the characters for the name of your bank, QuickBooks moves to the appropriate listing.)

FIGURE 15-3   The first step is to select your bank.

ProAdvisor Tip: If your bank has a nationwide presence with regional headquarters, after you select the bank you may see a second dialog asking you to select the appropriate bank region. For example, if your bank is BigAsTheNation, you may have to select BigAsTheNation-Massachusetts if the bank you use is part of that division.

QuickBooks contacts the bank over the Internet (to determine the information your bank requires to configure your bank account for online access), and then displays information about the bank's online access. As you can see in Figure 15-4, this bank requires a PIN (it offers Direct Connect). QuickBooks reminds you that if you signed up for your bank's own website-based online banking features, the User ID and password required to enter that website may be different from the User ID and PIN/password required for access via QuickBooks (your financial institution sets these rules).

FIGURE 15-4 This bank requires a PIN for Direct Connect.

Click Next and use the information the bank sent you to fill in the fields for your Customer ID and PIN/password (see Figure 15-5). Depending on the way your bank maintains account information to configure online services, you may be asked to enter a routing number for the bank and the account number for your bank account instead of only the Customer ID and PIN.

FIGURE 15-5 Enter the data the bank sent you.

Click Sign In to access your bank account online. QuickBooks contacts the bank over the Internet and downloads the transactions for your bank account, displaying a dialog that tells you how many transactions were downloaded. Click Finish to open the Online Banking Center automatically, where you can view the downloaded transactions (using the Online Banking Center and matching transactions is covered later in this chapter).

Enabling Online Access for Web Connect

After you receive your login information from your bank, you can enable a bank account for online access with Web Connect in any of the following ways:

- Choose Banking | Online Banking | Setup Account For Online Services and select the bank account you want to configure for online services.
- Open an existing bank account (select the account in the Chart of Accounts List and press CTRL-E) and click Set Up Online Services.
- Click Yes in the Set Up Online Services dialog that asks you whether you want to enable this new account for online services.

QuickBooks opens the Set Up Account For Online Services For *<Name you used for your bank account in the chart of accounts>* dialog. Select your bank from the drop-down list. You don't have to scroll through the list; instead, as you type the characters for the name of your bank, QuickBooks moves to the appropriate listing.

Click Next to have QuickBooks connect to your bank's website to check the bank's type of online services (which will be Web Connect). QuickBooks displays the dialog seen in Figure 15-6.

FIGURE 15-6 To enable a bank account for Web Connect online services, you must download a transactions file from the bank's website.

Click the button labeled Go To My Bank's Web Site. QuickBooks opens its Help files with instructions, information, and explanations about connecting to banks that offer Web Connect.

If you see a message telling you that QuickBooks must launch a browser and connect to the Internet, click OK (no, wait, click the option labeled Do Not Display This Message In The Future, *then* click OK).

When QuickBooks connects to your bank's website, use the login information the bank gave you when you signed up for online services. Depending on the type of software the bank uses, you may be asked for a company ID and a User ID (or both), as well as a password. Some bank software doesn't present the password field on the same web page as the sign-in ID; instead, you must click Continue or Next to move to the web page that asks for your password.

Click the button or link that connects you to your account transactions. The label might be Reports, Reporting, Download Statements, Download Transactions, Exports, or any other terminology that indicates, "Get a report on account activity."

In the options or criteria page, select QuickBooks File as the report type. Your bank may have several choices for QuickBooks files, for instance, according to the version (year). Some banks use a file named "QBO file" instead of "QuickBooks File."

Your bank probably displays criteria selections for a date range (yesterday, today, or a From Date To Date range of dates) and may also offer an option labeled Since Last Download (which you can select after this initial download).

After you make your selections and click the appropriate button (Generate, Download, or some other similar label), your bank generates the file and displays a File Download dialog asking whether you want to open the file or save it to your computer.

- If you click Save, QuickBooks downloads the file to your computer and saves it in a folder you select. When you're ready to import the file and view it in the Online Banking Center, choose File | Utilities | Import | Web Connect Files and select the file you saved.
- If you click Open, QuickBooks asks if you want to import the file into your bank account now, or save it and import it later.

In addition, the first time you import your Web Connect file into QuickBooks, the Select Bank Account window will appear where you'll be given two options to link the downloaded file to a QuickBooks bank account:

- If you've already created this bank account in QuickBooks, select the option Use An Existing QuickBooks Account, and then select the account from the drop-down list. Click Continue and QuickBooks enables the account for online access.

- If you haven't created this bank account in QuickBooks, select the option Create A New QuickBooks Account, and then click Continue. QuickBooks creates a new bank account automatically, naming it Checking At <*Name of Bank*> and enables the account for online access.

QuickBooks displays a message telling you the data has been imported.

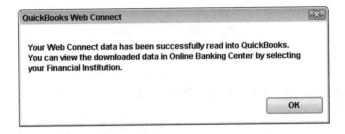

Click OK to open the Online Banking Center so you can view the downloaded data and match it to your bank register. Hereafter, you use the Online Banking Center to download your transaction data.

Using the Online Banking Center

To connect to your financial institution, choose Banking | Online Banking | Online Banking Center to open the Online Banking Center window.

If you've just enabled an account for online banking and downloaded transactions for the first time, the Online Banking Center opens automatically and you can skip the beginning of this section that tells you how to effect a transaction download— go right to the section on viewing the downloaded transactions. From now on you'll both download and view transactions from the Online Banking Center.

If you have online banking at more than one financial institution, select the appropriate one from the drop-down list in the Financial Institution field at the top of the window. For example, you may have online bank account access at one financial institution and online credit card access at another.

ProAdvisor Tip: If your financial institution supports Web Connect and not Direct Connect, you can only download transactions; all the other functions covered in this section (such as exchanging electronic messages, making online payments within QuickBooks, and so on) are available only for Direct Connect.

Downloading Transactions

To download transactions from your bank, open the Online Banking Center and click Send/Receive Transactions.

- For Direct Connect, QuickBooks opens the Access To *<Name of Bank>* dialog. Enter your PIN and click OK. QuickBooks automatically downloads new transactions.
- For Web Connect, QuickBooks connects to the bank's website, where you must log in and then select a QuickBooks download (as described earlier in this chapter).

Viewing the Downloaded Transactions

When your data has been downloaded, the Online Banking Center dialog displays a summary of the items received from your bank in the Items Received section. There are two ways to view and enter transactions: Side-by-Side mode (as shown in Figure 15-7) and Register mode. If you used online banking in a previous QuickBooks version—specifically, QuickBooks 2008 and earlier—then you're already familiar with Register mode, which lets you see your full register when matching transactions. Both modes offer the same functionality, with the exception that the renaming rules created in Side-by-Side mode are not available in Register mode. Likewise, aliases created in Register mode are not available in Side-by-Side mode. To switch between online banking modes, choose Banking | Online Banking | Change Online Banking Mode. If this is your first time using QuickBooks Online Banking, I recommend you choose Side-by-Side mode.

ProAdvisor Tip: After the first time you download transactions, QuickBooks checks your company file to see which transactions were already downloaded and downloads only transactions not downloaded previously. This means you don't have to worry about duplicate transactions.

Matching Transactions

To match downloaded transactions to your QuickBooks bank register, click the button labeled Add Transactions To QuickBooks and select the account. QuickBooks displays the downloaded transactions (see Figure 15-7).

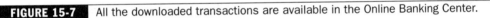

Add Transactions To QuickBooks

Change Online Banking Mode   Contact Info   Video Tutorial   Renaming Rules

Downloaded Transactions
Checking

1 Matched to existing QuickBooks/register transactions   Show
0 New transactions created using renaming rules
6 Unmatched Transactions

7 Total to be reviewed and added to QuickBooks

Status	▲ Date	No.	Desc	Pmt	Dep
Unmatched	11/13/2012		ATM With...	200.00	
Unmatched	11/13/2012	239		1,297.75	
Unmatched	11/14/2012	242		3,200.00	
Unmatched	11/14/2012	243		850.00	
Unmatched	11/15/2012		Deposit		2,080.
Matched	11/30/2012		Bank Seve...	9.00	

Add Multiple...   Select Items To Delete...

Add Transactions to QuickBooks

Select a transaction in the Downloaded Transactions list...

...then match or create transactions such as:
- Checks or credit card charges
- Bill payments
- Deposits
- Credit card payments or credits
- General journal entries

Note: Go to the appropriate QuickBooks form to create sales receipts or expenses with items.

Finish Later

FIGURE 15-7   All the downloaded transactions are available in the Online Banking Center.

QuickBooks automatically tries to match the transactions in the file to the transactions in your register and marks the status of each transaction with one of the following conditions: In the example shown in Figure 15-7, all but one of the transactions are unmatched.

- **Matched**   Means the downloaded transaction matches a transaction already entered directly in the register. To attempt a match, QuickBooks looks at check numbers, amounts, dates, and the payee name.
- **Unmatched**   Means no match was found in your register for the downloaded transaction.

By default, only the unmatched transactions are listed in the left pane of the window. The top of the left pane displays the number of matched transactions but doesn't display the details. If you have matched transactions and want to see the details, click the link labeled Show and QuickBooks displays the matched transactions (as shown in Figure 15-7). To hide the matched transactions listings, click the Hide link that appears at the top of the window. (Since you don't need to do anything with matched transactions, it's easier to work with the list when those transactions are removed.)

The top of the left pane also displays the number of transactions matched via Renaming Rules (see the "ProAdvisor Recommends: Renaming Rules").

▶ ProAdvisor Recommends

Renaming Rules

A renaming rule is what you use to tell QuickBooks that you want to use a particular name for a vendor or payee when a transaction is downloaded into QuickBooks from them. For example, if you use a credit card (from which you download transactions) to purchase gas for your car at four different Exxon stations, these four transactions can be presented as four different payees when downloaded via the Online Banking Center: ExxonStation #100001, ExxonStation#1000002, ExxonStation#1000003, and ExxonStation#1000004. In QuickBooks, you probably want to refer to that vendor as Exxon. When you download your credit card transactions and there is no matching vendor in your register, QuickBooks will assign it the name you designate (rather than create four new vendors) and will post it in your register to the category you intended.

If all the downloaded transactions are matched, you have nothing else to do except tell QuickBooks to confirm the match. QuickBooks inserts a lightning bolt in the Cleared column of your bank register (the column with a check mark heading) for every matched transaction, indicating that the transaction has cleared the bank. Whenever you open the register, you know which transactions have been matched with downloaded transactions:

- A check mark indicates a transaction has been through bank reconciliation.
- A lightning bolt indicates a transaction has been downloaded as cleared but has not been through a bank reconciliation.

Chapter 14 covers the topic of bank reconciliations.

Adding Transactions to the Bank Register

Many users (especially those who don't print checks in QuickBooks) don't bother to enter all transactions in the bank register. They use the download file to accomplish the task. This isn't a good way to keep accounting records, because you don't know which transactions are outstanding.

Even if you enter all your checks and customer receipts in QuickBooks, sometimes you have to wait for your bank to tell you whether the transaction has cleared to learn the amount of the transaction (such as merchant card receipts or payments taken out of your bank automatically by a vendor).

To add an unmatched transaction to the bank register, select its listing in the left pane of the Add Transactions To QuickBooks window. Depending on the type of transaction (payment or deposit), the right pane displays options for adding the transaction to the bank register.

Adding a Downloaded Payment to the Register

When you select an unmatched payment, QuickBooks opens the Record An Expense window in the right pane (see Figure 15-8).

If the vendor exists in your company file, select the vendor from the drop-down list in the Payee field.

FIGURE 15-8   A downloaded payment is assumed to be an expense.

If the vendor name on the downloaded transactions doesn't exist in your company file, you have several options:

- Select <Add New> to add the vendor name to your company file and then finish entering the transaction.
- Enter the transaction without a vendor name (which is appropriate only for those payments to vendors you don't care about tracking, such as monthly payments for merchant account charges or your bank's monthly service charges).
- Enter the transaction without a vendor name, and create the vendor after you're finished with the Online Banking window. Then edit the transaction to add the vendor name.
- Link the vendor name on the downloaded transaction to a vendor name in your company file via a renaming rule.

If the payment is posted to multiple accounts, or should be linked to a customer (or both), clicking the link Show Splits, Memo, Date, Number opens an entry window that looks like Figure 15-9.

FIGURE 15-9   Enter the payment with the details you need.

If the downloaded payment represents a check or online payment you created to pay a vendor bill that is entered in your system, click the link More Matching Options and select the option Select Open Bills To Pay In QuickBooks.

In the Vendor field, select the vendor with an open A/P bill that this downloaded payment is linked to. QuickBooks displays the open bills for the vendor.

Select the bill to pay with this transaction, and change the paid amount if the transaction represented a partial payment. You can also select multiple bills for this vendor, if you paid more than one bill with this payment. QuickBooks does some quick arithmetic to make sure that all the bills you select total up to match the downloaded amount.

Adding a Downloaded Deposit to the Register

When you select a downloaded deposit, the right pane of the Online Banking Center displays the Record A QuickBooks Deposit window, which could have either or both of the following tabs:

- Undeposited Funds, which contains all the current transactions waiting for deposit (the transactions you see when you open the Make Deposits window). If no entries exist in Undeposited Funds, the tab isn't displayed.
- Open Invoices, which lists all the current open invoices in your company file. If no open invoices exist, the tab isn't displayed.

Choose the appropriate tab, and then choose the matching transaction (or multiple transactions that total up to the amount of the downloaded transaction).

If the merchant card company deducts fees before depositing the sale, the downloaded transaction amount is lower than the amount received for the sale. To match the amount, enter those fees in this window, in the next blank row. Click the From Account column and select the merchant account fees expense account. Then, in the Amount column, enter the difference between the original transaction and the downloaded deposit (it's a minus amount). The net amount matches the downloaded transaction, which you can deposit into your account by clicking the Add To QuickBooks button at the bottom of the window.

Deleting Unmatched Transactions

Sometimes the download file contains transactions that can't be matched. This usually occurs when you don't download transactions frequently, and some of the transactions you download have already been cleared during a reconciliation. You can't match transactions (even manually) that have already been reconciled within QuickBooks.

You should delete these transactions; otherwise, they'll be there waiting for you every time you download new transactions. Click the button labeled Select Items To Delete at the bottom of the left pane. QuickBooks opens the Select Items To Delete dialog, where you can get rid of the transactions you don't want to see again.

The top of the dialog offers two options:

- Select Individual Transactions, which leaves the selection check boxes unchecked until you manually click each box to delete its transaction.
- Select All Download Transactions Older Than *<Date>*, which automatically adds check marks to the check boxes of transactions that are older than the specified date.

C a u t i o n : The Select Items To Delete dialog includes matched transactions, so pay attention to the Status column to avoid deleting transactions you've matched.

Using QuickBooks to Pay Your Bills Online

When you pay your bills or write checks, QuickBooks gives you the option of sending these payments electronically to your vendors. You can either use your own bank to transmit these payments to your vendors (if it offers online bill payment services or Direct Connect), or use the QuickBooks Bill Pay Service and have QuickBooks send these payments for you. Refer to the section "Finding Your Bank Online" earlier in this chapter to determine if your bank offers a bill payment service.

Using the QuickBooks Bill Pay Service

From the Banking menu, select Online Banking | Participating Financial Institutions. When the Financial Institutions list appears, scroll through the list to find "QuickBooks Bill Pay–New!" in the left pane (see Figure 15-10).

When you select this option, the right pane displays some information about the service. Click the Apply Now button to start the sign-up process.

Once you've completed the sign-up process, you can use either the Write Checks or Pay Bills feature in QuickBooks as you normally would. If you are writing a check instead of selecting To Be Printed, select Online Payment. Be sure to fill in the date that you want the payment to be delivered (you can only schedule a payment up to one year in advance). If you are using the Pay Bills feature, pay your bills as you normally would and select Online Payment as your payment method. Again, choose the date that you want the payment delivered.

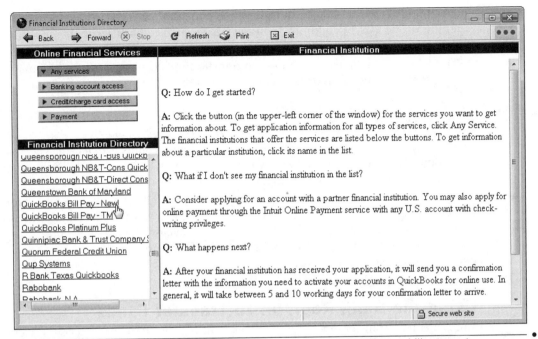

FIGURE 15-10 Sign up for the QuickBooks Bill Pay Service to simplify your bill payment process.

After you've entered your checks or paid your bills, open the Online Banking Center and click the Send/Receive Transactions button.

If your vendor is set up to receive electronic payments (meaning that the company is part of the national electronic payment database), QuickBooks will electronically transfer your payments from your bank to your vendor/payee on the date you've specified. If your vendor is not able to receive electronic payments, a paper check (generated by the QuickBooks Bill Pay Service) is sent via U.S. mail.

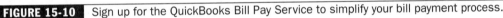

Transferring Money Between Accounts Online

If you have multiple accounts at your financial institution and the financial institution uses Direct Connect, you can transfer money between those accounts within QuickBooks. For example, you may have a money market account for your business in addition to your checking account.

To transfer money online, you must have applied at your financial institution for online banking for both accounts. You'll probably have a unique PIN for each account. (To make your life less complicated, you should make changes while you're online to ensure both accounts have the same PIN, so you don't inadvertently enter the wrong PIN.) In addition, you must have enabled both accounts for online access within QuickBooks.

There are two methods you can use to transfer funds between online accounts: the transfer funds function or direct data entry in the register for either account.

Using the Transfer Funds Function

The simplest way to move money between your online accounts is to use the QuickBooks Transfer Funds Between Accounts window, which you reach by choosing Banking | Transfer Funds from the menu bar.

Specify the sending and receiving accounts (remember, both must be enabled for Direct Connect online access) and enter the amount you want to transfer. Be sure to select the option for Online Funds Transfer. Click Save & Close. Then choose Banking | Online Banking Center, make sure the transaction has a check mark, and click Send/Receive Transactions.

Using the Bank Register to Transfer Funds

You can enter a transfer directly into the account register of the bank account from which you are sending the money. The significant data entry is the one in the Check Number column; instead of a check number, type the word **SEND**. Don't enter a payee; enter the amount, and then enter the receiving bank account in the Account field. Then choose Banking | Online Banking | Online Banking Center, make sure the transaction is listed in the Items To Send section and has a check mark, and click Send/Receive Transactions.

Receiving Customer Payments Online

Besides the online activities that permit you to track your own bank account activity, transfer money, and pay your own bills, QuickBooks offers a way for your customers to pay you online. This is a fee-based service provided by the Intuit PaymentNetwork service.

If you sign up for this service, you can notify your customers about this feature by e-mailing the invoice with the online service URL in the cover note, or by snail-mailing the invoice and sending an e-mail message with the online service URL. The customer clicks the link to the URL to travel to the QuickBooks website and arrange for payment by either their credit card or bank account.

To learn more about this service or to sign up, from the Online Services menu select Intuit PaymentNetwork | About PaymentNetwork.

Tracking Time
and Mileage

I n this chapter:

- Track time in QuickBooks
- Work with QuickBooks timesheets
- Track mileage

You can track time and mileage and use this information to recover reimbursable costs from customers, develop an accurate job costing system, prepare tax returns, analyze expenses, and pay employees. All the tools you need to perform these functions are available in QuickBooks, and they are covered in this chapter.

Your QuickBooks software includes built-in time-tracking that lets you record the amount of time you and your staff spend completing a project or doing work for a customer or for your company, such as administrative tasks. This chapter covers how to configure and use this feature. For businesses that need the ability to have their employees or consultants enter their time from anywhere and at any time, QuickBooks offers an online time-tracking solution called QuickBooks Time Tracker.

You can use this fee-based QuickBooks Time Tracker service to let timekeepers fill out their timesheets online (a real convenience for off-site workers). QuickBooks Time is easy to use and administer for both the company bookkeeper and the workers. To fill out timesheets, workers only need access to a computer that can reach the Internet. The computer they use does not need QuickBooks or any other software. This means workers who are performing tasks at customer sites or working at home can easily track and report their time.

To learn more about this service, and to sign up for a free 60-day trial, choose Employees | Enter Time | Let Your Employees Enter Time.

Setting Up Time Tracking

When you create a company in QuickBooks, if you respond "yes" when asked if you want to track time, QuickBooks turns on the built-in time-tracking features.

If you're not sure whether you turned on time tracking when you installed your company, choose Edit | Preferences from the QuickBooks menu bar. Select Time &

Expenses by scrolling to the last category in the left pane, and click the Company Preferences tab. Make sure the Yes option is selected.

By default, QuickBooks assumes your workweek starts on Monday. However, some businesses use a different workweek, such as a Sunday-to-Saturday pattern for tracking time. If you're tracking time for employees and you plan to use the timesheets for payroll, it's a good idea to match the workweek to the week your pay period covers.

Configuring Timekeepers

You can track time for your employees, outside contractors (vendors), or yourself. Everyone who must keep track of his or her time has to first exist in the system and, of course, must fill out a timesheet.

Setting Up Employees

If you're running the QuickBooks payroll feature, you already have employees in your QuickBooks system, and you can use timesheets to track their time. Optionally, you can also use their timesheet data to create a paycheck, using the number of hours reported on the timesheet. For this to work, however, you must modify the employee record as follows:

1. Open the Employee Center.
2. Click the Employees tab to display the list of employees.
3. Double-click the listing of the employee you want to link to time tracking.
4. In the Change Tabs field at the top of the window, select Payroll And Compensation Info from the drop-down list.
5. Select the Use Time Data To Create Paychecks check box (see Figure 16-1).
6. Click OK.

You don't have to link employees to time tracking in order for them to use timesheets to record their time—your employees can track time unconnected to the preparation of paychecks in order to make it possible to create job costing reports, or to invoice customers for their time.

FIGURE 16-1   Link employees to time tracking if you want to use timesheets to prepare paychecks automatically.

Even if you're not doing your own payroll in QuickBooks, you can create employees (in the Employee Center) for the purpose of tracking time, and you can use the timesheet data for an outside payroll service.

Tracking Vendor Time

Any vendor in your system who is paid for his or her time can have that time tracked for the purpose of billing customers. Most of the time, these vendors are outside contractors or subcontractors. You don't have to do anything special to the vendor record to enable time tracking; you just need to record their time in a timesheet. If you want to bill the customer for those hours for which the service was performed, mark their time as "billable" on their timesheet (covered in the "Working with Timesheets" section).

Tracking Other Worker Time

You may need to track the time of people who are neither employees nor vendors. QuickBooks provides a system list called Other Names, and you can use this list to collect names that don't fit in the other QuickBooks lists. Following are some situations in which you'll need to use the Other Names list:

- You have employees and use QuickBooks payroll, but you are not an employee because you take a draw instead of a paycheck. In this case, you should add your name to the Other Names list if you want to track your own time.
- You have employees and are not using QuickBooks payroll, so there is no Employee List in your system. You should add each employee name to the Other Names list to track employee time.
- You have no employees and your business is a proprietorship or a partnership. Owner or partner names should be entered into the Other Names list in order to track time.

Configuring the Tasks

Most of the tasks you track in timesheets already exist in your system as service items. These are the items you use when you invoice customers for services. However, because you can use time tracking to analyze the way people in your organization spend their time, you may want to add service items that aren't connected to tasks performed for customers.

For example, if you want to track the time people spend performing administrative tasks for the business, you can add a service item called Administrative to your items list. If you want to be more specific, you can name the particular administrative tasks you want to track (for example, bookkeeping, equipment repair, new sales calls, public relations, and so on).

To enter new items, choose Lists | Item List from the menu bar. When the Item List window opens, press CTRL-N to open the New Item dialog. Select Service as the item type (only service items are tracked in timesheets) and name the new item. Here are some guidelines for administrative items:

- If you're specifying administrative tasks, create a service named Administration and then make each specific administrative task a subitem of Administration.
- Don't put an amount in the Rate box unless every employee and outside contractor performing this service has the same hourly pay rate (highly unlikely). You can enter the amount when you make the payment (via payroll or vendor checks).
- Because QuickBooks insists that you assign an account to a service, choose or create a "dummy" (or placeholder) revenue account (such as Other Revenue or Time Tracking Revenue). Don't worry, no money is ever posted to the account because you don't ever sell these services directly to customers.

Working with Timesheets

The built-in QuickBooks timesheet feature offers two methods for recording the time your timekeepers spend on tasks: Single Activity and Weekly Timesheet.

- Single Activity is a form you use to enter what you did when you performed a single task at a specific time on a specific date. For example, a Single Activity form may record the fact that you made a telephone call on behalf of a customer, you repaired some piece of equipment for a customer, or you performed some administrative task for the company.
- Weekly Timesheet is a form in which you indicate how much time and on which date you performed work. Each Weekly Timesheet entry can also include the name of the customer for whom the work was performed.

Your decision about which method to use depends on the type of work you do and how often you intend to generate invoices to your customers based on your employees' time.

ProAdvisor Tip: After you fill out and save a Single Activity form, you can open a Weekly Timesheet to view all the single activities that have been entered within that week—they are automatically inserted there for you.

Setting the Format for Displaying Time

When you enter time in the various timesheet forms, you can use either the hh:mm format or a decimal format such as 6.5. To establish a default, choose Edit | Preferences and click the General category. Then select the Company Preferences tab and use the options in the Time Format section of the dialog to select the format you prefer.

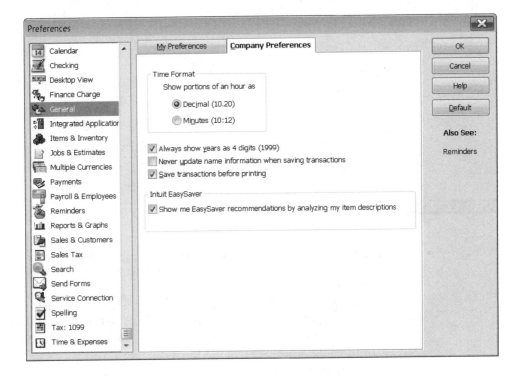

If you set the preference to decimal, and then enter time as 1:30, when you press TAB to move to the next field, QuickBooks changes the entry to 1.50 (or the other way around).

Tracking a Single Activity

To track one event or task with a Single Activity form (see Figure 16-2), choose Employees | Enter Time | Time/Enter Single Activity. Use the following guidelines to use this form.

FIGURE 16-2 Fill out the details to indicate how you spent your time.

- The Date field is automatically filled in with the current date. If this activity took place previously, you can change the date (but you cannot change the date if you're using the stopwatch).
- Click the arrow to the right of the Name field and select the name of the person who performed the work from the drop-down list. The list contains vendors, employees, and names from the Other Names list. Most of the time, the worker who performed the work is filling out the form.
- Select the customer or job in the Customer:Job field. Do this whether or not the customer is going to be billed for the time.
- In the Service Item field, select the task, and in the Duration box, enter the amount of time you're reporting.
- If this time is billable to the customer, the Billable check box should be marked (it is by default). If the time is not going to be billed to the customer (it's going to be tracked for job costing), click the box to remove the check mark.
- If the Payroll Item field appears, select the payroll item that applies to this time (for example, salary or hourly wages). This field appears only if the selected name is an employee and the employee record has been linked to the time-tracking system (explained earlier in this chapter).
- If the Class field appears, you can optionally assign the time to a class.

ProAdvisor Tip: If you've linked the employee to the time tracking system and you've also enabled class tracking, you won't see the Class field unless you turn on the "Earnings Item" option in Payroll & Employee Preferences (see Figure 16-3).

FIGURE 16-3 Enable the Earnings Item option in Payroll & Employee preferences if you want to assign an employee's payroll expense to a class.

- Use the Notes box to enter any comments or additional information you want to record about this activity. You can then transfer those notes onto the invoice that you generate using this timesheet data and they can be included in job reports as well.

When you've finished creating the activity, click Save & New to fill out another Single Activity form (many workers perform multiple single activities each day) or click Save & Close to finish.

Caution: The first time you select an employee that is not configured for using time data to create paychecks, QuickBooks asks if you'd like to change that configuration. If the employee is just tracking time for job-costing purposes and is not paid from these timesheets, click No.

Using the Stopwatch

You can let QuickBooks track the time you're spending on a specific task. Click the Start button in the Duration box of the Activity window when you begin the task to start the stopwatch. QuickBooks tracks hours and minutes as they elapse.

- To pause the counting when you're interrupted, click Pause. Then click Start to pick up where you left off.
- To stop timing, click Stop. The elapsed time is displayed.

The stopwatch always displays time in the hh:mm:ss format. If you set your format preference to decimal, QuickBooks converts the time when the stopwatch is stopped.

Using Weekly Timesheets

A Weekly Timesheet records the same information as the Single Activity form, except that the information is recorded in week-at-a-time blocks and you have the option to "batch" enter the same timesheet information for multiple timekeepers (both employees and nonemployees).

To use this form (shown in Figure 16-4), choose Employees | Enter Time | Use Weekly Timesheet. Use the instructions that follow to fill out the timesheet.

1. Select either an individual employee or vendor name from the drop-down list in the Name field. Optionally, choose either Payroll or Nonpayroll Multiple Names to create multiple timesheets with the same information for the names you've selected in your list. This latter option is useful if you've got a team of employees or contractors working on the same project and performing the same work for the week.

2. The current week appears by default; click the calendar icon if you need to select a different week.

3. In the Customer:Job column, select the customer or job connected to the activity (or select the in-house listing to enter administrative work unconnected to a customer).

Customer:Job	Service Item	Payroll I...	Notes	Class	M 3	Tu 4	W 5	Th 6	F 7	Sa 8	Su 9	Total	Billable?
Access Appliances	Custom Work				8.00	8.00	8.00					24.00	☑
Baker's Professional Lighting ▾	Custom Work ▾	▾		▾				8.00	8.00			16.00	☑

Totals 8.00 8.00 8.00 8.00 8.00 0.00 0.00 40.00

FIGURE 16-4 Some people find it easier to enter information on a weekly basis.

4. In the Service Item column, select the appropriate service item.

5. For an employee whose paycheck is linked to timesheets, use the Payroll Item column to select the Payroll Item that fits the activity. (If the name selected in the Name field is not an employee whose paycheck is linked to timesheets, the Payroll Item column disappears.)

6. In the Notes column, enter any necessary notes or comments.

7. Click the column that represents the day in which an activity occurred and enter the number of hours worked on this task. Repeat across the week for each day that the same activity was performed for the same customer or job.

8. Move to the beginning of the next row to enter a different activity, or the same activity for a different customer, repeating this action until the timesheet is filled in for the week.

9. For each row, indicate whether the time is billable in the Billable column. By default, all time entries linked to a customer are marked as billable (except for vendor time entries, which default to not billable). Click the check box to remove the check mark in the Billable column if the time on this row is not billable.

10. Click Save & New to use a timesheet for a different week. Click Save & Close when you are finished entering time.

Copying Previous Timesheets

You can copy the previous week's timesheet by clicking the Copy Last Sheet button after you enter the current date in the timesheet window and select a name. This is useful for workers who have similar timesheet data every week. This description frequently applies to your office staff or to outside contractors who are performing a large job that takes multiple weeks.

For some employees, whose work is usually for the office and not charged to a customer, the timesheet may be identical from week to week.

Reporting Timesheet Information

Before you use the information on the timesheets to invoice customers (covered later in this chapter in the section "Invoicing Customers for Time") or pay workers, you should go over the data on the timesheet reports. You can view and customize reports, edit information, and print the original timesheets.

Running Timesheet Reports

To run reports on timesheets, choose Reports | Jobs, Time & Mileage. You'll see a long list of available reports, but the following reports provide information on time tracking:

- **Time By Job Summary** Reports the amount of time spent for each service on your customers and jobs.
- **Time By Job Detail** Reports the details of the time spent for each customer and job, including dates and whether or not the time was marked as billable. A billing status of Unbilled indicates the time is billable but hasn't yet been used on a customer invoice.
- **Time By Name** Reports the amount of time each user tracked.
- **Time By Item** Provides an analysis of the amount of time spent on each service your company provides, including the customers for whom the services were performed.

Editing Entries in a Report

While you're browsing the report, you can double-click an activity listing to navigate to the original entry. You can make changes in the original entry, such as selecting or deselecting the billable option or change the Notes field by adding a note or editing the content of the existing note.

Editing the Original Timesheets

Before you use the timesheets for customer billing or payroll, make sure you examine them and make any needed corrections. In fact, you may want to take this step before you view any of the Jobs & Time reports.

The most common revision is the billable status. If you have outside contractors or employees filling out timesheets, it's not unusual to have some confusion about which customers receive direct time billings. In fact, you may have customers to whom you send direct time bills only for certain activities and provide the remaining activities as part of your basic services.

To check timesheets, just open a new weekly timesheet and enter the name of the person connected to the timesheet you want to view. Use the Previous or Next arrows at the top of the timesheet window or use the calendar icon to move to the timesheet you want to inspect. Then edit the information as necessary:

- If needed, change the number of hours for any activity item.
- Change the billable status.
- View (and edit if necessary) any notes.

C a u t i o n : If you've already used the timesheet data to create an invoice for the customer or to pay the employee, the changes you make to the timesheet do not automatically update these documents.

Printing the Weekly Timesheets

It's a common practice to have employees print their weekly timesheets and deliver them to the person responsible for monitoring and managing employee hours. And it's not uncommon for this person to handle your payroll-related activities as well.

To print timesheets, choose File | Print Forms | Timesheets from the QuickBooks menu bar to open the Select Timesheets To Print window shown in Figure 16-5.

- Change the date range to match the timesheets you want to print.
- By default, all timesheets are selected. To remove a timesheet, select its listing and click the column with the check mark to deselect that listing. You can click Select None to deselect all listings, then select one or more specific users.
- To see any notes in their entirety, select the Print Full Activity Notes option. Otherwise, the default selection to print only the first line of any note is enabled.

FIGURE 16-5 Print the timesheets for every person who tracks time.

The Select Timesheets To Print dialog has a Preview button, and clicking it displays a print preview of the selected timesheets. If you click the Print button in the Preview window, the timesheets are sent to the printer immediately, giving you no opportunity to change the printer or any printing options. Clicking the Close button in the Preview window returns you to the Select Timesheets To Print dialog. Click OK to open the Print Timesheets window, where you can change the printer or printing options. You should change the number of copies to print to match the number of people to whom you're distributing the timesheets.

One thing you should notice about printed (or previewed) timesheets is the last column, which indicates the billing status. The entries are codes, as follows:

- **B** Billable but not yet invoiced to the customer
- **N** Not billable
- **D** Billable and already invoiced to the customer

Invoicing Customers for Time

Now that you've entered time, marked it as billable, and reviewed it for accuracy, it's easy to invoice your customer for the hours spent on their project or job—and you can do this right from the Create Invoice window.

From the Customers menu, select Create Invoices, then select a customer name from the Customer:Job drop-down list. The first time you select a customer for which there is a timesheet entry, QuickBooks gives you a message informing you that the customer or job you've selected has outstanding billable time. You'll be prompted to either select the outstanding billable time (as well as any costs) to add to the invoice or exclude time and costs now and leave them available for invoicing at a later date. You can also have QuickBooks save your choice by checking the box Save This As A Preference.

If you choose the option to add the outstanding billable time to your invoice, QuickBooks displays the Choose Billable Time and Costs window (Figure 16-6). Select the Time tab to view all the unbilled time assigned to that customer or job. Use the Select All button to invoice your customer for all the time that appears in this window, or place a check mark next to only those hours that you're ready to invoice the customer for.

By default, each time entry that has a different service item will appear as a separate line item on the invoice. To combine the hours for all items in this window as one line item, place a check mark in the box next to Print Selected Time And Costs As One Invoice at the bottom of the window. The Options button gives you additional ways to customize how information from timesheets is included in invoices.

Tracking Mileage

QuickBooks provides a way to track the mileage of your vehicles. You can use the mileage information to track the expenses connected to vehicle use, to use mileage as part of your job-costing efforts, to bill customers for mileage expenses, or to maintain records for your vehicle-use tax deduction.

FIGURE 16-6 The Choose Billable Time and Costs window makes invoicing a customer for time an easy task.

ProAdvisor Tip: Your accountant may be able to use the vehicle mileage data on your income tax return. You can deduct either the actual mileage expense or your other vehicle expenses; you can't deduct both. Your accountant, working with the figures you provide as a result of mileage tracking, will make the decision.

To track a vehicle, you must add that vehicle to your Vehicle list (covered in Chapter 7). Once the vehicle is in your QuickBooks system, you can begin tracking its mileage. Of course, you also need to make sure that everyone who uses the vehicle is tracking mileage properly. Create, print, and distribute a form for this purpose, with the following categories to fill in:

- Trip Start Date
- Trip End Date
- Starting Odometer
- Ending Odometer
- Customer:Job

Entering Mileage Rates

To track the cost of mileage, you must make sure you have accurate mileage rates in your system. These change frequently, so you'll have to keep up with the latest IRS figures. QuickBooks calculates the cost of mileage based on the information you enter. To get the current rate, check with the IRS (www.irs.gov) or ask your accountant. To enter mileage rates for your own use, use the following steps:

1. Choose Company | Enter Vehicle Mileage to open the Enter Vehicle Mileage dialog.
2. Click the Mileage Rates button on the toolbar to open the Mileage Rates dialog.
3. Select a date from the calendar as the Effective Date.
4. Enter the IRS rate for that date.
5. Click Close.
6. Close the Enter Vehicle Mileage dialog (unless you're using it to enter mileage).

The Mileage Rates dialog accepts multiple dates and rates. When you track mileage, QuickBooks uses the appropriate rate, based on the date of your mileage entry, to calculate costs.

Creating a Mileage Item

If you plan to invoice customers for mileage expenses, you must create an item (call it mileage, travel, or something similar). The item you create can be either a Service or Other Charge type.

- If you want to charge your customers for mileage as a reimbursable expense and post your reimbursements as income (as explained in Chapter 11), use an Other Charge item type and select the option This Item Is Used In Assemblies Or Is A Reimbursable Charge. Then enter the appropriate expense and income accounts.
- If you want to charge your customers for mileage and reduce your mileage expenses with reimbursed amounts, select the expense account to which you post your mileage expenses.

It's important to understand that the mileage rate you entered in the Mileage Rates window (described in the previous section) is *not* automatically transferred to the item you create for mileage. Therefore, you must manually fill in the rate for the item and update it when the IRS rate changes. You can use the same rate you used in the Mileage Rates window or enter a different rate to create a markup (or a markdown, if you wish to take that approach).

Entering Mileage

After you've configured your company file for mileage charges, you can track the mileage in the Enter Vehicle Mileage dialog as follows:

1. Choose Company | Enter Vehicle Mileage.
2. Select the appropriate vehicle from the drop-down list in the Vehicle field and enter the following data:
   - The dates of the trip.
   - The odometer readings (QuickBooks calculates the total miles for you). You can skip the odometer readings and enter the total mileage manually, but entering the odometer numbers creates a report entry that's closer to what an IRS auditor wants to see (the IRS likes "logs" that include odometer readings).
   - If you want to bill the customer for mileage, place a check mark in the Billable check box and select the Customer:Job, the item you created for mileage, and the Class (if you're tracking classes).
   - If you don't want to bill a customer but you want to track job costs, select the Customer:Job, but don't place a check mark in the Billable check box.

Mileage charges can be added to customer invoices in the same fashion as time (see the earlier section, " Invoicing Customers for Time"). Reimbursable expenses are covered in Chapter 9.

Creating Mileage Reports

QuickBooks includes four vehicle mileage reports, which you can access by choosing Reports | Jobs, Time & Mileage and selecting the appropriate mileage report from the submenu. If you're working in the Enter Vehicle Mileage dialog box, the reports are available in the drop-down list you see if you click the arrow next to the Mileage Reports button.

Mileage By Vehicle Summary

Use the Mileage By Vehicle Summary report to see the total miles and the mileage expense for each vehicle you're tracking. You can run this report for any date range that you want to check, which is a way to determine whether vehicles need servicing. For example, you may need to change the oil and filter every 6,000 miles, or schedule a 50,000-mile checkup. If you deduct mileage expenses on your income tax form, use the entire year as the date range.

Mileage By Vehicle Detail

Use the Mileage By Vehicle Detail report to view details about each mileage slip you created. For each vehicle, the report displays the following information:

- Trip End Date
- Total Miles
- Mileage Rate
- Mileage Expense

No customer information appears in the report, but you can double-click any listing to open the original mileage slip, which shows you whether the trip is linked to a job and whether it's marked billable.

Mileage By Job Summary

Use the Mileage By Job Summary report to view the total number of miles linked to customers or jobs. The report displays total miles for all customers or jobs for which you entered an item and displays billable amounts for any mileage entries you marked billable.

Mileage By Job Detail

Use the Mileage By Job Detail report to see the following information about each trip for each customer or job:

- Trip End Date
- Billing Status
- Item
- Total Miles
- Sales Price
- Amount

To gain more insight, you can modify the report by clicking the Customize Report button on the report window to open the Modify Report dialog. In the Display tab, select additional columns to reflect what you want to see in this report. For example, you may want to add the Mileage Rate or Mileage Expense (or both). Memorize the report so you don't have to repeat the modifications next time.

Running Payroll

In *this chapter:*

- Choose a payroll service

- Run a manual payroll

- Set up payroll items

- Set up employee information

- Enter historical data

- Issue payroll checks

- Use the Employee Center

Chapter 17

If you plan on processing your payroll through QuickBooks, the information you need to set it up is in this chapter. This may also be a good time to consult with your accountant for advice on choosing the payroll option that best fits your business needs and to ensure that your setup is fully compliant with your local and state taxing authorities.

QuickBooks Payroll Services

QuickBooks offers a variety of do-it-yourself payroll services, and if you want to do your payroll in-house, here's a brief overview of the offerings:

- Basic Payroll, which provides tax tables and automatic calculations of paycheck deductions and employer expenses for up to three employees. No tax forms are included, so you either need to work with your accountant on tax filings or prepare your tax forms manually. QuickBooks makes it easy to prepare tax forms manually by providing detailed reports in Excel (covered in Chapter 18).
- Enhanced Payroll, which adds tax forms and e-filing for both federal and state reporting.
- Assisted Payroll, which lets you run payroll and then turns the job of depositing withholdings, paying employer contributions, and printing and filing government forms over to QuickBooks.

Additional plans are available such as Intuit's Online Payroll service, which does not require you use QuickBooks for your accounting, and Enhanced Payroll for Accountants, which lets you prepare payroll for up to 50 companies (including preparing Federal and State forms) and includes After The Fact payroll data entry capability. If you're looking for a complete solution, consider the Intuit Full Service option—you enter your employees' time, and Intuit handles the rest.

Direct Deposit

With any of the payroll services, you can purchase direct deposit services for your employees. Employees must sign a form giving permission for direct deposit, and you can print those forms directly from your QuickBooks software (QuickBooks provides a link to display and print the forms during the sign-up process). Employees can opt to deposit their entire paychecks into one bank account or split the amount between two bank accounts.

Signing Up for Payroll Services

To learn about the QuickBooks payroll offerings, choose Employees | Payroll and then, from the submenu, choose either Learn About Payroll Options or Order Payroll Service (both menu choices produce the same result).

After you've used the links on the Payroll Services website to learn about all the payroll offerings, follow the prompts to sign up.

When the sign-up process is completed, download the files you need to run payroll. The new files are automatically added to your QuickBooks system; you don't have to do anything to install them. In addition to the payroll software, the current tax table is added to your system. After payroll is installed, your Employees menu has all the commands you need to run payroll.

➥ ProAdvisor Recommends

Processing Your Payroll Manually in QuickBooks

Unless you've signed up for QuickBooks payroll services, no withholding or tax will automatically be calculated for any paycheck you create. You can, if you wish, use your own printed tax table (Employer's Circular E from the IRS), calculate the deductions, and enter them manually. However, you'll need to set up your file to allow you to enter these amounts manually, and the only way to tell QuickBooks you want to exercise this option is via the Help menu.

Select QuickBooks Help from the main Help menu to open the Have A Question? window. In the Search field, type **manual payroll**, then click the magnifying glass (search) icon. QuickBooks will display several Help articles—click the article titled "Process Payroll Manually (Without A Subscription To QuickBooks Payroll)." Within this article, click the topic titled "If You Prefer to Process Your Payroll Manually." Then click the link "manual payroll calculations" that's embedded within the topic.

From here, you'll be brought to a new Help article called "Are You Sure You Want to Set Your Company File to Use Manual Calculations?" Within this article, click the link at the end called "Set my company file to use manual calculations."

Whew! Seems like quite a lot to go through. But the decision to run a manual payroll should only be made after careful consideration and consultation with your accountant and if you're running a very simple payroll for only a few employees. Be sure you have the resources to ensure that the calculations are correct and you have a system in place to remit your withholdings to the appropriate agency in a timely manner.

Setting Up Your Payroll

To produce accurate paychecks, you need to complete setup tasks, including adding accounts to your chart of accounts, creating payroll items (salary, wages, and so on), identifying the payroll taxes you have to withhold, the payroll taxes you have to pay as an employer, and the deductions or company contributions for benefits. And you also need to set up tax information for each employee, such as dependents and deductions.

You can set up these payroll elements in either of two ways:

- Manually
- Using the Payroll Setup Wizard

The following sections cover all the steps involved in setting up payroll manually, and later in this chapter there's a walk-through of the Payroll Setup Wizard. You can read both to decide the way you want to approach setup.

Accounts

You may need to create new accounts in your chart of accounts for payroll. If you want to use a bank account specifically for payroll instead of using your main bank account (generally a good idea), you must open the account at your bank and also add the new bank account to your chart of accounts. In addition, you'll need at least the following accounts:

- Payroll Liabilities, which tracks the deductions from paychecks
- Payroll Expenses, which tracks company payroll expenses (company social security, Medicare, pension, medical, and so on)

QuickBooks automatically adds the Payroll Liabilities and Payroll Expenses accounts when you enable payroll. You can use each account for all payroll transactions or create subaccounts to track individual payroll liabilities and expenses.

You should use subaccounts for payroll liabilities and payroll expenses, because it's much easier to determine the current status of individual liabilities and expenses (see Figure 17-1). Link your payroll items to the subaccounts and never post to the parent account. (When you create reports, any balances in the subaccount are totaled in the parent account.)

Name	⚡	Type ▲	Balance Total	Attach
◆ Customer Deposits		Other Current Liability	3,500.00	
◆ Line of Credit		Other Current Liability	104,618.08	
◆ Payroll Liabilities		Other Current Liability	4,967.43	
◆ Medicare Withheld		Other Current Liability	0.00	
◆ FWT		Other Current Liability	0.00	
◆ FICA Withheld		Other Current Liability	0.00	
◆ 401K Payable		Other Current Liability	0.00	
◆ Payroll Taxes Payable		Other Current Liability	4,767.43	
◆ SEC125 Payable		Other Current Liability	200.00	

Account ▼ Activities ▼ Reports ▼ Attach ☐ Include inactive

FIGURE 17-1   It's easy to track payroll financial data if you use subaccounts.

Vendors

Running payroll creates liabilities for payroll taxes, other deductions that your company must remit, and possibly employee benefits that must be paid. To be able to send the money you owe to the appropriate vendors, set up those vendors before you set up payroll items so that you can assign the payroll items to the proper vendors. (Payroll items are discussed in the next section.)

For withholding of federal income taxes, Medicare, FICA, and the matching employer Medicare and FICA payments, you can assign the United States Treasury Department as the vendor.

For local and state income tax, unemployment, disability, workers comp, and deductions for benefits such as health insurance, set up a vendor for each agency you need to pay. Most states now offer electronic payments for payroll remittances on their websites, but if you use checks you probably have forms or coupons for the required payment interval (usually monthly or quarterly).

> **ProAdvisor Tip:** Beginning January 1, 2011, the IRS requires that all payroll tax deposits be made electronically using the Employer Federal Tax Payment System (EFTPS). If you haven't already done so, you'll need to go to the EFTPS website (www.eftps.gov) to learn more and enroll.

Payroll Items

A QuickBooks *payroll item* is any element that is part of a payroll check. The number of individual elements that go into a paycheck may be more than you thought. Consider this list, which is typical of many businesses:

- Salaries
- Wages (hourly)
- Overtime (time and a half)
- Double-time
- Federal tax withholdings (including FIT, FICA, and Medicare)
- State tax withholdings
- State unemployment and disability withholdings
- Local tax withholdings
- Pension plan deductions
- Medical insurance deductions
- Life insurance deductions
- Garnishes (such as child support)
- Union dues
- Reimbursement for auto expenses
- Bonuses
- Commissions
- Holiday pay
- Sick pay
- Advanced Earned Income Credit

Whew! And don't forget that you also have to track company-paid payroll items, such as matching FICA and Medicare, employer contributions to unemployment (both state and federal), state disability funds, pension and medical benefit plans, and more!

You can view your payroll items and create new payroll items by choosing Lists | Payroll Item List to open the Payroll Item List seen in Figure 17-2. QuickBooks adds some items to the list automatically when you enable payroll services. Usually, local taxes, medical benefits deductions, and other payroll items are missing (and the items that *do* exist may be missing information about the vendor, so you'll have to edit them to add that information).

FIGURE 17-2 The payroll items created automatically don't include everything you need.

To add a new payroll item, from the Payroll Item List window, press CTRL-N to open the Add New Payroll Item Wizard shown in Figure 17-3.

The two options presented on the first wizard window don't offer full explanations of their differences. Here's an explanation of what happens with each option.

EZ Setup of Payroll Items

If you select the EZ Setup option, when you click Next you see a list of payroll item types. The descriptions are brief, but essentially you can create any type of pay, deduction, or company benefit, including payroll items that are paid in full by the company, deducted in full from employees, or paid by both the company and the employee. The only types of payroll items you cannot create in the EZ Setup are state and local payroll taxes, including state unemployment and/or disability taxes.

FIGURE 17-3 This wizard helps you create a payroll item.

When you use the EZ Setup option, after you select the type of item, QuickBooks loads the Payroll Setup Wizard and then displays the Add New dialog from that feature. (The Payroll Setup Wizard is an alternate method of setting up all the elements in your payroll system—see "Using the QuickBooks Payroll Setup Wizard" later in this chapter.)

The questions and explanations you see in the Payroll Setup Wizard are more basic than the questions you're asked if you select the Custom option for setting up a payroll item. You need less knowledge of payroll processing to complete the setup, but you'll spend more time moving through more wizard windows, because most of the data you provide is entered one wizard window at a time. Most of the wizard windows ask one question or require a single answer.

This does not mean you can set up a payroll item accurately if you know nothing about deductions, benefits, or about the accounting and legal issues involved with payroll benefits and deductions (which is why it's always a good idea to consult with an accounting professional when payroll is involved). What it does mean, however, is that the explanations you see when you're asked to provide information are user-friendly.

For example, if you're setting up a benefit such as health insurance, pension benefit, or any form of a benefit in a cafeteria plan, the wizard asks you if the benefit cost is borne entirely by the company, entirely by the employee, or shared between both parties. Depending on your answer, the wizard moves through the ensuing windows to set up the necessary payroll item (or multiple items if you require the employee deduction and the employer contribution). If the employee contributes some or all of the cost, you have to know whether it's a pre-tax or after-tax deduction, and you have to know how the deduction affects the employee's W-2 form. This means that even if you choose the EZ Setup option, you can't do this properly if you have no familiarity with payroll issues—yet another reason to discuss the payroll items required for your QuickBooks company file with your accountant.

Custom Setup of Payroll Items

If you select the Custom Setup option, the list you see when you click Next is all inclusive, because you can set up all the payroll item types offered in the EZ Setup list of payroll types, and you can also set up state and local payroll items.

When you select a payroll item type, the wizard moves through information windows without asking the kind of easy-to-understand questions the EZ Setup presents; on the other hand, each window contains all the fields for the required information instead of walking you through multiple windows to answer questions and fill out a single field.

For example, if you have a health benefit with costs shared between the company and the employee, the wizard isn't going to remind you that you have to set up two items, one for the company payment and another for the employee deduction. You just have to know that both tasks must be completed (they are separate items). In the second wizard window, you select Deduction and establish the employee contribution (and you have to know which types of deductions are pre-tax and which are after-tax, and whether the deduction affects the W-2 form). Then you have to start the wizard again to select Company Contribution in the second wizard window to set up the company side of the health benefits item. If you have detailed instructions from your accountant, the Custom option is a quicker way to set up all your payroll items.

Setting Up Employees

The information about your employees *must* be accurate; otherwise, you may find yourself having to adjust payroll information inside QuickBooks and then having to report these changes to the IRS—which means more work for you and potential confusion with the IRS about your payroll withholding data.

Create an Employee Template

There is a great deal of information to fill out for each employee, and some of it is probably the same for all or most of your employees. For example, you may have many employees who share the same type of pay (salary or hourly wage) or the same deductions for medical insurance.

To avoid entering the same information over and over, you can create a template and then apply the information to all the employees who match that data. You'll save yourself lots of time, even if you have to edit one or two entries for some employees because their data differs from the template.

To get to the template, you have to open the Employee Center by choosing Employees | Employee Center from the menu bar.

Click the button labeled Manage Employee Information at the top of the window, and choose Change New Employee Default Settings from the submenu that appears.

This opens the Employee Defaults window, where you can enter the data that applies to most or all of your employees.

The information you put into the template is automatically added to the Payroll Info tab for each employee you create hereafter (discussed in the next section, "Creating Employees"). You can skip any field for which there isn't a common payroll item.

- Click in the Item Name column of the Earnings box, and then click the arrow to see a list of earnings types that you've defined as payroll items. Select the one that is common enough to be suitable for a template.

- In the Hourly/Annual Rate column, enter a wage or salary figure if there's one that applies to most of your employees. If there's not, just skip it and enter each employee's rate in the individual employee record later.

- Use the arrow to the right of the Payroll Schedule field and select a schedule (if you've established payroll schedules). See the section "Payroll Schedules" later in this chapter for more information.

- Select a pay frequency (if you created schedules and selected one, QuickBooks automatically uses that schedule to fill in the Pay Frequency field).

- Use the Class field if you've enabled classes to track data.

- If you're using QuickBooks' time tracking features to pay employees, you also see a check box labeled Use Time Data To Create Paychecks. Put a check mark in the check box to enable the feature.

- If all or most of your employees have the same additional adjustments (such as insurance deductions, 401(k) deductions, or reimbursement for car expenses), click in the Item Name column in the Additions, Deductions, And Company Contributions box, and then click the arrow to select the appropriate adjustments.
- Click the Taxes button to open the Taxes Defaults dialog and select those taxes that are common and therefore suited for the template. The State tab and the Other tab (usually local payroll taxes) contain tax data that probably applies to all or most of your employees.
- Click the Sick/Vacation button to set the terms for accruing sick time and vacation time if your policy is similar enough among employees to include it in the template.

When you are finished filling out the template, click OK to save it.

Creating Employees

Now you're ready to tell QuickBooks about your list of employees. Open the Employee Center and click New Employee to open a New Employee form.

The New Employee form opens with the Personal Info tab selected in the Change Tabs drop-down list at the top of the form. This selection displays three tabs: Personal, Address And Contact, and Additional Info.

Additional tab sets exist, and you use the drop-down list in the Change Tabs field at the top of the window to access them. The following tab categories are available in the drop-down list:

- **Personal Info** A three-tab dialog where you enter personal information about the employee.
- **Payroll And Compensation Info** Where you enter information about earnings, taxes, deductions, and other financial data.
- **Employment Info** Where you enter information about the employee's hiring date and other employment history.
- **Workers Compensation** Only available if you signed up for Enhanced Payroll. If so, workers comp is automatically enabled (you can disable it in the Payroll & Employees category of the Preferences dialog).

All of these tabs are covered in the following sections.

Personal Info Tab Set

The Personal Info tab set (see Figure 17-4) is the place to record personal information about this employee. It has three tabs because the information is divided into three categories.

FIGURE 17-4 Start by entering personal information about the employee.

Personal Tab Enter the employee's name, social security number, and the way the name should be printed on paychecks. Enter the gender and/or date of birth if you have a company policy of recording this information, or if any tax or benefits agency requires it. For example, your state unemployment form may require you to note the gender of all employees; your medical or life insurance carrier may require the date of birth.

Address And Contact Tab Use this tab to record the employee's address, as well as information about contacting the employee (phone number, e-mail, fax, and so on). The address is required for W-2 forms.

Additional Info Tab Use this tab to enter the employee number (if your company uses employee numbers). This tab also contains a Define Fields button, so you can create custom fields for employee records.

Payroll And Compensation Info Tab Set

This tab set has only one tab (Payroll Info), and it contains the information QuickBooks needs to pay employees (see Figure 17-5). Where the employee's payroll items and amounts match information already filled in from the default template, just accept the items. Otherwise, make additions and changes as necessary for this employee.

FIGURE 17-5   Enter information about this employee's compensation and deductions (excluding tax deductions).

If the amount of the earnings or the deduction is the same every week, enter an amount. If it differs from week to week, don't enter an amount on the employee card. Instead, you'll enter that information when you create the payroll check.

Employee Tax Information   Click the Taxes button to open the Taxes dialog, which starts with Federal tax information, as seen in Figure 17-6. Fill in any data that wasn't automatically filled in from the Employee Template, and modify data that is different for this employee.

FIGURE 17-6 Configure the employee's tax information.

Move to the State tab and configure the employee's status for the state. QuickBooks has built in a great deal of state information and, depending on the state, you should see the appropriate withholdings and company-paid items. For example, states that don't deduct SUI from employees have a check box for SUI (Company Paid), while states that collect disability funds from employees will display the appropriate check box.

In the Other tab, apply any local payroll tax that applies to this employee. If you haven't already configured that tax in the Payroll Item List, you can click <Add New> in the Item Name column to enter it now.

Click OK to save the tax status information and return to the Payroll Info tab.

Sick and Vacation Pay Information   Click the Sick/Vacation button and enter the configuration for this employee (which may include data from the Employee Template). When you are finished, click OK to return to the employee card.

Direct Deposit   The Payroll Info tab has a Direct Deposit button, which you can use to establish direct deposit of the employee's paycheck to his or her bank account. If you haven't signed up for direct deposit, the window that opens offers the chance to enroll.

Employment Info Tab Set

Select Employment Info in the Change Tabs drop-down list to see the Employment tab, which lets you track the following information about the employee:

- Hire date
- Release date (fill this in when an employee leaves your company)
- Employee type

For more information on employee types, see the section "Understanding Employee Types."

Workers Compensation Tab Set

For Enhanced Payroll subscribers, if you haven't disabled workers comp tracking in the Payroll & Employees category of the Preferences dialog, choose Workers Compensation from the Change Tabs drop-down list. Assign the workers comp code that applies to the employee, or select Exempt if this employee is exempt from workers comp.

Understanding Employee Types

The Type field on the Employment Info tab offers four choices, which are explained in this section. The selection you make has an impact on the way your tax returns are prepared. You must check with your accountant if you have any questions about the type you should assign to any employee.

Regular Employee

A regular employee is exactly what it seems to be: a person you hired for whom you deduct withholdings, issue a W-2, and so on. It's important to have every employee fill out a W-4 form every year (even if nothing has changed from last year).

> **ProAdvisor Tip:** If you need extra W-4 forms, you can download them from the IRS at www.irs.gov. Go to the forms section, select W-4, and print the form or download it and print as many copies as you need.

Officer Employee

An *officer* is someone who is an officer of a corporation. If your business isn't incorporated, you have no officers. On federal corporate tax returns, you are required to report payroll for officers of the corporation separately from the regular payroll amounts. Selecting Officer as the type has no impact on running your payroll (calculations, check printing, and so on); it only affects reports.

Statutory Employee

A *statutory employee* is someone who works for you that the IRS has decided qualifies as an employee instead of as an independent contractor. The list of the job types that the rules cover and the definition of *independent contractor* is the subject of much debate (especially in IRS audit hearings). The IRS has a list of criteria that must be met in order to qualify as an independent contractor (which means you don't have to put that person on your payroll, you don't have to withhold taxes, and you don't have to pay employer taxes). The rules that govern this change frequently, so it's important to check the rules in Circular E or with your accountant.

Owner Employee

Owner and Employee are mutually exclusive terms to the IRS. If you own a company, that means the company is a proprietorship; it's not a corporation (a corporation doesn't have owners; it has officers and directors). The same thing is true of a partnership, which has multiple owners. You cannot put yourself on the payroll; when you draw checks they cannot be paychecks. Post the checks against a Draw account in the Equity section of your chart of accounts.

QuickBooks puts this type in the list in case it's too late and you've already listed the proprietor or partners in the Employee List. The QuickBooks payroll program won't perform payroll tasks for any employee of this type. If you did add a proprietor or partner name to the Employee List, delete it rather than assign this type.

Entering Historical Data

If you're not starting your use of QuickBooks at the very beginning of the year, you must enter all the historical information about paychecks that have been issued thus far. This is the only way to perform all of the required year-end tasks. You cannot give your employees two W-2 forms, one from your manual system and another from QuickBooks, nor can you file your annual tax reports on a piecemeal basis.

No matter what your fiscal year is, your payroll year is the calendar year. Even though you can start using payroll for the current period before you enter the historical data, remember that the absence of historical data may affect some tax calculations. Also, year-to-date payroll information on pay stubs for the employees will be incorrect until you enter historical payroll data. If there are withholding amounts that cease after a certain maximum (perhaps your state only requires SUTA/SUI for the first $8,000.00 in gross payroll), you'll have to adjust the deductions on the current paychecks manually. If the historical data is entered, QuickBooks can calculate the maximum deduction properly and stop deducting these amounts.

ProAdvisor Tip: To make historical data entry easier, go live with payroll at the beginning of a calendar quarter.

How to Enter Historical Data

The historical data is the payroll you issued before the date on which you let QuickBooks take over your payroll chores (which is called the *go live date*). Starting with the go live date, you'll be entering payroll checks in QuickBooks. It's important to understand how the go live date affects the task of entering historical data, so here are some guidelines:

- Payroll records are summarized quarterly, because your 941 reports are due quarterly.
- You can't enter summarized data for the quarter that's current (the quarter that the go live date falls in). Instead, for the current quarter, you must enter data for each individual pay period (weekly, biweekly, semimonthly, or monthly). For previous quarters, you can enter quarterly totals.
- If your go live date is any date in the first quarter, you have to enter historical data for each pay period because you don't have a full quarter to summarize.
- If your go live date is in the second quarter, enter a quarterly total for the first quarter and then enter the individual pay period numbers for the second quarter, up to the go live date.
- If your go live date is in the third quarter, enter quarterly totals for the first two quarters and then enter each pay period up to the go live date.
- If your go live date is in the fourth quarter, you can follow the same pattern, but it might be just as easy to wait until next year to begin using QuickBooks payroll.

Entering Payroll History in Batches

Here's a little known shortcut for entering year-to-date payroll information (you must have created all your employees to use it).

Choose Help | About QuickBooks Pro 2012 to display the Product Information window. Then press the keyboard combination CTRL-SHIFT-Y. The Set Up YTD Amounts Wizard opens to walk you through the steps of entering year-to-date summary information for each employee (see Figure 17-7).

Set Up YTD Amounts

You are about to enter year-to-date (YTD) amounts for payroll.

YTD amounts are summaries of employee paychecks and associated company liabilities for this calendar year to date.

After you have set up these amounts you can do the following:

- Print accurate year-to-date summaries on employee paychecks.
- Create accurate payroll reports.
- Create accurate W-2 forms for the current calendar year.
- Track how much you owe for payroll taxes and other liabilities.

Back   Next   Leave

FIGURE 17-7 This is a quick way to use your manual payroll records to summarize year-to-date payroll information.

Click Next to begin. The wizard replicates the historical balance entry information that the QuickBooks Payroll Setup Wizard offers, but most people find this easier to use, especially if they've chosen to enter basic components manually.

The wizard asks you to specify three dates:

- The date your payroll liability and expense accounts are affected. That means, "When should the data you're entering be posted to liability and expense accounts that are associated with payroll items?"
- The date your payroll bank accounts are affected. That means, "When should the net paycheck amounts be posted to your payroll bank account?"
- The check date of the first paycheck you'll create using QuickBooks payroll. This paycheck posts to all relevant accounts; there are no historical balances.

The correct dates might not be the same for all three categories. Following are some examples of possible scenarios that should help you understand how to enter the dates in these categories. For the purpose of these explanations, let's assume you're entering historical information as of the end of April; your first QuickBooks-produced paychecks will be the first payday in May.

If you've been doing payroll manually or through an outside service, and you've remitted your liabilities and expenses, those amounts should have been posted when you set up your opening QuickBooks balances. You don't want QuickBooks to post the liabilities, expenses, and net check amounts again; instead, you're entering historical data for the purpose of producing accurate reports and W-2 forms. Tell QuickBooks that the first date of your liability, expense, and bank accounts is the day of your first May paychecks. Enter the first quarter payroll totals for each employee, and then enter the individual payroll data for April (so you have running totals for your quarterly reports). Your "first paycheck using QuickBooks" date is the first payday in May.

If you've been using an outside payroll service, you should already have been posting the payroll totals to the bank account you use for payroll, but you might not have been posting liabilities and expenses to date, because the payroll service was taking care of it and you wait for the quarterly reports to post amounts. Your last journal entry for liabilities and expenses was at the end of the quarter (March 31). Your first posting of liabilities and expenses should be April 1, and your first posting of bank account amounts should be May (the date of the first QuickBooks-produced paycheck). Your "first paycheck using QuickBooks" date is the first payday in May.

These "rules for entering historical payroll totals" also apply when you use the QuickBooks Payroll Setup Wizard.

Using the QuickBooks Payroll Setup Wizard

QuickBooks provides assistance for setting up payroll in the form of a wizard. You can use the wizard to set up all the components required for payroll, or set up your payroll items and employees manually and then use the wizard to enter your historical data.

Regardless of whether you use the Payroll Setup Wizard to set up all your components or to enter historical data only, be sure to set up all the vendors and accounts you need to remit payroll withholding and employer payroll expenses before using the wizard.

To use the wizard, choose Employees | Payroll Setup from the QuickBooks menu bar. The wizard window opens with all the tasks listed in the left pane (see Figure 17-8).

FIGURE 17-8   The QuickBooks Payroll Setup Wizard is divided into logical sets of tasks.

If you're using the wizard to set up your payroll from scratch (you didn't preconfigure any of the components as described in the previous sections of this chapter), the setup process can take more time than it takes to perform those tasks manually, but the wizard is rather user-friendly and demands no knowledge of accounting jargon, so you may prefer to use it. The wizard has a Finish Later button, which you can click if you have to do other work, get tired, or get bored. When you open the wizard again, you pick up where you left off.

The first few wizard screens are informational, indicating the data you need to complete the wizard (the same information about employees, payroll items, deductions, etc., discussed earlier in this chapter). The real work starts with Section 2, where the wizard starts configuring payroll for your company.

Company Setup for Payroll

In the Company Setup section, the wizard starts with compensation, which means payroll items that are compensation—salary, hourly wages, and so on. When you've finished with that section, the wizard moves on to other payroll item types.

If you've configured payroll items manually, they appear in the wizard window, and you can click Edit to view or change the settings.

If you haven't yet set up payroll items, click Add New to open a mini-wizard that walks you through the process (the same process initiated if you choose EZ Setup of Payroll Items, which is covered earlier in this chapter).

The types of payroll items the wizard offers to set up include the following:

- Types of compensation, such as salary, hourly wages, overtime, bonuses, commissions, tips, and so on.
- Benefits, such as insurance, pension, and so on. For each benefit you select, you configure the employee/employer contribution rates.
- Paid time off, such as sick leave and vacations. You can configure how QuickBooks calculates vacation time and sick time (if you let employees accrue time according to time worked).
- Other additions and deductions, such as workers comp, auto expense reimbursement, garnishments, union dues, and so on.

Setting Up Employees in the Wizard

In Section 3, the wizard moves on to the task of setting up employees. If you didn't set up your employees manually, you can add each employee in the wizard, moving through a series of windows in which you enter information about the employee's personal information, pay structure, and tax status. For each employee, you designate the taxes and benefits that affect the employee.

When you finish entering your employee information, the wizard displays the list of employees. If any employee is missing information, the wizard indicates the problem (if you entered your employees manually, the wizard automatically finds the employee records and displays the same list if problems exist).

Some missing information isn't critical to issuing paychecks, but QuickBooks requires the information in the employee record. If any employee in the list has the notation Fix This Error Now, it means critical information is missing, and the system either won't be able to issue a paycheck or won't be able to issue a W-2 form at the end of the year. Regardless of whether the missing information is critical or not, select the employee and click Edit to move through the wizard and fix the problem.

Incidentally, if you use the wizard to set up employees, when you fail to fill in required information the wizard displays a reminder, something that doesn't happen when you set up employees manually.

Setting Up Payroll Taxes in the Wizard

In Section 4, you tell the wizard about the federal, state, and local taxes you're responsible for. These are payroll items, so if you haven't set up all these items beforehand, you can use the wizard.

If you're setting up your taxes in the wizard, as you finish each section, the wizard displays a list of all the taxes for that section. If you set up your taxes as payroll items manually, the wizard finds those entries and uses them to populate the list.

If the wizard finds anything amiss in your setup of any tax, the problem is displayed in the Description column. Choose Edit to make the needed changes.

Entering Payroll History in the Wizard

In Section 5, you enter your historical payroll data. The wizard presents a set of windows, starting with a window that asks if you've issued paychecks this year (meaning outside of QuickBooks, of course). If you answer Yes, the next window displayed is the Payroll Summary window, where you have access to three preformatted tables into which you'll enter the following year-to-date information:

- Paychecks (monthly totals for each employee)
- Payroll tax payments
- Nonpayroll tax payments (company contributions to benefits, and so on)

Data Review and Payroll Checkup

Section 6 is the Data Review, which you can run if you choose. If you do, QuickBooks asks if you'd like to go over your payroll settings; if you select Yes, the wizard runs a Payroll Checkup routine.

Finishing Up

At this point, your setup is complete, and you're prompted to run a backup of your file to ensure that all the payroll setup information you just entered is protected. Making a backup is always a good idea. You can also choose to go straight to the Payroll Center, where you'll have access to essentially everything that relates to managing your payroll.

➡ ProAdvisor Recommends

Running a Payroll Checkup

You can run a Payroll Checkup whenever you make changes to your payroll components (employees, taxes, etc.) by choosing Employees | My Payroll Service | Run Payroll Checkup. The QuickBooks Payroll Setup Wizard walks through all the elements required for running payroll (a task list). Each section of the wizard's task list is checked for errors. The errors the checkup may find include missing information, invalid information (the format of an EIN number or state reporting number may be incorrect), or any other data that doesn't match the standards built into the QuickBooks payroll feature.

The program displays a report on the integrity of the data for prior quarters (unless you're working in the first quarter, of course), and then, separately, the integrity of the data for the current quarter.

Then, the program asks you about the federal and state forms you've filed to remit withholdings and pay employer taxes. After you've filled in the information, the program reconciles the totals against the payroll totals you entered previously. If there are errors, the specifics are displayed, and you can correct the problem and re-run the checkup.

Payroll Schedules

A payroll schedule is a way to separate different payroll intervals. For example, if your company pays salaried employees and officers on a weekly basis and pays hourly workers on a biweekly basis, you can run payroll by selecting the appropriate schedule in order to make sure you pay the right employees on the right dates.

When you create a payroll schedule, you define how often you pay your employees (weekly, biweekly, semimonthly, and so on), the pay period (the workdays covered by the paycheck), the date on the paycheck, and the date you prepare the payroll.

C a u t i o n : The date you prepare the payroll differs from the paycheck date if you're using direct deposit, which requires you to transfer payroll information two days before the paycheck date.

Creating a Payroll Schedule

To create a payroll schedule, choose Employees | Add Or Edit Payroll Schedules. When the Payroll Schedule List window opens, press CTRL-N to create a new payroll schedule. In the New Payroll Schedule dialog, fill out the required information as follows:

- A name for this schedule. Use descriptive text if you're setting up multiple payroll schedules, such as "weekly-checks," "weekly-DirDep," "CommissionsOnly," and so on.
- The pay period frequency for this schedule.
- The next pay period end date. This is the time period covered by the paycheck, which often is not the same as the paycheck date. For example, you may issue paychecks on Thursday for the period ending the previous Friday.
- The next paycheck date.

If your payroll is monthly or semimonthly, the dialog includes additional fields. For example, if you issue paychecks semimonthly, you can select specific dates, such as the 10th and the 25th, or you can select one midmonth date and then select Last Day Of Month for the second check in that month.

After you create the schedule, QuickBooks offers to assign the schedule automatically to any employees who are configured for the same pay frequency as the new schedule.

Assigning Payroll Schedules to Employees

Each employee record has a field for the applicable payroll schedule in the Payroll And Compensation Info tab. When you link the payroll schedule to the appropriate employees, those employees appear when you select the schedule on the day you're preparing paychecks.

Special Payroll Runs

QuickBooks offers a way to issue a paycheck, or multiple paychecks, outside of the schedules you create. When you choose Employees | Pay Employees, in addition to the subcommand Scheduled Payroll, you see two commands you can use for special payroll runs:

- Unscheduled Payroll
- Termination Check

Unscheduled Payroll   Select this special payroll category if you need to create bonus checks, commission checks, or any other type of paycheck that differs from a regularly scheduled payroll run. You also have the option of adding the additional compensation to a "regular" paycheck instead of running an unscheduled payroll.

Termination Check   Selecting this special payroll type, the use of which is rather obvious from its name, opens the Enter Payroll Information dialog. Select the terminated employee (put a check mark in the column to the left of the employee name), the pay period ending date, the check date, the termination date, and the hours (or amount if the employee is salaried). Click Continue, approve or change the paycheck details; then print the check, assign a check number for a manual check, or issue a direct deposit check. You must enter a Release Date in the Employment Info tab of the employee's record or QuickBooks will not create a termination check.

Running Payroll

It's payday. All the historical data is entered. It's time to run the payroll. Begin creating payroll checks as follows:

- If you don't use payroll schedules, choose Employees | Pay Employees to open the Enter Payroll Information dialog seen in Figure 17-9.
- If you have payroll schedules, choose Employees | Pay Employees | Scheduled Payroll to open the Employee Center with the Payroll tab selected (the Pay Employees function appears in the right pane). Select the appropriate schedule and click Start Scheduled Payroll to open the Enter Payroll Information dialog, which looks the same as Figure 17-9 but lists only the employees linked to this payroll schedule.

Select the employees to pay. If all the employees are receiving paychecks (the usual scenario), click Check All.

- For hourly employees who are configured for automatic payroll amounts using timesheets, the number of hours is prefilled.
- For hourly employees who are not paid from timesheets, you must fill in the number of hours for this paycheck.

FIGURE 17-9 Begin configuring paychecks in the Enter Payroll Information dialog.

Changing Paycheck Data

If you want to make changes to the paycheck, click the employee's name to open the Preview Paycheck dialog. You can add a payroll item such as a bonus, assign the paycheck to a customer or job, or add a deduction such as a repayment of a loan or garnishment. Click Save & Next to move to the next employee or click Save & Close to return to the Enter Payroll Information dialog. (There's also a Save & Previous button in case you think you should go back to a previous check.)

Reviewing the Payroll Run

Click Continue in the Enter Payroll Information dialog to display the Review And Create Paychecks window (see Figure 17-10), which displays all the financial information for this payroll run. If anything is amiss, click Back to reconfigure the paychecks or make other needed corrections.

FIGURE 17-10 The details for each paycheck have been entered.

Fill out the options for producing the paychecks (print the checks or automatically assign check numbers in the bank account register for manual checks), and then click Create Paychecks. QuickBooks creates the checks and displays the Confirmation And Next Steps dialog.

If you're printing paychecks, you can click Print Paychecks, or you can wait and print them from the Print Forms command in the File menu (in case you have another payroll schedule to process today, and you want to load the payroll checks and process them in one fell swoop).

If you have direct deposit employees, click Print Pay Stubs. When the pay stubs are printed, click the Send Payroll Data button on the Confirmation And Next Steps dialog. This opens the Send Center window and you can upload the direct deposit data to Intuit for processing. You can e-mail the pay stubs using the security standards built into the process (see the Help files for details).

If you have another payroll schedule to run today (perhaps both weekly and biweekly employees are paid today), repeat all the processes as outlined here.

Net to Gross Calculations for Enhanced Payroll Subscribers

If you subscribe to Enhanced Payroll, you can enter the net amount of a check and let QuickBooks calculate the gross amount. This is useful for bonus checks or another special payroll check for which you need to make sure the employee receives a net check of a certain amount.

During the payroll run (either a regular payroll or a special payroll for this individual paycheck), select the employee for this payroll run. In the Preview Paycheck window, select the option Enter Net/Calculate Gross, located in the lower-right corner, and then enter the net amount for this paycheck. QuickBooks automatically calculates the gross amount and the deductions to arrive at the net amount you entered.

The Employee Center

The Employee Center, seen in Figure 17-11, contains all the information about your payroll components and also provides links to all the functions in the payroll system. It's a central location for everything you need to do or need to know. To open this window, choose Employees | Employee Center from the menu bar.

FIGURE 17-11 The Employee Center is the repository of all payroll information and functions.

> **ProAdvisor Tip:** Users who do not have QuickBooks permissions to see payroll or other sensitive information do not see payroll financial information when they open the Employee Center.

If you subscribe to a QuickBooks payroll service, the left pane of the Employee Center contains three tabs: Employees, Transactions, and Payroll. If you don't have a payroll plan subscription, the pane lacks a Payroll tab.

Employees Tab

When you select an employee on the Employees tab, QuickBooks displays information from the employee's record on the top part of the right pane and displays transaction information for that employee on the bottom part of the right pane. You can change the choices in the Show and Date fields to filter the transactions information.

You can open any listed transaction by double-clicking its listing. For example, if you open a paycheck, you can see the original check along with a summary of the financial information. If you need to check any of the details, click Paycheck Detail to see all the calculated amounts.

Transactions Tab

The Transactions tab (see Figure 17-12) lists all payroll-related transaction types. Select a type to display the transactions you've created. You can use the Date field to narrow the breadth of information.

Payroll Tab

The Payroll tab provides a one-stop center for all your payroll tasks (see Figure 17-13). You can view transactions, create transactions, and generate the payroll forms you need. Visit this tab periodically to make sure you don't miss any deadlines.

Customizing the Employee Center

You can tailor the way the Employee Center displays information. Resize the panes by moving your mouse pointer over the edge of any pane; when the pointer changes to a vertical bar with right and left arrows, drag the pane in either direction. In addition, you can expand the pane to show the full list view by clicking the arrow button located next to the View drop-down list. Use the same button to collapse the pane to show both the Employee List and the detail panes.

FIGURE 17-12 The Transactions tab lets you view transactions of the selected type.

FIGURE 17-13 The Payroll tab is the place to access the tasks involved in payroll—the links and messages change depending on the QuickBooks payroll service you purchased.

You can customize the columns that QuickBooks displays in the left pane of the Employees tab by right-clicking anywhere on the list and choosing Customize Columns.

You can also customize the information displayed in the right pane when you select an employee's name in the Employees tab. Right-click anywhere in the right (Transaction) pane and select Customize Columns.

Of course, after you create and deliver paychecks to employees, you have to send the government agencies, insurance companies, and other vendors the money you're holding for them. Instructions for those tasks are in Chapter 18.

Payroll Reports and Liability Payments

In *this chapter:*

- Confirm payroll liability payment schedules

- Pay liabilities

- Prepare quarterly and annual returns

- Print W-2 forms

There's a logical order to all the tasks involved in reporting on and paying your payroll liabilities using QuickBooks, although the steps may differ depending on the state and municipality you're in. These tasks, and the order in which most businesses have to perform them, are covered in this chapter.

Confirming Payroll Payment Schedules

When you run payroll, QuickBooks maintains a payment schedule behind the scenes that keeps track of the amounts and due dates for all the payroll liabilities and employer expenses that are accumulating. You'll use this payment schedule to make sure you remit your payroll obligations on time. Most of the information required for scheduling payments is probably already in your system as a result of the information you provided when you set up payroll items. To view the schedule and correct any problems, choose Employees | Payroll Taxes And Liabilities | Edit Payment Due Dates/Methods.

This action opens the Payroll Setup Wizard's Schedule Payments window, and if any data is missing or does not match the content or format the payroll system expects, the wizard highlights the listing with a problem (see Figure 18-1).

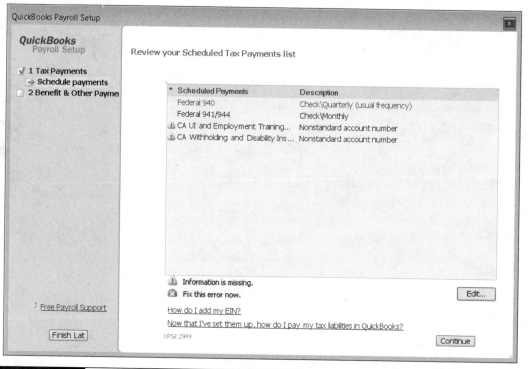

| **FIGURE 18-1** | If a listing has an icon, there's a problem with the configuration of that listing. |

Double-click the errant listing so you can edit its configuration to correct the problem. QuickBooks usually provides a hint about the problem in the window that opens for editing. For example, in Figure 18-1 the problem with the two listings is the format of the account numbers for state unemployment and withholding in California.

QuickBooks knows that the account number has to follow a specific format, and this data was originally entered in the wrong format.

Using the Scheduled vs. Unscheduled Liabilities Window

In the following sections covering paying payroll liabilities, you have a choice of methods for performing each task:

- For liabilities that have a schedule configured, choose Employees | Payroll Taxes And Liabilities | Pay Scheduled Liabilities. Select the payments to remit from the schedule that displays.
- For liabilities that don't have a schedule configured, choose Employees | Payroll Taxes And Liabilities | Create Custom Liability Payments. Select the paycheck date range you need, and then select the payments to remit. All your liabilities (both scheduled and unscheduled) are included in the list.

Remitting Liabilities

When you create payroll checks, QuickBooks tracks the liabilities you accrue as a result of those checks. To see your scheduled liabilities, choose the appropriate command (as described in the preceding section). QuickBooks displays the currently owed liabilities (see Figure 18-2).

Select the liability you want to pay, and click View/Pay. The first time you pay liabilities, QuickBooks asks you to select the right bank account (if you have more than one bank account).

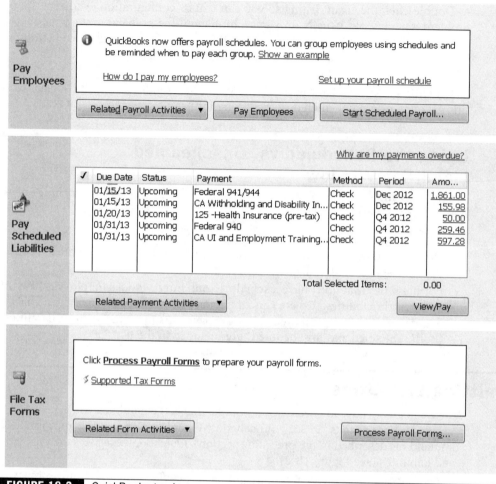

FIGURE 18-2 QuickBooks tracks your payroll liabilities automatically.

The payment transaction window opens, as seen in Figure 18-3. Continue to view and pay until all the current liabilities are remitted. The following sections cover the details involved in remitting common payroll liability payments.

Liability Payment - Company Checking Account

Payment 1 of 1   Print

Bank Account Company Checking Account ▼   Ending Balance   89,670.81

| | No. | EFTPS |
| | Date | 01/15/2013 |

Pay to the Order of Dept of the Treasury ▼ $ 1,861.00

One thousand eight hundred sixty-one and 00/100* Dollars

Address

Memo 55-5555555

Period: 12/01/12 - 12/31/12   How do I e-pay?   ○ E-payment ● Check

| Expenses | $0.00 | **Payroll Liabilities** | $1,861.00 | ☐ To be printed

Payroll Item	Amount	Memo	Class
Federal Withholding	912.58		
Social Security Comp...	318.66		
Social Security Emplo...	452.47		
Medicare Company	74.24		

Recalculate   Save & Close   Save & Next   Cancel

FIGURE 18-3   This liability check is posted to the right accounts and is ready to print.

Sending Federal Tax Payments

Payments to the federal government involve two payroll taxes:

- 941/944/943 taxes, which cover withholding, Social Security, and Medicare
- 940 taxes, which are the federal unemployment taxes

ProAdvisor Tip: This section is specific to liabilities payments made by companies that file Form 941/943 on a quarterly basis. If you use Form 944, you file annually.

941/943 Payments

The federal government requires you to deposit the withheld amounts, along with the matching employer contributions, at a specified time. That time period is dependent upon the size of the total withholding amount you've accumulated. You may be required to deposit monthly, semimonthly, weekly, or within three days of the payroll. Check the current limits with the IRS or your accountant.

There's a formula for determining the size of the 941/943 payment—it's the sum of the following amounts for the period:

- Federal withholding
- FICA withholding
- Medicare withholding
- FICA matching contribution from employer
- Medicare matching contribution from employer

You don't have to do the math—QuickBooks does it for you. But it's a good idea to know what the formula is so you can check the numbers yourself (and make sure you have sufficient funds in your bank account to cover the next payment).

Creating a Check for 941/943 Payments

If you write or print the 941/943 payment check and deposit it at the bank in which you have your payroll account, use the coupons the federal government sent you (Form 8109). Fill out a coupon and take it, along with your check, to the bank in which you have your payroll account. Make the check payable to the bank. Don't forget to fill in the little bullets on the coupon: one to indicate the type of deposit (941 or 943), the other to indicate the quarter for which this payment is remitted.

E-paying 941/943 Payments

If you remit your payments electronically (either through QuickBooks Enhanced Payroll or by using the Electronic Federal Tax Payment System (EFTPS) operated by the IRS), the payee is the IRS. The payment appears in your bank register as an e-payment, either automatically (if you're using QuickBooks e-pay) or manually (if you use EFTPS).

Employers who e-pay directly through EFTPS usually enter text in the check number field such as "ACH," which is the method the IRS uses to take the payment out of your bank account. ACH stands for *Automated Clearing House*, which is a network operated by the Federal Reserve and the Electronic Payments Network that provides a way for financial institutions to exchange funds electronically. You can also leave the check number field blank.

940 Payments

The Federal Unemployment Tax Act (FUTA) provides unemployment compensation to workers who have lost their jobs, usually after the workers' state benefits have been exhausted. The FUTA tax is paid by employers; no deductions are taken from employee wages. Companies must make FUTA payments if either of the following scenarios exists:

- During this year or last year you paid wages of at least $1,500 in any calendar quarter.
- During this year or last year you had one or more employees for at least part of a day for a period of 20 weeks (the weeks do not have to be contiguous).

You don't have to make the deposit until you owe the entire amount, but you can make deposits until you reach that amount if you wish.

Technically, FUTA tax is 6.2 percent of gross wages up to $7,000 per employee, but the federal government gives employers a 5.4 percent credit for paying their state unemployment taxes. Therefore, unless you deliberately ignore your state unemployment payments, you can calculate FUTA at the rate of 0.8 percent of gross wages (0.008 × $7,000), which is $56 per employee who reaches the $7,000 goal. QuickBooks assumes you're paying your state unemployment taxes and calculates your FUTA liability accordingly.

Remitting State and Local Liabilities

Your state and local payroll liabilities vary depending upon where your business is located and where your employees live (and pay taxes). Besides income taxes, you may be liable for unemployment insurance and disability insurance.

Remitting State and Local Income Taxes

Most states have some form of an income tax, which might be calculated in any one of a variety of ways:

- A flat percentage of gross income
- A sliding percentage of gross income
- A percentage based on the federal tax for the employee

Local (municipal or county) taxes are also widely varied in their approach:

- Some cities have different rates for employees of companies that operate in the city. There may be one rate for employees who live in the same city and a different rate for nonresidents.
- Your business might operate in a city or town that has a *payroll head tax* (a once-a-year payment that is a flat amount per employee).
- You may have a head tax for the town in which your business operates and still be required to withhold local taxes for employees who live in another city.

QuickBooks Enhanced Payroll supports most state forms. State and local taxing authorities also provide coupons or forms or an online service for remitting income tax withholding. The frequency with which you must pay might depend on the size of your payroll, or it might be quarterly, semiannual, or annual, regardless of the amount. Some municipal authorities have e-pay available.

Remitting Other State Liabilities

If your state has SUI or SDI or both, you have to pay those liabilities when they're due. Commonly, these are quarterly payments.

ProAdvisor Tip: It's a good idea to create different vendor names for SUI, SDI, and state income tax withholding to make sure you don't accidentally send checks for the wrong component and to prevent QuickBooks from issuing a single check for the grand total. The vendor record for each vendor name may have the same payee (State Department of Revenue), but the vendor names are different.

Not all states have SUI or SDI, and some have one but not the other. Some states collect SUI and SDI from the employee and the company; some collect only from the company. Check the rules for your state.

Remitting Other Payroll Liabilities

The rules for remitting the paycheck deductions and employer contributions for other reasons—such as health benefits, pension, and workers compensation—are specific to your arrangements with those vendors.

There are a great many ways to handle the way these payments are posted, and you have to decide what makes sense to you (or to your accountant). For example, if you pay a monthly amount to a medical insurer, you may want to post the employee deductions back to the same expense account you use to pay the bill. That way, only the net amount is reported as an expense on your taxes.

Workers Comp

QuickBooks Enhanced Payroll offerings include workers comp, and the setup options are available in the Payroll & Employees category of the Preferences dialog. Click the Workers Compensation button on the Company Preferences tab to open the Workers Comp Preferences dialog. Select Track Workers Comp to enable the feature.

When workers comp is enabled, you can also opt to see reminder messages to assign workers comp codes when you create paychecks or timesheets. In addition, you can select the option to exclude an overtime premium from your workers comp calculations (check your workers comp insurance policy to see if you can calculate overtime amounts as regular pay).

Preparing Your 941/943 Form

Unless you've been notified that you're a Form 944 filer, you must file a 941 or 943 form every quarter to report the total amount you owe the federal government for withheld taxes, FICA, and Medicare. If you have been paying the deposits regularly, no check is remitted with the 941/943. Instead, it's a report of amounts due and amounts paid, and they should match so that Line 12 is $0.00.

- If you underpaid, use the payment voucher to send your check for the underpaid amount. The vendor for the check is the United States Treasury (you do not take this check to the bank; only deposits accompanied by Form 8109 are deposited at your bank). Use the address provided on the form instructions (QuickBooks prints the instruction page).
- If you overpaid, you can select the option to take a credit toward the next 941/943, or you can select the option for a refund.

The 941/943 is concerned with the following data:

- Gross wages paid
- Federal income tax withholding
- FICA (Social Security) withholding and matching employer contributions
- Medicare withholding and matching employer contributions

Creating a 941/943 Form

QuickBooks will prepare your 941/943 report using the information in your QuickBooks registers.

If QuickBooks isn't preparing your federal forms (either because you're doing payroll manually or you subscribed to the QuickBooks Basic Payroll service), you can prepare your forms manually with the use of Excel worksheets that QuickBooks provides. See the section "Tax Form Worksheets in Excel" at the end of this chapter. Creating the form is quite easy.

Follow these steps to create a 941/943 form:

1. Choose Employees | Payroll Tax Forms & W-2s | Process Payroll Forms.
2. In the Select Form Type dialog, select Federal Form and click OK.
3. In the Select Payroll Form dialog, select Quarterly Form 941 or Annual Form 943.
4. Select the filing period and click OK.

The Payroll Tax Form window opens with Form 941 or 943 selected. This process is a wizard, so you fill out information and click Next to move through all the steps in the process. The first window is an interview; enter the appropriate data (see Figure 18-4), and click Next to continue.

> **ProAdvisor Tip:** Schedule B is the Employer's Record of Federal Tax Liability. If you are a semiweekly depositor or your payroll tax liability on any day in the quarter exceeds the standard amount for a monthly depositor, you must file Schedule B with Form 941/943.

Move through the wizard, following the prompts, using the guidelines presented in the following sections.

Filling In Blank Fields

To enter information in a blank field, click your cursor in the field to activate it, and then type the data. The typed text appears in blue, but that's just a signal to you that the data was entered manually; QuickBooks doesn't print the form in color.

Tax Form for EIN: 00-1111100

Interview for your Form 941/Schedule B
Employer's Quarterly Federal Tax Return

Instructions: Use this interview to help you fill out your Form 941 and Schedule B (if applicable).
* QuickBooks uses your answers to complete your Form 941.

Do you need a Schedule B?

Are you a semiweekly depositor **OR** a monthly depositor required to file **Schedule B**? .... [X] Yes   ☐ No
Note: Only monthly depositors accumulating tax liability of $100,000 or more on any given day
in the reporting period are required to file Schedule B.
Check this box to print **Schedule B** regardless of applicability .... ☐

To find out if you need a Schedule B, click the "Details about this form" link.

Answer the following questions for Form 941

Select the state code for the state where you made your deposits OR select 'MU' if you made your
deposits in multiple states .... CA

If you do not have to file returns in the future, check here .... ☐
and enter the date that final wages were paid ....
*You would not have to file returns in the future if you went out of business or stopped paying wages
this quarter, for example.*

If you are a seasonal employer, check here .... ☐

View details about this form   View filing and printing instructions

[<<< Previous]   [Next >>>]

[Save and Close] [Save as PDF...] [Print for Your Records...]   [Check for Errors] [Submit Form...]
☑ Automatically create an archive when I e-file or print

FIGURE 18-4 Start by answering questions; the answers are transferred to the form in the appropriate places.

Editing Prefilled Data
Follow these steps to edit data:

1. Right-click the field and choose Override from the menu that appears.
2. Enter the replacement data in the Override box and press the TAB key.
3. The new data replaces the original data in the field, and it's green (to remind you that you manually replaced the data that was exported from QuickBooks).

If you change your mind and decide that the data automatically supplied by QuickBooks should remain in the form, right-click in the field and choose Cancel Override.

Data You Cannot Change

Do *not* edit the following types of data on the Form 941 (or on any payroll tax form for that matter):

- Federal Employer Identification Number (EIN)
- Filing period (if you're trying to change the filing period, start the process again and select the appropriate date range)
- Totals (these are calculated by QuickBooks; if a total is wrong, edit the erroneous number and QuickBooks will recalculate the total)

Checking for Errors

Before you finalize the contents of Form 941/943, click the Check For Errors button. QuickBooks examines the content and displays any errors in the Errors box that opens at the top of the form. If there aren't any problems, the Errors box reports this, too.

Click the error to move automatically to the field that's causing the problem, and correct the information.

- If the problem is in a field you filled out, correct the data and press TAB.
- If the problem is in a field that was prefilled but you changed the content by overriding the data, right-click the field and select Cancel Override.

When you press TAB to replace the data in the field, the error listing should disappear from the Errors box. If it doesn't, you have to do some homework to figure out what's wrong with the data in the affected field and then correct it.

Close the Errors box by clicking the Close Errors button.

Saving and Reopening an Unfinished Form

If you get interrupted or confused while you're preparing your 941, 943, or 940 form, you can save the form with the data you already filled in, so you don't have to start from scratch when you resume your work. Click Save And Close to save the form with its current contents. To return to work on the saved form, go through the steps enumerated earlier in this section to select the form and its date range. QuickBooks asks if you want to use the saved draft.

If you open a saved draft, QuickBooks does not examine your files and refresh the data, so if you made changes to payroll data, you have to start a new form instead of opening a saved draft. Changes could include an additional paycheck being issued within the date range for some reason or a payment you made to the bank or IRS as a deposit for this report period.

Printing Form 941/943

You can print the form from QuickBooks and send it to the IRS if you use these printing criteria:

- The form must be printed with black ink on white or cream paper.
- The paper must be 8.5" × 11".
- The paper must be 20-lb. weight or heavier.

The printed report doesn't look exactly like the blank form you received, but it's close. More importantly, it's perfectly acceptable to the government. Print two copies: one to mail and one for your files.

ProAdvisor Tip: You could also use the information in the printed report to fill in the blank 941/943 form you receive if you don't want to send the QuickBooks printout. Save the printed report as your file copy.

If you're signed up for e-payments, you can e-file your 941/943. Save the printed report as your file copy.

ProAdvisor Tip: If you subscribe to QuickBooks Enhanced Payroll service, you can archive a copy of the form as a PDF file by clicking the Save As PDF button on the form.

Preparing Annual Returns

All taxing authorities want annual returns. The feds, state, and local folks need reports in the form of coupons or longer forms. Some of them want money; some just want reports because the payments were made earlier in the year. You can get all the information you need from QuickBooks; all the standard QuickBooks payroll reports work just fine, as long as you remember to set the Dates field to the entire year.

Preparing State and Local Annual Returns

The state and local taxing authorities usually send you a form that asks for a reconciliation for the year. You may have to present quarterly totals as you fill out the form, which you can accomplish by changing the date range in the QuickBooks payroll reports. For example, if your state returns require totals for each quarter, run payroll reports for January 1 through March 31, followed by April 1 through June 30, and so on.

Finish your state unemployment annual report or fourth quarter report as soon as possible, because the payments you make to the state are relevant to the federal unemployment report (Form 940). In many states, the year-end or fourth quarter report doesn't require a check because there's a limit to the wages that are eligible for applying the unemployment contribution rate, and it's common to meet that limit fairly early in the year.

Preparing the 940 Form

The 940 form (FUTA) is filed annually; there are no quarterly forms to file. To create your Form 940, choose Employees | Payroll Tax Forms & W-2s | Process Payroll Forms from the QuickBooks menu bar. Select Federal Form, and then select 940 and fill in the year.

The Payroll Tax Form window (it's the first window of a wizard) opens with the Form 940 Interview displayed. The top section of the interview window asks about your state and federal unemployment payments. Below that section is a series of questions aimed at determining whether any of your payroll expenses covered exempt payment types. Exempt payments are wages you paid that are exempt from FUTA taxes. QuickBooks checks your payroll items to track several categories of exempt payments, and if you've used these payroll items, QuickBooks fills in the amounts. If you had any exempt payments that are not in the payroll items that QuickBooks automatically checks, fill in the amount directly on the appropriate field. Check the IRS rules for preparing Form 940, or check with your accountant. You can also get more information about this form by clicking the link "View details about this form" located at the bottom of the Payroll Tax form window.

Click Next to see the form itself. Fill out any fields that aren't automatically prefilled by QuickBooks from your payroll records. Continue to click Next and follow the instructions that appear on the screen.

Preparing the 944 Form

If your annual payroll withholding liability is less than $1000 per year, you may be eligible to file Form 944—a simplified version of the 941 form. If you were notified by the IRS that you should file Form 944 instead of Form 941, follow the instructions in the previous sections to open the federal form list and select Form 944. You can remit your liabilities when you send the form, or, if you wish, you can make deposits against your 944 liability by using the deposit coupon (8109), filling in the circle for Form 944, and taking the check to the bank.

You cannot use Form 944, even if you qualify financially, unless you've been notified by the IRS that you are a Form 944 filer. This form is shorter than Form 941, has no additional schedules, and has an annual filing frequency, all of which combine to make this a desirable filing method. If you think you qualify financially but you didn't receive a notification to use Form 944, you can contact the IRS to request a notification at www.irs.gov.

> **Caution:** If the IRS notified you to file Form 944, use it even if your payroll liabilities exceed the Form 944 threshold. The IRS will notice and will switch you back to Form 941/943. You cannot make the decision on your own.

Preparing W-2 Forms

You must print W-2 forms for your employees and send or e-file copies to the appropriate government agencies as well. You start by selecting the form and the employees, and then move to the process of creating and printing or electronically sending the forms.

Follow these steps to produce W-2 forms:

1. Choose Employees | Payroll Tax Forms & W-2s | Process Payroll Forms to open the Select Form Type dialog.
2. Select Federal Form and click OK (if you subscribe to an enhanced payroll service, state forms are also listed).
3. In the next dialog, make sure the filing period year is correct, select Annual Form W-2/W-3, and then click OK.

The Select Employees For Form W-2/W-3 window opens, listing all your employees that have received a paycheck during the year (see Figure 18-5). By default, all employees are selected and the current status of the W-2 printing process is noted.

Click Review/Edit to display the Payroll Tax Form window, which explains the steps you'll go through as you step through the wizard (see Figure 18-6). Click Next to move through the wizard.

Each employee's W-2 form is presented on the screen. If there is nonfinancial data missing (such as an address or ZIP code), you must fill it in. If prefilled information is incorrect, right-click the appropriate field and select Override. Enter the correct information, and press TAB to put that information into the field.

Caution: Changes you make to nonfinancial information are not written back to the employee record. You must make the same changes there.

FIGURE 18-5 When you begin, none of the W-2s have been reviewed or printed.

FIGURE 18-6 The wizard takes you through an interview to produce your W-2/W-3 forms.

Click Check For Errors to see if anything is amiss on any employee's form. If errors appear in the Errors box at the top of the form, click the error's listing. QuickBooks automatically takes you to the appropriate field to correct the information.

When everything is correct, load your W-2 forms in the printer (even if you're e-filing, you'll likely be printing the copy that goes to the employee) and click Submit Form to open the Print/E-file Form dialog. If you enrolled in an agency's e-filing program, have an active Enhanced Payroll subscription, and there are no errors on the form, the option to e-file these forms will be available to you. Otherwise, only the Print button will be active. Select the option to open the Print W-2 And W-3 Forms window. From here, you can tell QuickBooks about the type of form you'll be printing on and the printer you'll be using. Click Print when all of these settings are just the way you want them. You must also print or e-file the W-3 form, which is a summary of your W-2 forms.

ProAdvisor Tip: You can make your employees' W-2s available online at no extra charge if you have a QuickBooks payroll subscription. Using this service eliminates the need for you to print and mail W-2s to your employees since they can view and print their own W-2 information directly from an Intuit website called ViewMyPaycheck.com. Also, if your employees use TurboTax to prepare their own personal tax returns, they can view and download their W-2s directly into TurboTax. To learn more about this service, click the "Tell me more" link at the bottom of the Print W-2 and W-3 forms window.

Tax Form Worksheets in Excel

If QuickBooks isn't preparing your payroll forms (either because you're doing payroll manually or you subscribed to the QuickBooks Basic Payroll service), you can prepare your forms manually with the use of Excel worksheets that are available from QuickBooks.

To access the worksheets, choose Reports | Employees & Payroll | More Payroll Reports In Excel | Tax Form Worksheets. Because this Excel file has macros (programming code to accomplish the required tasks), you might have to tell Excel to let the macros run (depending on how you've configured Excel's security options).

When the QuickBooks Tax Worksheets dialog appears, select the form and date range you need.

> **ProAdvisor Tip:** In Excel 2010 and earlier versions, if you see a dialog warning you that the file contains macros, follow the instructions (which are dependent on your version of Excel) to open the file with macros enabled. Depending on your version of Excel, you may have to choose Always Trust Macros From This Source before the Enable Macros button becomes available.

Setting Report Options

Click the Options/Settings button on the QuickBooks Tax Worksheets dialog to configure the report using the guidelines discussed in the following sections.

Configuring Worksheet Headers

By default, the option to update headers is selected. This means that the header of a printout of the worksheet contains the company name and address information, as well as the date range of the report (the date range you selected in the previous dialog). If you are planning to print the report, it's important to know the date range, so make sure this option is selected.

Configuring the Level of Detail

By default, the Hide Detailed Data Returned From QuickBooks option is selected, which means that the workbook displays only the information connected to the report you selected. For example, Figure 18-7 displays a workbook with a single worksheet (the 941 report).

	A	B	C	D	E
	QB_Taxform_Link1 [Compatibility Mode]				
1	**941 Summary**				
2	**Wages, Tips, and other Compensation**				
3	*Payroll Category*	*Item Type*	*Tax Tracking Type*		*Amount*
4	Hourly Wage	Hourly salary	Compensation		9,800.00
5	Salary-Officers	Salary	Compensation		2,000.00
6	Salary-Staff	Salary	Compensation		6,000.00
7					17,800.00
8	*Federal Tax Withholding*	*Subject Income*	*Taxed Wages*		*Tax*
9	Federal Withholding	17,800.00	17,800.00		3,075.00
10	*Social Security & Medicare*	*Subject Income*	*Taxed Wages*	*Tax Rate*	*Tax*
11	Social Security	17,800.00	17,800.00	0.124	2,207.20
12	Medicare Employee	17,800.00	17,800.00	0.029	516.20
13					2,723.40
14	**Total Tax (Calculated)**				5,798.40
15	*Advance Earned Income Credit*	*Subject Income*	*Taxed Wages*		*Tax Credit*
16					0.00
17	**Total Tax After AEIC (Calculated)**				5,798.40
	941				

FIGURE 18-7   Hide detailed data to produce only the report.

If you deselect the option to hide the detail, QuickBooks adds a second worksheet named Data to the workbook. This worksheet contains all detailed information about the employees (every field on the employee record), the payroll items, and the job-costing links (if you use timesheets to do job costing for payroll).

This is an enormous amount of information and should be used only if you need to troubleshoot the numbers you saw when you produced a report without detailed data. In fact, most of this information is available through other QuickBooks reports, such as the detail reports available in the Employees & Payroll section of the Reports menu.

Journal Entries

n this chapter:

- The QuickBooks Journal Entries window
- Make adjustments to the general ledger
- Depreciate fixed assets
- Use journal entries to post to outside payroll services

As you work in QuickBooks, the amounts involved in the financial transactions you complete (like invoices and bills) are transferred to your general ledger. In addition to transaction data, changes can be made to the general ledger directly. QuickBooks refers to this transaction as general journal entry and uses GJE as the abbreviation.

Journal entries should be used only to enter financial data that cannot be added to an account via a standard transaction.

The QuickBooks Journal Entry Window

The Make General Journal Entries window is shown in Figure 19-1 and is accessed from the Company menu. The format of the transaction window follows a standard approach to viewing the general ledger: columns for account numbers, debit amounts, and credit amounts. In addition, QuickBooks provides columns you can use to link the data you enter to customers and classes and also enter a memo.

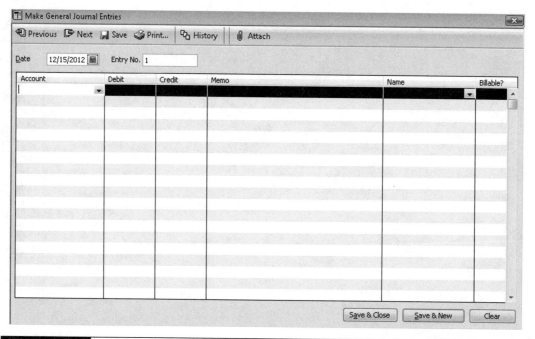

FIGURE 19-1 The QuickBooks Make General Journal Entries window has extra columns so you can track additional information about your entry.

To create a journal entry, follow these steps:

1. Choose Company | Make General Journal Entries. QuickBooks displays a message telling you that automatic numbers are now assigned to journal entries. (You can select the option Do Not Display This Message In The Future before you click OK.) You can enable or disable the automatic numbering feature in the Accounting category of the Preferences dialog.
2. In the Account column, select the account you need.
3. Move to the Debit or Credit column (depending on the data you're entering), and enter the amount for this account.
4. Optionally, enter the appropriate data in the other columns.
5. Repeat for all the accounts in the journal entry.

As you enter each amount, QuickBooks presents the offsetting total in the next line. For example, if the line items you've entered so far have a higher total for the credit side than the debit side, the next entry presents the balancing offset (see Figure 19-2).

FIGURE 19-2 QuickBooks keeps the running offset figure available so you don't have to enter an amount for the last entry.

Here are the guidelines for using the columns QuickBooks adds to a traditional journal entry window:

- Use the Memo column to write a comment about the reason for the journal entry. The memo text appears in the entry of the account's register and on reports, so you should enter the text on every line of the entry in order to see the explanation no matter which account register you're viewing.

- Use the Name column to assign a customer, vendor, employee, or other name to the amount on this line of the entry, if you're linking the entry to a name. If the account you're posting to is an A/R or A/P account, an entry in the Name column is required.

- The Billable? column indicates whether the amount is billable to the name in the Name column, if you are using an expense account and you enter a customer name in the Name column.

- If you are using the Classes feature, a Class column is present and you can link the entry to a class. This can be useful if, for example, you'd like to allocate certain overhead costs or assets to different classes. (See Chapter 7 for information about setting up classes.)

➡ ProAdvisor Recommends

Creating Journal Entries for Changed Accounts

I've had many clients who decided, after they'd been using QuickBooks for a while, that they wanted to track income differently. For example, instead of using only one income account for all the products and services they sell, they determine that having separate income accounts for service fees and for products sold makes analyzing their business easier.

You can use a journal entry to split out these amounts. Create the new account and then take the appropriate amount of funds out of the original account and put it into the new account. Revenue is a credit-side item, which means:

- Debit the original account for the amount that belongs in the new account.
- Credit the new account for that same amount.

Then, of course, you'll have to go to the Item List and change the necessary items by linking them to the new income account so you don't have to keep making journal entries.

The same decision is frequently made about expenses as well. Maybe you feel your insurance accounts should be separated for car insurance, equipment insurance, building insurance, malpractice insurance, and so on.

> ➡ **ProAdvisor Recommends** *(Continued)*
>
> For expense accounts, the journal entry goes to the opposite side of the ledger, so do the following:
>
> - Credit the original expense account for the amount you're taking out of it and putting into the new account(s).
> - Debit the new account(s) for the appropriate amount(s).
>
> This logic also applies to fixed asset accounts. For example, you may have a fixed asset account named Vehicles that you want to divide to track the truck separately from the car—especially if they were purchased in different years. This means you can also separate out any accumulated depreciation so it's assigned to the correct asset. You can also assign the asset as well as the accumulated depreciation to a class if you're using that feature. Refer to the following section to learn about JEs for depreciation.

Creating Journal Entries for Depreciation

Depreciation is a way to track the current value of a fixed asset that loses value as it ages. The basis of an asset's depreciation from an accounting point of view is determined by a complicated set of rules, including IRS rules, and the rules change frequently. Most small businesses enter the depreciation of their assets at the end of the year, but some companies perform depreciation tasks monthly or quarterly.

Depreciation is a special journal entry because the accounts involved are very specific. The account that is being depreciated must be a fixed asset, and the offset entry is to a Depreciation Expense account found in the expense section of your chart of accounts.

Creating Accounts for Tracking Depreciation

It's not uncommon to have multiple fixed-asset accounts if you want to track different types of fixed assets separately. For instance, a chart of accounts could have three fixed-asset account categories: Equipment, Furniture & Fixtures, and Vehicles.

It's very useful to have a separate subaccount to capture the depreciation entries for each of your fixed assets as well as the purchase of an asset for that asset category.

For example, the fixed-asset section of the chart of accounts for the three categories just described would look like this:

Parent Accounts	Subaccounts
Equipment Assets	
	Equipment Purchases
	AccumDepr-Equipment
Furniture & Fixtures Assets	
	Furn & Fixtures Purchases
	AccumDepr-Furn & Fixtures
Vehicle Assets	
	Vehicle Purchases
	AccumDepr-Vehicles

If you use numbers for your chart of accounts, create a numbering system that makes sense for this setup. For example, if Equipment is 16000, the subaccounts start with 16010; Furn & Fixtures starts with 16100, and the subaccounts start with 16110; Vehicle starts with 16200, and so on.

Post asset purchases to the subaccount created for purchases, and make the journal entry for depreciation in the AccumDepr subaccount. Avoid using the "parent" accounts. There are several reasons for this:

- The transactions posted to both the asset subaccount and the AccumDepr subaccount should be consistent so that you (or your accountant) can look at either one to see a running total instead of a calculated net total.
- Tracing the year-to-year depreciation is easier. Just open the AccumDepr subaccount register—each line represents a year.
- The net value of the fixed assets is correct. A Balance Sheet report shows you the details in the subaccounts and automatically displays the total of the subaccounts in the parent account.

You can further refine this example by creating subaccounts and classes for specific fixed assets. For instance, you may want to create a subaccount for each vehicle asset (or one that covers all cars and another that manages all trucks) and its accompanying accumulated depreciation. If your equipment falls under a variety of depreciation rules (for example, manufacturing equipment versus computer equipment), you may want to have a set of subaccounts for each type. You can then use classes to categorize these assets by location or division.

Now, if you're really particular, you can create a different subaccount for each year of depreciation; for instance, under your AccumDepr-Vehicle subaccount, you could have Vehicle-Depr 2009, Vehicle-Depr 2010, Vehicle-Depr 2011, and so on. Then your balance sheet shows a complete year-by-year depreciation schedule instead of accumulated depreciation—and the math still works properly.

Creating a Depreciation Entry

To depreciate fixed assets, you'll need to have a depreciation offset account in the Expense section of your chart of accounts. Once that account exists, open the Make General Journal Entries window and choose the first asset depreciation subaccount (for example, the AccumDepr account under the fixed asset "Equipment"). Enter the depreciation amount in the Credit column.

Choose the next asset depreciation subaccount and enter its depreciation amount in the Credit column. (QuickBooks automatically puts the offsetting amount in the Debit column, but just keep moving to the Credit column as you work.) Continue until all your depreciation figures are entered in the Credit column.

Choose the Depreciation Expense account. The total amount of the credits you've entered is automatically placed in the Debit column. Click Save & Close.

For example, here's a typical journal entry for depreciation. Notice the colon in the account names for the asset accounts—that's the QuickBooks indication of a subaccount.

Account	Debit	Credit
Equipment:AccumDepr-Equip		5,000.00
Furn & Fix:AccumDepr-Furn & Fix		700.00
LeaseholdImprov:AccumDepr-LeasImprov		1000.00
Depreciation Expense	6,700.00	

Using Journal Entries to Post to Outside Payroll Services

If you have an outside payroll service, you have to tell QuickBooks about the payroll transactions that took place. You get a report from the service, so all the numbers are available. It's just a matter of entering them.

It's common for businesses to perform this task via a journal entry. Like all other journal entries, this one is just a matter of entering debits and credits. There are three parts to recording payroll:

- Transferring money to the payroll account
- Entering the payroll figures
- Entering the employer expense figures

Transferring Money to the Payroll Account

It's a good idea to have a separate bank account for payroll if you have an outside payroll service—actually, a separate payroll account is a good idea even if you do your own payroll. Having a separate account makes it easier to record, keep track of, and reconcile payroll-related transactions.

To transfer the money you need for this payroll, choose Banking | Transfer Funds. Then, transfer the money from your regular operating account to your payroll account. Be sure to transfer enough money for the gross payroll plus the employer payroll expenses, which include the following:

- Employer-matching contributions to FICA and Medicare
- Employer-matching contributions to pension plans
- Employer-matching contributions to benefits
- Employer state unemployment assessments
- Employer FUTA
- Any other government or benefit payments paid by the employer

Even though some of these aren't transmitted every payday, you should transfer the amounts at that time anyway. Then, when it's time to pay them, the correct amount of money will have accumulated in the payroll account.

Recording the Payroll

Running your payroll produces a fairly complicated set of debits and credits. Many businesses record a journal entry for the run, then a separate journal entry for the employer expenses when they're transmitted.

- If your payroll service takes care of remitting payroll liabilities, you can journalize those payments.
- If your payroll service doesn't remit your liabilities, when you create those checks your check-writing activity will record the payments, so you don't need a journal entry.

Account	Debit	Credit
Salaries and Wages (expense)	Gross Payroll	
FWT (liability)		Total Federal Withheld
FICA (liability)		Total FICA Withheld
Medicare (liability)		Total Medicare Withheld
State Income Tax (liability)		Total State Tax Withheld
Local Income Tax (liability)		Total Local Tax Withheld
State SDI (liability)		Total State SDI Withheld
State SUI (liability)		Total State SUI Withheld
Benefits Contrib. (liability)		Total Benefits Withheld
401(k) Contrib. (liability)		Total 401(k) Withheld
Other Deductions (liability)		Total Other Deductions Withheld
Payroll Bank Account (asset)		Total of Net Payroll

TABLE 19-1 Typical Journal Entry to Record Payroll by an Outside Service

Table 19-1 shows a typical template for recording the payroll run as a journal entry. It's possible that you don't have all the expenses shown in this table (for instance, not all states have employee unemployment assessments). And you may have additional withholding categories such as union dues, garnishments against wages, and so on. Be sure you've created a liability account in your chart of accounts for each withholding category you need and a vendor for each transmittal check.

Recording Liabilities

You need to journalize the employer remittances of payroll liabilities if your payroll service is taking care of them for you (if you do it yourself, just write the checks from the payroll account and each item will post to the general ledger). Table 19-2 is a sample journal entry for recording payroll remittances.

The entry involving the transmittal of withholdings is posted to the same account you used when you withheld the amounts. In effect, you "wash" the liability accounts; you're not really spending money—you're remitting money you've withheld from employees.

Account	Debit	Credit
Federal Payroll Expenses (expense)	Employer FICA and Medicare	
Federal Withholdings (liability)	All federal withholding	
State and Local Withholdings (liability)	All local withholding	
SUTA (expense)	Employer SUTA	
FUTA (expense)	Employer FUTA	
Employer Contributions (expense)	All employer benefit, pension, etc.	
Payroll Bank Account (asset)		Total of checks written

TABLE 19-2   Typical Journal Entry for Employer-side Transactions

You can have as many individual employer expense accounts as you think you need, or you can post all the employer expenses to one account named "Payroll Expenses."

ProAdvisor Tip: Most outside payroll services take their fee from the payroll account. The fee for the service is really not a payroll expense; it's an operating expense. If your payroll service takes their payroll processing fee from the payroll account, include the amount in your JE and post it to the appropriate operating expense.

Creating Your Own Payroll Entry Template

You can save a lot of time and effort by creating a template for the payroll journal entries. Open a Make General Journal Entries window and fill out the Account column only. Enter the first account, then press the DOWN ARROW key and ENTER the next account, and keep going until all accounts are listed.

Press CTRL-M to open the Memorize Transaction dialog. Name the memorized transaction Payroll (or something similar), and select the Do Not Remind Me option (the reports from the payroll company are your reminder).

Close the Make General Journal Entries window. QuickBooks displays a message asking if you want to save the transaction you just created. Click No (you don't have to save a JE to memorize it). Do the same thing for the boilerplate journal entry you create to record employer remittances.

When you're ready to record payroll, open the memorized transaction by pressing CTRL-T to open the Memorized Transaction List. Double-click your payroll boilerplate JE, enter the appropriate date, and then enter the data.

Click Save & New if you have to create another JE for the employer expenses; otherwise, click Save & Close.

Reconciling the Payroll Account

When you use journal entries to enter your payroll, the reconciliation process is a bit different. You don't have a record of the individual check numbers and payees. When you open the payroll account in the Reconcile window, you see the journal entry totals instead of the individual checks.

Reconciling Outside QuickBooks

You should have a report from the payroll service that lists each check number. You can reconcile the account outside of the QuickBooks Reconcile window using a manual system or Excel, or you can use the method described in the sidebar "ProAdvisor Recommends: Entering Your Payroll Check Details for Your Banks Reconciliation."

➡ ProAdvisor Recommends

Entering Payroll Check Details for Your Bank Reconciliation

If you want to perform the reconciliation in QuickBooks, you can enter the checks and post them back to the payroll account. (The journal entry took care of all the real postings.) You have a little bit of setup to do, and then you can perform this task every payday.

Create a name in the Other Names List, and name the new entity Payroll. You can use this name for every check and put the employee's name in the memo field.

Alternatively, you can create a name for each employee in the Other Names list using initials, last name only, or some other name that isn't the same as the original employee name as it exists in your Employee List.

⇥ ProAdvisor Recommends *(Continued)*

Get the report from the payroll service and open the Payroll bank account register. Then enter the payroll checks using these guidelines:

- The date is the date of the payroll check.
- The number is the first check number on the payroll service report.
- You can use "Payroll" as the payee name (unless you've entered all of your employee names as Other Names, in which case enter the appropriate name, which you can match to the right check number, too).
- The amount is the net paycheck (not the gross payroll amount).
- The account is the same bank account you're currently working in.

When you enter the account data, QuickBooks flashes a message warning you that you're posting the payment to the source account. Click OK (because that's exactly what you want to do), and click the check box that tells QuickBooks to omit this warning in the future.

You can also enter the checks the payroll service wrote to transmit your withholdings or pay your taxes. As long as each entry you make here was included in your initial journal entry, you can post everything back to the payroll account. You're "washing" every transaction, so the net effect on your bank account is zero. Then, when you want to reconcile the payroll account, the individual checks are in the Reconcile window. The fact is that this procedure is quite easy and fast, and you have to do it only on payday (or once a month if you want to wait until the bank statement comes in).

Financial Planning and Reporting

Part Three of this book covers all the steps you need to gain insight into your company's finances. You'll learn about the accountant's copy, which is a feature that lets your accountant examine your books and adjust entries when necessary while allowing you to keep working in your QuickBooks file. You'll also learn how to run the reports you need to analyze your business and pay your taxes, along with instructions for customizing reports so they produce exactly the data you want to see (or need for your accountant or your tax return).

This part also covers setting up budgets and comparing them to your actual income and expenditures.

Accountant's Copy

In *this chapter:*

- Understand the accountant's copy

- Create an accountant's copy

- Merge the accountant's changes into your file

Many accountants specialize in supporting QuickBooks, which means they understand the software and know how to use it. Many have a specialized version of QuickBooks for accountants on their own computers.

At various times during the year, your accountant might want to look at your books. There might be quarterly reports to analyze and adjustments to make, a physical inventory that resulted in serious changes in your balance sheet, expenses that should be posted to different accounts, or any of a hundred other reasons to examine your transactions. Almost definitely this will occur at the end of the year when you close your books and prepare your tax returns.

This could result in your accountant showing up and sitting in front of your computer, making the necessary changes (frequently journal entries), moving this, reversing that, and generally making sense out of your daily transaction postings. By "making sense," I mean fixing transactions that were posted incorrectly or moving postings into categories that better fit your tax-reporting needs.

Some accountants may ask for a copy of the company file, a backup of your company file (which they restore onto their computer), or a portable company file in order to review and make changes to your QuickBooks file. If they use this method, while they have the file, you can't do any work. If you continue to work, the transactions you enter won't be in the company file you restore when your accountant returns it to you because it overwrites the company file you continued to use. Not a good solution.

Understanding the Accountant's Copy

QuickBooks has a better solution. Give your accountant a specially designed copy of your company file called the *accountant's copy*. Let your accountant do the work back at his or her office while you continue to work in your copy. When the file comes back to you with the accountant's changes, QuickBooks can merge the changes from the accountant's copy into your copy of the company file, which means the work you do while the accountant is working isn't replaced by the work your accountant does.

When you create the accountant's copy, QuickBooks imposes restrictions on the type or extent of transactions you and your accountant can perform to make sure you don't work at cross purposes. All of this is discussed in this chapter.

Creating an Accountant's Copy

QuickBooks provides two methods for delivering an accountant's copy to your accountant.

Send the File to Your Accountant You can save an accountant's copy on removable media (CD, DVD, or flash drive) and send or deliver it to your accountant. Sometimes people can't e-mail the file because of the limits imposed by their ISP (Internet service provider) and/or their accountant's ISP.

Upload the File to a QuickBooks Secure Server If your accountant has subscribed to this service, you can upload (at no cost to you) an accountant's copy to a secure server provided by QuickBooks and have your accountant download the file. QuickBooks notifies the accountant of the existence of the file by e-mail and provides a link to the file in the e-mail message.

ProAdvisor Tip: Only the Admin user can create an accountant's copy, and the company file must be operating in Single-User mode to accomplish this task.

Saving the Accountant's Copy on Removable Media

To create an accountant's copy and save it on removable media, choose File | Accountant's Copy | Save File. In the Save Accountant's Copy dialog, be sure the Accountant's Copy option is selected.

Click Next to move to the window in which you set the dividing date for this accountant's copy. Your accountant will be able to work on transactions dated on or before that date in their copy while you can continue to work and create transactions that are dated after the dividing date in your company file. To learn more about this important date, be sure to read the section "Choosing the Dividing Date."

Click Next to save the file. QuickBooks opens the Save Accountant's Copy dialog and creates a filename that incorporates your company filename as well as the date and time of the file's creation. That's an excellent filename and there's no reason to change it. By default, QuickBooks saves the accountant's copy to your desktop, but you can change the location if you wish.

If you're sending the file on a flash drive, change the location by choosing the flash drive in the Save In field at the top of the dialog. If you're planning to send the file on a CD or DVD, save the file to your hard drive and then transfer the file to the CD/DVD. After you save the file, QuickBooks displays a message reminding you of the dividing date and also reminding you to send the file to your accountant.

If you've password-protected your QuickBooks data file, you must give your accountant the Admin password so he or she can open it.

Sending an Accountant's Copy to the QuickBooks Server

To create an accountant's copy that is uploaded to a secure server maintained by QuickBooks from which your accountant can download the file, choose File | Accountant's Copy | Send To Accountant, which opens the Send Accountant's Copy dialog that explains the process.

Click Next to establish a dividing date. Your accountant will be able to work on transactions dated on or before that date in their copy while you can continue to work and create transactions that are dated after the dividing date in your company file. To learn more about this important date be sure to read the next section, "Choosing the Dividing Date."

In the next window, enter your accountant's e-mail address (twice, to confirm the data), your name, and your e-mail address. If an e-mail address exists in the e-mail field of the Company Info dialog (in the Company menu) window, that address is automatically entered as your e-mail address, but you can change it.

In the next window (see Figure 20-1), enter a password for the upload/download of this file. This is not the Admin password your accountant needs to open the

FIGURE 20-1 Secure the file's transfer over the Internet with a strong password.

company file; it's a password required to download the file from the server. It must be a *strong password,* which means it contains at least seven characters, a mixture of letters and numbers, and at least one letter is in a different case from the other letters (usually this means one letter is uppercase).

If your Admin password is a strong password (because you enabled credit card security, as explained in Chapter 3), you can use the Admin password for the upload/download server access.

You can also enter a message for your accountant that will appear in the body of the e-mail message, notifying your accountant that you've uploaded the file. E-mail text is not encrypted as it travels around the Internet, so don't use this message to give your accountant the password.

Click Send to upload the file to the server. QuickBooks displays a message telling you it must close all windows to create an accountant's copy; click OK to continue. When the accountant's copy has been created and uploaded, QuickBooks displays a success message.

QuickBooks sends an e-mail to your accountant (see Figure 20-2) and to you (see Figure 20-3). (The text in both of the messages displayed in these figures has been edited to protect secure information.)

Choosing the Dividing Date

The text in the Set The Dividing Date window (see Figure 20-4) explains that your accountant works on transactions dated on or before the dividing date, and you work on transactions dated after the dividing date. You and your accountant should discuss the dividing date you select.

ınTuıT.

Accountant's Copy File Available

An Accountant's Copy Transfer File is now available for <u>download</u> on the Intuit Accountant's Copy File Transfer secure server. Click the link and then click **Save** in the File Download dialog. Save the file in any convenient location.

About this Accountant's Copy Transfer File:

File Name:	<u>Original sample wholesale-distribution business</u> <u>(QuickBooks2012 Acct Transfer Aug 22,2012</u> <u>10 35 AM).QBX</u>
Sent by:	Leslie, <u>info@samplecompany.com</u>
Note:	Here's our file for your quarterly review.
Uploaded:	08-22-2012 07:36 AM
Expires:	**09-05-2012**

What Next?

No automatic notification is sent to your client when you download the file. Please contact your client to confirm receipt of this file.

To use the transfer file, start QuickBooks Accountant Edition. On the **File** menu, choose **Accountant's Copy** and then choose **Open and Convert Accountant's Copy Transfer File**. The system will prompt you for a password to decrypt the file. Your client must give you that password.

FIGURE 20-2	QuickBooks notifies your accountant that the file is available and explains what to do next.

While your accountant is working with the accountant's copy, you can continue to work in your QuickBooks file, adding transactions dated *after* the dividing date. There are some limitations, however, in what you can change in your file while an accountant's copy is outstanding.

- You can add a new account but not subaccounts. You can also make new accounts inactive. But you cannot add a subaccount to an account that existed prior to creating the accountant's copy.
- If you perform a reconciliation of your bank account (or other account) and clear transactions dated on or before the accountant's copy dividing date, be sure to advise your accountant that you're performing a reconciliation. Otherwise, if the accountant performs a reconciliation for the same month and/or clears the same transactions, the reconciliation will be undone in your QuickBooks file when you import the accountant's changes.

INTUIT

Upload Successful

Your Accountant's Copy file has been successfully uploaded to the Intuit Accountant's Copy File secure server. Your accountant has been notified by email to download the file. The file is available on the server for 14 days, through **09-05-2012**

File Transfer Password
Please be sure to let your accountant know the file transfer password that is required to open the file.

Just in Case...
Please save this message, in case you need it in the future. If your accountant does not receive the notification message, you can forward this message to your accountant. Your accountant can download your Accountant's Copy Transfer File from the Intuit Accountant's Copy File Transfer secure server by clicking the link and then clicking **Save** in the File Download dialog.

About your file:

File Name:	Original sample wholesale-distribution business (QuickBooks2012 Acct Transfer Aug 22,2012 10 35 AM).QBX
Sent to:	samplecompany.com
Note:	Here's our file for your quarterly review.
Uploaded:	08-22-2012 07:36 AM
Expires:	**09-05-2012**

FIGURE 20-3   QuickBooks also sends you information about the file transfer.

The dividing date you select should be the period for which you need your accountant to examine your books and make needed changes, which may not be a year-end date.

Some people send an accountant's copy with a dividing date matching the date of a report they need for a special reason—such as an income statement and/or balance sheet the bank wants to see because of an existing or potential line of credit. Other users may need an "accountant-approved" detailed report of transactions for the company's partners or a nonprofit association's board (usually a month, quarter, or year-end date).

To give your accountant a period in which to insert changes, such as adjusting journal entries or reversing journal entries, set the dividing date about two weeks after the end date you need. For example, if the report you need is as of the end of the last quarter, set the dividing date for two or three weeks after the last quarter end date.

FIGURE 20-4 The dividing date establishes boundaries and limits for the type of work you and your accountant can perform.

Merging the Accountant's Changes into Your File

The file your accountant sends back is not a complete QuickBooks company file; it contains only the changes made by your accountant. The file is encrypted so it can be imported only into the company file you used to create it.

ProAdvisor Tip: The file is quite small and can easily be sent as an e-mail attachment. Because it's encrypted, transferring this type of file by e-mail is perfectly safe.

Use the following steps to open the file and import it into the original company file:

1. Be sure the company file from which you created the accountant's copy is open.
2. Choose File | Accountant's Copy | Import Accountant's Changes From File (if the file is on removable media) or From Web (if your accountant is using Intuit's file transfer service).

3. Navigate to the location where you saved the file your accountant sent, and double-click the file listing; the file has the naming format *<CompanyName> (Acct Changes).qby.*

4. The Incorporate Accountant's Changes window opens so you can preview the changes that will be merged into your company data file and read any notes your accountant wrote. (Before you import the changes, you can save the report as a PDF file or print it.)

5. Click Incorporate Accountant's Changes. QuickBooks walks you through the process of backing up your current file before importing the changes and then merges the changes into your company data file.

After the changes have been incorporated into your file, QuickBooks displays a window (which looks like the window displayed before you selected the option to incorporate the file, except the window indicates that the transactions are "incorporated" instead of "pending"). If any transactions failed to merge with your company file, a message appears informing you of the failure.

The window includes buttons you can click to save (as PDF) or print the information. But QuickBooks will automatically create a PDF and save it in the same location as your QuickBooks data file.

Click Close. QuickBooks displays a message asking if you'd like to set a closing date and password-protect the closed period as of the dividing date you set.

If the dividing date on this accountant's copy was the last day of the previous fiscal year, this is a good idea, so click Yes; if not, use your own judgment. (You can learn about setting a closing date to protect data in the previous fiscal year in Chapter 24.)

QuickBooks opens your company file, the text on the title bar changes back to its normal contents (instead of displaying a notice that an accountant's copy is outstanding), and you can work in the file with no restrictions.

ProAdvisor Tip: After you're up and running again normally, you can delete the file your accountant sent you, and you can also delete the accountant's copy file you created (if you saved it instead of uploading it).

Canceling the Accountant's Copy

If you're not going to get a file back from your accountant, you can cancel the accountant's copy in order to work normally in your company file.

Sometimes accountants report that they have no changes to make, sometimes accountants send you e-mail to notify you of a small change and ask you to enter the transaction manually, and sometimes you decide you made the accountant's copy in error and don't want to wait for a file to come back (don't forget to tell the accountant about your decision).

Another reason to cancel the accountant's copy is because you don't want to import the changes you saw in the Incorporate Accountant's Changes window. Call your accountant and discuss the problem. If the end result is that you prefer not to import the changes, close the Incorporate Accountant's Changes window without importing the changes and cancel the accountant's copy.

To return everything to normal, choose File | Accountant's Copy | Remove Restrictions. QuickBooks asks you to confirm your decision. Select the Yes, I Want To Remove The Accountant's Copy Restrictions option, and click OK.

Caution: If you cancel the accountant's copy and then later decide you want to import and accept the changes, you cannot import the copy you've just canceled. You'll have to create a new accountant's copy, send it to your accountant again and he or she, in turn, will need to redo whatever changes were made in the accountant's copy.

Creating Reports and Analyzing Your QuickBooks Information

Chapter 21

In this chapter:

- The QuickBooks Report Center
- Standard financial reports
- Financial activity reports
- Company Snapshot
- Client Data Review tool
- The External Accountant

If QuickBooks is your first accounting software program and you've been using a manual bookkeeping system, you've already discovered how much easier it is to complete your day-to-day bookkeeping tasks. But in my opinion, the reports you get out of the software are what's really worth the investment of buying and learning QuickBooks. You'd spend hours using a manual bookkeeping system to create these reports, and, in fact, a good deal of the data you obtain from QuickBooks reports wouldn't be available from a manual system. What's more, QuickBooks makes it easy to change, customize, and manipulate reports to get all sorts of information about your business. (See Chapter 22 to learn about customizing reports.)

Using the Report Center

In the Report Center, you can get a dynamic preview of the built-in reports that are available in QuickBooks. It's also where you can access reports that have been contributed by other QuickBooks users and keep track of reports that you especially like by adding them to your list of favorites. Choose Reports | Report Center or click the Reports icon on the toolbar to get there.

As you can see in Figure 21-1, there are many ways you can view samples of the reports that belong to a particular category. Start by selecting a report category from the Standard tab on the left. QuickBooks displays either a sample or a description

FIGURE 21-1   The Profit & Loss Standard Report as seen in the Carousel View.

of the reports available for that category in the main window. Next, select the view in which you want to display the category. The Report Center has three view types: Carousel, List, and Grid. All views provide the same options and quick access to multiple reports, but they're arranged in different ways. Experiment with the different views to find the one that works best for you.

If you double-click the report display itself, the report opens (see Figure 21-2); it's not a sample report, it's an actual report on your company.

		Jan - Dec 12
Ordinary Income/Expense		
Income		
4100 · Revenue		415,428.89
Total Income		415,428.89
Cost of Goods Sold		
5100 · Direct Labor		
5130 · Wages - Sales-Inside	8,800.00	
5120 · Wages - Warehouse	18,655.00	
Total 5100 · Direct Labor		27,455.00
5500 · Freight Costs		1,810.00
5300 · Packaging Materials		1,752.50
5000 · Purchases (Cost of Goods)		180,527.05
5200 · Sales Commission (outside reps)		7,981.60
Total COGS		219,526.15
Gross Profit		195,902.74
Expense		
6237 · Outside Services		2,327.50
6251 · Office Supplies		314.45
6100 · Advertising Expense		2,000.00
6115 · Bank Service Charges		60.00
6120 · Business License & Fees		710.23
6130 · Car/Truck Expense		
6131 · Car Lease	6,756.00	
6132 · Gas	907.64	

FIGURE 21-2   The Profit & Loss report can be launched from the Report Center.

In addition to the Standard tab that is displayed by default when the Report Center opens, four other tabs give you quick access to reports that you've memorized (learn how to memorize reports in Chapter 22), chosen as a favorite (clicking the star associated with a report adds it to your Favorites list), and viewed most recently. You can also see reports that have either been shared by you or contributed by others.

Drilling Down for Details

When you create a report, you can investigate the information that's presented by drilling down to the details behind the displayed totals.

Position your mouse over a total, and your mouse pointer turns into a magnifying glass with the letter "Z" (for zoom). Double-click to see the details behind the number.

- If the report is a summary report, the detail report that opens is a list of transactions that made up the total on the original report. You can drill down into each listing to see the original transaction.
- If the report is a detail report, the list of individual transactions is displayed. You can drill down into each listing to see the original transaction.

Standard Financial Reports

Accountants, bookkeepers, and business owners can keep an eye on the company's health and financial status with a group of reports that are generally referred to as the *standard financial reports*.

These are also likely the reports your banker will ask to see for loans and lines of credit, and if you're selling your business, these are the initial reports the potential buyer wants to see.

Profit & Loss Report

Your P&L report is probably the one you'll run most often. It's natural to want to know if you're making any money. A P&L report is sometimes called an *income statement*. It shows all your income accounts (and displays the total), all your expense accounts (displaying the total), and then puts the difference between the two totals on the last line. If you have more income than expenses, the last line is a profit; if not, that last line is a loss.

There are several variations of the P & L report available in QuickBooks. The ones most widely used are covered in the following section and can be accessed by choosing Reports | Company & Financial.

Profit & Loss Standard Report

The P&L standard report is a straightforward document that follows the normal format for an income statement.

- The income is listed and totaled.
- The Cost of Goods Sold accounts are listed (if any exist), and the total is deducted from the income total to show the gross profit.
- The expenses are listed and totaled.
- The difference between the gross profit and the total expenses is displayed as your net ordinary income (or loss).

> **ProAdvisor Tip:** If you don't sell inventory items, you may not have a Cost of Goods Sold section in your P&L.

While the format is that of a normal income statement, the date isn't. The default date range for the QuickBooks Standard P&L is the current month to date. This is not a year-to-date figure; it uses only the transactions from the current month, and it's almost certainly not what you want to see. Click the arrow to the right of the Dates field and change the date range to This Fiscal Year-To-Date. The resulting display is what you want to see—an income statement for your business so far this year.

Profit & Loss Detail Report

The P&L Detail report lists every transaction for every account in the P&L format. It goes on and on.

This report is a good one to run if you notice some numbers that seem "not quite right" in the standard P&L. I don't recommend it as the report to run when you just need to know whether you're making money.

Profit & Loss YTD Comparison Report

The YTD (year-to-date) Comparison report compares the current month's income and expense totals with the year-to-date totals. Each income and expense account is listed.

Profit & Loss Prev Year Comparison Report

If you've been using QuickBooks for more than a year, this is a great report! If you recently started with QuickBooks, next year you'll say, "This is a great report!"

This is an income statement for the current year to date, with a column that shows last year's figures for the same period. This gives you an instant appraisal of your business growth (or ebb). So that you don't have to tax your brain doing the math, two additional columns show you the difference between the years in dollars and in percentage.

Balance Sheet

A Balance Sheet report is specifically designed to show only the totals of the Balance Sheet accounts (assets, liabilities, and equity) from your chart of accounts—information that's critical to understanding your business's financial health.

The Balance Sheet balances because it's based on the age-old accounting formula:

Total Assets = Total Liabilities + Total Equity

QuickBooks offers several Balance Sheet reports, and each of them is explained in this section. Select the one you want to see from the Report Center, or choose Reports | Company & Financial and then click one of these reports.

Balance Sheet Standard Report

The Balance Sheet Standard report lists the balance in every Balance Sheet account (unless the account has a zero balance) and subtotals each type of asset, liability, and equity in addition to reporting the totals of those three categories. By default, the report displays totals as of the fiscal year-to-date figures, but you can change the As Of date.

Balance Sheet Detail Report

This report displays every transaction in every Balance Sheet account. By default, the report covers a date range of the current month to date. Even if it's early in the month, this report is lengthy. If you change the date range to encompass a longer period (the quarter or year), the report goes on forever.

If you want to see a Balance Sheet report just to get an idea of your company's financial health, this is probably more than you wanted to know.

Balance Sheet Summary Report

This report is a quick way to see totals, and it's also the easiest way to answer the question, "How am I doing?" All the Balance Sheet accounts are subtotaled by type, as shown in Figure 21-3.

FIGURE 21-3 Check your financial health with the Balance Sheet Summary report.

Balance Sheet Prev Year Comparison Report

This report is designed to show you what your financial situation is compared to a year ago, and it displays the following four columns:

- The year-to-date balance for each Balance Sheet account
- The year-to-date balance for each Balance Sheet account for last year
- The amount of change in dollars between last year and this year
- The percentage of change between last year and this year

If you've just started using QuickBooks this year, there's little reason to run this report. Next year, however, it'll be interesting to see how you're doing compared to this year.

Trial Balance

A *trial balance* is a list of all your general ledger accounts and their current balances. It's a quick way to see what's what on an account-by-account basis. Most accountants ask to see a trial balance when they're preparing your taxes or analyzing the health of your business.

To see a trial balance, choose Reports | Accountant & Taxes | Trial Balance. Your company's trial balance is displayed on your screen, and you can scroll through it to see all the account balances. The bottom of the report shows a total for debits and a total for credits, and they're equal.

By default, the trial balance displays every account (including inactive accounts), even if an account has a zero balance. That's because most accountants want to see the entire list of accounts, and sometimes the fact that an account has a zero balance is meaningful.

Cash Flow Reports

The list of reports in the Company & Financial submenu includes two cash flow reports: Statement of Cash Flows and Cash Flow Forecast. The difference between them is that the Statement of Cash Flows reports history based on the data in your company file, and the Cash Flow Forecast looks ahead and forecasts cash flow, based on the history in your company file.

Statement of Cash Flows

The Statement of Cash Flows report displays the history of your cash position over a given period (by default, the Dates field is set to This Fiscal Year-To-Date, but you can change the interval). This is one of the reports you'll probably be asked for by a banker or a potential buyer; it's not a report that provides quick analysis about whether you're making a profit.

This is an accrual report that self-modifies to report on a cash basis, and the lines on the report show you the adjustments that were made behind the scenes to provide cash-based totals. If you have no asset accounts that involve money owed to you (such as accounts receivable (A/R), or loans you made to others) and no liability accounts that involve money you owe (such as accounts payable, or loans), then no adjustments have to be made, because you're essentially operating your business on a cash basis.

A cash flow report has several categories and, depending on the general ledger postings, QuickBooks provides category totals as follows:

- **Operating Activities** The postings involved with general business activities
- **Investing Activities** The postings involved with the acquisition and sale of fixed assets
- **Financing Activities** The postings involved with long-term liabilities and, if the business is not a C-Corp, postings of owner/partner investments in the business and draws from the business

QuickBooks uses specific accounts for this report, and you can view and modify those accounts as follows:

1. Choose Edit | Preferences and select the Reports & Graphs category in the left pane.
2. Move to the Company Preferences tab, and click the Classify Cash button.
3. In the Classify Cash dialog, you can add or remove accounts or move an account to a different category.

	Operating	Investing	Financing
Classify Cash			
Assign accounts to a section of the Statement of Cash Flows:			
* You can move a balance sheet account but you cannot remove it.			
* You can add or remove an income or expense account but make sure that the account only tracks non-cash transactions.			
Account Name	Operating	Investing	Financing
1210 · Accounts Receivable	✓		
1121 · Inventory Asset	✓		
1122 · *Inventory Asset	✓		
1250 · Prepaids	✓		
1250 · Prepaids:1255 · Prepaid Insurance	✓		
1310 · Employee Advances	✓		
1330 · Security Deposit	✓		
1510 · Automobiles & Trucks		✓	
1520 · Computer & Office Equipment		✓	
1530 · Office Equipment (Over $500)		✓	
1550 · Accumulated Depreciation		✓	
2010 · Accounts Payable	✓		

OK   Cancel   Help   Default

Cash Flow Forecast

The Cash Flow Forecast report predicts your cash flow as of a specific date range (by default, the next four weeks, but you can change this). The forecast predicts cash in and cash out and then displays the cash balances that result from those cash flows.

This report is based on income predicted from current receivables and outgo predicted by current payables. If your business operates mostly on a cash basis (you usually collect payment from customers at the time of the sale and you usually write direct disbursement checks instead of entering vendor bills), there's not much future cash flow for QuickBooks to predict.

This report assumes that both you and your customers pay bills based on their terms. If your customers pay late, you can tell QuickBooks to "re-predict" the flow of cash and the dates you can expect that cash by using the Delay Receipts field at the top of the report window. Enter the number of days after the due date you expect to receive money from your customers. For example, if your terms to customers are 30 Days Net, and you know from experience that most of your customers pay you in 60 days, enter **30** in the Delay Receipts field. (QuickBooks has no field on the report window for you to enter the number of days you take beyond the terms your vendors offer; this report assumes you always pay on time.)

Other Useful Reports

QuickBooks offers many other financial reports on your transactions that are categorized by the type of activity for those transactions. Following is a brief overview of those reports.

Sales Reports

If you choose Reports | Sales, you'll see a list of built-in reports you can open to see sales reports summarized by a variety of categories. Table 21-1 explains the contents of each report. Keep in mind that all these reports can be customized to include additional data and various sort totals. See Chapter 22 to learn how to customize reports.

Report	Contents
Sales by Customer Summary	Total sales for each customer and job; does not include reimbursed expenses or sales tax
Sales by Customer Detail	Each transaction that's included in the Sales by Customer Summary report
Sales by Item Summary	Summary of sales, subtotaled by item type
Sales by Item Detail	Each transaction that's included in the Sales by Item Summary report
Sales by Rep Summary	Summary of sales totaled by sales rep; does not include reimbursed expenses or sales tax
Sales by Rep Detail	Each transaction that's included in the Sales by Rep summary report
Sales by Ship To Address	Totals for each unique address you ship to.
Sales Graph	Bar and pie graphs of sales totals (you can display data by customers, items, and reps)
Pending Sales	All sales transactions currently marked "Pending"

TABLE 21-1　All of These Sales Reports Are Already Built into QuickBooks

Vendor Reports

Choose Reports | Vendors & Payables to track financial data related to vendor payments. The list of reports in the submenu includes A/P aging, Form 1099 data, and other useful information.

A/P Aging Summary
A/P Aging Detail
Vendor Balance Summary
Vendor Balance Detail
Unpaid Bills Detail
Accounts Payable Graph
Transaction List by Vendor

1099 Summary
1099 Detail

Sales Tax Liability
Sales Tax Revenue Summary

Vendor Phone List
Vendor Contact List

Inventory and Purchasing Reports

If you've enabled inventory tracking, QuickBooks provides the following useful reports:

- **Purchases Reports** Purchases sorted and totaled by vendor or item, open POs
- **Inventory Reports** Inventory reports on inventory value and stock status

Employees & Payroll Reports

The Employees & Payroll submenu provides a number of reports that range from important to useful, depending on how you and your accountant want to analyze your financials.

Summarize Payroll Data in Excel
More Payroll Reports in Excel ▶
Intuit 401(k) Reports

Payroll Summary
Payroll Item Detail
Payroll Detail Review
Employee Earnings Summary
Employee State Taxes Detail
Payroll Transactions by Payee
Payroll Transaction Detail
Payroll Liability Balances

Employee Contact List
Employee Withholding
Payroll Item Listing
Paid Time Off List

Banking Reports

To track your banking/cash activities, you can display reports on them, including check and deposit detail data, missing check numbers, and reconciliations. (See Chapter 14 to learn about reconciliation processes and troubleshooting reconciliation problems with the reconciliation reports in this Reports submenu.)

Reporting by Class

If you've enabled class tracking and have assigned classes to all of your income and expense transactions, you can run two types of reports:

- Individual class reports
- Reports on all classes

Reporting on a Single Class

To report on a single class, open the Class list and select the class on which you want to report. Then press CTRL-Q to open a QuickReport on the class. This report will give you a list of all the transactions that have been assigned to that class. When the Class QuickReport appears, you can change the date range or customize the report as needed. Using the Sort By drop-down list, you can also sort the report by type to group together transactions of the same type (such as invoice, bill, and so on).

Reporting on All Classes

If you want to see one report in which all classes are used, open the Class list and click the Reports button at the bottom of the list window. Choose Reports On All Classes, and then select either Profit & Loss By Class, Profit & Loss Unclassified, or Graphs. The Graphs menu item offers a choice of an Income & Expenses graph or a Budget Vs. Actual graph.

Profit & Loss By Class Report   The Profit & Loss By Class report is the same as a standard Profit & Loss report, except that each class uses a separate column. The Totals column provides the usual P&L information for your company for each class that you've created. This report is also available on the submenu by choosing Reports | Company & Financial.

Profit & Loss Unclassified Report   This report displays P&L totals for transactions in which items were not assigned to a class. You can drill down to the transactions and add the appropriate class to each transaction. (This will likely be a rather lengthy report if you enable class tracking after you've already begun using QuickBooks.)

Graphs That Use Class Data   You can also display graphs for income and expenses sorted by class, or a graph that compares budget versus actual figures sorted by class.

Accountant & Taxes Reports

The reports that you or your accountant will need for year end or to identify entries that may need adjusting can be found on this submenu under the Reports menu. Using the Audit and Transaction detail reports (see the details on these reports next), you can investigate user actions and changes to previously saved transactions. And, of course, you can generate the reports you and your accountant need to begin tax preparation. Chapter 24 covers the year-end procedures you should follow to prepare for filing your taxes.

Voided and Deleted Transactions Reports

QuickBooks offers two reports you can use to track voided and deleted transactions. Both reports are available by choosing Reports | Accountant & Taxes and then selecting either of these reports: Voided/Deleted Transactions Summary or Voided/Deleted Transactions Detail.

Voided/Deleted Transactions Summary Report

This report displays a summary of all voided and deleted transactions in the selected period. The report shows the current state (void or deleted) and the original state (including the amount) of each affected transaction.

Voided/Deleted Transactions Detail History Report

This report provides more information about both the original transaction and the change. In addition to the information provided by the Voided/Deleted Transactions Summary report, this report displays the credit and debit postings and the posting accounts. If items (including payroll items) were involved in the transaction, they're also displayed.

Company Snapshot

You can get a quick answer to the question, "How's business?" in the Company Snapshot window (see Figure 21-4). Click Snapshots from the Icon Bar to open this window.

In addition to displaying an easy-to-understand summary of the money that's moved in and out, this customizable window provides information on tasks you should perform, account balances, and A/R and A/P data by customer/vendor. Clicking the Add Content link at the top of the window allows you to add reports to your "dashboard." You can then modify the report content (such as date ranges), rearrange positions, or completely remove a report.

To view more detail, double-click an element in this window. For example, to see details about a specific customer's A/R balance, mouse over the customer name in the "Customers Who Owe Money" listing to display an Open Balance report for that customer, sorted and totaled by job.

In addition, selecting the Payments or Customer tab opens new snapshot windows that give you quick access to the details on money due your business and the particulars on the customers that you do business with (like how long they've been customers and how long, on average, they take to pay you). To view more detail on any of the information presented in the snapshot view, just mouse over and double-click an element.

FIGURE 21-4 View a summary of your financial status.

The data displayed in the Company Snapshot window is always appropriate for the permissions granted to the current user. If the user does not have permission to see sensitive financial data, no bank balances appear in the Account Balances section of the window. In addition, the Income And Expense Trend graph section has no data; instead, the user sees a message explaining that he or she needs permission to view the area. Various elements of the window are displayed or hidden depending on the current user's permissions. (Learn about configuring users and permissions in Chapter 26.)

Client Data Review

When your accountant comes to your office to work on your books, he or she can use the Client Data Review tool to examine the data and troubleshoot data entry problems (or potential problems) in a company file. Client Data Review (see Figure 21-5) provides a central place for investigating these problems.

Accessible from the Company menu, the Client Data Review is available only for a user who has logged in as an "External Accountant" (discussed next).

FIGURE 21-5 Your accountant can review your data to make sure your financial information is correct.

External Accountant

You should create an External Accountant user so that when your accountant (or a bookkeeper from your accountant's office) comes to your office, the Client Data Review tools are available. An External Accountant is a specific type of user who has the same rights as the QuickBooks Admin but with the following exceptions:

- The External Accountant cannot create, edit, or remove users.
- The External Accountant cannot view customer credit card numbers if the QuickBooks Credit Card Protection feature is enabled (covered in Chapter 3).

Creating an External Accountant

To create a user who is an External Accountant, you must be logged into QuickBooks as the Admin (only the QuickBooks Admin can create users).

1. Choose Company | Set Up Users And Passwords | Set Up Users.
2. In the User List dialog, select Add User.

3. Enter the user name and password, and click Next.
4. Select External Accountant and click Next.
5. QuickBooks asks you to confirm this action—click Yes.
6. Click Finish to create the External Accountant.

Converting an Existing User to an External Accountant

Many companies have already set up a user name for the accountant. Even if the accountant's login provides full permissions, the Client Data Review tool isn't available on the Company menu unless an External Accountant is logged in (except in Premier Accountant Edition). You can edit the accountant's user account to convert it to an External Accountant.

Select the accountant's user account and click Edit User. Don't change the user name and password data. Click Next, and in the next window, select External Accountant and follow the prompts to save this user name as an External Accountant.

Customizing Reports

In *this chapter:*

- Understand report customization tools

- Memorize customized reports

- Share report templates

QuickBooks offers built-in report customization features that give you the tools you need to work with and view your financial information in the way that makes the most sense for you. When you learn how to use the customization tools, you can select and sort almost any piece of information stored in your QuickBooks company file, from the smallest detail to the broadest overview. This chapter covers where to find and how to use these report customization tools.

Customization Starts with a Built-in Report

All report customization efforts start with opening one of the standard QuickBooks reports. For this discussion, the Sales By Customer Detail report is opened with the date range set for the first half of the year. Figure 22-1 shows you what it looks like before any customization.

Click the Customize Report button to open the Modify Report dialog. This is where you can customize the format and content of the report. Each part of the Modify Report dialog is discussed in the following sections.

FIGURE 22-1 This report has a lot of detail, but sometimes you won't need all this information, and other times you may need slightly different data.

Customizing Report Display Settings

The Display tab (see Figure 22-2) is in the foreground when you open the Modify Report dialog, and it's filled with customization options. Some of the options are also right on the report window, such as the Dates and Sort By fields.

FIGURE 22-2 Use the Display tab to determine what type of data appears on the report and how it's sorted.

➤➤ ProAdvisor Recommends

QuickBooks Report Types

Built-in QuickBooks reports come in two flavors: summary and detail. A summary report displays summarized transactions that are grouped together and show a single total for a reporting group. The Display tab in this type of report will show customization options that allow you to compare current and previous periods, calculate percentages of an account total in relation to others listed in a row or a column, and change how the information is totaled and displayed in the report.

Detail reports display the individual transactions that make up the totals for a reporting group. In addition to allowing you to change how the information is totaled and displayed in a report, the Display tab allows you to add or remove columns from the report that make up the report totals.

Selecting the Report Basis

You can select accrual or cash basis for most QuickBooks reports.

- When you create a cash basis report, the data is calculated by considering actual cash transactions. This means that revenue doesn't exist in the report until a customer pays you and expenses don't exist until you pay the vendor.
- When you create an accrual basis report, the data is calculated to reflect all the transactions you've entered. This means that revenue is reflected in the report when you send an invoice to a customer and expenses are reflected when you enter a vendor bill.

By default, QuickBooks displays financial reports as accrual-based reports because accrual-based reports are more useful for getting an overview of the state of your business. However, if you file taxes on a cash basis, a cash-based report is easier to use for tax preparation.

Selecting Columns

The real power in the Display tab is in the Columns list (which exists only in detail reports, not in summary reports). You can select and deselect columns so the report displays only the information you need.

For example, in this report you may not care about the contents of the Memo field but you'd like to know whether the invoice is paid. In the Columns list, deselect Memo and select Paid, and then click OK to return to the report where the Memo column is gone and the appropriate data ("Paid" or "Unpaid") appears in the Paid column.

ProAdvisor Tip: Any custom fields you created appear in the Columns list, which adds even more power to your ability to customize reports in a meaningful way.

Advanced Options

Some reports have an Advanced button on the Display tab of the Modify Report dialog to open the Advanced Options dialog, which lets you specify the way QuickBooks selects data for the report.

This dialog varies depending on the report, and the following discussion covers the various options you might encounter.

Include Option

The following options determine which accounts appear in transaction detail reports:

- **All** All accounts, whether or not the account had postings in the date range selected for the report
- **In Use** Only those accounts that had postings in the date range selected for the report

Open Balance/Aging Options

The following options specify the way QuickBooks calculates an open balance in an aging report:

- **Current (Faster)** Displays the open balance as of today, including all payments received through today's date
- **Report Date** Displays the open balance as of the ending date of the report, and payments received after the ending date of the report are not included in the calculation

Display Rows Options

These options (typically found in summary reports) specify the rows to include or exclude, as follows:

- **Active** Only rows in which some financial activity occurred, which includes amounts of $0.00 if that total resulted from financial transactions
- **All** All rows regardless of activity or balance
- **Non-Zero** Only rows in which activity occurred and where the amounts are other than zero

Display Columns Options

These options specify whether to include or exclude columns based on whether financial activity occurred in the time frame specified for the report, as follows:

- **Active** Only columns in which some financial activity occurred, which includes amounts of $0.00 if that total resulted from financial transactions
- **All** All columns regardless of activity or balance
- **Non-Zero** Only columns in which activity occurred and where the amounts are other than zero

Reporting Calendar Options

These options specify the calendar basis of the report, as follows:

- **Fiscal Year**   Uses the fiscal year as specified in the Company Info window, starting with the first month of the fiscal year. For example, if your fiscal year begins in October, configuring the report's date range to First Fiscal Quarter displays transactions from October through December.
- **Calendar Year**   Uses the calendar year (starts in January).
- **Tax Year**   Uses a year that starts in the first month of your company's tax year, as specified in the Company Info window.

ProAdvisor Tip: Some reports have a Show Only Rows And Columns With Budgets option, which you can use to customize a report so it displays only accounts that are used in your budgets.

Filtering Report Data

The Filters tab (see Figure 22-3) gives you a full complement of tools that you can use to customize a report to display the exact information that you want it to. Some examples are covered here, but I encourage you to explore all the options in this tab to get a feel for its capabilities and power.

FIGURE 22-3   Change what's reported by filtering the data to meet your own criteria.

For the sales report currently under discussion, suppose you want to see only those transactions that are higher than a certain amount.

1. Select Amount in the Filter list. The filter changes to reflect the options available for the Amount item (see Figure 22-4).
2. Select the greater than or equal to (> =) option.
3. Enter the amount on which to filter the transaction.
4. Press TAB to add the filter to the Current Filter Choices list.
5. Click OK to return to the report, where the contents of the report have changed to match your filter.

FIGURE 22-4   You can create filters to show precisely the information you want to see.

If you want to see only certain types of transactions on the report, use the Transaction Type filter to select the type you want to see; for example, in this report on sales and customers, you might want to see only credit memos. At that point, you've effectively created a "Credit Memos by Customer Detail" report (see Figure 22-4). This is an example of the kind of report you memorize so you can use it frequently (memorizing customized reports is covered later in this chapter).

If you select multiple filters, make sure they don't interfere with each other. In this discussion, I mentioned filtering for amounts and also for transaction type. If you were following along creating the same filters I created, at this point you're seeing only credit memos that exceed the amount you entered in the amount filter. If you want to see all credit memos, select the Amount filter in the Current Filter Choices list and click Remove Selected Filter.

Keep in mind that each filter has its own options. As you add and configure filters and notice the effect on your reports, you'll learn to use filters effectively.

Customizing Report Headers and Footers

You can customize what appears on the header and footer of your report by changing the options on the Header/Footer tab, shown in Figure 22-5.

FIGURE 22-5 Customize the information that appears on the top and bottom of the report page using the Header/Footer tab.

The options you set here have no bearing on the figures in the report; this is just information about the report that appears in the header or footer. Most of the fields are self-explanatory, but the Date Prepared field bears mentioning. The date you see in this tab has nothing to do with the current date or the dates on the report; it's just a sample format. Click the arrow to the right of the field to see other formats for displaying the date.

Customizing Report Fonts and Numbers

The Fonts & Numbers tab, shown in Figure 22-6, lets you spiff up your report by changing fonts and also provides options for the way numbers display on the report.

FIGURE 22-6 Change the fonts and format of the data in the report.

The Change Font For list lets you select elements of the report and change their fonts. Select an element and click Change Font, and then select a typeface, a style (bold, italic, and so on), a size, and a special effect such as underline.

On the right side of the Fonts & Numbers tab, you can configure the way numbers display and print on your report. Select a method for showing negative numbers. If you wish, you can also select a method for displaying all the numbers on the report.

- **Divided By 1000**   Reduces the size of the numbers by showing them as multiples of 1,000. This is useful for companies that report seven- and eight-digit numbers.
- **Without Cents**   Eliminates the decimal point and the two digits to the right of the decimal point from every amount. Only the dollars show, not the cents. QuickBooks rounds the cents to the nearest dollar. (Accountants frequently enter numbers in this manner for tax preparation purposes.)

Memorizing Customized Reports

After you've customized a report to display the information you want in the manner in which you want it, you can avoid the need to go through all this work again by memorizing the report.

ProAdvisor Tip: Before you memorize a report, change its name in the Header/Footer tab so when you use it in the future you know exactly what you're looking at.

Click the Memorize button on the report's button bar to open the Memorize Report window, where you can give this customized report a name. QuickBooks gives you the option to save the report in a report group and to share the report you've just customized with others (both of these options are discussed in this chapter).

By default, QuickBooks uses the report name in the Header/Footer tab. If you didn't change that title, be sure to use a reference to the report type in the memorized name. If you use a name such as My Report, you'll have no idea what the report displays.

Using a Memorized Report

Open a memorized report by choosing Reports | Memorized Reports from the QuickBooks Menu bar and selecting the report from the submenu.

When you open the report, all your customized settings are the way you configured them, but the data changes to reflect up-to-date information. Incidentally, it's not uncommon for experienced QuickBooks users to open a memorized report, look at the data, and think, "Hmm, this makes me think that I'd like to know more about X than Y when I do my quarterly analysis." When that happens, use your memorized report as the basis of another customized report, and memorize that one, too.

Using Memorized Report Groups

After you discover the power available in creating and memorizing customized reports, you may find yourself creating special-data reports like crazy. After a while, it can become difficult to select the report you need in the list of memorized reports. To save time and confusion, you have to get more organized in the way you store these reports. QuickBooks provides a nifty feature called Memorized Reports Groups to help. These report groups let you store reports by category, which makes it easier to locate exactly the report you need.

Creating a Memorized Report Group

Memorized report groups are displayed in the Memorized Report List window, as well as on the submenu you see when you select Memorized Reports on the Reports menu. However, to create or manipulate groups, you have to work in the Memorized Report List window. Choose Reports | Memorized Reports | Memorized Report List to open the Memorized Report List window.

Click the Memorized Report button at the bottom of the window to display the window's menu, and choose New Group. Enter a name for this group in the New Memorized Report Group dialog and click OK. The group you created appears in the window list, and its listing is boldfaced. Continue to add groups to reflect the types of memorized reports you've already created or expect to create in the future.

> **ProAdvisor Tip:** Choose a name that fits the category for the group you're creating. Common names for these groups are Year-End, Monthly, and so on. The more straightforward the name, the easier it is to place reports in the group and find those reports when you need them.

Moving Existing Memorized Reports into Groups

Start by moving your existing memorized reports into the appropriate groups, and then you can save reports you memorize directly in the right group (covered next). You can use either of the following methods to move a report into a group:

- **Edit each report to add the name of the group.** Select the report's listing and press CTRL-E. Select the Save In Memorized Report Group option, and then select the appropriate group from the drop-down list.
- **Drag each report to a group by indenting the report name under the group name.** First, drag each report listing (by the diamond icon to the left of the report name) so it's under the group listing, and then drag to the right, indenting the report name under the group name.

Note that any report listing indented under a group listing is automatically a member of that group.

> **ProAdvisor Tip:** You can drag listings to groups only if the Report Name column heading bar at the top of the window is the only column heading. If you see a column to the left that has a diamond as the heading, click the diamond to hide that column. (To reverse the process, click the Report Name heading to reveal the diamond.)

Saving a Memorized Report in a Group

After you've created groups, you can save memorized reports directly to a group. When you've perfected the customizations you need, click Memorize on the report window. In the Memorize Report dialog, enter the report name, select the Save In Memorized Report Group option, and then select the appropriate group from the drop-down list.

Processing Report Groups

One of the cool things about creating groups for your memorized reports is that QuickBooks makes it easy to process all the reports in a group at once. You can print all the reports in one fell swoop or display all the reports (and then export them to Excel for your accountant).

For example, if you've created reports that are important at the end of each month or each quarter and placed them in a group named End of Month or End of Quarter, you can display or print all the reports with a single mouse click.

To process a group of reports, double-click the group's listing in the Memorized Report List window to open the Process Multiple Reports dialog shown in Figure 22-7. You can deselect any report you don't need at the moment.

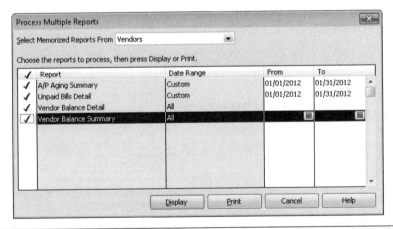

FIGURE 22-7 When it's time to review your businesses performance at month's end, print everything you need.

Adding Standard Reports to Memorized Reports Groups

Often, the report you want to include in a group is a standard, built-in report, available on the Reports menu. To add the report to a group, open the report and click the Memorize button. In the Memorize Report dialog, put the report into the appropriate group.

Sharing Reports You've Customized

It's nice to share—and when you modify a report you can share its template (meaning only the customized report structure you've created and not your company's actual financial data) with other QuickBooks users. Simply click the Share Template button at the top of the report window and give your report a title and description. You can decide if you want to share the name of the report with the rest of the QuickBooks world.

Your shared report will then be listed on the Memorized tab in the Report Center (covered in Chapter 21). What's more, you can access reports that others have decided to share. In the Report Center, select the Contributed tab. Be sure to check in from time to time to see what reports may have been added by other QuickBooks users in your industry.

▶▶ ProAdvisor Recommends

Exporting Your Report Data to Excel

This chapter points out many ways you can work with and customize standard reports inside QuickBooks. But there may be times when you'll need to perform some additional analysis of your QuickBooks data or even change the appearance of a report in ways that QuickBooks itself doesn't allow. The ability to easily send the contents of a QuickBooks report to Excel enhances the power of QuickBooks reports and the value of all the important information that you enter into QuickBooks every day.

At the top of every report window is an Excel drop-down menu that has two options: Create New Worksheet or Update Existing Worksheet (as shown below). If you choose the first option, QuickBooks can either create a new file (workbook) that contains a new worksheet, or it can create a new worksheet in an existing workbook. If you choose the second option, QuickBooks opens a window that allows you to browse to an existing Excel workbook. QuickBooks can send the report information and update the existing Excel report data accordingly, using much of the existing formats and formulas in the workbook.

Budgets and Planning Tools

Chapter 23

In this chapter:

- Configure a budget
- Report on budget versus actual figures
- Export budgets
- Project cash flow

A budget is a tool for tracking your business's progress against your plans. A well-prepared budget can also help you decide when it's best to make a major business purchase, hire additional staff, or draw money out of your business account.

For general planning, the ability to project cash flow by using actual data and then applying "what if" scenarios helps you decide whether you can increase or decrease expenses and prices.

Making these tools work for you is covered in this chapter.

How QuickBooks Handles Budgets

Before you begin creating a budget, you need to know how QuickBooks manages budgets and the processes connected to them. This section presents an overview of the QuickBooks budget features so you can understand them and keep them in mind when you create your budgets.

Types of Budgets

QuickBooks offers several types of budgets:

- Budgets based on your Balance Sheet accounts
- P&L budgets based on your income and expense accounts
- P&L budgets based on income and expense accounts and a customer or job
- P&L budgets based on income and expense accounts and a class. P&L budgets can be created from scratch or by using the actual figures from the previous year. The latter option, of course, works only if you've upgraded to QuickBooks 2012 from an earlier version.

Budget Data Is Saved Automatically

In QuickBooks, a budget is the data you enter in a budget window. Once you begin creating a budget, the data you record is stored in the budget window and reappears whenever you open that budget window. You create a budget by choosing Company | Planning & Budgeting | Set Up Budgets.

You can create only one of each type of budget for the same year. For example, if you create a P&L budget, enter and record some figures, and then decide to start all over by launching the Create New Budget Wizard, you can't create a new P&L budget. Instead of creating a new budget, the wizard displays the data you already configured. You have no way of telling QuickBooks, "Okay, save that one; I'm going to do another one with different figures." You can change the figures, but the changes replace the original figures. You're editing a budget; you're not creating a new budget document.

Creating Multiple Budgets

Once you've created your first budget, regardless of type, the next time you select Company | Planning & Budgeting | Set Up Budgets, the budget window opens with the last budget you created.

If the budget is a P&L or Balance Sheet budget, you cannot create a second budget of the same type for the same year. However, you can create a budget of a different type (P&L with Customer:Job or P&L with Class). To do so, click the Create New Budget button in the budget window and go through the wizard to select different criteria (Customer:Job or Class).

After you've created a Customer:Job budget or a Class budget, you can create another budget using a different customer or job or a different class (or using different accounts for the same customer, job, or class). See the sections "Customer:Job Budgets" and "Class Budgets" for instructions on creating multiple budgets of those types.

Deleting a Budget

QuickBooks lets you delete a budget. This means if you want to create multiple budgets of the same type (perhaps you feel better if you have a "Plan B" budget), you have a workaround to the "no two budgets of the same type" rule. Export the original budget to Microsoft Excel, and then delete the original budget and start the process again. See the section "Exporting Budgets" later in this chapter.

To delete a budget, choose Edit | Delete Budget from the QuickBooks Menu bar while the budget window is open.

Understanding the Budget Window

Before you start entering figures, you need to learn how to manage your work using the buttons on the budget window.

- **Clear** Deletes all figures in the budget window—you cannot use this button to clear a row or column.
- **Save** Records the current figures and leaves the window open so you can continue to work.
- **OK** Records the current figures and closes the window.

- **Cancel**   Closes the window without offering to record the figures.
- **Create New Budget**   Starts the budget process anew, opening the Create New Budget Wizard. If you've entered any data, QuickBooks asks if you want to record your budget before closing the window. If you record your data (or have previously recorded your data with the Save button), when you start anew, the budget window opens with the same recorded data, and you can change the figures.

The other buttons in the budget window are used when you're entering data, and I go over them later in this chapter. See the section "Enter Budget Amounts."

Tasks to Perform Before You Start Your Budget

Before you create a budget, you need to check the following details:

- Make sure the accounts you need exist; adding accounts while you're working in a budget doesn't work properly because you won't see the accounts unless you close and reopen the budget.
- The first month of the budget must be the same as the first month of your fiscal year.
- All the accounts you want to include in the budget must be active; inactive accounts aren't available in the budget window.

▶▶ ProAdvisor Recommends

A Word About Balance Sheet Budgets

A Balance Sheet budget can be challenging to build because it's difficult to predict the amounts for most Balance Sheet accounts—with the exception of fixed assets and loans. In fact, the transactions that affect fixed assets and loans are usually planned and therefore don't need budget-to-reality comparisons to allow you to keep an eye on them.

If you still feel you need to create a Balance Sheet budget, choose Company | Planning & Budgeting | Set Up Budgets. If this is your first budget, the Create New Budget Wizard opens. Otherwise, when an existing budget appears, click the Create New Budget button. When the Create New Budget Wizard opens, select the year for which you want to create the budget and select the Balance Sheet option. Then click Next, and because the next window has no options, there's nothing for you to do except click Finish. The budget window opens, listing all your Balance Sheet accounts, and you can enter the budget figures.

See the following sections on creating P&L budgets to learn the detailed procedures for entering budget figures.

P&L Budgets

The most common (and useful) budget is based on your income and expenses. After you've set up a good chart of accounts, creating a budget is quite easy.

Create the Budget and Its Criteria

To create a P&L budget, choose Company | Planning & Budgeting | Set Up Budgets. If this is the first budget you're creating, the Create New Budget Wizard opens to walk you through the process. (If you've already created a budget, the Set Up Budgets window appears with your existing budget loaded. Click Create New Budget to launch the Create New Budget Wizard.) Enter the year for which you're creating the budget and select the Profit And Loss option. If you're not operating on a calendar year, the budget year field spans two calendar years, for instance 2011–12, to accommodate your fiscal year.

Click Next to select any additional criteria for this budget. You can include customers (and jobs) or classes in your budget.

This discussion covers how to generate regular P&L budgets (unconnected to customers or classes). Budgeting for customers and jobs and for classes is covered a bit later in this chapter. Click Next to choose between creating a budget from scratch or from the figures from last year's activities, and then select the option to create a budget from scratch. Click Finish to open the budget window, where all your income and expense accounts are displayed (see Figure 23-1).

Enter Budget Amounts

To create budget figures for an account, select the account and then click in the column of the first month for which you want to budget. Enter the budget figure, press TAB to move to the next month, and enter the appropriate amount. Repeat until all the months for this account have your budget figures. As you enter each monthly amount and press TAB, QuickBooks automatically calculates and displays the annual total for the account (see Figure 23-2).

Using Budget Entry Shortcuts

To save you from having to complete some of the more mundane budgeting tasks, QuickBooks provides some shortcuts for entering budget figures.

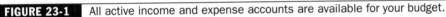

Account	Annual Total	Jan12	Feb12	Mar12	Apr12	May12	Jun12	Jul12	Aug12	Sep12	Oct12	Nov12	Dec12
40400 · Reimbursa...													
40402 · Reimburs...													
40401 · Reimburs...													
40500 · Discounts o...													
49900 · Uncategori...													
4100 · Revenue													
4800 · Vendor Refu...													
5100 · Direct Labor													
5130 · Wages - S...													
5120 · Wages - ...													
5500 · Freight Costs													
5300 · Packaging M...													
5000 · Purchases (...													
5200 · Sales Commi...													
6237 · Outside Ser...													
6251 · Office Supplies													
Inventory Adjustm...													
6273 · Subcontract...													
69800 · Uncategori...													
6100 · Advertising ...													
6115 · Bank Service...													

FIGURE 23-1 All active income and expense accounts are available for your budget.

Copy Numbers Across the Months

To copy a monthly figure from the current month (the month where your cursor is) to all the following months, enter the figure and click Copy Across. The numbers are copied to all the rest of the months of the year.

You can perform this shortcut as soon as you enter an amount (but before you press TAB), or you can return to the month you want to designate as the first month by clicking its column (useful if you've entered figures for several months and then remember this shortcut).

This is handier than it seems at first glance. It's obvious that if you enter your rent in the first month and click Copy Across, you've saved a lot of manual data entry.

FIGURE 23-2 QuickBooks takes care of tracking the running totals.

However, suppose your landlord sends you a notice that your rent is increasing beginning in July. To adjust the July–December budget figures, just move your cursor to July, enter the new rate, and click Copy Across.

The Copy Across button is also the only way to clear a row. Delete the figure in the first month (or enter a zero) and click Copy Across. The entire row is now blank (or filled with zeros).

Automatically Increase or Decrease Monthly Figures

After you've entered figures into all the months on an account's row, you can raise or lower monthly figures automatically. For example, you may want to raise an income account by an amount or a percentage starting in a certain month because you expect to sign a new customer or a new contract.

Select the first month that needs the adjustment, and click Adjust Row Amounts to open the Adjust Row Amounts dialog.

Choose 1st Month or Currently Selected Month as the starting point for the calculations.

- You can choose 1st Month no matter where your cursor is on the account's row.
- You must click in the column for the appropriate month if you want to choose Currently Selected Month (you can click the first month to make that the currently selected month).
- To increase or decrease the amount in the selected month and all the months following by a specific amount, enter the amount.
- To increase or decrease the amount in the selected month and all columns to the right by a percentage, enter the percentage rate and the percentage sign.

Compound the Changes

If you select Currently Selected Month, the Adjust Row Amounts dialog adds an option named Enable Compounding.

> **ProAdvisor Tip:** Although the Enable Compounding option appears only when you select Currently Selected Month, if your cursor is in the first month and you select the Currently Selected Month option, you can use compounding for the entire year.

When you enable compounding, the calculations for each month are increased or decreased based on a formula starting with the currently selected month and taking into consideration the resulting change in the previous month.

For example, if you entered $1,000.00 in the current month and indicated a $100.00 increase, the results differ from amounts that are not being compounded.

Compounding Enabled?	Current Month Original Figure	Current Month New Figure	Next Month	Next Month	Next Month	Next Month
Yes	1,000.00	1,000.00	1,100.00	1,200.00	1,300.00	1,400.00
No	1,000.00	1,100.00	1,100.00	1,100.00	1,100.00	1,100.00

Creating a Budget from Last Year's Data

If you used QuickBooks last year, you can create a budget based on last year's figures. To use last year's real data as the basis of your budget, open the Create New Budget Wizard by choosing Company | Planning & Budgeting | Set Up Budgets. When the Create New Budget Wizard opens, enter the year for which you're creating the budget, and select the P&L budget option. In the next window, select any additional criteria, such as a customer, job, or class. (I'm skipping additional criteria for this example.) In the next window, select the option to create the budget from the previous year's actual figures, and click Finish.

The budget window opens with last year's actual data used for the budget figures. For each account that had activity, the ending monthly balances are entered in the appropriate month. You can change any figures you wish using the procedures and shortcuts described earlier in this chapter.

Customer:Job Budgets

If you have a customer or a job that warrants it, you can create a P&L budget to track the financials for that customer or job against a budget.

Creating the First Customer:Job Budget

To create your first budget for a customer or a job, choose Company | Planning & Budgeting | Set Up Budgets. I'm assuming you're creating the budget from scratch, not from last year's P&L figures.

- If you already created another budget of a different type (P&L or Class), the budget window opens with the last budget you created. Click the Create New Budget button in the budget window to launch the Create New Budget Wizard.
- If this is your first-ever budget, the Create New Budget Wizard appears automatically.

Follow these steps to create a Customer:Job budget:

1. Select the year for your budget, and choose Profit And Loss as the type.
2. In the next wizard window, select the option Customer:Job.
3. In the next window, specify whether you want to create the budget from scratch or from last year's data. Then click Finish.

In the Set Up Budgets window, select the Customer:Job for this budget from the drop-down list. Enter budget figures using the following guidelines:

- The expenses you track depend on the scope of the job. For example, you may only want to budget the cost of outside contractors or supplies, so if prices rise you can have a conversation with the customer about overruns.
- Enter a monthly budget figure for each account or for each month the project exists, or enter a total budget figure in the first month. The last option lets you compare accumulated data for expenses against the total budgeted figure by creating modified reports, where you change the report date to reflect the elapsed time for the project and filter the report for this job only.
- If the project is lengthy, you may budget some accounts for some months and other accounts for other months. For example, if you have a project that involves purchases of goods, followed by installation of those goods, or training for the customer's employees, you might choose to budget the purchases for the first few months and then the cost of the installation or training (either by tracking payroll or outside contractors) for the months in which those activities occur.
- If you want to track payroll costs against a job, use the QuickBooks Time and Billing features that are discussed in Chapter 16.

C a u t i o n : Customer:Job budget reports aren't accurate unless you're faithful about assigning every appropriate transaction to the customer or job.

Creating Additional Customer:Job Budgets

After you've created one budget based on a customer or job, creating a budget for a different customer or job requires different steps.

To create a budget for another customer immediately while the Customer:Job budget you just created is still in the budget window, select another customer from the drop-down list. When QuickBooks asks if you want to record (save) the budget you just finished, click Yes. Then begin entering data for the new budget.

To create a budget for another customer later, choose Company | Planning & Budgeting | Set Up Budgets. The budget window opens immediately with the last budget you worked on.

- If the budget that appears is a Customer:Job budget, select a different customer or job from the Current Customer:Job drop-down list and begin entering data.
- If the budget that appears is a different type of budget, click the arrow to the right of the Budget field and select Profit And Loss By Account And Customer:Job as the budget type. Then select a customer from the Current Customer:Job drop-down list and begin entering data.

Class Budgets

You can link your budget to any class you've created (if you're using class tracking). If you're using classes to track branch offices, company divisions, or company departments, you can create very useful class budgets. If, on the other hand, you're using classes to divide your transactions in some esoteric way, budgeting may not work well.

Look at your class-based reports, and if you find yourself asking, "Aren't those expenses higher than they should be?" or "Why is one class less profitable than the other classes?" you might want to budget each month to get a handle on where and when expenses got out of hand. Also, if you ask, "Is this department contributing the income I expected?" include income accounts in your budget. You can use income accounts in class budgets to provide incentives to your employees—perhaps a bonus to a manager if the reality is better than the budget.

To create a class-based budget, use the steps described earlier to create a budget and choose Class in the Additional Profit And Loss Budget Criteria Wizard window. When the budget window opens, a Current Class field appears. Select the class for which you're creating a budget from the drop-down list. Then begin entering data.

To create additional class budgets (for other classes, of course), use the same approach discussed in the previous section on creating additional customer or job budgets.

Budget Reports

QuickBooks provides a number of budget reports you can use to see how you're doing. I'll discuss each of them in this section. To get to the reports, choose Reports | Budgets from the Menu bar, and then select one of the following reports:

- Budget Overview
- Budget vs. Actual
- Profit & Loss Budget Performance
- Budget vs. Actual Graph

Budget Overview

This report shows the accounts you budgeted and the amounts you budgeted for each month. Accounts that you didn't include in the budget aren't displayed.

Profit & Loss Budget Overview

If you created multiple budgets, select the budget you want to view from the drop-down list and click Next. In the next window, select a report layout (the options differ depending on the type of budget). Click Next, and then click Finish. Essentially, the Overview report type produces the display you'd see if the window you use to create a budget had a button labeled Print The Budget.

This report includes inactive accounts if an account was used when preparing the budget and then subsequently made inactive. This may be confusing if you print this report as the "official" budget for your company.

If you use subaccounts in your budget but only want to see parent account budget totals, you can click the Collapse button at the top of the report window. The button name changes to Expand, and clicking it puts the subaccount lines back into the display.

To condense the numbers, use the Columns drop-down list to select a different interval. The default is Month, but you can choose another interval and QuickBooks will calculate the figures to fit. For example, you might want to select Quarter to see four columns of three-month subtotals (and a Total column).

If you want to tweak the budget, or play "what if" games by experimenting with different numbers, click the Export button to send the report to Microsoft Excel.

Balance Sheet Budget Overview

If you created a Balance Sheet budget, select Balance Sheet By Account in the first window, and then click Next. QuickBooks displays a graphical representation of the report's layout (it's a monthly layout similar to the layout for the P&L budget). Click Finish to see the report.

Customer:Job Budget Overview

If you created budgets for customers or jobs, select Profit & Loss By Account And Customer:Job in the first window and click Next. Select a report layout from the drop-down list (as you select each option from the list, QuickBooks displays a diagram of the layout). The following choices are available:

- **Account By Month**   Lists each account you used in the budget and displays the total budget amounts (for all customer budgets you created) for each month that has data. No budget information for individual customers appears.
- **Account By Customer:Job**   Lists each account you used in the budget and displays the fiscal year total for that account for each customer (each customer has its own column).
- **Customer:Job By Month**   Displays a row for each customer that has a budget and a column for each month. The budget totals (for all accounts—individual accounts are not displayed) appear under each month. Under each customer's row is a row for each job that has a budget.

ProAdvisor Tip: The name of each layout is a hint about the way it displays in the report. The first word represents the rows, and the word after "by" represents the columns. So, for Customer:Job By Month, Customers:Jobs are shown in rows and months are displayed as columns.

Class Budget Overview

If you created a Class budget, select Profit & Loss By Account And Class in the first window and click Next. Select a report layout from the drop-down list. You have the following choices:

- **Account By Month**   Lists each account you used in the budget and displays the total budget amounts (for all Class budgets you created) for each month that has data. No budget information for individual classes appears.
- **Account By Class**   Lists each account you used in the budget and displays the yearly total for that account for each class (each class has its own column).
- **Class By Month**   Displays a row for each class that has a budget and a column for each month. The total budget (not broken down by account) appears for each month.

Budget vs. Actual

This report's name says it all—it shows you how your real numbers compare to your budget figures. For a standard P&L budget, the report displays the following data for each month of your budget, for each account:

- Amount posted
- Amount budgeted
- Difference in dollars
- Difference in percentage

The choices for the budget type are the same as the Budget Overview report, so you can see account totals, customer totals, or class totals to match the budgets you've created.

When the report opens, only the accounts you used in your budget show budget figures.

You can also use the options in the Modify Report window to make the following changes:

- Change the report dates.
- Change the calculations from Accrual to Cash (which means that unpaid invoices and bills are removed from the calculations and only actual income and expenses are reported).

You should memorize the report so you don't have to make these modifications the next time you want to view a comparison report. Click the Memorize button at the top of the report window and then give the report a meaningful name. Only the formatting changes you make are memorized, not the data. Every time you open the report, it displays current data. To view the report after you memorize it, choose Reports | Memorized Reports from the QuickBooks Menu bar.

Profit & Loss Budget Performances

This report is similar to the Budget vs. Actual report, but it's based on the current month and the year to date. For that time period, the report displays your actual income and expenses compared to what you budgeted.

By default, the date range is the current month, but you can change that to see last month's figures or the figures for any previous month. This report is also available for all types, as described in "Budget Overview," earlier in this section, and can also be modified to customize the display.

Budget vs. Actual Graph

This report just opens; you have no choices to select first. All the choices are in the graph that displays, in the form of buttons across the top of the report window. Merely click the type of report you want to see.

Exporting Budgets

If you need to manipulate your budgets, you can export them to Excel. A good use of this export feature is to change the budget dates to the following year so you can import your budgets back into QuickBooks and use them as the basis of next year's budgets.

You have two methods for exporting your budgets:

- Export all your budgets to a delimited text file that can be opened in Excel or Access (or another database program).
- Export a Budget Overview report to Excel.

Exporting Budgets to Delimited Text Files

When you export budgets to a delimited text file (the delimiter is a tab character), you can't select specific budgets to export—it's all or nothing. Use the following steps to export your budgets:

1. Choose File | Utilities | Export | Lists To IIF Files from the QuickBooks Menu bar.
2. When the Export dialog opens, it displays all the QuickBooks lists. Select the item named Budgets, and click OK.
3. Another Export dialog opens (this one looks like the Save dialog you're used to seeing in Windows software). Select a folder in which to save this exported file, or leave it in your QuickBooks folder (the default location). I usually change the folder to the location where I keep files for the program I'm going to use for the exported file.
4. Give the exported list a filename (for example, 2012Budgets). QuickBooks will automatically add the extension .IIF to the filename.
5. Click Save. QuickBooks displays a message telling you that your data has been exported successfully.
6. Click OK.

Exporting a Budget Report to Excel

You can export any budget report to Excel, although it's common to use the Budget Overview report. Click the Excel button at the top of the report window. From here you can choose to create a new worksheet or update an existing work sheet (Chapter 22 covers how to use the Excel export feature on all reports). Select Create New Worksheet if this is the first budget you're exporting. If you're exporting multiple budgets in this manner, you can select an existing workbook and create separate worksheets for each budget.

Importing Budgets Back into QuickBooks

The only practical reason you'd import budgets back into QuickBooks is to copy a budget to another year. If you wanted to edit figures, you'd work in the QuickBooks budget window. To play "what if" games or to sort the budget differently, it's easier to work in Excel, because QuickBooks doesn't provide those features.

Before you can import the file, you must save it as a delimited text file, choosing Tab as the delimiter. You must also change the filename extension to .IIF. Then follow these steps to bring the budget into QuickBooks:

1. Choose File | Utilities | Import | IIF Files from the Menu bar to open the Import dialog.
2. Locate and double-click the file you saved.
3. When QuickBooks displays a message telling you the import was successful, click OK.

You can view the imported budgets in any budget report or in the budget window. QuickBooks checks the dates and changes the budget's name to reflect the dates. Budget filenames start with FY*xxxx*, where *xxxx* is the fiscal year.

When you select a budget report or choose a budget to edit in the budget window, the available budgets include both the budgets you created in QuickBooks (FY2011) and the budgets you imported after changing the date (FY2012). Next year, you can delete the FY2011 budgets.

Projecting Cash Flow

The Cash Flow Projector is a tool you can use to build a report that projects your cash flows using your own criteria. This tool uses data in your company file and then lets you remove and add accounts and even adjust figures. These features make it easier to achieve the projection parameters and results you need.

The Cash Flow Projector is rather powerful if you understand the accounting terminology and principles of determining cash flows. You can design specific cash flow scenarios, which might be useful in planning for an expansion or other major business events.

It's beyond the scope of this book to provide a detailed explanation of the best ways to use this tool, but this section gives you an overview.

To ensure accuracy, make sure you've entered all transactions, including memorized transactions, into your QuickBooks company file. Then launch the Cash Flow Projector by choosing Company | Planning & Budgeting | Cash Flow Projector. The program operates like a wizard, and the opening window (see Figure 23-3) welcomes you and offers links to information you should read before you begin.

FIGURE 23-3 Use the links to familiarize yourself with the information the wizard needs.

ProAdvisor Tip: Each ensuing wizard window has a button labeled Preview Projection. Click it to see your results so far.

Click Next to display the Beginning Balance window (see Figure 23-4), and select the cash accounts you want to include in your projection.

FIGURE 23-4   Select the accounts to use to project your cash flow.

The software calculates a beginning balance by adding together the balances of all the accounts you select. You can make an adjustment to that calculated balance to change the beginning balance of the cash flow projection. This is useful if you know the current balance of any account contains an amount that you don't want included in the projection, such as an income item that is earmarked for spending today or tomorrow and therefore shouldn't be counted.

Click Next to move to the Cash Receipts window (see Figure 23-5). You must select a projection method from the drop-down list. If you don't understand the terminology in the list, discuss it with your accountant. One of the choices is I Want To Project Cash Receipts Manually, which is useful if your accountant has some particular paradigm in mind or if you don't have A/R totals to guide you because you run a retail business.

FIGURE 23-5 Summarize your projected cash receipts on a weekly basis.

The next two wizard windows look similar to Figure 23-5, but they deal with expenses, starting with expenses that are not accounts-payable expenses (expenses for which you write direct checks instead of entering bills, and any unique expenses that qualify as "one-time-only"), and moving on to accounts-payable expenses (including recurring bills you've entered into your system). In both windows you can enter specific expenses or adjusted total expenses.

This brief discussion should help you examine the explanations and instructions and understand the possibilities when using this tool. If you need a variety of cash flow scenarios, you should work with this tool with your accountant to see all the ways it can be applied to suit your business needs.

Year-End Procedures

n this chapter:

- The year-end To Do list

- Run financial reports

- Print 1099 forms

- Make year-end journal entries

- Get ready for taxes

- Close the books

- Create a year-end backup

Chapter 24

The end of the year brings with it several inevitable tasks, and that's true for major corporations as well as for small businesses. There is so much to do: so many reports to examine, corrections to make, entries to create, adjustments to apply—whew!

You can relax a bit. You don't have to show up at the office on January 1 (or the first day of your new fiscal year if you're not on a calendar year). Everything doesn't have to be accomplished immediately. QuickBooks is date-sensitive so you can continue to work in the new year without affecting the totals of the previous year. As long as the dates of new transactions are after the last day of your fiscal year, the transactions won't work their way into your year-end calculations.

The Year-End To Do List

Most of the topics in this chapter are instructions for printing reports and creating transactions to make sure your company file is accurate at the end of the year (so your tax return is accurate). In addition to creating the specific year-end tasks covered in this chapter, you should create a year-end To Do list so you don't miss anything important. The tasks discussed in this section should be a part of that list.

Reconciling All Bank, Cash, and Credit Card Accounts

In January, when your December statements arrive from your bank and credit card company, be sure to either set those aside or print extra copies. Your cash position at year's end is important for planning, applying for credit, tax returns, and other purposes. It's also a good time to gather and enter all those petty cash receipts in your petty cash account register (see Chapter 13).

ProAdvisor Tip: If your fiscal year is not a calendar year, substitute the appropriate months for January and December.

Inventory Stock Status

Perform a physical inventory immediately after the end of the year. Adjust the physical count to remove stock changes (sales and receipt of goods) that occurred after the last day of the year, and then create an inventory adjustment dated the last day of the previous year. (See Chapter 6 to learn about using the QuickBooks inventory count processes and inventory adjustments.)

Fixed Assets

Create a report on your fixed asset accounts to see purchases for the year, as well as accumulated depreciation totals for fixed assets that were purchased in prior years.

The easy way to create this report is to select any fixed asset account in your chart of accounts and press CTRL-Q to open a QuickReport on that account. Click Customize Report, move to the Filters tab, and select Account in the Choose Filter list. Then select All Fixed Assets from the drop-down list in the Account field. The resulting report displays information about all your fixed assets, including purchases and accumulated depreciation.

Payroll

Payroll reports are always relevant as of the end of the calendar year, regardless of your company's fiscal year setup. (See Chapter 18 to learn about year-end payroll processes, including W-2 forms.)

If you run your payroll in-house, QuickBooks primarily uses the paycheck date as the basis for calculating payroll totals. (However, the pay period dates are used in some forms to calculate the number of employed workers working on the 12th of key months.) For example, if you pay employees on Friday for the pay period ending the previous Saturday, all payroll reports are based on the Friday paycheck date. That means for 2012, the last payroll figures are reported as of the last Friday in December. Paychecks issued in January 2013 for the period covering the end of December 2012 are not part of your payroll totals.

Some businesses (and accountants) prefer to track gross salaries and wages as a liability based on the work period and pay off that liability with the paycheck, so they create journal entries to track accrued salaries and wages. In 2012, that accrued entry covers December 24 through December 29 (and will be paid with the paycheck issued January 4, 2013).

If you're accruing payroll entries and you file taxes on a cash basis, you need to make a journal entry for the accrued amounts that won't be paid by the end of the year. A reversing journal entry (dated December 31, 2012, and reversed on January 1, 2013) takes care of maintaining the figures you need.

This is also the time to review any employee benefits that should be reported in W-2 forms and make sure that you're up to date with changes in employee names and mailing addresses. This is important information to verify/gather, whether you'll be printing your own year-end payroll forms or passing that information on to an outside payroll processor.

Running Year-End Financial Reports

The standard financial reports you run at year-end provide a couple of services for you:

- You can see the financial health of your business.
- You can examine the report to make sure everything is posted correctly before you organize information for paying taxes.

Don't forget that reports have date ranges such as "current year" and "last fiscal year." If you perform these tasks before the end of your fiscal year, you're still in the current year. However, if you're working after the last date of your fiscal year (which is quite common), the current year isn't the year of interest. Instead, choose Last Fiscal Year.

Profit & Loss Reports

Start with a Profit & Loss Standard report (also called an *income statement*) by choosing Reports | Company & Financial | Profit & Loss Standard. When the report opens, be sure the date range is the entire fiscal year—either the current fiscal year or the last fiscal year, depending on when you're generating the report (by default, the date range is the current month to date).

The report displays the year-end balances for all the income and expense accounts in your general ledger that had any activity this year. Examine the report, and if anything seems out of the ordinary to you, double-click the line to see a list of the postings to that account. If the data you see doesn't reassure you, double-click any of the individual posting lines to see the original transaction.

If a transaction seems to be in error, you can take corrective action. You should not delete or void a bill you paid or a customer invoice for which you received payment without consulting first with your accountant.

You may also find that you posted an expense or income transaction to the wrong general ledger account. If so, you can either change the posting account in the transaction or create a journal entry to correct it. (See Chapter 19 for information on creating journal entries.) Then run the year-end P&L report again and print it.

Year-End Balance Sheet

Your financial position is best represented on your balance sheet, and you should look at this report toward the end of your fiscal year. To run a year-end balance sheet, choose Reports | Company & Financial | Balance Sheet Standard. Your year-end balance sheet figures can lead to a list of chores if you take the time to review them carefully. Here are some examples:

- Perform a "reality check" with the balances that QuickBooks shows for your bank accounts with your bank's records: Are they in sync?
- Try to pay your payroll withholding liabilities in the current year (the year in which they were accumulated) to clear them from the balance sheet. Also pay employer contributions.
- Check to see if your accounts payable and accounts receivable need some housekeeping: Is QuickBooks still showing some open customer invoices or vendor bills that you're sure have been paid?
- If you have an A/P balance, pay as many bills as you can afford in the current year. Even if this means you pay vendor bills earlier than their due dates (if those dates fall in the next year), you can gain the expense deduction for this year.

Issuing 1099 Forms

If any vendors are eligible for 1099 forms, you need to print and mail the forms to them by January 31st. QuickBooks supports only the 1099-MISC form. Most of the work involved in issuing 1099 forms is done during company setup, where you set up the conditions for 1099 tracking. Then, during the year, you need to make sure the transactions you enter are posted to the proper accounts so that your configuration settings are met. It's also a very good idea to check the latest IRS rules about which vendors should receive a 1099 from you and about any other guidelines that you should be aware of.

Checking the 1099 Setup

First, make sure your file is set up to track and process 1099 forms: choose Edit | Preferences, click the Tax: 1099 icon, and move to the Company Preferences tab to see your settings (see Figure 24-1).

Be sure you've clicked Yes next to the Do You File 1099-MISC Forms? question. Optionally, you can click the first link (located at the top of the 1099 preference window), which opens to the Report 1099 Vendor Payments window (see Figure 24-2).

QuickBooks lists for you the accounts that have payment transactions to 1099 vendors for the previous calendar year. From here, you tell QuickBooks which box(es) on the 1099-MISC form you want the totals from each account to appear in, or you can simply have all amounts appear in Box 7 (nonemployee compensation). To assign an account to a 1099 category, select the category from the drop-down menu. Click Save & Close to assign all the accounts you've mapped.

FIGURE 24-1 QuickBooks supports Form 1099-MISC. The links in the 1099 Preference window guide you through mapping your accounts to the categories (boxes) on the form.

You can assign multiple accounts to a 1099 category, but you cannot assign any account to more than one 1099 category. For example, if you have an expense account Maintenance/Janitorial and an expense account Outside Services, both of the accounts can be linked to the same 1099 category (Box 7–Nonemployee Compensation). However, once you link those accounts to that category, you cannot use those same accounts in any other 1099 category.

Note that you can also access this window via the 1099 Wizard, which is covered in the following section.

FIGURE 24-2 The Report 1099 Vendor Payments window lets you tell QuickBooks which boxes you want the totals from each account to appear in.

Using the 1099 Wizard

Before you print the forms, you need to run a checkup—it's essential to make sure everything is correct before you send forms to vendors and the government.

QuickBooks provides a wizard that walks you through the process to make sure every step is covered and every amount is correct. You can launch the QuickBooks 1099 wizard from 1099 Preferences (see the previous section) or by choosing Vendors | Print/E-File 1099s (see Figure 24-3).

To prepare and file your 1099-MISC/1096 forms

1. **Verify your 1099 vendors**
   Review and edit vendors selected to receive 1099 forms.

2. **Report 1099 vendor payments**
   Choose which payments to report in each box on Form 1099-MISC.

3. **Review 1099 summary**
   Review the amounts to be reported on each vendor's Form 1099-MISC.

4. **Choose a filing method**
   - **Print** 1099s and 1096 on preprinted forms to file by mail.
   - **E-file** 1099s electronically with the IRS using the Intuit 1099 E-File Service. You can also print copies on plain paper.

   ⓘ Learn more about these options

   Get Started

FIGURE 24-3   The QuickBooks 1099 Wizard makes it easy to issue 1099 forms.

This wizard walks you through three important steps: verifying your 1099 vendor information, ensuring that the expense accounts that you associated with 1099 vendor payments are reported in the correct box on form 1099-MISC, and choosing a filing method.

Verify Your 1099 Vendors

In this window, you'll see a list of all of the vendors you've entered into your QuickBooks company file. You'll also see if they've already been set up to receive a 1099. Use the drop-down arrow in the 1099? column to change the 1099 status of a vendor. If you're switching from No to Yes, QuickBooks will warn you if the required address and tax ID information is missing. You can then enter this information directly in the appropriate field(s). Click Continue when you're ready to advance to the next window.

Report 1099 Vendor Payments

This is the same window discussed in the previous section, "Checking the 1099 Setup," but the steps are worth repeating here.

QuickBooks lists for you the accounts that have payment transactions to 1099 vendors for the previous calendar year. In this window, you tell QuickBooks which box(es) on the 1099-MISC form you want the totals from each account to appear in, or you can have all amounts appear in Box 7 (nonemployee compensation). To assign an account to a 1099 category, select the category from the drop-down menu. Click Continue to assign all the accounts you've mapped and to move onto the Review 1099 Summary window.

Review 1099 Summary

The Review 1099 Summary page of the 1099 Wizard shows all the vendors for which a form 1099-MISC will be created (see Figure 24-4). To the right of each vendor name, the following information appears:

- The payment amounts applied to each box on the 1099
- The total of all payments included on the 1099
- The total of all payments excluded on the 1099
- The total of all payments made to the vendor

To see the details behind the amounts being displayed for each vendor, double-click anywhere on the row that contains the vendor's information. The 1099 Detail report for that vendor opens, listing all payment transactions that make up the 1099 reporting balance. If you want to investigate—or modify—an individual payment, double-click the transaction in question on the report.

When you're satisfied that the amounts you'll be reporting are accurate, click Continue.

QuickBooks 1099 Wizard

Review 1099 summary

Review the amounts QuickBooks will report on each vendor's Form 1099-MISC.
Double-click an amount to view details.

Verify Vendors — Report Payment — Review Form → Choose Filing

Vendor Name	Tax ID	Box 7: Nonemployee compensation	Total Included on 1099	Total Excluded from 1099	Total Paid
Jeff's Janitorial	123-45-6789	2,527.50	2,527.50	314.45	2,841.95
Michael Kretchmar	555-55-5555	3,990.80	3,990.80	0.00	3,990.80
TOTAL		6,518.30	6,518.30	314.45	6,832.75

Need more information?

Back   Save & Close   Continue

FIGURE 24-4   Make sure your vendor information is correct for 1099 forms.

Choose a Filing Method

You have two options when choosing how to file your 1099-MISC information to your vendors, your state, and the IRS: e-file your federal and state forms with a printed copy to send to your vendor, or print all copies.

Click the Go To Intuit 1099 E-File Service button to use this method or to learn more about it (additional fees may apply). Click the Print 1099s button if you prefer to file using this method.

Printing 1099s

The 1099 Print Wizard asks you to confirm the year for which you're printing. You'll likely be performing this task in January of the next year. In this case, you'll choose Last Calendar Year as the date range.

Click OK to move to the Select 1099s To Print dialog. QuickBooks displays the vendors for whom you should be printing 1099s.

✓	Vendor	Valid...	Valid Add...	Total	
✓	Jeff's Janitorial	Yes	Yes	2,127.50	
✓	Michael Kretchmar	Yes	Yes	3,990.80	

1096 Summary Information
Number of vendors selected: 2
Total for vendors selected: 6,118.30

Buttons: Preview 1099 · Print 1099 · Print 1096 · Cancel · Help · Select All · Select None

Click Preview 1099 to see what the form will look like when it prints. Zoom in to make sure your company name, address, and employer ID number (EIN) are correct, and also check the vendor's information to make sure it's up to date.

Click Close on the Print Preview window to return to the Select 1099s To Print window. Then load the 1099 forms into your printer and click Print 1099. If you're using a laser or inkjet printer, set the number of copies at three. Dot-matrix printers use three-part forms.

When the forms are printed, click Print 1096 in the Select 1099s To Print dialog. Enter the name of the contact person in your company who can answer questions about these forms (the name is printed on the 1096 form).

Print two copies of the 1096 so you have one for your files. Send each vendor a copy of the 1099 form by January 31. Send the government a copy of each 1099, along with a 1096 Transmittal Form.

Repeat these procedures for each box number of the 1099-MISC form you are required to print (most small businesses need only Box 7).

Making Year-End Journal Entries

Your accountant may want you to make some journal entries before you close your books for the year, such as the following:

- Enter depreciation.
- Move retained earnings to an account created to hold prior retained earnings, or move retained earnings to owner or partner equity retained earnings accounts.
- Create adjustments needed for cash versus accrual reporting (these are usually reversed on the first day of the next fiscal year).
- Adjust prepaid expenses from asset accounts to expense accounts.

You can send the P&L and Balance Sheet reports to your accountant by exporting the reports to Excel.

You can also send your accountant an accountant's copy of your company data and let him or her make the journal entries. You import the changes when the file is returned. (See Chapter 19 for detailed instructions on creating journal entries and Chapter 20 to learn how to use the accountant's copy feature.)

Getting Ready for Taxes

Most small businesses turn over the tax preparation chores to their accountants, but some business owners prepare their own taxes manually or use a tax software program such as TurboTax.

No matter which method you choose for tax preparation, you should run the reports that tell you whether your QuickBooks data files are ready for tax preparation. Is all the necessary data entered? Do the bottom-line numbers call for some special tax planning or special tax considerations? Even if your taxes are prepared by your accountant, the more organized your records are, the less time the accountant spends on your return (which makes your bill from the accountant smaller).

Check Tax Line Information

If you're going to do your own taxes, every account in your chart of accounts that is tax related must have the right tax form in the account's tax line assignment. To see if any tax line assignments are missing, choose Reports | Accountant & Taxes | Income Tax Preparation. When the report appears, all your accounts are listed, along with the tax form assigned to each account. If you created your own chart of accounts instead of accepting a chart of accounts during company setup, the number of accounts that lack a tax form assignment is likely to be quite large.

Before you can prepare your own taxes, you should edit each account to add the tax information. To do so, you can double-click each account listed as <Unassigned > on the Income Tax Preparation report to open the Edit Account dialog, or open the chart of accounts and select an account. Press CTRL-E to edit the account and select a tax form from the Tax-Line Mapping drop-down list.

Your selections vary depending upon the organizational type of your company (proprietorship, partnership, S-Corp, C-Corp, and so on).

ProAdvisor Tip: Be sure the Income Tax Form Used field is filled out properly on the Company Information dialog (on the Company menu). If it's blank, you won't see the tax information fields on any accounts.

Calculate Other Important Tax Information

Some taxable numbers aren't available through the normal QuickBooks reports. One of the most common is the report on company officer compensation if your business is incorporated.

If your business is a C-Corporation, you file tax Form 1120, while a Subchapter S-corporation files tax Form 1120S. Both of these forms require that you separate compensation for corporate officers from the other employee compensation. You will have to add those totals from payroll reports (either QuickBooks payroll or an outside payroll service).

You can avoid the need to calculate this by creating a separate Payroll item called Officer Compensation and assigning it to its own account (named something like Salaries & Wages—Officers, which you'll also have to create). Then open the Employee card for each officer and change the Earnings item to the new item. Do this for next year; it's probably too late for this year's end-of-year process.

Using TurboTax

If you purchase TurboTax to do your taxes, you don't have to do anything special in QuickBooks to transfer the information. Open TurboTax and tell it to import your QuickBooks company file.

Almost everything you need is transferred to TurboTax. You'll have to enter some details directly into TurboTax (for example, home-office expenses for a Schedule C form). You can learn more about TurboTax at www.turbotax.com.

Closing Your Books

After all the year-end reports have been run, any necessary journal entries have been entered, and your taxes have been filed, it's customary to go through the exercise of closing the books. Typically, closing the books occurs some time after the end of the fiscal year, usually within the first couple of months of the next fiscal year, as soon as your business tax forms have been filed.

The exercise of closing the books is performed to lock the books so no user can add, remove, or change any transactions. After taxes have been filed based on the information in the system, nothing should ever be changed.

Understanding Closing in QuickBooks

QuickBooks does not require you to close the books in order to keep working in the software. As a result, "closing the books" in QuickBooks does not automatically set the information for that year in cement; it can be changed and/or deleted by users with the appropriate permissions.

You can work forever, year after year, without performing a closing process. However, many QuickBooks users prefer to lock the transactions for the previous year as a way to prevent any changes to the data except by users with the appropriate permissions who know the password (you create the password when you close the books).

When transactions are locked, existing transactions can't be changed and new transactions cannot contain a date that is on or before the closing date. Users who know the password can overcome these restrictions, so make sure anyone given the password understands the bookkeeping ramifications of changing a transaction in a way that might change the totals you used for tax preparation.

Closing the Year

In QuickBooks, you close the year by entering a closing date. This very important action essentially locks users out of the previous year's transactions. At the same time, you can configure user rights to enable or disable a user's ability to see, or even manipulate, closed transactions.

1. Choose Company | Set Closing Date.
2. In the Closing Date section of the dialog, click Set Date/Password.
3. In the Set Closing Date And Password dialog, enter the closing date (the last date of your fiscal year) and a password.

> **ProAdvisor Tip:** If you've set up users and passwords for access to your QuickBooks data file, only the QuickBooks user named Admin can set the closing date and password.

Creating a Year-End Backup

After all the numbers are checked, all the journal entries are made, and the books have been closed by entering a closing date as described in the preceding section, do a separate backup in addition to your normal daily backup. Don't put this backup on the same media you use for your normal backups—the best option is a CD or DVD, which you can label "Year-End Backup 2012" and store off-site. See Chapter 27 to learn about backing up your QuickBooks files.

Part Four

Managing QuickBooks

The software that you use in both your personal and business life needs regular maintenance. But accounting software, in particular, needs some extra attention in order to ensure its integrity.

In Part Four of this book, you'll learn how to set up and customize QuickBooks so that the documents it creates project your businesses image. There's also an entire chapter devoted to securing your QuickBooks file, where you'll learn how to control who can do what in your company file. The "Managing your QuickBooks Files" chapter includes an in-depth discussion about how to protect and maintain your file using built-in tools and utilities. And finally, in Chapter 28 you'll gain an understanding of how to customize QuickBooks using both user-specific and company-wide preferences.

Printing, E-mailing, and Managing Documents in QuickBooks

n this chapter:

- Set up printers for QuickBooks

- Print transaction forms and checks

- E-mail transaction forms

- QuickBooks document management

Many of the transactions that you create in QuickBooks need to be communicated to either your customers, vendors, or employees. In some cases, this is in the form of a printed document; in other cases, the communication happens over the Internet. This chapter covers your options for both sending and storing the key forms and documents related to running your business.

Setting Up Printing

If you choose to send printed versions of your documents, you have to link each type of document you print to a specific printer and configure the way the printer processes each document type.

To begin setting up forms, choose File | Printer Setup. The Printer Setup dialog opens with the drop-down list of the Form Name field displayed, as shown in Figure 25-1. The form types you see may differ from those shown in Figure 25-1 because the available forms depend on the features you've enabled (for instance, if you haven't enabled Timekeeping, the Timesheet form won't appear).

FIGURE 25-1   Start by selecting the form you want to configure.

The form type you select determines the contents of the Printer Setup dialog, where the tabs, fields, and options vary depending on the form. Many of the forms you print come out of the printer perfectly without any (or much) customization; however, some forms (such as checks) should be tweaked to make sure the output is what you want it to be. If you use multiple printers, you can assign specific printers to specific types of forms, and QuickBooks will always select the appropriate printer when you print those forms.

Configuring Form Printing

This section covers setting up forms, with the exception of checks. See the section "Using QuickBooks to Print Checks" to learn how to set up check printing.

You must assign a printer and configure settings for the forms you print. Start by selecting the appropriate form in the Form Name field at the top of the Printer Setup dialog; the fields in the dialog change to match the needs of the form you selected. For example, Figure 25-2 shows the setup options for invoices; other forms have different (and sometimes fewer) options available.

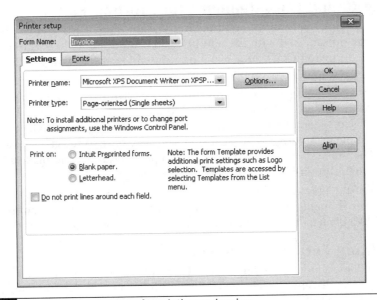

FIGURE 25-2 Configure the settings for printing an invoice.

Choosing a Printer for a Form

The drop-down list in the Printer Name field displays the printers installed on your computer. Select the appropriate printer for this form.

Selecting the Paper for Printing a Form

For transaction forms, the setup offers three types of paper: Intuit preprinted forms, blank paper, and letterhead.

Intuit Preprinted Forms You can order these forms from Intuit or your favorite form supplier (who carries forms specifically designed for QuickBooks). All the fields are preprinted and aligned to match the way QuickBooks prints the form. When you print, only the field data prints, not the field names.

Blank Paper If you use blank paper to print transaction forms, QuickBooks prints your company name and address at the top of the paper and prints the field names in addition to the data. Lines to separate fields and columns are also printed. You can select the option not to print the lines, but without the column and field lines, the invoice may be hard to read or understand.

Letterhead This setting is the same as the Blank Paper setting, except QuickBooks does not print the company name and address information at the top, and the top of the form begins printing two inches below the top of the paper to make sure the data doesn't print over your preprinted letterhead text.

Fine-tuning the Alignment for Printing Forms

To make sure that everything prints in the right place (or to change the placement if you're not satisfied with the output), you can fine-tune the alignment of text. It's important to do this if you're using preprinted forms, but you should also check the way the printout looks on blank paper or letterhead.

Click Align to open the Align Printer dialog. Choose the template that you want to work with and click OK. This opens the Fine Alignment dialog in which you can print a sample and then move text up, down, left, or right to make adjustments to the sample printout. (For some forms, you may have to select a specific form before the Alignment dialog opens.) Continue to print a sample and make adjustments until the printout looks the way you want it to.

Adjustments affect all the text as a block. You cannot adjust individual fields, rows, or other elements in the printed form. If you adjust the alignment by moving up 10/100th of an inch, everything that prints on the form moves up 10/100th of an inch.

Printing Forms as PDF Files

QuickBooks automatically installs a PDF printer driver when you install the software. The printer driver is used by QuickBooks when you click Send to e-mail transaction forms to customers or vendors (covered in this chapter in the section, "E-mailing Forms and Reports"). If you want to print your forms as PDF documents, open the form and choose File | Save As PDF.

Using QuickBooks to Print Checks

If you want to print your checks from within QuickBooks instead of creating checks manually, you must use checks that are designed specifically for QuickBooks.

Purchasing Checks That Work with QuickBooks

QuickBooks checks come in several varieties and in a wide range of colors and designs. You can order any of the following check types directly from Intuit by choosing Banking | Order Checks & Envelopes | Order Checks:

- Voucher
- Standard business checks
- Wallet-sized checks

Setting Up Your Printer for Checks

To configure your printer to manage check printing, choose File | Printer Setup from the Menu bar. Select Check/PayCheck as the form, and then select the printer you're using for checks. Your Printer Setup window should look similar to Figure 25-3.

FIGURE 25-3   Set up your printer for check printing.

Choosing a Check Style

You have to select a check style, and it has to match the check style you purchased, of course. Three styles are available for QuickBooks checks, and a sample of each style appears in the dialog to show you what the style looks like.

- **Voucher checks**   These have a detachable section on the check form. QuickBooks prints voucher information if you have voucher checks, including the name of the payee, the date, and the individual amounts of the bills being paid by this check. The voucher is attached to the bottom of the check. The check is the width of a regular business envelope.
- **Standard checks**   These are just checks. They're the width of a regular business envelope (usually called a *#10 envelope*). If you have a laser or inkjet printer, there are three checks to a page. Continuous (dot-matrix) feed printers just keep rolling, since the checks are printed on a continuous sheet with perforations separating the checks.
- **Wallet checks**   These are narrower than the other two check styles so they fit in your wallet. The paper size is the same as the other checks (otherwise, you'd have a problem with your printer), but there's a perforation on the left edge of the check so you can tear the ledger portion off the check.

Adding a Logo and Signature

If your checks have no preprinted logo and you have a file of your company logo, select Use Logo or click the Logo button to open the Logo dialog. Click the File button to locate the graphics file. If you want to print a signature on your checks, select the Print Signature Image check box; then click the Signature button and locate the signature file that you want to use.

There's also a selection box for printing your company name and address, but when you buy checks, you should have that information preprinted.

Changing Fonts

Click the Fonts tab in the Printer Setup window to choose different fonts for printed check. Use the Font button to change the font for all check information, with the exception of your company's name and address. To change the font for this information, click the Address Font button. Click the appropriate button and then choose a font, a font style, and a size from the dialog that opens.

Handling Partial Check Pages on Laser and Inkjet Printers

If you're printing to a laser or inkjet printer, you don't have the advantage that a continuous feed printer provides—printing a check and stopping, leaving the next check waiting in the printer for the next time you print checks. QuickBooks has a handy solution for this problem on the Partial Page tab (see Figure 25-4). The solution that matches your printer's capabilities is preselected.

FIGURE 25-4 The Partial Page solution is based on the way your printer handles envelopes.

Aligning the Printout

Click the Align button to print a sample check and see where the printing lines up on the physical check. You can move the starting points for printing up/down or left/right to make sure everything prints where it's supposed to. When you're finished, click OK in the Printer Setup window to save the configuration data.

Printer Settings vs. Printer Options

When you configure a printer by assigning it to a form (or multiple forms) and customize the printing setup for that form, QuickBooks memorizes the selection. If you change printers when you're ready to print, the next time you print the same form, QuickBooks returns to the original printer and printer settings linked to that form type, unless you reconfigure the setup to change printers.

➡ **ProAdvisor Recommends**

Print Settings May Not Work for Multiple Companies

QuickBooks printer settings are applied to the software, not to the company file that's open when you set up printers. That means that if you work in multiple company files and they require different print settings, you'll need to set up the printer and the printing options each time you change the company file.

So, for example, if one company file has payroll and buys voucher checks for all their check printing, but the other company uses wallet-size checks, you must go through a complete printer setup every time you switch company files and want to print checks. In addition, QuickBooks doesn't let you perform separate setups for payroll checks (with vouchers) and vendor checks (without vouchers). You can solve that problem for a single company by buying voucher checks for both types of check printing. If you've repositioned printing with the Align feature, you should write down your saved settings so you can enter them again each time you switch between companies.

Every printer has its own set of options to control the way printing occurs. When you're ready to print a document, such as an invoice, you can set the printing options when you print. The Print dialog has an Options button that opens an additional dialog for selecting options for the selected printer. You can change the tray (or select manual feed), change the resolution of the printing, and perform other tweaks.

QuickBooks does not memorize these options; it uses the printer's defaults the next time you print the form type. If you want to make printer options permanent, you must change the printer configuration in the Windows Printers folder.

Printing Checks

If you print checks in QuickBooks, you can print each check as you create it in the Write Checks window, or wait until you've finished creating all your checks and then print them in a batch. When you use the Pay Bills window to create checks, check printing is treated as a batch process, even if only one check is created.

Printing Each Check As You Create It

If you use the Write Checks window to create a check, when you've finished entering all the data, you can click the Print icon at the top of the window. The Print Check dialog opens, and the next printed check number is entered as the default.

Peek at the checks in your printer to make sure this is the next check number; if not, change the number in the dialog. Then click OK to open the Print Checks dialog and click Print. After sending the check to the printer, QuickBooks displays the Print Checks–Confirmation dialog.

►► ProAdvisor Recommends

How QuickBooks Numbers Checks

QuickBooks tracks two sets of check numbers for each checking account:

- **Numbers for checks that are entered manually**   The next available number is automatically inserted when you enter checks in the check register or deselect the To Be Printed option in the Write Checks or Pay Bill window.
- **Numbers for checks that are printed in QuickBooks**   The next available number is used automatically when you print checks.

This is a useful feature if you have preprinted checks in the office for printing checks and a checkbook you carry around so you can write checks when you're not in the office.

If the check printed properly, click OK. If not, click Cancel to fix the problem and print the check again; see "Reprinting Checks After a Problem," later in this section. If you have additional checks to create in the Write Checks window, you can repeat these steps. However, if you're creating multiple checks, it's faster to create all the checks and then print them in a batch.

Printing Checks in Batches

You can print all your checks in a batch after you've completed the task of creating them. If you've been working in the Write Checks window, use the Save & New button to continue to create checks. When you're finished, use one of the following options to print all the checks you've prepared:

- On the last check, click Save, then click the arrow to the right of the Print icon on the check window and select Print Batch.
- Click Save & Close when you create the last check, and then choose File | Print Forms | Checks to print the batch.

Either option opens the Select Checks To Print dialog.

By default, all the unprinted checks are selected for printing, which is almost always what you want to do, but you can deselect checks if there's a reason to do so (they remain in the batch and will be waiting for you the next time you print checks). Click OK to open the Print Checks window.

ProAdvisor Tip: The first time you print checks, the first check number is 1; just replace that number with the first check number in the printer, and QuickBooks will track printed check numbers thereafter.

If your checks were written on different bank accounts (perhaps you pay bills from your operating account and you use the Write Checks window to send checks to vendors for special purchases, using a different bank account), the Select Checks To Print window displays only the checks ready for printing from a specific bank account. After you print those checks, use the same steps to get to the Select Checks To Print window and change the bank account to see those checks. Don't forget to put the correct checks in your printer.

If you use the Pay Bills window to create checks for vendors, when you finish selecting the bills and amounts to pay, click Pay Selected Bills. QuickBooks displays a Payment Summary window with a Print Checks button. (If you don't print checks, before you see the summary you must assign check numbers in the Assign Check Numbers dialog.)

- If these are the only checks you're creating at the moment, click Print Checks.
- If you have additional checks to print (checks you have to create in the Write Checks window for vendors that do not have bills entered in your file), you can click Done and print all your checks at once from the File menu, as described earlier in this section.

In the Print Checks dialog, click Print to begin printing your checks. When all the checks have been sent to the printer, QuickBooks displays the Print Checks–Confirmation window. If all the checks printed correctly, click OK.

Reprinting Checks After a Problem

Sometimes things go awry when you're printing. The paper jams, you run out of toner, an ink cartridge is empty, the dog chews the paper as it emerges—all sorts of bad things can occur.

If anything bad happens, select the check(s) that didn't print properly in the Print Checks–Confirmation window, click OK, and put more checks into the printer. Then click OK and choose File | Print Forms | Checks. Your unprinted checks are listed in the Select Checks To Print dialog, and the first check number is the next available check number (well, it should be; if not, change it).

Printing Transaction Forms

Many of the transactions you create in QuickBooks, like invoices and purchase orders, for example, need to be sent to the customer or vendor involved in the transaction. (See the section "E-mailing Forms and Reports" if you prefer electronic delivery.)

You can print each transaction as you create it, or wait and print all your transactions in a batch.

Printing Transactions As You Create Them

For your security and the integrity of your QuickBooks file, it's best to save the transaction before printing; that way, you have a record of the transaction in your QuickBooks file. However, if you want to print the current transaction as soon as you finish filling in the data (before you click Save & Close or Save & New), click the Print button at the top of the transaction window. QuickBooks opens the Print dialog (Figure 25-5 displays the dialog for Print One Invoice). Click Print to send the transaction form to the selected printer.

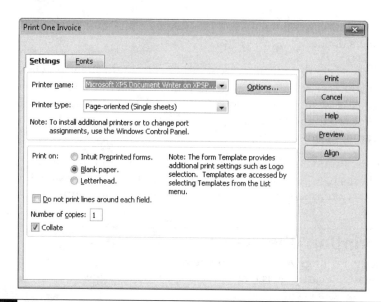

FIGURE 25-5 Printing a single invoice transaction is quick and easy.

Previewing Form Printouts

If you want to see what the printed document looks like, click the arrow to the right of the Print icon at the top of the document window and select Preview.

Often, the printed form differs from the form shown onscreen. For example, if you're creating a packing slip, the onscreen form shows prices, but the printed form doesn't. If you create custom fields for lists or items, the custom field data may appear only in the onscreen form to help you prepare the transaction (such as backorder preferences for customers, advance payment requirements for vendors, and so on).

To learn how to customize transaction forms and decide which fields are seen only onscreen, only in the printed form, or on both, read Chapter 28.

Printing Transaction Forms in Batches

To print transactions in batches, make sure the To Be Printed check box is selected on each transaction you create. Then follow these steps to batch-print the documents:

1. Choose File | Print Forms | *<Transaction Type>* (substitute the transaction type for <Transaction Type>).

2. In the Select *<Transaction Type>* To Print window, all your unprinted transaction forms are selected with a check mark. Click the check marks to remove them from any forms you don't want to print at this time (it's a toggle).

3. Click OK to print. A Print *<Transaction Type>* dialog appears where you can change or select printing options. Click Print to begin printing. After sending the documents to the printer, QuickBooks asks you to confirm that all the documents printed properly.

4. If everything printed properly, click OK; if not, click Cancel. If you have to reprint one or more forms, select the appropriate listing(s) and go through the steps to print batch forms again; the forms you selected for reprinting are listed in the Select *<Transaction Type>* To Print dialog, and you can finish printing your batch. (Of course, before taking this step, you need to unjam the printer, put in a new ink cartridge, or correct any other problem that caused the original print job to fail.)

E-mailing Forms and Reports

You can e-mail documents and reports directly from QuickBooks as PDF attachments to e-mail messages. E-mailing works exactly the same as printing forms and reports, as described earlier in this chapter. That is, you can e-mail each individual transaction as you create it, or save the transactions and e-mail them in a batch.

If you're using Outlook or a compatible web-based e-mail service, QuickBooks can send e-mail to your customers either directly through your e-mail software or your e-mail service. If you use e-mail software other than the supported software, you can use QuickBooks E-mail, which provides a server-based e-mail service. This is a service that you have to sign up for and additional fees may apply.

You can e-mail any report (either as a PDF file or as an Excel file), and you can also e-mail all of the following QuickBooks transaction forms:

- Invoices
- Estimates
- Sales receipts
- Credit memos
- Statements
- Purchase orders
- Pay stubs (if you use QuickBooks payroll and have signed up for direct deposit)

Setting Up E-mail

If QuickBooks finds a copy of one of the supported e-mail software applications (such as Outlook) on your computer with an active profile installed, your QuickBooks e-mail is automatically sent using that software. (An *active profile* is an e-mail account established in the software, and the software is the default e-mail software on your computer.) In that case, the Send Forms category of the Preferences dialog shows the default e-mail method, as shown in Figure 25-6. If these options aren't displayed, you must use the QuickBooks e-mail service to send transaction forms and reports.

If Outlook doesn't appear on this dialog, it means QuickBooks didn't find supported e-mail software configured as the default e-mail software on your computer.

The dialog also contains an option to instruct QuickBooks to select To Be E-mailed automatically on every transaction linked to a customer that is configured for e-mail as the preferred method for sending transaction forms. (The Preferred Send Method

FIGURE 25-6 QuickBooks selects your e-mail software by default.

field is on the Additional Info tab of the customer record.) If you configure a customer for e-mail, make sure you enter the e-mail address in the customer's record.

On the Company Preferences tab (see Figure 25-7), you see the preset text for the e-mail message that's used for sending transaction forms and reports (the text differs depending on the form you select at the top of the dialog). You can change the text to suit yourself.

Sending E-mail

To send a transaction form by e-mail, click the Send Or E-mail button at the top of the transaction form (to send the e-mail immediately), or select the To Be E-mailed option at the bottom of the form before saving the transaction (to send the e-mail in a batch).

FIGURE 25-7 The text for the message body is the same whether you use Outlook, web-based e-mail, or QuickBooks e-mail.

Using Your E-mail Software

If QuickBooks is using Outlook to send transaction forms (or reports), the standard Create Message window appears.

- If the customer's e-mail address is in the customer record, it's automatically inserted into the To: field.
- If the customer's e-mail address is not in the customer record, QuickBooks searches your e-mail software address book. If the customer is found, the entry in the To: field is underlined to indicate the name has been matched to an existing address book entry.
- If the customer's e-mail address is not available in either place, you'll need to add the customer's e-mail address to your QuickBooks file.

The Subject field is prefilled with the text "Invoice from <*YourCompanyName*>" (if the file you're attaching isn't an invoice, the correct form type is automatically inserted). The Attachment field is prefilled with the name of the PDF file of the transaction form. The text of the message is prefilled by QuickBooks, using the text in the Send Forms Preferences dialog, discussed in the previous section.

Using QuickBooks E-mail (Billing Solutions)

If you're not using one of the supported e-mail applications and you've activated the QuickBooks E-mail service, QuickBooks fills out the message and attaches the document in the same way described when using your own e-mail software.

When you click Send Now, QuickBooks opens a browser window and takes you to the QuickBooks Billing Solutions website. If this is the first time you're e-mailing invoices, follow the prompts to complete the sign-up process, and then QuickBooks sends the e-mail. Thereafter, your e-mail is sent automatically. An additional feature of this Billing Solutions service is the ability to accept online payments from your customers that receive an invoice from you via this service (additional fees may apply).

ProAdvisor Tip: If you use the QuickBooks Billing Solutions, enter your own e-mail address in the CC: or BCC: field of the message window so you have a record of the e-mail. (If you use your own software, you have a copy in the Sent Messages folder.)

Document Management: Using the Attach Documents Feature

The Attach Documents feature allows you to attach files of any type to a QuickBooks list record or transaction. You'll see the Attach icon in all QuickBooks centers as well as at the top of all transaction windows.

Once you've attached a file or scanned image, it is easily accessible via the Doc Center (which you can open using the Docs button on the Icon Bar). For example, you might want to attach a scanned copy of a customer's purchase order to the invoice that you generate for them in QuickBooks, or maybe you'll need to attach an e-mailed copy of a vendor's bill when you enter the bill into QuickBooks. Or you might want to attach a file or image to a vendor record.

To attach a file or image to a transaction (like invoices and estimates), open the transaction and click the Attach (paperclip) icon. To attach the same to a record, highlight a name in the appropriate Center, and then click on the Attach (paper clip) icon.

The Attachments window opens, giving you the option of attaching a document directly from your computer, your scanner, or the Doc Center.

A QuickBooks transaction or record that has an attachment will display a green paper clip Attach icon, indicating that an attached file or image exists. Click this icon to open the Doc Center to view this and other files and documents stored there.

Managing Users and Permissions

I n *this chapter:*

- Learn about the QuickBooks administrator

- Create QuickBooks users

- Set permissions for users

In many businesses, multiple users have access to the QuickBooks company file, either on the same computer (taking turns using QuickBooks), or by accessing the company file from other computers on a network. Refer to Appendix A for help with installing QuickBooks on a network. If this is the case with your business, you should create a user name and password for each of these users. This will help you keep track of who is making what changes to your company file. Even if you're the only one using QuickBooks, you should make sure that you log in with a password to ensure the security of the company file.

Why User Logins Are Important

If you run QuickBooks on a network with multiple users accessing a company file from other computers on the network, QuickBooks requires user logins. (You can't open a file in multi-user mode to permit simultaneous access by other users until you set up users.)

If you're the only QuickBooks user, it's tempting to avoid the extra step of logging in and remembering a password. Don't yield to that temptation because, without a login and password, if anyone else wanders into the room and accesses your computer, it's possible for him or her to open QuickBooks and easily view your financial information. Worse, it's possible for someone to create, delete, or modify transactions that you might not notice for a very long time.

If you have only one computer running QuickBooks but more than one user shares that computer to work in QuickBooks, you may need to know who did what. Without creating and enforcing separate login names, that information won't be available to you when you need it. The QuickBooks Audit Trail report (which tracks activities with a time and date stamp) displays the name of the logged-in user for every transaction it tracks, but if you and your staff are using "Admin" as the login name each time you use QuickBooks, the value of this report will be greatly diminished.

User names are linked to permission levels, which means you can limit the parts of QuickBooks that certain users can access to create or view transactions and reports. For example, you can keep users from seeing payroll information or sensitive reports that contain information about your profits, debt, and so on.

Understanding Passwords

Most of us who use computers on a regular basis know that passwords are very important when it comes to protecting our personal and business information. You shouldn't use passwords that are based on information that someone else may know, such as your child's name, your dog's name, your nickname, your license plate, or your birth date because many computers and databases have been hacked by intruders who successfully guessed a password.

Creating Complex Passwords

If you've enabled the credit card protection feature in QuickBooks (covered in Chapter 3), you must create a complex password (sometimes called a *strong password*) if you're the Admin or a user who has permission to view customer credit card information. The rules for the complex password are

- A minimum of seven characters is required.
- At least one character must be a number.
- At least one letter must be uppercase.

However, even if you're not using the credit card protection feature, you should still consider using a complex password; after all, if you're going to use passwords, you might as well be serious about security.

The longer the password and the more complicated it is, the harder it is for someone else to guess. For example, Xyyu86RDa is a great password, but it would be very difficult to remember. You must strike a balance between complexity and your ability to remember the password.

The QuickBooks Admin

The QuickBooks user initially named Admin is the administrator of the QuickBooks company file. The administrator is in charge of all QuickBooks users and is the only user who can set up additional users. The person who creates the company file becomes the administrator automatically because he or she is the first person to open the file. QuickBooks lets you change the name Admin to any other name without losing the administrator power.

As mentioned previously in this chapter, it is never a good idea to use QuickBooks without the security of having users log in to a company file with a user name and a password. Even if you're the only person who works in QuickBooks, and therefore you're automatically the administrator, be sure the user named Admin has a password.

ProAdvisor Tip: The administrator's (Admin) privileges in QuickBooks are totally unrelated to your Windows logon name and privileges. Even if you're an ordinary user in Windows and can't install software or manage users on the computer, you can be a QuickBooks administrator.

The way the administrator account is configured, and whether you have to log in to your company file, depends on the way you created your company file. Here's how QuickBooks establishes the administrator account:

- If you use the Advanced Setup option to set up your company file and you create a password for the administrator account when the wizard offers that option, every time you open the company file you have to log in as Admin and enter the password.

- If you use the Advanced Setup option to set up your company file and you do *not* create a password for the administrator account when the wizard offers that option, the Admin account is established. However, because there's no password, when you open the company file you don't see a Login dialog.

- If you use the Express Start option to create your company file, you do not have an opportunity to set up the administrator's password (although the Admin user is created automatically). When you open the company file, you don't see a Login dialog.

Adding or Changing the Administrator Password

If you didn't create a password for the user named Admin when you set up the company file, you can create a password at any time. If you did create a password and you think the existing password may have been discovered by someone else, you can create a new password.

To add or change the password for the user named Admin, log in to QuickBooks as Admin and choose Company | Set Up Users And Passwords | Change Your Password to open the Change QuickBooks Password dialog seen in Figure 26-1. If the Admin account is already password-protected, and you're merely changing the password, you have to enter the current password to proceed to this dialog. Enter the new password, enter it again in the Confirm Password field, and select a challenge question (and the answer).

Creating a Challenge Question for the Admin Account

If you don't remember your Admin password, you can't get into your company file. If Admin is the only user, that means you can't use QuickBooks. If there are other users, they can open the company file, but they can't perform administrative tasks in the file (many QuickBooks functions can be performed only by the Admin user). Essentially, this brings your QuickBooks work to a screeching halt.

To prevent this inconvenience, QuickBooks gives the Admin user the opportunity to create a reminder about the password.

Select a question from the drop-down list in the Challenge Question field and then enter the answer to that question in the Answer field. Be careful about the

FIGURE 26-1 You can easily add or change an Admin password.

answer you enter. You cannot see what you're typing, so type carefully. (QuickBooks treats this the same way it treats password entry; you see bullet characters instead of the characters you're typing.)

Resetting the Admin Password When You Forget It

If you forget your Admin password, you can reset it, using the challenge question you created. In the QuickBooks Login dialog, click the I forgot my password button.

The challenge question is displayed in the Reset QuickBooks Administrator Password dialog. Enter the answer you recorded in the Answer field (this time you can see what you're typing).

Reset QuickBooks Administrator Password

Enter the answer to your challenge question. When you answer correctly, you'll be asked to create a new password.

If you are not an administrator, you can't reset your password. Ask your administrator to reset it for you.

Challenge Question   **City where you went to high school**

Answer   Boston   I forgot my answer

OK   Cancel   Help

When you answer the question correctly, all of your password information is removed from the company file and you can start all over with a new password (and a new challenge question and answer).

Password Removed

Your password and challenge answer and question have been removed, and your company file is no longer password-protected.

When you close this window, you will be asked to create your new password and select and answer your challenge question.

Close

If you can't remember your challenge question, click the "I forgot my answer" link. The Reset QuickBooks Administrator Password window opens, where you'll have to fill out information about your QuickBooks installation, company file, license information, and other data. Once this information is completely filled in, your password will be reset.

Adding Users

Only the Admin user can add users. To add a new user to your company file, choose Company | Set Up Users And Passwords | Set Up Users. QuickBooks asks you to enter your Admin password to proceed, and it then opens the User List dialog. Click Add User to open the Set Up User Password And Access wizard that assists you in setting up the new user.

Use the following guidelines to create a new user:

- The user name is the name this user must type to log into QuickBooks.
- A password is optional, but it's much less secure to omit passwords. Enter the same password in both password fields. (Later, the user can change the password—see the section "Users Can Change Their Own Passwords.")
- Assign permissions for this user to access QuickBooks features. See "Setting User Permissions."

Deleting a User

If you want to remove a user from the User List, select the user name and then click the Delete User button. QuickBooks asks you to confirm your decision. Note that you can't delete the Admin.

Editing User Information

You can change the user settings for any user. Select the user name in the User List window and click Edit User. This launches a wizard similar to the Set Up User Password And Access Wizard, and you can change the user name, password, and permissions.

The Edit User feature is handy when one of your QuickBooks users comes to you because they cannot remember their password—and you don't have it handy either. You can create a new password for the user, who will then have the option to change the password to something of their own liking. See the section "Users Can Change Their Own Passwords" later in this chapter for more details.

Setting User Permissions

When you're adding a new user or editing an existing user, the wizard walks you through the steps for configuring the user's permissions. Click Next on each wizard window after you've supplied the necessary information.

The first permissions window (see Figure 26-2) asks if you want this user to have access to selected areas of QuickBooks or all areas. If you give the user access to all areas of QuickBooks, or you select the option to make this user an External Accountant, when you click Next you're asked to confirm your decision, and there's no further work to do in the wizard. Click Finish to return to the User List window. (See Chapter 21 to learn about the External Accountant user type.)

If you want to limit the user's access to selected areas of QuickBooks, select that option and click Next. The ensuing wizard windows take you through all the QuickBooks features (Sales and Accounts Receivable, Check Writing, Payroll,

The Set Up User Password And Access window gives you control over a user's access to your QuickBooks data.

FIGURE 26-2

and so on) so you can establish permissions on a feature-by-feature basis for this user. You should configure permissions for every component of QuickBooks. Any component not configured is set as No Access for this user (which means the user cannot work in that part of QuickBooks). For each QuickBooks component, you can select one of the following permission options:

- **No Access** The user is denied permission to open any windows in that section of QuickBooks.
- **Full Access** The user can open all windows and perform all tasks in that section of QuickBooks.
- **Selective Access** The user will be permitted to perform tasks as you see fit.

If you choose to give selective access permissions, you're asked to specify the rights this user should have. Those rights vary slightly from component to component, but generally you're asked to choose one of these permission levels:

- Create transactions only
- Create and print transactions
- Create transactions and create reports

You can select only one of the three levels, so if you need to give the user rights to more than one of these choices, you must select Full Access instead of configuring Selective Access.

Special Permissions Needed for Customer Credit Card Data

If you provide Full Access permissions to a user for the Sales And Accounts Receivable area, by default, the user is not able to view customer credit card data. A separate option for this permission appears on the wizard window.

- If you've enabled the Customer Credit Card Security feature (explained in Chapter 3), the next time this user logs in to the company file, he or she will be asked to create a strong password.
- If you haven't enabled the Customer Credit Card Security feature, this user, and any other user you configure to have access to customer credit card information, does not have to set up a strong password and can view credit card numbers you store in your customers' records.

Configuring Special Areas of QuickBooks

Two wizard windows are used for setting permissions that are not directly related to any specific area of the software: sensitive accounting activities and sensitive accounting reports.

Sensitive accounting activities are those tasks that aren't directly related to QuickBooks transactions, such as the following:

- Making changes to the chart of accounts
- Manipulating the register for any balance sheet account
- Using online banking
- Transferring funds between banks
- Reconciling bank accounts
- Creating journal entries
- Preparing an accountant's copy
- Working with budgets

Sensitive financial reporting reveals important financial information about your company, such as the following:

- Profit & Loss reports
- Balance Sheet reports
- Budget reports
- Cash flow reports
- Income tax reports
- Trial balance reports
- Audit trail reports

Configuring Rights for Existing Transactions

If a user has permissions for certain areas of QuickBooks, you can limit his or her ability to manipulate existing transactions within those areas. This means the user can't change or delete a transaction, even if that user created it in the first place.

You can also prevent the user from changing transactions that occurred prior to the closing date you set (even if the user knows the password to access transactions that were created before the closing date). See Chapter 24 to learn about setting a closing date and password-protecting access to transactions that predate the closing date.

When you have finished configuring user permissions, the last wizard page presents a list of the permissions you've granted and refused. If everything is correct, click Finish. If there's something you want to change, use the Back button to return to the appropriate page.

Users Can Change Their Own Passwords

Any user can change his or her password by choosing Company | Set Up Users And Passwords | Change Your Password to open the Change QuickBooks Password dialog. The dialog opens with the name of the current logged in user in the User Name field, and that text cannot be changed.

To change the password, the user must enter the old password, and then enter the new password (twice). That's an excellent security device, because it prevents other users from changing a user's password (which can happen if a user leaves the computer without logging out of QuickBooks).

Theoretically, it's a good idea for the QuickBooks administrator to know all user passwords and to ask users to notify the administrator when a password is changed. However, tracking passwords can be burdensome if you have more than just a couple of users. It's perfectly acceptable to decide that you don't want to know user passwords, because if a user forgets a password, you can edit the user's record to create a new one (as described earlier in this chapter) and tell the user the new password.

QuickBooks Login Dialog

The QuickBooks Login dialog appears whenever you open a company file, unless you have not configured any users in addition to the built-in administrator named Admin, and the Admin user has not been assigned a password.

The Login dialog displays the name of the last user who logged in to this company file on this computer. If the same user is opening the file, entering the correct password opens the file.

If a different user is opening the file, replace the text in the User Name field with the login name of the new user, enter the password, and click OK.

Managing Your QuickBooks Files

In this chapter:

- Delete unneeded company files

- Back up and restore company files

- Create a portable company file

- Verify data files

- Condense data

- Update QuickBooks software

The bookkeeping chores you complete in QuickBooks ensure that you're tracking important information about your business and how it's performing. Just as important as these tasks is the need to take care of the "health" of your QuickBooks company data file. In particular, it's important to keep your software up to date and make sure your data is not cluttered with very old or irrelevant transactions and list items. Finally, it's critical that you decide on and adopt a backup routine that you can rely on.

Deleting Company Files

Sometimes you have a valid reason to get rid of a company file. Perhaps you created a company to experiment with and you no longer use it, or someone is taking over your job and you no longer need to keep a QuickBooks company file on your local computer.

QuickBooks doesn't have a Delete File command from within the program itself, but you can delete the file from your hard drive through Windows Explorer or My Computer. Before you delete the file, however, read the following sections carefully so you don't encounter a problem the next time you open QuickBooks.

How QuickBooks Loads Company Files

QuickBooks automatically opens the company file that was loaded when you last exited the software. It's best to make sure that you don't have the about-to-be-deleted company file loaded when you close QuickBooks. Otherwise, the next time you open the program it will try to "find" the deleted file, which can be confusing to both you and the software. To prevent this, take one of the following actions:

- Choose File | Open Or Restore Company or File | Open Previous Company to select another company file and then exit the program.
- Choose File | Close Company to close the current file and have no company loaded if you shut down QuickBooks and reopen it.

Deleting the File

To delete a company file, open My Computer or Windows Explorer and navigate to the folder that holds your company files. Then delete the file *companyname*.QBW. Deleting the QBW file will also remove the associated *companyname*.DSN and *companyname*.ND files. To complete the task, you'll also need to delete the *companyname*.TLG file separately (you may also see an LGB file that can be removed as well).

Alternatively, you can delete the file while you're working in QuickBooks, as long as the file you want to delete isn't the file currently open in QuickBooks. To accomplish this, choose File | Open Or Restore Company and click through the wizard to get to the Open A Company dialog. Click the file's listing to highlight it, and press the DELETE key. QuickBooks asks you to confirm your action. You'll need to delete the TLG file separately, however, as described above. Then, from the same Open A Company dialog, open the company file you want to work on.

ProAdvisor Tip: It's a good idea to create a separate folder on your hard drive for your QuickBooks company files. Store all the import and export files you create that are associated with your QuickBooks files in that folder, too. Having a separate folder makes it easy to find files, and you can back up everything simply by backing up the folder.

Eliminating Deleted Files from the Company File List

QuickBooks tracks the company files you've opened and lists the most recently opened files on the Open Previous Company submenu (under the File menu) to make it easier to move among files. You don't have to open a dialog to select one of those files, you just click the appropriate listing. The submenu lists the company files you've opened starting with the most recent (it's a duplicate of the listing displayed in the No Company Open dialog).

After you delete a company file, its "ghost" listing may still appear on the Open Previous Company submenu or in the No Company Open dialog. A user could inadvertently select it, which produces a delay followed by an error message, and then possibly followed by a user panic attack.

To eliminate this possibility, open another company file and choose File | Open Previous Company | Set Number Of Previous Companies. Change the data for the number of companies to list from its current setting to 1, and click OK.

This changes the company files that are listed in the Open Previous Company menu to the current company file only. The next time you open QuickBooks, repeat these steps and change the number back to the number that's efficient (depending on the number of companies you work with). QuickBooks begins tracking your work; as you open different company files, it rebuilds the list.

Backing Up and Restoring Files

Backing up your QuickBooks data is an incredibly important task and should be done on a daily basis. In addition, once a week, use removable media to make an extra backup, and take that backup off site.

If you need to use a backup file, you don't open it the way you open a regular company file; instead, it has to be restored, using the QuickBooks Restore command as discussed in the following section.

Backing Up

Do this every day! You don't have to create a manual backup every day, as described here, if you set up scheduled backups (covered later in this section); you'll still be making a daily backup, you just won't have to do the work.

▶▶ ProAdvisor Recommends

Backing Up a Remote Company File

If you're working on a network, and the company file is on a computer that's acting as a data file server only (QuickBooks is not installed on the computer; instead, only the QuickBooks database engine is installed), don't use the QuickBooks backup feature when the company file is open on your own computer.

If you back up a remote company file, the backup that's created is not as complete as a backup made when the company file is on the same computer as the QuickBooks user. Some important files are not included in the backup file, and you'll have to restore, rebuild, and reconfigure some of the file.

Instead of creating a backup of the company file using the QuickBooks backup function, back up (copy) the entire folder on the server that holds your company files to a removable drive (flash drive or CD/DVD).

The sidebar, "Backing Up a Remote Company File," mentions that backing up a file across the network results in a backup that isn't a full backup. Unfortunately, backing up a company file that is located on your computer can also result in a backup file that's missing some information, although the problem isn't as severe. If you do payroll in-house, any payroll forms you saved (940, 941, W-2, etc.) are not backed up. Luckily, you can back up those forms separately by copying them to your backup media. Look for a folder named <*YourCompanyFile*> Tax Forms in the folder that holds your company files; all the forms you saved are in that folder. To create a backup of the company currently open in QuickBooks, choose File | Create Backup. This opens the Create Backup Wizard window seen in Figure 27-1. If you select Online Backup, QuickBooks opens a browser and takes you to a website with information about the QuickBooks online backup service (a fee-based service).

Create Backup

Make a backup copy of everything you need to recreate your

Do you want to save your backup copy online or

○ Online backup
Get automatic, online backup for your QuickBooks data and other important documents using Intuit's online backup solution (fees may apply).

Try now or learn more

◉ Local backup
Save locally to a removable storage device (such as a CD or USB flash drive) or to a folder on your network.

[Options]   Click **Options** to change your current backup settings.

[Back] [Next] [Finish]   [Help] [Cancel]

FIGURE 27-1   Select the type of copy you want to create—in this case, it's a local backup.

From there, you can learn more about the service (which allows you to back up not only your QuickBooks data, but also your entire computer) or sign up for the service.

Choose Local Backup and click the Options button to set the location of the backup in the Backup Options dialog seen in Figure 27-2. Use the guidelines in the following sections to select options in this dialog.

Selecting a Location for the Backup

Click the Browse button to select the location for this backup. The optimum location is a USB drive, a CD/DVD, or a drive on another computer on your network (if you have a network). (The location shown in Figure 27-2 is a stand-alone network drive attached to a remote computer on the network, and the folders on that drive are

Backup Options

Use this window to set default options for your manual and automatic backups.

Local backup only

Tell us where to save your backup copies **(required)**

F:\2012\QBFiles   [Bro_w_se...]

☑ Add the date and time of the backup to the file name (recommended)

☑ Limit the number of backup copies in this folder to 3

Online and local backup

☑ Remind me to back up when I close my company file every 1 times.

Select an option to verify that your company data is OK (that is, not corrupted) when you save.

⦿ Complete verification (recommended)

◯ Quicker verification

◯ No verification   Help me choose

[OK]   [Cancel]   [Help]

FIGURE 27-2   Configure the options for this backup.

burned to CDs and taken off site.) If you select a local drive that also holds your QuickBooks company file, QuickBooks issues a warning message when you click OK.

QuickBooks

⚠ You've told us to save backup copies to the same hard drive (drive: D:) that holds your company file. We do not recommend this.

Instead, we recommend that you save to a different drive or to a removable storage device to avoid losing the backup due to an unexpected hard-drive failure.

[_C_hange Location]   [Use _t_his Location]

Unless you're saving the file to a folder on the drive that is going to be backed up later in the day or at night, heed the warning. Putting a backup on your hard drive could make your backup irretrievable if your hard drive experiences a catastrophic failure.

Adding Time Stamps to Backup Filenames

You can select the option to append a date/time stamp to the filename, which lets you tell at a glance when the backup file was created. The backup filename has the following format:

```
CompanyFilename(Backup Jun 01,2012 04 36 PM).QBB
```

When you select the time stamp option, you're creating multiple backups in the same location, and you can limit the number of backups you save in a specific location. Multiple backups over continuous days provide an option to restore a backup from two days ago (or longer) if you think the backup you made yesterday may have some corrupted data. During backup, QuickBooks notes the number of backups you opted to keep and, when a backup is made that exceeds that number, QuickBooks asks if you want to delete the extra backup (always choosing the oldest backup as the one to delete).

Click OK in the Options dialog to return to the wizard.

Setting Backup Reminders

You can ask QuickBooks to remind you about backing up when you close a company file by selecting that option and then indicating the frequency. Hopefully, this prompt won't be necessary, because you are already backing up every day. However, if you think you'll still need to be reminded to back up your file, use this option.

Choosing File Verification Options

If you wish, you can ask QuickBooks to verify the data in your company file before backing up (by selecting either verification option). This can increase the amount of time it takes to complete the backup, so if you're performing a quick backup because you want to make changes in your file, or you're about to perform some other action that makes you think you want a quick safety backup, you can select the option No Verification.

If you choose this option, however, you'll want to be sure that when time permits, you run the verify utility by selecting File | Utilities | Verify Data. See the section "Verifying and Rebuilding a Company File," later in this chapter, for more information on completing this very important task.

Choosing When to Save the Backup

Click Next to choose when to create this backup. You have three choices:

- Save It Now
- Save It Now And Schedule Future Backups
- Only Schedule Future Backups

The second and third choices are concerned with scheduling automatic and unattended backups, a subject that's covered later in this chapter in the section, "Scheduling Backups."

Assuming you're creating a backup now (the option chosen by default), click Next. QuickBooks opens the Save Backup Copy dialog with your location selected and the backup filename in the File Name field. Click Save.

Backing Up to a CD

If you're using QuickBooks on a computer running Windows XP, Windows 2003 Server, Windows Vista, or Windows 7, you can select your CD drive as the backup target (assuming your CD drive is capable of writing CDs).

QuickBooks saves the backup to the default folder on the hard drive that holds files waiting to be written to a CD, and the software displays a message telling you your data has been backed up successfully to that location. When you click OK, QuickBooks may display a dialog offering online backup (you can choose to learn more about this service or close the dialog to proceed). From here, you can choose to burn the CD using the Windows CD Wizard (Burn Now) or using your own CD burning software (Burn Later).

You may see a balloon over the notification area of your taskbar, telling you that files are waiting to be written to the CD (the standard notification when you burn CDs in Windows). You don't have to click the balloon to open the folder that holds the file, because the QuickBooks backup feature automatically opens the Windows CD Writing Wizard and copies the file to the CD.

If you choose Burn Later, when you're ready to burn your CD, Windows looks in the folders under your name in C:\Documents and Settings and uses the backup files that QuickBooks created to burn to the CD. You can open your CD burning software and direct it to that location, or you can use the Windows CD Writing Wizard by following these steps:

1. Select the CD drive in My Computer, where Windows displays the file(s) waiting to be written to the CD.
2. Choose File | Write These Files To CD (in Windows 7, you see a Burn To Disc command).
3. When the Windows CD Writing Wizard appears, follow the prompts to move your backup file to the CD.

Scheduling Backups

QuickBooks offers both automatic backups and unattended backups (which are also automatic). You can schedule either or both of these types of backups from the same wizard that walks you through the backup process (described in the previous sections). Click through the wizard windows until you get to the window titled Create Backup. You'll see two options that allow you to schedule future backups:

- Select Save It Now And Schedule Future Backups if you want to create a manual backup and also set up automatic and/or unattended backups.
- Select Only Schedule Future Backups if you just want to set up automatic and/ or unattended scheduled backups.

Clicking Next after either selection brings you to the wizard window shown in Figure 27-3.

FIGURE 27-3   Set up automatic backup procedures to make sure your data is always safe.

Configuring Automatic Backups

An automatic backup is one that takes place whenever you close the company file. Closing a file is an action that can take place under any of the following circumstances:

- You open another company file.
- You choose File | Close Company (or File | Close Company/Logoff if you've set up users for the company).
- You close QuickBooks with this company file loaded.

Set the frequency of automatic backups to match the way you use QuickBooks and the way you work in this company file. For example, if you open QuickBooks with this company file loaded in the morning and keep QuickBooks open all day without changing companies, set a frequency of 1 to make sure you have at least one backup each day (and you can also set up another scheduled backup for that evening). The automatic backup is created using the settings, including the location, you configured in the Options dialog.

Configuring Scheduled Backups

You can configure QuickBooks to perform a backup of your company files at any time, even if you're not working at your computer. This is a cool feature, but it doesn't work unless you remember to leave your computer running when you leave the office. Before you leave, make sure QuickBooks is closed so all the files are available for backing up (open files are skipped during a scheduled backup).

To create the configuration for an unattended backup, click New to open the Schedule Backup dialog seen in Figure 27-4.

FIGURE 27-4 Configure the specifications for an unattended backup.

You can give the backup a descriptive name (it's optional), but if you're going to create multiple unattended backup configurations, it's a good idea to identify each by name. For example, if you're backing up to a USB stick drive that's had its drive letter assigned as F:, a good description of a backup scheduled for 10 P.M. is "10PM to F."

C a u t i o n : Be sure the target drive is available—insert the Zip, USB, or other removable drive before leaving the computer; or be sure the remote network computer you're using for backup storage isn't shut down at night.

If you don't want to overwrite the last backup file every time a new backup file is created, select the option Number Of Backup Copies To Keep, and specify the number. QuickBooks saves as many backup files as you specify (up to 99), each time replacing the first file with the most recent backup and copying older files to the next highest number in the filename. These backup files are saved with the file extension .QBB and include a date and time stamp.

Create a schedule for this unattended backup by selecting a time and a frequency. In the example shown in Figure 27-4, the backup occurs every night.

If you're on a network, QuickBooks displays the Enter Windows Password dialog. The password in question is not to your QuickBooks user and password configuration; it's your Windows logon name and password. You can create multiple unattended backups and configure them for special circumstances. For instance, in addition to a nightly backup, you may want to configure a backup every four weeks on a Saturday or Sunday (or during your lunch hour on a weekday) to create a backup on a removable drive that is earmarked for off-site storage. Be sure to bring your backup media to the office on that day and take it back to the off-site location when the backup is finished.

Mapped drives are unique to your Windows login name. If you log off of Windows before you leave the office (not the same as shutting down the computer, which would prevent the backup from running), you cannot use a mapped drive to create your backup. While it's not common to take the trouble to log off of Windows, if you do normally log off, use the full path to the remote folder you're using as the target backup location instead of the mapped drive letter. The format of the full path (called *Universal Naming Convention* or UNC) is

```
\\ComputerName\ShareName
```

Restoring a Backup

You just turned on your computer and it sounds different—noisier. In fact, there's a grinding noise. You wait and wait, but the usual startup of the operating system fails to appear. Eventually, an error message about a missing boot sector appears (or some other equally chilling message). Your hard drive has gone to hard-drive heaven. You have invoices to send out, checks to write, and tons of things to do, and if you can't accomplish those tasks, your business suffers.

Don't panic; get another hard drive or another computer. If you buy a new hard drive, it will likely take some time to install your operating system. If you buy a new computer, it probably comes with an operating system installed.

If you're running on a network and you were backing up your QuickBooks files to a network drive, create the mapped drive to the shared folder that holds your backup. Then install your QuickBooks software.

Maybe your computer is fine, and it's your QuickBooks program that won't open, or it opens but reports a corruption error when it tries to open your file. In this case, you don't have all the work of rebuilding hardware. If QuickBooks won't open or opens with error messages about a software problem, try reinstalling. If the new installation of QuickBooks opens but your company file won't open, restore your backup. Here's how:

1. Start QuickBooks. If the opening window tells you there's no company open and suggests you create one (if this is a fresh installation of the software), ignore that message.

2. If you backed up to removable media, put the disc or USB flash drive that contains your last backup into its slot. If you backed up to a network share, be sure the remote computer is running. If you purchased the QuickBooks online backup service, be sure you've configured your Internet connection in QuickBooks.

3. Choose File | Open Or Restore Company. Or, if your backup file is stored on your computer or a network computer, choose Restore Previous Local Backup and skip to Step 9.

4. Choose Restore A Backup Copy and click Next.

5. Select Local Backup if your backup files are on removable media or on a remote computer on the network. Select Online Backup if you subscribe to that QuickBooks service. Then click Next. (If you use the QuickBooks online backup service, at this point follow the prompts to restore your backup.)

6. If you selected Local Backup, the Open Backup Copy dialog appears. Navigate to the folder or drive where your backup is stored.

7. Select the backup file—if you store multiple backups with time stamps embedded in the filename, select the most recent backup.

8. Click Open, and then click Next to continue with the Restore Wizard.

9. In the Save Company File As dialog, select the folder to which you're restoring the file and click Save.

10. If you're restoring to an existing company (because the problem was a corrupt data file), QuickBooks asks if you want to replace the existing file. Click Yes. Then, just to make sure, QuickBooks displays a warning that you're about to overwrite/delete the existing file. That's fine; it's what you want to do, so type **Yes** in the dialog and click OK.

QuickBooks displays a message that your data files have been restored successfully and opens the file (if you have to log in, the login dialog displays first, and the success dialog appears after you log in).

Using a Portable Company File

A portable company file is a copy of your QuickBooks company file that has been condensed to save disk space to make it "portable," that is, smaller than a backup (QBB) copy. Portable files are designed to move data between computers (such as your home computer and your office), so you can work at home and then bring the updated file back to the office.

Creating a Portable Company File

To create a portable company file, choose File | Create Copy, select Portable Company File, and click Next. In the Save Portable Company File dialog, select a location for the file (by default, QuickBooks selects the Desktop as the location).

If you're taking the file to another computer (perhaps you're taking it home), choose removable media such as a Zip or USB drive, and take the media with you. Or, save the file on your hard drive and then send it to the person who will be working with the file (such as your accountant), either by e-mail or by burning it to a CD and sending the CD to the recipient.

> **ProAdvisor Tip:** Do not substitute making a full backup as part of your regular backup routine with creating a portable company file. Why? Because a portable company file does not contain an important transaction log file that a full backup (QBB) file has. This file is located in the same folder as your company file (the QBW file) and its filename is <*YourCompanyFilename*>.TLG. In many cases, Intuit Technical Support can use the log file and your most recent backup to recover data up to the point of the transactions saved at the time of the backup file you supply.

QuickBooks automatically names the file using the following format:

```
CompanyFilename (Portable).QBM
```

Click Save. QuickBooks displays a message telling you it has to close the company file to create the portable file. Click OK.

It takes a while to create the file, and when it's done, QuickBooks issues a success message.

▶▶ ProAdvisor Recommends

Overwriting Your Data File by Restoring a Backup or Portable File

When you restore a portable or backup file to a computer that has an existing QuickBooks company file, replacing the existing file may cause you to lose any work you've performed in the existing file. The process of overwriting the existing file with the portable or backup copy deletes the existing file and replaces it with the data in the portable or backup copy.

If you're the only person who works in the company file, and you take a portable or backup file to another computer (such as your home computer), work on the file and bring it back to the office; it's safe to overwrite the office copy with the changes that are made when you restore. Nobody has created any transactions since you created the portable or backup file, so deleting the original file doesn't delete any new transactions.

However, if you send a portable or backup file to someone else and then continue to work in the original file, you can't restore the file when it's returned unless you're prepared to lose all the work you did in the meantime. You have four ways to avoid this situation:

- Stop working on the file until the portable or backup file is returned. Then, when you restore to the company file, you don't lose any data.
- Have the person who's performing work in the portable or backup file send you a list of the transactions that were entered, instead of returning the file, and enter those transactions in the existing company file.
- Restore the file to a different location, or use a different filename (or both). You can open the restored company file and see what's new, then add that data to your real company file.
- Send an accountant's copy to the person doing the off-site work (this person needs to be using QuickBooks accountant edition). Creating and working with an accountant's copy is covered in Chapter 20.

To restore a portable company file, either on your home computer or on the office computer after you've worked on the file at home and saved it as a portable file, follow these steps to use the wizard that guides you through the process:

1. Choose File | Open Or Restore Company.
2. In the Open Or Restore Company window, select Restore A Portable File and click Next.
3. In the Open Portable Company File dialog, navigate to the folder or removable media drive that holds the file, select the file, and click Open.
4. The next window that appears is the informational window about where to restore the file. Click Next.
5. The Save Company File As window opens, which allows you to choose where you want to save the restored file. Use one of the guidelines described next to select a location and filename.

Replacing the Existing Company File with the Portable File   If you're deliberately replacing a company file, select the folder that holds the original company file and use the same filename as your company file. QuickBooks displays a warning that you're about to overwrite the existing file and asks if you want to replace it; click Yes. To make sure you really understand what you're about to do, QuickBooks displays the Delete Entire File dialog and asks you to confirm your action. Type **Yes** and click OK to continue.

Creating a Different Company File from the Portable File   If you want to create a separate company file to avoid overwriting the work you did in your real company file, change the location or the filename (or both) before you click Save.

After the portable company file is uncompressed, it's loaded in the QuickBooks window so you can work in it.

Verifying and Rebuilding a Company File

QuickBooks includes utilities to verify and rebuild the data in your company file. They're both found on the File | Utilities submenu.

Verifying a company file checks the data and the accuracy of the file's contents. If QuickBooks does find any issues with your data, you're prompted to rebuild the file. Before you start the rebuild, QuickBooks asks you to make a backup and reminds you *not* to use your existing backup disk (or location)—heed this advice!

In many cases, the Rebuild routine will resolve the issue with the data (the best way to determine this is to run the Verify routine again). If it does not, the problems that are encountered are written to a log file named QBWIN.LOG. If you wish, you can view the contents of the log within QuickBooks by pressing F2 to open the Product Information window and then pressing F3 to open the QuickBooks Tech Help window. Click the tab named Open File, select QBWIN.LOG, and click Open File.

Sometimes the log file has clear, helpful information about the problem and you can remove the troublesome record from the data file. However, at this point you should call Intuit support for help. The support technician may ask you to send the log file, along with other files available in the QuickBooks Tech Help window, using the button labeled Send Log Files To Intuit Support on the Open File tab.

Condensing Your Data

To help reduce the size of your data file, QuickBooks provides a feature that enables you to remove certain transaction and list data in your company file that you no longer use or need. While this seems to be a handy feature, it carries some significant side effects in the loss of details about transactions.

Understanding the Data Removal Procedure

The data removal process deletes closed transactions and replaces them with a journal entry that shows totals posted to accounts. (If you subscribe to any QuickBooks payroll services, no current year transactions are condensed.) Open transactions (such as unpaid invoices and bills and estimates that are not marked "Closed") are not removed. Before removing the data, QuickBooks creates an archive copy of your company file (which you can open to see the original transactions that were removed).

Choosing a Date

QuickBooks asks you for the date you want to use as the cutoff date. Everything you no longer need before that date is removed, if it can be safely removed without interfering with transactions that remain. No open transactions are removed; only those data items that are completed and safe to remove are targeted. Also, any transactions before the cutoff date that affect current transactions are kept, so the details are maintained in the file.

Understanding Summary Transactions

The transactions that fall within the parameters of the condensing date are deleted and replaced with summary transactions. Summary transactions are nothing but journal entry transactions that show the totals for the removed transactions, one for each month. The account balances are not changed by removing data, because the summary transactions maintain those totals.

Understanding the Aftereffects

After you clean up the file, you won't be able to run detail reports for those periods before the cutoff date. However, summary reports will be perfectly accurate in their financial totals. You will be able to recognize the summary transactions in the account registers because they will be marked with a transaction type GENJRNL. You can open the archived file if you need to see the original transaction details.

Running the Condense Data Utility

To run the Condense utility, choose File | Utilities | Condense Data. The Condense Data Wizard opens, offering two cleanup methods (see Figure 27-5). You may see a warning about losing your budget data when your file is condensed, because some budgets are based on detailed postings. Click Yes. (Chapter 23 explains how to export your budgets to Excel and import them back into QuickBooks.)

FIGURE 27-5   You can choose to clean up your file or empty it.

For this discussion, select the option Transactions Before A Specific Date. (Read "Removing All Transactions" later in this section, to learn about the other option.) By default, QuickBooks inserts the last day of the previous fiscal year as the date. Usually, it's a good idea to go back a bit more if you've been using QuickBooks for several years without performing a cleanup. Click Next when you've entered the cutoff date.

Condensing Inventory Transactions

If you're tracking inventory in your QuickBooks file, the next window will ask you how you want QuickBooks to handle the removal of transactions that involve inventory. If your file is not set up to track inventory, you'll be asked to tell QuickBooks about the transactions you want to remove from your file.

Selecting Additional Transactions to Remove

In the next wizard window, you can select one or more types of existing transactions to remove, even though they wouldn't be removed automatically during a file cleanup process (see Figure 27-6). For example, if you have a transaction marked "To Be Printed" that's more than a year old, you probably aren't planning to print it (and you probably forgot you ever created it). When you've made your selections, click Next.

FIGURE 27-6 You can remove transactions that QuickBooks would normally keep, but make these selections thoughtfully.

Removing Unused List Entries

In the next window, you can select the lists that may have entries that won't be used after old transactions are removed (see Figure 27-7). Click the list(s) you want QuickBooks to examine to determine whether there are unused listings, and if so, remove them.

Click Next to see an informational window in which the condense process is explained. Click Begin Condense to start the process. QuickBooks displays a message telling you that first your data file needs to be backed up. This is not an everyday backup; it's the last backup of a full data file before information is removed. Therefore, add text to the name of the backup file to indicate that it's special (for instance, *MyCompanyFile*-Condensed.QBB). Click Save to begin the backup.

As soon as QuickBooks finishes backing up, it starts removing data. You'll see progress bars on your screen as each step completes. When the job is complete, you're given the name of the archive copy of your data file.

The archive copy is intact, just the way your file was before you ran the cleanup feature. This means you can open it if you need to see transaction details the next time a customer or vendor calls to discuss an old, old transaction.

Removing All Transactions

The Condense Data feature offers an option to strip the file of all transactions, leaving behind only the lists and the configuration settings you created for printers and Edit | Preferences categories.

Often, this function is used shortly after you start using QuickBooks as a way to "start all over." The other reasons you may use this option, include the following:

- To start a new file at the beginning of a new year when the current company file has become so large that working in it is slower than you'd like.
- When a company changes its legal structure (from a proprietorship to a corporation or to an LLC), payroll, equity accounts, and other elements of the file must be changed to reflect the new organization type.

QuickBooks creates a backup of the file before beginning the process and creates an archive of the file before clearing the transactions, so you don't really wipe out the company's history permanently.

C a u t i o n : The Remove all Transactions choice won't run if you have payroll transactions for the current year or if your file contains bank or credit card accounts that are still enabled for online access.

Updating QuickBooks

QuickBooks provides an automatic update service you can use to make sure your QuickBooks software is up to date and trouble free. This service provides you with any maintenance releases of QuickBooks that have been created since you purchased and installed your copy of the software. A maintenance release is distributed when a problem is discovered and fixed, or when a new feature is added to the software. Note that this service does not provide upgrades to a new version; it just provides updates to your current version.

You can enable automatic updates, which means QuickBooks periodically checks the Intuit update site on the Internet for updates to your version of QuickBooks. If new files exist, they're downloaded to your hard drive. If you turn off automatic updates, you should periodically check for new software files manually. Use the Update Now tab to select and download updated files.

Configuring QuickBooks Update Service

Choose Help | Update QuickBooks and move to the Options tab to configure the Update feature. You can enable or disable the automatic check for updates.

If you're using QuickBooks on a network, you can configure the update service to share downloaded files with other users. When this option is enabled, QuickBooks creates a subfolder on the computer that holds the shared QuickBooks data files, and the other computers on the network use that subfolder as the source of updated files (instead of going online and downloading files).

For this to work, every user on the network must open his or her copy of QuickBooks and configure the Update options for Shared Download to reflect the folder location on the host computer. The folder location is displayed on the Options tab when you select the Shared Download option.

Customizing
QuickBooks

In *this chapter:*

- Configure preferences
- Customize transaction templates

The Preference settings you establish in QuickBooks allow you to control the way you complete tasks, how data is kept, and how it is reported. It's not uncommon for QuickBooks users to change or tweak these preferences periodically. In fact, the more you use QuickBooks and understand the way it works, the more comfortable you'll be about changing preferences.

In addition, by using templates you can customize some of the transaction windows in order to store additional information about those transactions. That information is available in reports, and it means you can get a better picture of your company's financials.

Customizing Settings and Options

Your settings and options for the available QuickBooks features are maintained in the Preferences dialogs, which you open by choosing Edit | Preferences from the QuickBooks menu bar.

Each category in the Preferences dialog is accessed by clicking the appropriate icon in the left pane. Every category has two tabs: My Preferences and Company Preferences.

- The My Preferences tab is where you configure your preferences as a QuickBooks user. Each user you create in QuickBooks can set his or her own My Preferences. QuickBooks will apply the correct preferences as each user logs into the company file. (Many categories lack options in this tab.)
- The Company Preferences tab is the place to configure the way the QuickBooks features work for the current company, regardless of which user logs in. Only the Admin or an External Accountant user can change settings in the Company Preferences tab.

As you configure options and move from one category of the Preferences window to another, you're asked whether you want to save the changes in the section you just left.

In the following sections, I'll briefly go over the Preferences categories, so the information is available in one place in this book. Many of the categories, settings, and options covered here are also discussed in detail throughout this book in the relevant chapters.

Accounting Preferences

Click the Accounting icon on the left pane of the Preferences dialog to open the Accounting preferences (see Figure 28-1). There are only Company Preferences available for this section; the My Preferences tab has no options available.

FIGURE 28-1 Configure the way basic accounting functions work.

You can select the option to use account numbers, and if so, you should also select the option Show Lowest Subaccount Only. The latter option is useful because it means that when you see an account number in a drop-down list (in a transaction window), you see only the subaccount. If the option is not selected, you see the parent account followed by the subaccount, and since the field display doesn't show the entire text unless you scroll through it, it's hard to determine which account has been selected.

The option to require accounts means that every item and transaction you create in QuickBooks has to be assigned to an account. If you disable this option, transaction amounts that aren't manually assigned to an account are posted to Uncategorized Income or Uncategorized Expense, and I don't know any way to produce accurate reports that analyze your business if you don't post transactions to accounts.

You can enable the class feature, which lets you create Profit & Loss reports for divisions, departments, or other categories by which you've decided to analyze your business.

The other options on this dialog are self-explanatory, except for the Closing Date section, which is discussed in detail in Chapter 24.

Bills Preferences

In the Bills category, you have the opportunity on the Company Preference tab to set options for the way you enter and pay vendor bills:

- You can set default terms (QuickBooks sets this at ten days but you can change this default). When you create terms and link those terms to vendors, QuickBooks ignores this default for any vendor that has terms configured.
- You can tell QuickBooks to take discounts and credits automatically when you're paying vendor bills. Be sure to enter the account in which you post those discounts.

Calendar Preferences

All the settings available in this preference area are found only on the My Preferences tab. This means that the choices you make here will apply to only your login name.

The Calendar Settings area in this preference gives you several alternatives on the view (daily, weekly, monthly) that should be set as your default. If you can't decide, you can tell QuickBooks to open the view that you were using the last time you had your calendar window open. Other options in the Calendar Settings area include the number of days you want to appear for each week and the type of transactions your calendar should display for you.

The Upcoming & Past Due Settings area gives you control over which future and past due transactions will make their way onto your calendar.

Checking Preferences

This category has options in both the My Preferences and Company Preferences tabs. On the My Preferences tab, you can select default bank accounts for different types of transactions. Skip these options if you only have one bank account.

The Company Preferences tab (see Figure 28-2) offers several options concerned with check printing, which are described in the following paragraphs.

Print Account Names On Voucher

This option is useful only if you print your checks and the check forms you purchase have vouchers (stubs). If so, selecting this option means that the text on the stub will display posting accounts. That information is of no interest to your vendors, so only use this option if you keep and file check vouchers instead of leaving them attached to the check.

FIGURE 28-2 Select the options you need to make check writing more efficient.

Change Check Date When Non-Cleared Check Is Printed

Selecting this option means that at the time you print checks, the current date becomes the check date. If you don't select this option, the check date you specified when you filled out the check window is used (even if that date has already passed).

Start With Payee Field On Check

Enabling this option forces your cursor to the Payee field when you first bring up the Write Checks window. If the option is not enabled, the bank account field is the first active field. If you always write checks from the same bank account, enable this option to save yourself the inconvenience of pressing TAB.

Warn About Duplicate Check Numbers

This option means that QuickBooks will warn you if a check number you've used in a check you've created already exists.

Autofill Payee Account Number In Check Memo

Most vendors maintain an account number for their customers, and your own account number can be automatically printed when you print checks. In order for this to occur, you must fill in your account number in the Vendor card (on the Additional Information tab). The printout appears in the Memo section on the lower-left section of the check.

Select Default Accounts To Use

You can set the default bank accounts for different types of payroll transactions, which is important if you have a separate bank account for payroll. Then, when you create these checks, you don't have to select the bank account from a drop-down list in the transaction window. This avoids the common error of printing the payroll checks on operating account checks, voiding the checks, and starting again with the right account.

Online Banking

If you use online banking, you can choose how you want to view and enter transactions. Side-by-Side mode allows you to see your account balances and the transactions that need to be processed and categorized all in one window. If you select Register mode, the work of processing and categorizing your transactions happens while in a register view. Register mode was the only method used in QuickBooks 2008 and earlier versions.

Desktop View Preferences

This is where you design the way the QuickBooks window looks and acts. The My Preferences tab (see Figure 28-3) contains basic configuration options.

In the View section, you can specify whether you always want to see one QuickBooks window at a time or view multiple windows.

- Choose One Window to limit the QuickBooks screen to show one window at a time, even if you have multiple windows open. The windows are stacked atop each other, and only the top window is visible. A convenient way to switch between multiple windows is by using the Open Window List. To use this view, select View | Open Window list.
- Choose Multiple Windows to make it possible to view multiple windows on your screen. Selecting this option activates the arrangement commands on the Windows menu item, which allows you to stack or arrange windows so that more than one window is visible at a time.

FIGURE 28-3 Configure the look and behavior of the QuickBooks window.

In the Desktop section, you can also specify what QuickBooks should do when you open and exit the software, choosing among the following options:

- **Save When Closing Company** Means that the state of the desktop is remembered when you close the company (or exit QuickBooks). Whichever QuickBooks windows were open when you left will reappear when you return. You can pick up where you left off. If you select the option Show Home Page When Opening A Company File, that option overrides this option, so if you close the company file after closing the Home page, the Home page appears on top of any open windows when you open the company file.

- **Save Current Desktop** Displays the desktop as it is at this moment every time you open QuickBooks. Select this option after you've opened or closed the QuickBooks windows you want to see when you start the software. If you select the option Show Home Page When Opening A Company File, that option overrides this option if you close the Home page.

- **Don't Save The Desktop**   Tells QuickBooks to display an empty QuickBooks desktop (unless you enable the Show Home Page When Opening A Company File option) when you open this company file or when you start QuickBooks again after using this company file. The desktop isn't really empty—the menu bar, Icon Bar, and any other navigation bars are on the desktop, but no transaction or list windows are open.
- **Keep Previously Saved Desktop**   Available only when you select Save Current Desktop, this option tells QuickBooks to display the desktop as it was the last time you used the Save Current Desktop option.
- **Show Home Page When Opening A Company File**   Tells QuickBooks to display the Home page when you open the company file.
- **Show Getting Started Window**   If you're new to QuickBooks and want some extra help with your setup, this window lets you click the Get Started Right button to learn about startup services provided by Intuit (additional fees may apply).

In the Color Scheme section, you can select a scheme from the drop-down list. In addition, buttons are available to configure Windows Settings for Display and Sounds. Clicking either button opens the associated applet in your Windows Control Panel. The display and sounds configuration options you change affect your computer and all your software, not just QuickBooks.

In the Company Preferences tab, you can customize the contents of the Home page. If you want to add an icon on the Home page for a particular feature (such as Estimates), this tab also tells you whether that feature has been enabled in your company file. If the feature hasn't been enabled, click the feature's name to open its category in the Preferences dialog. Turn the feature on to add its icon to the Home page, and then click the Desktop View icon to return to this window.

Finance Charge Preferences

In the Company Preferences tab, you can turn on, turn off, and configure finance charges. Finance charges can get complicated, so read the complete discussion about this topic in Chapter 10.

General Preferences

This dialog contains options for the way you work in QuickBooks. There are settings on both the My Preferences and Company Preferences tabs.

The My Preferences tab (as shown in Figure 28-4) offers a number of options that are designed to let you control the way QuickBooks behaves while you're working in transaction windows.

FIGURE 28-4 The My Preferences tab in General Preferences helps you control the way QuickBooks behaves when you're the logged in user.

Pressing Enter Moves Between Fields

This option exists for people who constantly forget that the default (normal, usual) key for moving from field to field in Windows software is the TAB key. Of course, when they press ENTER instead of TAB, the record they're working on is saved even though they haven't finished filling out all the fields. Rather than force you to get used to the way Windows works, QuickBooks lets you change the procedure.

Automatically Open Drop-Down Lists When Typing

This is a handy option that's used when you're making selections from drop-down lists. When you begin typing the first few letters of the listing you need, the drop-down list appears (and you move to the first listing that matches the character you typed).

Beep When Recording A Transaction

If you don't want to hear sound effects as you work in QuickBooks, you can deselect the option. On the other hand, you can use the Windows Sounds And

Audio Devices applet in Control Panel to configure the sounds so that some actions produce sound effects and other actions don't. You can even specify which sound you want for the actions that you've configured to play sounds.

Automatically Place Decimal Point

This is a handy feature once you get used to it (I couldn't live without it—and my desk calculator is configured for the same behavior). When you enter currency characters in a field, a decimal point is placed automatically to the left of the last two digits when you enable this feature. Therefore, if you type 5421, when you move to the next field the number changes to 54.21. If you want to type in even dollar amounts, type a period after you enter 54, and QuickBooks will automatically add two zeros to the right of the period (or you can enter the zeros, as in 5400, which automatically becomes 54.00).

Warn When Editing A Transaction

This option, which is selected by default, tells QuickBooks to flash a warning message when you change any transaction and try to close the transaction window without explicitly saving the changed transaction. This means you have a chance to abandon the edits. If you deselect the option, the edited transaction is saved as changed, unless it is linked to other transactions (in which case, the warning message explaining that problem appears).

Bring Back All One-Time Messages

One-time messages are those informational dialogs that include a Don't Show This Message Again option. If you clicked that Don't Show option on any message dialogs, select this check box to see those messages again (and you can once again select the Don't Show option).

Turn Off Pop-Up Messages For Products And Services

Selecting this option stops pop-up messages from QuickBooks that are connected to products and services available from Intuit. For example, when creating checks, Intuit displays a pop-up message explaining that you can buy checks at the Intuit Marketplace.

Show ToolTips For Clipped Text

Enabling this option means that if text in any field is truncated, hovering your mouse over the text displays the entire text. This saves you the trouble of selecting the field and using the arrow keys to read the entire text.

Warn When Deleting A Transaction Or Unused List Item

When selected, this option produces a warning when you delete a transaction or a entry that has not been used in a transaction—it's a standard message asking you to confirm your action.

If you try to delete an item or a name that has been used in a transaction, QuickBooks won't permit you to complete the deletion.

Keep QuickBooks Running for Quick Startups

When enabled, QuickBooks will start automatically and run in the background whenever you start your computer. When you close QuickBooks, it remains running in the background so it starts quickly the next time you open it.

Automatically Remember Account Or Transaction Information

Enabling this option tells QuickBooks to prefill information in a bill, check, or credit card transaction window, based on previous transactions for the same vendor. If this option is enabled, you can choose either of the suboptions:

- Automatically Recall Last Transaction For This Name, which duplicates the information in the last transaction. This is handy for transactions that don't change (or don't change often), such as the check to your landlord, which is always for the same amount and posted to the same account.
- Pre-Fill Accounts For Vendor Based On Past Entries, which examines the history of transactions for the current vendor. If the same information appears in all or most of the historical transactions, QuickBooks autofills the transaction window (same as the previous option). If historical transactions differ, QuickBooks does not prefill the transaction window, saving you the trouble of removing the data if it doesn't match this transaction.

P r o A d v i s o r   T i p : In addition to these "memory tricks" that QuickBooks provides for vendor transactions, you can prefill accounts for vendors right in the vendor record, which is a really handy feature. See Chapter 4 for details.

Default Date To Use For New Transactions

Use this option to tell QuickBooks whether you want the Date field to show the current date or the date of the last transaction you entered, when you open a transaction window. If you frequently enter transactions for the same date over a period of several days (for example, you start preparing invoices on the 27th of the month, but the invoice date is the last day of the month), select the option to use the last entered date so you can just keep going. QuickBooks resets this option when you close and reopen the program or the company file.

Keep Custom Item Information When Changing Item In Transactions

The selection you make for this option determines what QuickBooks does when you change the description text or the price for an item you insert in a sales transaction form, and then change the item. For example, you select an item named Widget, and then in the Description field, you type text to describe this widget, changing the default description that displayed when you selected the item. Or, perhaps the item had no default description, and you entered text to correct that omission. Then, you realize that you didn't really mean to sell the customer a Widget, you meant a Gadget, and the descriptive text you just typed was meant for the item named Gadget (which you thought you'd selected in the Item column). You return to the Item column (on the same line), click the arrow to see your item list, and select Gadget. Now, you think you have to type all that descriptive text again, because Gadget has its own descriptive text, and it will automatically replace your work. This option prevents that work going to waste.

- If you select Always, QuickBooks will keep the descriptive text you wrote, even though you changed the Item. This descriptive text is linked to this different item only for this invoice; no changes are made to any item's record.
- If you select No, QuickBooks just fills in the description that goes with the new item you selected.
- If you select Ask, as soon as you change the item, QuickBooks asks if you want to change only the item and keep your customized description on the invoice. You can answer Yes (or No), and you can also tell QuickBooks to change this Preferences option permanently to match your answer.

The same thing happens if you entered a different price (instead of, or in addition to, the description), and then changed the item.

The Company Preferences Tab in General Preferences

The Company Preferences tab in the General section has the following options:

Time Format Select a format for entering time, choosing between decimal (for example, 11.5 hours) or minutes (11:30).

Always Show Years As 4 Digits If you prefer to display the year with four digits (01/01/2012 instead of 01/01/12), select this option.

Never Update Name Information When Saving Transactions By default, QuickBooks asks if you want to update the original information for a name when you change it during a transaction entry. For example, if you're entering a sales receipt and you change the customer's address, QuickBooks offers to make that change on the customer's record (you can choose Yes or No when QuickBooks asks). If you don't want to be offered this opportunity and always want the record to remain as is, select this option.

Save Transactions Before Printing   The rule that a transaction must be saved before it's printed is a security device. Keeping this option enabled will help to prevent an employee (or others who have access to your QuickBooks file) from printing an invoice or check without the transaction being recorded. I recommend that you keep this default setting.

Intuit EasySaver   EasySaver is an Intuit service that reviews your items (only inventory and non-inventory items from your QuickBooks Item List) and offers you a comparison price with the EasySaver price list—all in an effort to save you money. The default setting for this preference is on, and you can check out the comparisons that EasySaver can offer you by clicking the Intuit EasySaver icon on the QuickBooks Home page.

Integrated Applications Preferences

You can let third-party software access and share the data in your QuickBooks files. Click the Integrated Applications icon and move to the Company Preferences tab to specify the way QuickBooks works with other software programs.

When you use a third-party program that links to QuickBooks, you're asked to approve that link. If you say Yes, the information for that program is recorded and appears in this dialog.

Items & Inventory Preferences

Use this dialog to enable the inventory function and set options for processing inventory transactions. Only the Company Preferences tab has options.

Inventory And Purchase Orders Are Active

Select this option to tell QuickBooks that you want to enable the inventory features; the purchase orders are automatically enabled with that action.

Warn About Duplicate Purchase Order Numbers

When this option is enabled, any attempt to issue a purchase order with a PO number that already exists will generate a warning.

Warn If Not Enough Inventory Quantity On Hand (QOH) To Sell

This option turns on the warning feature that is useful during customer invoicing. If you sell ten widgets but your stock of widgets is fewer than ten, QuickBooks displays a message telling you there's insufficient stock to fill the order. You can still complete the invoice; it's just a message, not a functional limitation, but you should order more widgets immediately.

(The option for Unit Of Measure is displayed, but the feature is only available in QuickBooks Premier editions.)

The Company Preferences tab of the Items & Inventory Preferences dialog also contains an Advanced Inventory Settings button. This feature, available only in QuickBooks Enterprise Solutions, allows you to track inventory across multiple locations. Click the "Learn about serial #/lots, FIFO and multi-location inventory" link to see if it's a fit for your business and learn how to upgrade to QuickBooks Enterprise Solutions.

Jobs & Estimates Preferences

Use the Company Preferences tab to configure the way your estimates work, as shown in Figure 28-5. The options are self-explanatory. Read Chapter 9 to learn everything about creating estimates and invoices for those estimates.

Multiple Currencies Preferences

The Company Preferences tab is where you enable the ability to do business in multiple currencies. The available options are Yes and No, but if you select Yes, QuickBooks prompts you to make a backup of your company file before finalizing your decision since this feature cannot be turned off once it's been turned on. From this window, you'll also tell QuickBooks what your home currency is.

Even if you're sure you want to work in multiple currencies in QuickBooks, make a backup, and use a name for the backup file that indicates what you're doing (such as *<Company Name>*PreMulticurrency.QBB). Then, if you decide you don't want to use this feature, you can restore your backup file and proceed as before. Using the multiple currencies feature in QuickBooks is covered in Appendix B.

Payments Preferences

Use the Payments preference (Company Preferences tab only) to learn more about or to sign up for the Intuit Payment Network. With this service, you can choose from credit card processing, paper check processing, or electronic check processing (additional fees may apply). In the Receive Payments section, you'll find three options.

FIGURE 28-5 Set up and configure estimates.

Automatically Apply Payments

This option tells QuickBooks to apply payments automatically to open invoices. If the payment amount is an exact match for an open invoice, it is applied to that invoice. If the payment amount is smaller than any open invoice, QuickBooks applies the payment to the oldest invoice. If the payment amount is larger than any open invoice, QuickBooks applies payments, starting with the oldest invoice, until the payment amount is used up.

Without this option, you must manually apply each payment to an invoice. That's not as difficult as it may sound, and in fact, is quite common because the customer's check almost always indicates the invoice the customer wants to pay (even if the check doesn't cover the entire amount of that invoice). Sometimes customers don't mark the invoice number on the check and instead enclose a copy of the invoice in the envelope. Read Chapter 10 to learn about receiving and applying customer payments.

Automatically Calculate Payments

When this option is enabled, you can begin selecting invoices to pay in the Receive Payments window before entering the amount of the customer's payment check. When you've finished selecting invoices, either paying them entirely or applying a partial payment, the amounts you've applied should equal the amount of the check you received.

This is efficient if a customer has many invoices (some of which may have credits or may have an amount in dispute) and has attached instructions about the way to apply the checks.

Use Undeposited Funds As A Default Deposit To Account

Selecting this option automates the process of depositing all cash received into the Undeposited Funds account. If the option isn't selected, each cash receipt transaction window (customer payment and sales receipt) offers the choice of depositing the cash into a bank account or into the Undeposited Funds account.

Invoice Payments

In this section, you can learn more about or sign up for the Intuit Payment Network. When you sign up for this service, a link (with a web address set up just for your business) is included on your invoices. Your customer can use this link to pay you online. Click the Learn More or Explain links to activate this service or to get more information about how it works. Additional fees may apply.

Payroll & Employees Preferences

Use the Company Preferences tab of this category to set all the configuration options for payroll. Read Chapter 17 to understand the selections in this window.

Reminders Preferences

The Reminders category of the Preferences dialog has options on both tabs. The My Preferences tab has one option, which enables the display of the Reminders List when you open the company file.

The Company Preferences tab lists all the available reminders, and you can select the ones you want to use (see Figure 28-6). Of course, these selections are meaningless unless you enabled Reminders in the My Preferences tab.

For each item, decide whether you want to see a summary (just a listing and the total amount of money involved), a complete detailed list, or nothing at all. You can also determine the amount of lead time you want for your reminders. (Some of the items are grayed out because they're only available in QuickBooks Premier editions.)

FIGURE 28-6 Decide which tasks you want to be reminded about.

Reports & Graphs Preferences

This is another section of the Preferences window that has choices on both tabs, so you can set your own user preferences and then set those options that affect the current company.

The My Preferences tab configures the following performance issues for reports and graphs.

Prompt Me To Modify Report Options Before Opening A Report

If you find that almost every time you select a report you have to customize it, you can tell QuickBooks to open the Modify Report window whenever a report is brought to the screen. If you find this feature useful, select this option.

Reports And Graphs Settings

While you're viewing a report or a graph, you can make changes to the format, the filters, or to the data behind it (by opening the appropriate transaction window and changing data). Most of the time, QuickBooks automatically changes the report or graph to match the changes. However, if there is anything else going on (perhaps you're also online, or you're in a network environment and other users are manipulating data that's in your report or graph), QuickBooks may not make changes automatically. The reason for the shutdown of automatic refreshing is to keep your computer running as quickly and efficiently as possible. At that point, QuickBooks has to make a decision about when and how to refresh the report or graph. You must give QuickBooks the parameters for making the decision to refresh.

- Choose Prompt Me To Refresh to see a message asking you whether you want to refresh the report or the graph after you've made changes to the data behind it. When the reminder appears, you can click Yes to refresh the data in the report.
- Choose Refresh Automatically if you want up-to-the-second data and don't want to bother to click the Refresh button. If you work with QuickBooks across a network, this could slow down your work a bit because whenever any user makes a change to data that's used in the report/graph, it will refresh itself.
- Choose Don't Refresh if you want to decide for yourself, without any reminder from QuickBooks, when to click the Refresh button on the report window.

Graphs Only

Give QuickBooks instructions about creating your graphs, as follows:

- Choose Draw Graphs In 2D (Faster) to have graphs displayed in two dimensions instead of three. This doesn't limit your ability to see trends at a glance; it's just not as high-tech. The main reason to consider this option is that the 2-D graph takes less time to draw on your screen.
- Choose Use Patterns to draw the various elements in your graphs with black-and-white patterns instead of colors. For example, one pie wedge may be striped, another speckled. This is handy if you print your graphs to a black-and-white printer.

Move to the Company Preferences tab of the Reports & Graphs category to set company preferences for reports (see Figure 28-7).

Summary Reports Basis

Specify whether you want to see summary reports as accrual-based or cash-based. You're only setting the default specification here, and you can always change the basis in the Modify Report dialog when you actually display the report.

Aging Reports

Specify whether you want to generate A/R and A/P aging reports using the due date or the transaction date.

FIGURE 28-7   Set the default options for reports.

Reports—Show Accounts By

Specify whether you want reports to display account names, account descriptions, or both. If you enabled account numbers, those numbers are part of the account names.

Setting Report Format Defaults

You can set the default formatting for reports by clicking the Format button and making changes to the default configuration options for parts of reports that aren't data related but instead control the look of the reports. Use this feature if you find yourself making the same modifications to the formats over and over.

Configuring the Cash Flow Report

A cash flow report is really a complicated document, and before the days of accounting software, accountants spent many hours creating such a report (and charged a lot of money for doing so). QuickBooks has configured a cash flow report format that is used to produce the Statement Of Cash Flows report available in the list of Company & Financial reports.

You can view the format by clicking the Classify Cash button, but you shouldn't mess around with the available selections until you check with your accountant. You can learn about cash flow reports in Chapter 23.

Sales & Customers Preferences

You can set options in the Sales & Customers category on both the My Preferences and Company Preferences tabs. On the My Preferences tab, set the options for invoicing customers for reimbursable expenses and billable time.

Prompt For Time/Costs To Add

Choosing this option tells QuickBooks to open a dialog that displays the current reimbursable expenses whenever you create an invoice or sales receipt for a customer with outstanding reimbursable costs. This is the option to select if you always (or almost always) collect reimbursable costs from customers.

Don't Add Any

Selecting this option prevents the automatic display of any dialogs about reimbursable expenses when you create a sales transaction. Choose this option if you rarely (or never) seek reimbursement from your customers. If you *do* want to collect reimbursable expenses during invoice creation, you can click the Add Time/Costs button on the sales transaction form.

Ask What To Do

Select this option to tell QuickBooks to ask you what you want to do whenever you create a sales transaction for a customer with outstanding reimbursable costs. Depending on your selection in that dialog, you can add the costs to the sales transaction or omit them. You can learn how to bill customers for expenses and time in Chapter 9.

Show Payment Toolbar On Receive Payment And Sales Receipt Forms

The default setting is on, which displays the customer payment options toolbar that lists the payment methods available to you and your customers when you use QuickBooks (additional fees may apply). Uncheck this option to remove the toolbar from these windows.

On the Company Preferences tab, set the default options for sales transactions.

Usual Shipping Method

Use this to set the default shipping method, if you use the same shipping method most of the time. This saves you the trouble of making a selection from the drop-down list unless you're changing the shipper for a particular invoice.

Usual FOB

Set the FOB language for invoices. FOB (Free On Board) is the location from which shipping is determined to be the customer's responsibility. This means more than just paying for freight; it's a statement that says, "At this point you have become the owner of this product." The side effects include assigning responsibility if goods are lost, damaged, or stolen. FOB settings have no impact on your financial records. (Don't let the size of the text box fool you; you're limited to 13 characters.)

Warn About Duplicate Invoice Numbers

This option tells QuickBooks to warn you if you're creating an invoice with an invoice number that's already in use.

Choose Template For Invoice Packing Slip

Select a default packing slip to use when you print packing slips. If you've created customized packing slips, you can make one of them the default.

Use Price Levels

This option turns on the Price Level feature, which is explained in Chapter 7.

Sales Tax Preferences

If you collect sales tax, you must set your sales tax options. These options are easy to configure because most of the selections are predefined by state tax laws and state tax reporting rules. Check with your accountant and read the information that came with your state sales tax license. For more information about managing sales taxes (a very complicated issue in many states), see Chapter 5.

Search Preferences

The Search feature allows you to quickly search in all areas of your company file for things like transactions, names, amount, dates, QuickBooks features, and so on. By default, the Search field is included on the QuickBooks Icon Bar. You can remove it by unchecking that option at the top of the My Preference tab. You can also tell QuickBooks whether to search the Help files or your QuickBooks file when a search term is entered in this field.

The preferences listed on the Company Preferences tab give you the option of updating your search information automatically (as often as every five minutes) or manually.

Send Forms Preferences

If you send transactions to customers via e-mail, the My Preferences tab offers the opportunity to automatically select the To Be E-Mailed option on a sales transaction if the current customer is configured for e-mail as the preferred send method. You can also choose whether to send this information via Outlook or a compatible web e-mail service like Yahoo or Gmail.

On the Company Preferences tab, you can design the message that accompanies the e-mailed transaction, which can be a customer or vendor transaction.

Service Connection Preferences

If you use QuickBooks services on the Internet, use this category to specify the way you want to connect to the Internet for those services.

The My Preferences tab contains options related to online banking if your bank uses the Web Connect method of online access. (Chapter 15 has detailed information about online banking services.)

- **Give Me The Option Of Saving A File Whenever I Download Web Connect Data** Select this option if you want QuickBooks to provide a choice to save Web Connect data for later processing instead of automatically processing the transactions. QuickBooks provides the choice by opening a dialog that lets you choose whether to import the data immediately or save it to a file so you can import it later (you have to supply a filename). The QuickBooks dialog also includes an option to reset this option. This option only works when you select Open on the File Download dialog. If you disable this option, the file is automatically opened and the data is imported into QuickBooks.
- **If QuickBooks Is Run By My Browser, Don't Close It After Web Connect Is Done** Selecting this option means that when QuickBooks is launched automatically when you download Web Connect data from your Financial Institution (after selecting Open on the Download dialog), QuickBooks remains open after you process the data. If you deselect this option, QuickBooks closes automatically as soon as your data is processed.

The following connection options are available on the Company Preferences tab (these options don't apply to payroll services or online banking):

- **Automatically Connect Without Asking For A Password** Lets all users log into the QuickBooks Business Services network automatically.
- **Always Ask For A Password Before Connecting** Forces users to enter a login name and password in order to access QuickBooks Business Services.
- **Allow Background Downloading Of Service Messages** Lets QuickBooks check the Intuit website for updates and information periodically when you're connected to the Internet.

Spelling Preferences

The Spelling section presents options only on the My Preferences tab. This is where you control the way the QuickBooks spell checker works. You can instruct QuickBooks to check spelling automatically before saving or printing any form.

In addition, you can specify those words you want the spelling checker to skip, such as Internet addresses, numbers, and solid capital letters that probably indicate an abbreviation.

Tax:1099 Preferences

Use the Company Preferences tab of this window to access a wizard that will help you establish the 1099 form options you need (see Figure 28-8). For each type of 1099 payment, you must assign an account from your chart of accounts. See Chapter 24 for detailed information about configuring and issuing 1099 forms.

FIGURE 28-8   Use the 1099 Preference window to launch the wizard that will guide you through the process of configuring your QuickBooks file for 1099 reporting.

Time & Expenses Preferences

Use this section in the Company Preferences tab to turn on Time Tracking and to tell QuickBooks the first day of your work week (which becomes the first day listed on your timesheets). Read all about tracking time in Chapter 16.

In addition, you can configure invoicing options, as explained in the following sections.

Track Reimbursed Expenses As Income

Selecting this option changes the way your general ledger handles customer payments for reimbursements. When the option is enabled, the reimbursement is assigned to an income account instead of posting back to the original expense account.

As a result of enabling this option, QuickBooks adds a new field to the dialog you use when you create or edit an expense account, so you can enter the associated income account.

Whenever you post a vendor expense to this account and also indicate that the expense is reimbursable, the amount you charge to the customer when you create an invoice for that customer is automatically posted to the income account that's linked to this expense account.

QuickBooks requires a separate income account for each reimbursable expense. If you have multiple expense accounts for which you may receive reimbursement (a highly likely scenario), you must also create multiple income accounts for accepting reimbursed expenses. See Chapter 11 to learn how to enter expenses as reimbursable.

Default Markup Percentage

You can preset a markup for reimbursed expenses and also for items that have both a cost and price. QuickBooks uses the percentage you enter here to automate the pricing of inventory items. When you're creating an inventory item, as soon as you enter the cost, QuickBooks automatically adds this percentage and displays the result as the price. If your pricing strategy isn't consistent, don't enable this option; you'll find this automatic process more annoying than helpful, because you'll constantly find yourself re-entering the item's price.

Customizing Transaction Templates

QuickBooks makes it very easy to customize the forms you use to create transactions. (Forms such as invoices, purchase orders, statements, and so on, are called *templates* in QuickBooks.) There are two customization options available when customizing templates. The first allows you to create brand-new template designs (choosing this option takes you online). You can then save these templates to your template list. My focus in this section is on the second option, which gives you the ability to work with and modify the appearance of an *existing* template or to create a new template based on an existing one.

You can use an existing template as the basis of a new template, copying what you like, changing what you don't like, and eliminating what you don't need. Existing templates can be customized in two ways:

- **Basic customization** Change the appearance by customizing the fonts, colors, and other output settings only—these are minor changes (a form of "window dressing") that can be made to built-in Intuit templates.

- **Additional customization** Customize the fields and columns that appear on the template—these are major changes and require you to create a new template with a new template name.

Basic Customization of Templates

To make minor changes to an existing template, select the template from the drop-down list in the Template field at the top right of the transaction window. Next, click the arrow next to the Customize button, select Manage Templates, choose the template, and click OK to open the Basic Customization window (see Figure 28-9).

FIGURE 28-9 Change the appearance of a template in the Basic Customization dialog.

ProAdvisor Tip: Templates that have the word "Intuit" in the template name are designed to work with preprinted forms you purchase from Intuit (although you can use them with blank paper or letterhead). Except for the Intuit Packing Slip, you can only perform basic customization on these templates. To use Intuit templates as the basis of additional customization, you must make a copy of the template and create a new template as shown next.

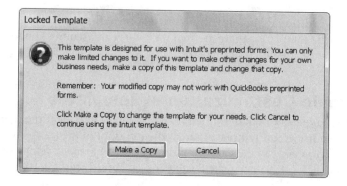

Manage Templates

Click Manage Templates to view, copy, or rename a template. The Preview pane (on the right) displays a layout of the template as it currently looks and displays the template name at the top. In the Template Name field at the top of the Preview pane, you can delete the current name (unless it's an original Intuit template) and replace it with the name you want for the new template. Clicking OK returns you to the Basic Customization dialog.

Adding a Logo to a Template

You can add your company logo to a template by selecting the Use Logo check box. Click the Select Logo button to open the Select Image dialog, navigate to the folder that has your logo graphic file, and select the file. Use the following guidelines to add a logo to a template:

- The logo should be a square shape to fit properly on the template.
- QuickBooks accepts all the common graphic formats for your logo. However, the graphic loads when you print the template, and graphic files saved with a BMP format tend to be larger than other formats and may take quite some time to load each time you print. The most efficient format, in terms of size and resolution, is JPG.
- Your logo appears in the upper-left corner of the form, unless you open the Layout Designer (covered later in this chapter) to reposition it.
- You won't see the logo on the screen version of the template.
- If you can't place the logo in the size and position you prefer, consider having stationery printed and using it as the paper source for the template.

Customizing Colors on a Template

You can change the color of the lines that appear on the template by selecting a color scheme from the drop-down list in the Select Color Scheme field. Click Apply Color Scheme to save the change and see its effect in the Preview pane on the right side of the dialog.

You can also change the color of any text that's printed on the form by using the features for changing fonts (covered next) and selecting a color for the font.

Customizing Fonts on a Template

To change the fonts for any elements on the template, select the element in the Change Font For list and click Change Font. Select a font, size, style (such as bold or italic), or color.

Customizing the Company Information on a Template

You can select and deselect the text that appears in the name and address block of your templates. The data is taken from the Company Information dialog, which you can open by clicking Update Information, to make sure that the data exists.

Printing Status Stamps on Templates

You can select or deselect the option to print the status stamp on a transaction template (PAID, RECEIVED, and so on). The status stamp prints at an angle across the center of the header section of the template. If you deselect the status stamp, you are only removing it from the printed copy of the form; the screen copy always shows the status.

➡ ProAdvisor Recommends

The List of Templates

If you've just started using QuickBooks, you may be confused by the template names you see in the Templates List because several types of templates aren't listed. The templates that appear in the list depend on the preferences you set and the transactions you've created.

By default, QuickBooks installs Invoice templates, a Statement template, and a Packing Slip template. You won't see a Purchase Order template unless you enable Inventory & Purchase Orders (covered earlier in this chapter) and also open the built-in Purchase Order template by choosing Vendors | Create Purchases Orders. As soon as the Create Purchase Orders transaction window opens, the Purchase Order template appears on the list (you can close the transaction window without creating a PO if your only purpose was to add the template to the list). The same convention applies to Sales Receipts, Estimates, and other QuickBooks templates.

Additional Customization of Templates

You can make major changes in templates to suit your needs as well as your taste. QuickBooks calls this the Additional Customization feature. Start your customization by selecting an existing template on which to base your new template. Select the Customize button at the top right of the transaction window and select the Customize Data Layout window. If you are attempting to modify an Intuit template, the Locked Template dialog appears instructing you to make a copy of the template; otherwise, the Additional Customization window opens (see Figure 28-10).

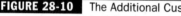

FIGURE 28-10 The Additional Customization dialog lets you point and click to redesign a template.

Notice that in Figure 28-10, the name of this template includes the text "BOPref," which refers to a custom field that was created for tracking customer preferences for back orders. This field will only display on the screen version of the template (the field serves as a guideline when filling an order), but not on the printed version that is sent to the customer.

Custom fields you create in a Names list appear in the Header section of transaction windows—custom fields you create in the Item List appear in the Columns section of transaction windows.

Customizing the Template Header

The Header section of the Additional Customization dialog includes all the fields that appear above the line items in a transaction form. You can add or remove fields on the screen form, the printed form, or both. The Preview pane on the right is a preview of the printed form, and as you add or remove fields from the printed form, you see the changes reflected there.

There are some changes to the Header section that are often effected by QuickBooks users (the data for the fields is automatically filled in using the data in the customer or vendor record when you use the template to create a transaction):

- If you assign account numbers to your customers, display the Account Number field (only available on the printed version).
- If you use Reps, either as commissioned salespersons or as customer support contacts, add the Rep field to both the screen and printed versions.
- If you're tracking jobs for the majority of your customers, add the job name to the form (only available in the printed version). QuickBooks uses the term "Project" because that's the commonly used term in most businesses (the exception is the construction trade, where "Job" is a common term). If you refer to jobs as "jobs" with your customers, you can change the text.

Customizing the Template Columns

On the Columns tab of the Additional Customization dialog (see Figure 28-11), you can add or remove columns that appear in the line item section of the transaction form. If you created custom fields for items, they're available for any template you design.

FIGURE 28-11 Add columns to specify details of the items you're including in the transaction.

If progress invoicing is turned on, another columns tab, called Prog Cols, is available for customizing the transaction form you use when you create a progress invoice against an estimate (to learn how to create estimates and progress invoices, read Chapter 9).

Customizing the Template Footer

The Footer tab (see Figure 28-12) contains the elements that appear at the bottom of the transaction form. If you want to add additional fields to this section of the printed transaction form, you'll have to use the Layout Designer to maneuver the positioning, because you don't have a lot of space to work with.

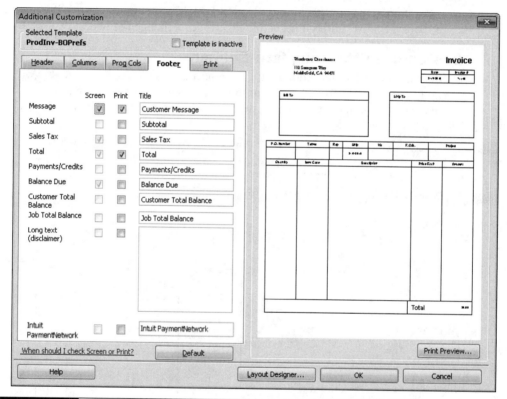

FIGURE 28-12   Add fields from the footer tab to add more information to the transaction form.

Using the Layout Designer

As you customize the printed forms, you can see the effects in the Preview pane. If you notice some overlapping fields, or you think the layout looks too crowded, you can use the Layout Designer to reposition the elements on the form. Click Layout Designer to open your template in the Layout Designer window, as seen in Figure 28-13.

FIGURE 28-13 You can reposition the elements in the form to create your own design.

The Layout Designer is a powerful and complicated feature, and it's beyond the scope of this book to go into deep detail about it. The more you work with it, however, the better you'll get at making it work for you. Don't be afraid to experiment!

If you use window envelopes to mail your invoices, be sure the option Show Envelope Window at the bottom of the Layout Designer is selected before you start. The areas of the form that appear in envelope windows are highlighted in green. This helps you avoid moving any fields into that area.

Select any element to put a frame around it. Now you can perform an action on the frame, as follows:

- To change the size of the element, position your pointer on one of the sizing handles on the frame, then drag the handle to resize the element.
- To move an element, position your pointer inside the frame and, when your pointer turns into a four-headed arrow, drag the frame to a different location on the form.

- Double-click an element's frame to see a Properties dialog that permits all sorts of changes for the selected element.

- To change the margin measurements, click the Margins button at the bottom of the Layout Designer.
- Click the Grid button to open the Grid And Snap Settings dialog where you can eliminate the dotted line grid, change the spacing between grid lines, or turn off the Snap To Grid option (which automatically aligns objects to the nearest point on the grid).
- Use the toolbar buttons to align, resize, and zoom into the selected elements.

There's also an Undo/Redo button, just in case.

When you finish with the Layout Designer, click OK to move back to the Additional Customization window. If everything is just the way you want it, save your new template by clicking OK. This new template name appears on the drop-down list when you create transaction forms.

▶▶ ProAdvisor Recommends

QuickBooks Live Community

The QuickBooks Live Community is a user forum where QuickBooks users can ask questions and get answers from other users (and sometimes from Intuit ProAdvisors and other experts). You can read all the questions and answers without joining the community, but if you want to post a question or answer you must join. Joining is free, and all you have to do is provide a user name and your e-mail address.

It's important to be aware that some of the answers and explanations you see are posted by users who have limited experience with QuickBooks. It's best to check with your accountant or create a test company file to experiment before implementing changes that can have a significant impact on your QuickBooks data.

Appendixes

Installing QuickBooks on a Network

In *this appendix:*

- License requirements

- Understand the different installation options

- Understand the multi-user hosting options

- Set up and configure QuickBooks in a multi-user environment

If you plan on giving more than one user access to your QuickBooks file, this appendix will provide you with the background information you need to know along with some tips to help ensure your multi-user installation goes as smoothly as possible.

Soon after you launch the QuickBooks installer on your computer—either from a QuickBooks CD or via a download link—you're asked to make some choices about how the program should be installed on your computer. The choices themselves are presented in a very clear and simple manner in the installation wizard. Yet sometimes there's confusion about what should be considered in order to make right choice. In most cases, this confusion has its roots in understanding how many user licenses you need and your network configuration.

License Requirements for a Multi-user Installation

You'll need to purchase a separate QuickBooks license for each computer that will have simultaneous access to your QuickBooks data file. In addition, all computers must use the same version—in this case, QuickBooks Pro 2012. QuickBooks Pro comes in one-, two-, or three-user license packs, allowing for up to three simultaneous users (with three unique user login names) to access a company file on a network. You can also purchase a two-user and a three-user pack that allows you to have up to five simultaneous users accessing the company file (again, each user is required to have a unique user login name). Setting up users and permissions is covered in Chapter 26.

Multi-user Installation Options

Multi-user installation options are dependent on the type of network configuration you plan to use. Specifically, it depends whether you plan on using a dedicated server to host your QuickBooks company file, or whether you plan on utilizing a peer-to-peer network, where one of the computers on the network runs QuickBooks and also stores the file.

It's beyond the scope of this appendix to give instruction on which configuration is best in your situation and the steps required for setup. You'll want to contact your system administration for that; if you don't have one, find a local IT expert.

Installing QuickBooks on a Peer-to-Peer Network

First, ensure that all the computers that need access to the QuickBooks file are on a network running Windows 7 (all editions except Starter and Basic), Vista, or XP. It's also a good idea to make sure your operating system is up to date with the latest release. Other important tasks to add to your preinstall checklist include:

- Deciding which computer on your network will hold the QuickBooks file. It should be the fastest computer on your network, and it will be the first computer that you install QuickBooks on.
- Ensuring that the other QuickBooks computers on the network have full read/write access to the folder that you plan on storing your QuickBooks data file.

Insert the QuickBooks CD in your CD drive or, if you downloaded the program, run the Download Manager to launch the Intuit QuickBooks Installer. A Welcome screen confirms the launch. Click Next and follow these steps:

1. Review and accept the terms of the Intuit Software End User License Agreement. Click Next.
2. In the Choose Installation Type window, select Custom And Network Options (see Figure A-1). Click Next.

Intuit QuickBooks® Installer   intuit.

Choose Installation Type

     ○ **Express (recommended)**
         Install using default settings.

     ● **Custom and Network options**
         Customize location and advanced
         server options.

         Need Help?
         ► **Let us install for you!**
         or access our Self Help tools.

     ⓘ Explain these choices in detail   ‹ Back   Next ›   Cancel

FIGURE A-1   Choose the installation type: Custom And Network Options.

3. The Custom And Network Options window opens, giving you three choices. Select the middle option, I'll Be Using QuickBooks On This Computer, And I'll Be Storing Our Company File Here So It Can Be Shared Over Our Network (see Figure A-2). Click Next.
4. Enter your license and product information (found either on your CD or in the e-mail received from Intuit that included your product download link).

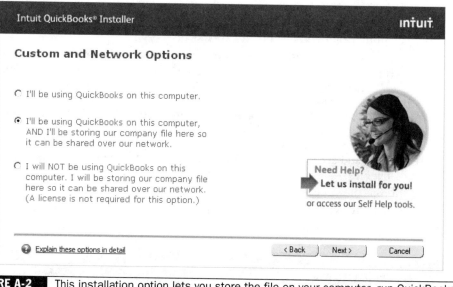

Intuit QuickBooks® Installer

Custom and Network Options

○ I'll be using QuickBooks on this computer.

◉ I'll be using QuickBooks on this computer, AND I'll be storing our company file here so it can be shared over our network.

○ I will NOT be using QuickBooks on this computer. I will be storing our company file here so it can be shared over our network. (A license is not required for this option.)

Need Help?
Let us install for you!
or access our Self Help tools.

 Explain these options in detail

< Back | Next > | Cancel

FIGURE A-2 This installation option lets you store the file on your computer, run QuickBooks, and give others access to your QuickBooks company file.

5. If this is your first version of QuickBooks, you can accept the suggested folder that the installer recommends. If you're upgrading from a previous version of QuickBooks, you'll have the option of replacing your previous version with QuickBooks 2012 or changing the install location (which keeps the existing version of QuickBooks on your computer). I recommend you select the option Change The Install Location (see the next ProAdvisor Tip). Click Next, then click the Install button.

ProAdvisor Tip: Most installations are trouble free. But there are times when a setting on your computer that you are not aware of—or even an emergency situation in your office—interrupts your installation. Whatever the reason, choosing to not overwrite and replacing your existing QuickBooks installation gives you the ability to continue working in your QuickBooks file until any issues with the installation have been resolved. Later, after you're up and running, you can confidently uninstall the previous version using the appropriate utility in Windows Control Panel.

6. For the next several minutes, you'll see a series of informational windows about various QuickBooks features and additional services. Each of these windows contains a status bar to keep you apprised of the progress of your installation. When the installation is complete, you'll receive a congratulations message and the option to open QuickBooks directly, get help getting started, or both. For the discussion that follows, select Open QuickBooks and click Finish.

ProAdvisor Tip: If you're brand new to QuickBooks, refer to Chapter 1 for what you need to know about creating a new company file. Return to this topic once you've created the file.

7. With your QuickBooks company file open, select File | Switch To Multi-user Mode. Click OK.

By switching to Multi-user mode, you also automatically configure this computer as the host for your QuickBooks company file.

File Hosting and the Database Server Manager

When you turn on Multi-user mode (as just described) on the first computer that you've installed QuickBooks on, you automatically designate this computer as the host of your QuickBooks data file. In addition, behind the scenes, QuickBooks installs a Database Server Manager program. Running this program along with QuickBooks ensures that other QuickBooks users will be able to access the company file even if the QuickBooks program is not open on this computer (the computer itself, however, has to be turned on).

To open and run the Database Server Manager, go to the Windows Start menu and select All Programs | QuickBooks | QuickBooks Database Server Manager. On the Scan Folders tab, click the Add Folder button to browse to the QuickBooks file you want to make available to other users. When your folder is listed in the Folders That Contain QuickBooks Company Files box, click the Scan button. Your file will be configured to ensure that others on the network can open your QuickBooks file (see Figure A-3).

Installing QuickBooks on the Client Computers

With your QuickBooks host computer up and running, you're ready install the program on the other networked computers. Follow these steps:

1. Complete steps 1 and 2 from the previous section.
2. In the Custom And Network Options window, select the first option I'll Be Using QuickBooks On This Computer (see Figure A-4). Click Next.

FIGURE A-3 Running the Database Server Manager makes your QuickBooks company file available to other users on your network.

FIGURE A-4 When you install QuickBooks on client computers, choose the option I'll Be Using QuickBooks On This Computer.

3. Enter your license and product information (found either on your CD or in the e-mail received from Intuit that included your product download link).

4. If this is your first version of QuickBooks, you can accept the suggested folder that the installer recommends. If you're upgrading from a previous version of QuickBooks, you'll have the option of replacing your previous version with QuickBooks 2012 or changing the install location (which keeps the existing version of QuickBooks on your computer). I recommend you select the option Change The Install Location. (See the preceding ProAdvisor Tip.) Click Next, then click the Install button.

5. For the next several minutes, you'll see a series of informational windows about various QuickBooks features and additional services. Each of these windows contains a status bar to keep you apprised of the progress of your installation. When the installation is complete, you'll receive a congratulations message and the option to open QuickBooks directly, get help getting started, or both. For the discussion that follows, select Open QuickBooks and click Finish.

6. In the No Company Open window, select the option Open Or Restore An Existing Company. In the Open Or Restore Company window, select the option Open A Company File. Click Next.

7. Browse to and open your QuickBooks company file located on the QuickBooks host computer.

ProAdvisor Tip: After you click Finish, and before proceeding to the No Company Open window, QuickBooks may ask if you want to use this computer to host multi-user access. Answer No to ensure that the first computer that you installed QuickBooks on remains the host computer. If you answer Yes to this question, this computer will become the host, which means that not only will QuickBooks need to be open on this computer, but also a user will need to be logged into the company file before any of the other users on the network can work in the file.

Multi-user hosting setup required

To allow multiple users to work on the company file at the same time, QuickBooks must set up this computer to host multi-user access. You may also need to purchase additional user licenses. Learn more. (H101)

Do you want to use this computer to host multi-user access?

Yes   No   Help

Installing QuickBooks on a Client-server Network

In order to use QuickBooks on a network with a dedicated server, you must be running one of the following: Microsoft Windows XP (SP2 or later), Vista (w/ UAC on), 7 (w/ UAC on), Windows Server 2003, Windows Server 2008, or Small Business Server 2008. Once you've confirmed that your server operating system meets one of these requirements, follow these installation instructions:

1. On the server computer, insert the QuickBooks CD into the CD drive; if you downloaded the program, run the Download Manager to launch the Intuit QuickBooks Installer. A Welcome screen confirms the launch. Click Next.

2. Review and accept the terms of the Intuit Software End User License Agreement. Click Next.

3. In the Choose Installation Type window, select the Custom and Network options. Click Next.

4. The Custom and Network Options window opens giving you three choices. Select the last option, I Will Not Be Using QuickBooks On This Computer. I Will Be Storing Our Company File Here So It Can Be Shared Over Our Network (see Figure A-5). Click Next.

| Intuit QuickBooks® Installer | ın†uı† |

Custom and Network Options

○ I'll be using QuickBooks on this computer. **[Current setting]**

○ I'll be using QuickBooks on this computer, AND I'll be storing our company file here so it can be shared over our network.

◉ I will NOT be using QuickBooks on this computer. I will be storing our company file here so it can be shared over our network. (A license is not required for this option.)

Need Help?
Let us install for you!
or access our Self Help tools.

Explain these options in detail   < Back   Next >   Cancel

FIGURE A-5 Choosing the option I Will Not Be Using QuickBooks On This Computer installs the Database Server Manager only.

▶▶ ProAdvisor Recommends

Installing Both QuickBooks and the Database Server Manager on Your Server

Selecting the "I Will Not Be Using QuickBooks On This Computer" option installs the QuickBooks Database Server Manager program and not the full version of QuickBooks. While this is a perfectly acceptable installation option when installing in a Client-Server environment, it's also acceptable to install both QuickBooks and the Database Server Manager on the server. This can be a good idea because two very important utilities are built into the full QuickBooks program: the verify and rebuild utilities (they are covered in Chapter 27). These utilities should only be run locally, meaning that the QuickBooks file being verified and rebuilt should reside on the same computer as the full QuickBooks program.

When both QuickBooks and the Database Server Manager are installed, the QuickBooks program will be "silent" and used only occasionally for maintenance purposes. As a result, it will not affect your licensing requirements, but it will give you peace of mind knowing that you can easily perform routine maintenance on your QuickBooks file when you need to.

5. QuickBooks suggests an installation location for the Database Server Manager Program. You can change the location if you wish by clicking Change The Install Location. Click Next, then click the Install button.

6. For the next several minutes, you'll see a series of informational windows about various QuickBooks features and additional services. Each of these windows contains a status bar to keep you apprised of the progress of your installation. When the installation of the Database Server Manager is complete, you'll receive a congratulations message and the option to get help getting started. For the discussion that follows, click Finish.

Configure the Database Server Manager

To open and configure the Database Server Manager, go to the Windows Start menu and select All Programs | QuickBooks | QuickBooks Database Server Manager. On the Scan Folders tab, click the Add Folder button to browse to the QuickBooks file you want to make available to other users. When your folder is listed in the Folders That Contain QuickBooks Company Files box, click the Scan button. Your file will be configured to ensure that others on the network can open your QuickBooks file (refer to Figure A-3).

You're now ready to install the QuickBooks program on the other client workstations by following the instructions in the earlier section, "Installing QuickBooks on the Client Computers."

Multiple Currencies

In this appendix:

- Set up and configure multiple currencies

- Set up and configure customers and vendors for multiple currencies

- Create transactions in other currencies

- Run reports

This appendix provides an overview of the Multiple Currencies feature in QuickBooks. If you do business with customers or vendors in other countries, this feature allows you to create transactions in their currency and track the exchange rate, so you always know what the transactions mean to you in US Dollars.

Setting Up and Configuring Multiple Currencies

Before you can begin creating transactions in different currencies, you have some configuration and setup tasks to attend to.

It's important to know that unlike most of the configuration preferences available in QuickBooks, once you enable multiple currencies, you can't disable it. If you're already using QuickBooks (either because you updated your company files from a previous version or because you began creating transactions before deciding to use multiple currencies), be sure to back up your company file before enabling this feature.

Creating a Special Backup

When you create your backup before turning on multiple currencies, don't use your normal backup routine. Instead, name the backup file differently so you can identify it easily and avoid having the backup file overwritten with "regular" backups. For example, when you save your backup file, change the name of the file from the usual *<CompanyFileName>*.QBB to *<CompanyFileName>*-BeforeMulticurrency.QBB. It's also a good idea to copy the backup file to a CD.

If you change your mind later and decide not to use multiple currencies and you don't want to restore the backup (because you'd have to re-enter all the transactions you'd created while multiple currencies was enabled), it's okay to keep using the company file with multiple currencies enabled as long as you use customers, vendors, and accounts that are not linked to another currency. Some windows and dialogs will continue to have an extra field for currency, but no financial information will be compromised.

Enabling Multiple Currencies

To enable the Multiple Currencies feature, choose Edit | Preferences and click the Multiple Currencies category icon in the left pane. In the Company Preferences tab (see Figure B-1), select Yes, I Use More Than One Currency.

FIGURE B-1   Enable multiple currencies and select your home currency.

When you select Yes, QuickBooks displays a warning message.

If you've already made a backup, as discussed in the previous section, you can continue. If not, stop the process and create your backup. Then enable multiple currencies.

The dialog offers the opportunity to change your home currency from US Dollars to another currency. Changing your home currency is not a good idea, because QuickBooks tracks payroll, sales tax, online banking, and other basic data in US Dollars only.

Selecting Currencies

QuickBooks provides a long list of currencies you can use, but by default only the commonly used currencies are active. You can change the list of active currencies to suit your own needs. Remember, only active currencies appear in the drop-down list when you're assigning a currency to a customer or vendor.

Choose Company | Manage Currency | Currency List to open the Currency List window seen in Figure B-2. (If the list includes only active currencies, select the check box labeled Include Inactive to see the entire list.)

Currency (1 unit)	Code	Exchange Rate	As of Date
Afghanistan Afghani	AFN		
Albanian Lek	ALL		
Algerian Dinar	DZD		
Angolan Kwanza	AOA		
Argentine Peso	ARS		
Armenian Dram	AMD		
Aruban Florin	AWG		
Australian Dollar	AUD		
Azerbaijani Manat	AZN		
Bahamian Dollar	BSD		
Bahraini Dinar	BHD		
Bangladesh Taka	BDT		
Barbados Dollar	BBD		
Belarussian Ruble	BYR		
Belize Dollar	BZD		
Bermudian Dollar	BMD		
Bhutan Ngultrum	BTN		
Bolivian Bolivianos	BOB		
Bosnia & Herz K. Marka	BAM		
Botswana Pula	BWP		
Brazilian Real	BRL		
British Pound Sterling	GBP	1.95215	08/24/...
Brunei Dollar	BND		
Bulgarian Lev	BGN		
Burundi Franc	BIF		
Cambodian Riel	KHR		
Canadian Dollar	CAD	.954335	08/24/...
Cape Verdean Escudo	CVE		
Cayman Islands Dollar	KYD		
Central African CFA Franc	XAF		
CFP Franc	XPF		
Chilean Peso	CLP		
Chinese Yuan Renminbi	CNY	.14562	08/24/...
Columbian Peso	COP		
Comorian Franc	KMF		
Congolese Franc	CDF		
Costa Rican Colon	CRC		
Croatian Kuna	HRK		
Cuban Peso	CUP		

Exchange rate: 1 unit foreign currency = x units home currency
Example: 1 AFN (foreign) = x units USD (home)

Currency ▾   Activities ▾   Reports ▾   ☑ Include inactive

FIGURE B-2   Activate the currencies you need.

To activate an inactive currency, click the X in the leftmost column to remove the X; to make an active currency inactive, click the leftmost column to place an X in the column.

Notice that each currency has a three-letter abbreviation; for example, US Dollar is USD.

You can, if necessary, create a currency if the one you need doesn't appear on the list. With the Currency List window open, press CTRL-N to open the New Currency dialog and configure the currency.

Tracking Exchange Rates

Because QuickBooks tracks both the customer/vendor currency and its worth in your home currency, you need to make sure the exchange rate is accurate. If the exchange rate isn't accurate, your financial reports, which use US Dollars, won't be accurate.

To update the exchange rate for all your active currencies, choose Company | Manage Currency | Download Latest Exchange Rates. QuickBooks travels to the Internet to get the current rates (you don't see an Internet page; all of this is done in the background). When your active currencies have been updated, QuickBooks displays a success message. You can see the updated exchange rates in the Currency List.

Managing Customers and Vendors with Foreign Currencies

You need to identify the currency of every customer and vendor in your company file. QuickBooks automatically assigns your home currency (USD) to all customers and vendors, so you only need to change those that do business in a different currency.

Creating Customers and Vendors with Currency Assignments

When you create customers and vendors who do business in another currency, the basic steps are the same as creating any new customer or vendor in QuickBooks. The only difference is the existence of a Currency Field in the New Customer or New Vendor dialog.

As you can see in Figure B-3, QuickBooks inserts US Dollar in the Currency field, but you can choose another currency from the drop-down list (which displays only those currencies you've marked Active).

FIGURE B-3   If the new customer or vendor you're creating uses a foreign currency, change the default data by selecting a currency from the drop-down list.

> **Caution** If you select a currency other than USD, the Opening Balance field is inaccessible, which is a good thing since you should never use that field when setting up a new customer or vendor. See Chapter 3 for information about creating customers and Chapter 4 for information about creating vendors.

Changing Currency for Existing Customers and Vendors

You can change the currency specification only for existing customers and vendors that have no transactions. It doesn't matter whether the current open balance is 0.00; the existence of any transaction prevents you from changing the currency. For those customers and vendors, you must create a new entity with the new currency. In addition, you cannot merge customers or vendors that have different currencies.

Editing Existing Customers and Vendors

To edit the currency of an existing customer or vendor that has no existing transactions, open the appropriate center, select the customer/vendor, and click the Edit Customer button in the right pane. Select the currency from the drop-down list in the Currency field, and click OK.

Creating New Customers and Vendors for Multiple Currencies

To create a new customer or vendor for existing accounts with a foreign currency specification, create the new entity using the following guidelines.

In the Name field, use the same name as the existing entity, but add text to make the name unique (QuickBooks does not allow duplicates in the Name field).

It's best to add text after the name, so the customer/vendor appears in the right place in drop-down fields in transaction windows. For example, in Figure B-4, a new customer is created in order to assign a new currency to an existing customer by adding a three-digit abbreviation for the customer's currency to create a unique name (you'll still see the existing customer name in the Customer & Jobs list).

Remember, the data in the Name field doesn't appear on transaction documents; instead, QuickBooks uses the data in the Company Name and Address fields (and, for Vendors, there's even a field labeled Print On Check As).

Managing Existing Open Transactions

When you create new customers and vendors, you have to manage existing open transactions using the original customer or vendor since you cannot accept or make a payment linked to the original entity using the new entity. When the open

FIGURE B-4   The new customer has the currency added to their name; everything else is the same as the existing customer.

balance for the original entity becomes zero, you can make the original customer or vendor inactive so the listing doesn't appear in drop-down lists in transaction windows. Be sure to use the new entity you created for all new transactions.

Currency Data in Customer and Vendor Centers

After you've enabled multiple currencies, the Customer Center and Vendor Center display currency information in both panes.

In addition, QuickBooks makes the following changes automatically:

- In the List pane, the currency is noted for each customer/vendor and the current balance total displays using the customer/vendor currency.
- In the Details pane, the Amount and Open Balance columns display amounts in the currency of the customer or vendor.

You can change these default settings to make it easier to understand the data you see in the centers.

Configuring the List Pane

In the List pane you can add the current balance total in USD to save yourself the need to calculate the "real money."

You can either remove the Balance Total column for the foreign currency or display both Balance Total columns. If you frequently talk to vendors or customers about current balances, it's handy to have the foreign currency balance in front of you, so having both amounts display makes sense. However, to save room in the List pane, remove the Currency column.

Chart of Accounts for Multicurrency Transactions

As you create transactions in other currencies QuickBooks adds accounts to your chart of accounts:

- An Accounts Receivable account for each currency
- An Accounts Payable account for each currency

Creating Transactions in Other Currencies

When you open a sales or payment transaction window, QuickBooks automatically takes care of the currency issues by adding fields to the transaction window.

If the customer or vendor currency is USD, you won't see much difference between the transaction window for multiple currencies and the same transaction window before you enabled multiple currencies. The only real difference is that the text "USD" appears for "Total" amounts.

If the customer or vendor is configured for another currency, the transaction window changes to provide the information you need. For example, Figure B-5 shows an invoice for a customer in Europe, and Figure B-6 shows a vendor bill for a vendor in the UK who does business in Euros.

FIGURE B-5 This invoice displays all the data needed to see the sales total for this invoice in both US Dollars and Euros.

FIGURE B-6 When the amount of the bill is entered in Euros (which is what the bill that arrived showed), QuickBooks also displays the amount in USD.

Notice the following about these transaction windows:

- The A/R or A/P account is specific to the currency.
- The amounts in the line items are displayed in the customer/vendor currency.
- There are two totals: one for the transaction currency and one for USD.
- The Exchange Rate field displays the exchange rate used when this transaction was created.

The printed versions of transactions that are sent to customers (invoices, credits, and so on) and vendors (checks) do not display any fields or data related to USD; those fields only appear on the screen for your convenience.

Decide on an exchange rate update schedule that makes sense to you. Keep in mind that if the exchange rate changes between the day you enter an invoice or bill and the day you receive a payment or make a payment, QuickBooks automatically adds an Other Expense account named Exchange Gain or Loss to track the net amounts that accrue from adjustments in exchange rates for current open balances.

Creating Reports on Multiple Currency Transactions

By default, all reports on customer and vendor transactions (such as Aging, Sales, Purchases, and so on) are displayed in your home currency (USD). You can modify the reports so they display the appropriate currencies.

- For Summary reports, click Customize Report, and in the section labeled Display Amounts In, select The Transaction Currency.
- For Detail reports, click Customize Report and select Foreign Amount in the Columns list. You may also want to add the Currency column.

Memorize these reports, using a name that reflects the contents (such as Transaction Currency), so you don't have to customize them each time you create them.

Index

• Numbers

940 forms
    preparing annual FUTA, 376–377
    saving and reopening, 374–375
940 tax payments, 369
941/943 forms
    archiving, 375
    checking for errors, 374
    creating, 372–374
    editing data on, 373–374
    filing quarterly, 367
    preparing, 371, 376
    printing, 375
    saving and reopening, 374–375
    Schedule B of, 372, 373
    uneditable information on, 374
941/943 tax payments, 367, 368
944 forms
    filing annually, 367
    preparing, 377
    when to use, 371, 377
1096 transmittal forms, 470
1099-MISC forms, 463–470
    about, 463
    configuring options for, 85, 463–465
    methods for filing, 469–470
    printing, 469–470
    reviewing, 468
    setting preferences for, 549
    tracking vendors requiring, 72, 73
    using QuickBooks 1099 Wizard, 465–468
1120/1120S forms, 471
8109 forms, 371

• A

access. *See* permissions
Account Prefill tab (New Vendor window), 73–74
accountants. *See also* accountant's copy
    checking 1099 reporting with, 86
    considering manual payroll option with, 333
    correcting customer's opening balance, 44
    creating accurate opening trial balance, 137–143
e-mail notification about accountant's copy for, 401, 402, 403
External Accountant user for, 421–422
    including vehicle mileage on tax return, 326, 327
    providing accountant's copy for, 398–406
    reports used by, 418
    tracking assets for, 123
    using Cash Flow Projector, 455–458
    using Client Data Review, 420–421

accountant's copy, 398–406
    about, 398
    canceling, 405–406
    created by Admin user, 399
    e-mail notifications about, 401, 402, 403
    merging changes from, 404–405
    methods for creating, 398–399
    saving on removable media, 399
    uploading to secure server, 399, 400–404
accounting
    accrual, 222, 426, 544
    cash, 222, 544
    changing accounts with journal entries, 386–387
    closing in QuickBooks, 472–473
    double-entry bookkeeping, 116
    formula for Balance Sheet, 411
    limitations while accountant's copy outstanding, 402
    restricting sensitive activities in, 501–502
    standard financial reports for, 410–415
Accounting Preferences dialog, 26–27, 528–529
accounts. *See also* chart of accounts;
    subaccounts; *and specific accounts*
    adding for payroll processing, 334–335
    assigning account numbers to customer, 48
    autofilling payee account number in check memo, 532
    creating and editing company, 12–13
    credit card, 271–272
    default bank, 532
    deleting, 38
    depreciation, 387–389
    designating for noncustomer deposits, 263
    entering opening balances in, 34
    hiding, 38–39
    Inventory Adjustment, 116–117
    making journal entries when changing, 386–387

    merging, 39
    naming, 30
    needed for payroll processing, 334
    numbering chart of, 26–29
    Opening Balance Equity, 143
    over and short, 195
    petty cash, 269
    posting reimbursable expenses to income, 239–241
    printing names on vouchers, 530
    Reimbursed Expenses, 240–241
    required inventory, 106
    selecting payment, 248
    showing only lowest subaccount, 28, 37, 529
    specifying display format on reports, 545
    tracking discounts in specific, 189
        year-end reconciliation of bank, cash, and credit card, 460
accounts payable. *See* A/P
accounts receivable. *See* A/R
accrual accounting
    about, 222
    selecting for reports, 426
    specifying for summary reports, 544
ACH (Automated Clearing House), 368
active profile, 488
Add/Edit Multiple List Entries window, 50–52, 75, 102
Add New Account dialog, 31–32
Add New Payroll Item (Payroll Setup Wizard), 337–338
Add Shipping Address Information window, 45
Add To Do window, 56, 81
Add Transactions To QuickBooks window, 302–303, 305
Additional Customization window, 228, 554
Additional Info tab
    New Customer window, 45–47
    New Vendor window, 72–73

Address Info tab
  New Customer window, 42–45
  New Vendor window, 70–71
addresses
  adding customer, 44
  entering vendor, 70–71
  multiple customer shipping, 44–45
  origin of invoice, 148
  selecting to use with QuickBooks Billing
    Solutions, 491
  updating customer name changes on
    shipping, 55
Adjust Quantity/Value on Hand window, 114,
  115, 142
Adjust Row Amounts dialog, 447
Admin user
  about, 495–496
  adding or changing password for, 11,
    496–497
  Challenge Question for, 65, 496–497
  configuring credit card protection, 65
  creating accountant's copy, 399
  creating user accounts, 498–499
  privileges in QuickBooks vs. Windows, 495
  resetting password, 497–498
Advanced Options dialog, 426
Advanced Setup, 9–13
  administrator account password
    setup in, 496
  choosing company's legal entity, 11
  designating administrator password, 11
  entering company information, 9–10
  fiscal year setup in, 11
  launching Easy Step Interview, 9
  saving and naming company file, 11
  selecting business type in, 10
aging reports. See A/R aging reports
aligning
  checks, 481
  forms, 478

alphabetical account order, 27
A/P (accounts payable)
  defined, 24
  entering unpaid, 139–140
  new accounts for multicurrency
    transactions in, 579
A/P accounts
  posting inventory receipts and bills to, 231
  reviewing balance of, 204
  selecting from multiple, 223, 247
App Center, 17
applications. See also Excel
  sharing QuickBooks data with other,
    37, 539
  using QuickBooks with your e-mail,
    488–489
Apply Credit To Invoices window, 163–164
A/R (accounts receivable). See also A/R aging
  reports; collections
  about, 24
  entering unpaid, 139–140
  making journal entries to A/R account, 204
  new accounts for multicurrency
    transactions in, 579
  running A/R aging reports, 203–209
  tracking, 201–203
A/R Aging Detail window, 206
A/R aging reports, 203–209
  A/R Aging Summary report, 204, 205
  configuring header/footer data, 208
  customizing columns, 205–206, 207
  defined, 203
  filtering information in, 206–208
  generating by due or transaction dates, 544
  including open balance in, 427
  memorizing, 209
  modifying appearance of, 209
  printing, 209
assemblies
  Pending Builds report for, 119
  using services in, 91

Assess Finance Charges window, 212
assets. *See also* fixed assets
    finding out value of A/R, 204
    gathering balance for, 4
    tracking with Fixed Asset Item list, 123
    types of, 24
asterisk (*), 213
ATM withdrawals, 270
Attach Documents feature, 491–492
auditing
    customer credit card access, 68
    using Audit Trail report, 494
Automated Clearing House (ACH), 368
automatic backups, 513–514
automatic markups, 238, 550
automatic payment calculation, 542
automatically applying and calculating
  payments, 180, 182, 541
automatically refreshing reports, 544
Available Estimates window, 167

• B

Backup Options dialog, 510
backups
creating before turning on Multicurrency
  feature, 125, 572
making company file, 507–515
managing or overwriting, 515
    portable company file vs., 517
    remote, 508–509
    restoring, 516–517
    scheduling, 512–515
    selecting location for, 509–510
    setting reminders for, 511
    time stamping filenames of, 511
    verifying data for, 511

    when to save, 511–512
    year-end, 473
balance forward invoice system, 180
Balance Sheet budgets, 442, 451
Balance Sheet reports, 411–413
    about, 411
    Balance Sheet Detail report, 412
    Balance Sheet Prev Year Comparison
      report, 413
    Balance Sheet Standard report, 412
    Balance Sheet Summary report, 412
    year-end, 462–463
bank accounts. *See also* bank register; online
  banking; reconciling bank accounts
    adjusting entries for, 285
    ATM and debit card withdrawals, 270
    changing during check printing, 484
    clearing reconciled transactions, 279
    depositing cash receipts into, 190
    enabling for online banking, 293
    entering balances for, 139, 140
    gathering reconciled balance for, 3–4
    getting cash back from deposits, 201
    giving up reconciliation search, 290
    handling bounced checks, 265–267
    making deposits to separate, 198
    preventing check posting to wrong, 270
    recording NSF charges, 267
    selecting for payroll liabilities, 365
    setting default, 532
    tracking all activity in, 260
    tracking cash disbursements, 268–271
    transferring funds between, 263–265,
      309–310
    undoing last reconciliation, 289
    voiding disbursements, 267–268
    year-end reconciliation of, 460

bank register
    adding downloaded transactions to, 304–305
    entering downloaded deposit to, 307
    entering noncustomer deposits in, 260–261
    matching downloaded transactions in, 302–308
    not used for sales tax payments, 257
    noting electronic payments in, 368
  recording downloaded payment in, 305–307
  transferring funds in, 310
  writing manual checks in, 252–253
bank statements
    data used for reconciling account, 276–277
    downloading, 293, 300–301, 302
banking reports, 417
banks. *See* financial institutions; bank accounts
Basic Customization window, 551
Basic Payroll service, 332
batching
    cash sales, 191, 193–194
    check printing, 254, 484–485
    form printing, 486–487
    invoices, 156–157
    payroll history entry, 348–349
beeping during transactions, 535–536
Begin Reconciliation window
    configuring, 277–278
    entering starting balance in, 276–277
beginning balances. *See also* opening trial balances
    gathering information on, 2, 3–5, 137
    making in General Journal entries, 137–138
    troubleshooting differences in, 286
benefit plan payments, 390–391
bill payments. *See* online payments; payments
billable time. *See also* reimbursable expenses
    including on customer invoices, 324–325
    invoicing options for, 546–547
    prompting for, 171

Billable Time/Costs dialog, 172, 325
bills. *See* invoices; statements; vendor bills
Bills Preferences dialog, 530
bounced checks
    creating NSF check and charge items, 265
    recording charges for, 267
    recovering fees for, 266
budget reports, 451–454
    Balance Sheet Budget Overview, 451
    Budget vs. Actual graph, 454
    Budget vs. Actual report, 453
    Class Budget Overview, 452
    Customer:Job Budget Overview, 452
    Profit & Loss Budget Overview, 451
    Profit & Loss Budget Performances, 453
    selecting, 451
budgets, 440–455. *See also* budget reports; P&L budgets
    Balance Sheet, 442
    before starting, 442
    class-based, 450
    compounding changes in, 447–448
    copying numbers across months, 445–446
    creating multiple, 441
    Customer:Job, 448–450
    deleting, 441
    entering amounts for P&L, 443
    exporting, 454–455
    importing back into QuickBooks, 455
    increasing or decreasing figures automatically, 446–447
    options in Create New Budget Wizard, 441–442
    P&L, 443–450
    setting up and saving, 440–441
    taking from last year's data, 448
    types of QuickBooks, 440

• C

C-Corporation businesses, 471
calculating
 compensation for corporate officers, 471
 gross pay from net, 359
 merchant fees for credit cards, 200
 payments automatically, 180, 182, 542
Calendar, 17
Calendar Preferences dialog, 530
calendar year
 fiscal vs., 460
 running reports for, 428
canceling accountant's copy, 405–406
capital, 24
Carousel View, 408, 409
cash. See also cash sales
 about, 268
 ATM and debit card withdrawals, 270
 depositing into Undeposited Funds or bank account, 190
 gathering balances for, 3–4
 handling sales in, 191–194
 reconciling cash accounts, 460
 recording payments with petty, 269–270
 replacing spent petty, 270
 tracking money put in petty, 269
cash accounting
 about, 222
 selecting for reports, 426
 specifying for summary reports, 544
cash back from deposits, 201
cash drawer
 over and short problems, 195–196
 ways to track receipts, 194–195
Cash Flow Projector, 455–458
Cash Flow reports, 413–415
 about, 413
 Cash Flow Forecast, 415

 configuring, 545–546
 Statement of Cash Flows report, 413–414
Cash On Hand account, 24
cash sales
 batching, 191, 193–194
 customizing template for receipts, 193
 defined, 191
 entering data for, 192
 methods for handling, 191–192
 printing receipts for, 193
 tracking cash drawer, 194–196
CDs
 creating portable company file on, 517–519
 making backup onto, 508, 512
 selecting as backup location, 509–510
Challenge Question, 65, 496–497
Change Item Prices window, 96–97
Change QuickBooks Password dialog, 503
chart of accounts, 24–39. See also subaccounts; and specific accounts
 accounts added for multicurrency transactions, 579
 adding fields in, 33–34
 adding payroll accounts, 334–335
 alphabetical sorting of, 27
 checking tax line assignments for, 471
 creating and editing, 12–13
 creating petty cash account, 269
 defined, 24
 deleting accounts in, 38
 depreciation tracking in, 387–389
 discount tracking in, 189
 editing, 37
 entering opening balances in, 34
 hiding accounts, 38–39
 illustrated, 36
 merging accounts, 39
 multiple subaccounts for, 36–37

numbering accounts in, 26–29

re-sorting, 29

selecting new accounts for, 31–33

setting up, 30–34

showing only lowest subaccount, 28, 37, 529

types of accounts in, 24–26

check printing

batching, 484–485

setting up QuickBooks and printer for, 479–482

as you create check, 483–484

Checking Account window, 139, 140

Checking Preferences dialog, 530–532

checks. *See also* bank register; running payroll

adding outstanding, 139, 140

aligning before printing, 481

assigning numbers to, 252, 484, 485

autofilling account number in memo, 532

batch printing of, 254

bounced, 265–267

changing date when printed, 531

changing paycheck data, 356

creating before running payroll, 355–356

duplicate numbers for, 531

effect of changing timesheet data on, 323

forcing cursor to Payee field for, 531

handling partial check pages, 480–481

logos and signatures on, 480

manual, 252–254

numbering, 252, 483, 484

paying payroll liabilities with, 365–367

preferences for, 530–532

preventing posting to wrong bank account, 270

printing, 479–481, 482–485

purchasing QuickBooks, 479

re-configuring employee for time data on, 320

reprinting, 485

resolving missing, 281–282

reviewing payroll, 357–358

style of, 480

termination, 355

transferring funds between accounts, 263–265, 309–310

unscheduled printing of payroll, 354–355

using Write Checks window, 253–254

voiding, 267–268

writing for people on Other Names list, 127, 128

writing without entering bill, 252

Choose Bank Account dialog, 365

Choose Billable Time And Costs dialog, 172, 173, 326

Class list, 126

classes

about, 126

class-based budgets, 450, 452

creating, 126–127

individual class reports, 417

reports for all, 428

tracking, 319

using subclasses, 127

Classify Cash dialog, 414

clearing

downloaded transactions, 304

rows in copied budget, 446

transactions during reconciliation, 279

client computer QuickBooks installations, 565–567

Client Data Review, 420–421

client-server networks, 568–569

closing the books, 472–473

collections

Collection Center reports, 203

sending customer statements, 215–220

tracking accounts receivable, 201–203

using A/R aging reports for, 203–205

Collections Center, 201–203
color
    desktop color scheme, 534
    template, 552
Column Labels dialog, 432
columns
    adding to journal entry window, 386
    customizing cash sales receipts, 193
    customizing report, 426, 427
    designing aging report, 205–206, 207
    modifying template, 555–556
company file. *See also* accountant's copy;
  Advanced Setup
    accountant copy of, 398
    Advanced Setup steps for, 9–13
    backing up, 125, 507–515
    CD backup of, 512
    configuring preferences for, 528
    creating, 6, 7–14
    creating new files from portable file, 519
    customizing, 12
    deleting, 506–507
    designing with Express Start, 8
    making folder for, 507
    merging accountant's changes with,
      404–405
    modifying company info on templates, 553
    opening last loaded, 506
    opening or restoring existing, 6
    password-protecting, 494
    portable, 517–519
    printer hardware settings for multiple, 482
    rebuilding, 519–520
    remote backups of, 508–509
    removing old files from list of, 507
    replacing with portable file, 519
    restoring, 6, 507, 516–517

    saving and naming, 11
    setting permissions for data, 12
    sharing with third-party applications,
      37, 539
    Single-User mode for, 399
    task reminders for, 542–543
    using multiple, 7
    verifying, 519
    working with sample, 7
Company Information dialog, 471
Company Preferences tab (Preferences dialog)
  about, 529
    customizing project tracking terms, 59
    General preferences on, 538–539
Company Setup section (QuickBooks Payroll
  Setup Wizard), 351
Company Snapshot window, 419–420
compensation. *See also* payroll
    configuring payroll, 351
    setting up payroll taxes for, 352
    sick and vacations pay, 344
complex passwords, 65, 66, 401, 495
computers. *See also* Windows operating system
    designating file host, 565, 567
    installing QuickBooks on client,
      565–567
Condense Data Wizard, 521–523
condensing data, 520–524
  about, 520
  effect of, 520–521
  running Condense Data Wizard, 521–523
Confirmation And Next Steps dialog, 358
corporate officers
    calculating compensation for, 471
    designating as officer employees, 346
Cost of Goods Sold (COGS) account, 25,
  106, 249

counting inventory, 110–117
    adjusting quantities and values, 117
    effects of adjustments, 116
    making count adjustments, 113–115
    making inventory adjustments, 112–116
    planning physical count, 112
    printing Physical Inventory Worksheet, 110–111
    types of inventory adjustments, 117
    valuation adjustments, 115–116
Create Backup window, 509, 513
Create Estimates window, 165
Create Invoices window, 146, 580
Create Item Receipts window, 230
Create New Budget Wizard, 441–444
Create Progress Invoices Based on Estimate window, 167
Create Purchase Order, 227
Create Statements window, 217
credit card accounts, 271–272, 460
credit cards
    calculating merchant fees for, 200
    creating account for, 271–272
    depositing payments by, 198
    entering customer's number, 49
    managing, 271
    online services for, 293
    permissions to view data on, 67–68, 501
    protection features for, 65, 66
    security log of access to, 68
    security standards for, 64
    treating as bill, 273
credit limits
    assigning customer, 48
    blank vs. zero in field, 48
credit memos. *See also* credits
    applying, 162–164
    creating against invoice, 160–161

    e-mailing, 488
    issuing customer refunds, 162–163
    without previous invoice, 161
credits
    applying, 185–187, 250
    enabling, 248
    equal to or less than invoice amount, 186
    larger than invoice amount, 186–187
    recording vendor, 233–234
    specifying different job for, 187
    using, 150
currency. *See also* multicurrency option
    changing in open transactions, 577–578
    decimal point placement in, 536
    editing customer and vendor, 577
    enabling use of multiple, 125, 540, 572–574
    exchange rates for, 575
    reports in different, 582
    selecting multiple, 574–575
    setting customer's, 43
    transactions using non-USD, 579–582
    vendor settings for, 70
Currency list, 125, 574–575
current liabilities, 24
current window icon, 20
Customer:Job budgets, 448–450
    accuracy of, 449
    additional, 450
    creating, 449
    Customer:Job Budget Overview report, 452
Customer & Vendor Profile Lists, 128–133
    about, 128
    Customer Message list, 131
    Customer Type list, 129
    Job Type list, 130
    Memorized Transaction list, 133

Customer & Vendor Profile Lists (*cont.*)
    Payment Method list, 131–132
    Sales Rep list, 129
    Ship Via list, 132
    Terms list, 130–131
    Vehicle list, 132–133
    Vendor Type, 129
Customer Center
    about, 52–53
    adding customer To Do notes, 55–56
    Collections Center in, 201–203
    customizing Customers & Jobs list, 53–54
    defined, 15
    displaying currency data in, 578–579
    editing customer records, 55–56
    filtering data in Customer Information pane of, 54
    location of, 201
    opening, 42
    using, 202–203
Customer Credit Card Audit Trail, 68
Customer Credit Card Protection Setup window, 65, 68
Customer Information pane (Customer Center), 54
Customer Message list, 131
customer payment options toolbar, 546
Customer Snapshot report, 203
Customer Type list, 46, 129
customers, 42–68. *See also* Customer:Job budgets; Customer Center; invoices; jobs
    about jobs and, 42
    adding finance charges to invoices, 213
    adding multiple records, 50–52
    address for, 44
    applying credits to invoices, 185–187
    applying special pricing for, 123–124
    assessing finance charges to, 210–214
    assigning account numbers to, 48

assigning sales tax codes to, 101–102
billing for reimbursable expenses, 170–177
cautions for Opening Balance field, 44
changing currency in open transactions, 577–578
collecting sales tax from, 47
credit card information for, 49
credit limits for, 48
custom fields for, 47
customizing list of, 53–54
deleting, 60–62
discounting untimely payments for, 189
editing records during invoicing, 149
editing records of, 55–56
entering name of, 42–43, 55
finding data on, 52–53
gathering balance for, 4
giving credit larger than invoice, 186–187
hiding inactive, 60–62
importing lists of, 13–14
including custom name field for, 62–64
incurring reimbursable expenses for, 237
invoicing for employee time, 324–325
issuing refunds to, 162–163
linking price levels to, 124
making payments online, 542
merging, 62
multiple shipping addresses for, 44–45
opening balance for, 44
payment terms for, 46
preferred payment method for, 49
preventing sales to, 48
price levels for, 47
printing payment receipts for, 190
receiving online payments from, 310
recording payments from, 181–182
remitting sales tax from, 254
reports for jobs and, 210
retaining credits for, 162

reviewing finance charge history for, 213–214

sales representatives for, 46–47

selecting currency for, 43

selecting to receive statements, 218

send methods for invoices, statements, and estimates, 47

setting default shipping method for, 546

splitting reimbursable expenses among, 241–242

supplying estimates to, 164–166

taking timely payment discounts, 187–189

To Do notes for, 55–56

tracking jobs for, 56–60

types of, 46

underpayments by, 184–185

using credit for different job, 187

using multicurrency option for, 576–577

Customers & Jobs tab (Customer Center), 52, 53

Customize Columns window

adjusting displayed customer data in, 54

customizing vendor columns displayed, 77–78

filtering vendor information displayed, 78–79

modifying Employee Center columns, 362

using, 51

Customize Icon Bar Dialog, 20

customized reports, 432–436

preparing header and footer before memorizing, 432

sharing, 436

using memorized, 433

customizing. *See also* customized reports; Preferences dialog

cash sales template, 193

company file, 12

customer price levels, 47

Customers & Jobs list, 53–54

Excel tax form worksheets, 381–382

Favorites menu, 21

Icon Bar, 18–20

name field for customers, vendors, and employees, 62–64

New Jobs window, 58

QuickBooks by industry, 10

reports, 424, 432–436

statements, 220

templates, 550–558

using Preferences dialog options, 528

Vendor Center, 77–79

• D

data

about summary transactions, 520–521

accuracy of Customer:Job budgets, 449

adding to custom vendor fields, 83, 84

checking payroll, 352, 353

condensing, 520–524

copying budget, 445–446

displayed in Company Snapshot, 419–420

editing 941/943 form, 373–374

entering cash sales, 192

entering company, 9–10

entering payroll compensation, 351

exporting to Excel, 437

filling for custom name fields, 63–64

filtering report, 428–430

found in memorized reports, 209

gathering accounting, 2, 3–5

hiding on Excel tax form worksheets, 381–382

overwriting with restored backup or portable file, 518

setting permissions for company, 12

sharing with other applications, 37, 539

taking budget from last year's, 448

verifying backup, 511

Database Server Manager
    configuring client-server networks with, 569
    installing on same server with QuickBooks, 569
    opening and running, 565, 566
Date Stamp button (Notepad window), 80
dates. *See also* start date
    changing check date when printed, 531
    choosing finance charge assessment, 213
    closing, 473
    dividing, 399, 401–403
    formatting display of, 538
    generating aging reports by due or transaction, 544
    go live, 347
    paycheck vs. payroll preparation, 353
    picking for data removal, 520
    scheduling backup, 512–515
    selecting date range for statements, 217
debit card withdrawals, 270
decimal point placement, 536
default bank accounts, 532
deleting
    accountant's copy, 405
    accounts, 38
    budgets, 441
    company file, 506–507
    customers and jobs, 60–62
    invoices, 159–160
    transactions, 536
    transactions during account reconciliation, 280
    transactions with reimbursable expenses, 177
    unmatched downloaded transactions, 307–308
    users, 499
    vendors, 81–82

delimited text file budgets, 454
deposit slips, 201
deposits. *See also* Make Deposits window
    adding items to, 199–200
    adding outstanding, 139, 140
    cash back from, 201
    choosing payments for, 196–198
    credit card payment, 198
    designating default account for, 542
    Direct Deposit service, 332, 344
    during account reconciliation, 280
    electronic payroll tax, 335
    entering downloaded, 307
    handling petty cash, 269
    making from Receive Payments window, 189–190
    making to separate bank accounts, 198
    noncustomer, 260–263
    options for cash receipts, 190
    selecting items for, 198
    separating items by payment method, 198
depreciation journal entries, 387–389
Description field, 33
Desktop View Preferences dialog, 532–534
detail reports. *See also* reports
    about, 425
    drilling down in, 410
    effect of data removal on, 521
Direct Connect
    defined, 292
    enabling access for, 296–298
    illustrated, 295
    services available with, 301
Direct Deposit service, 332, 344
disabling. *See* enabling/disabling
disbursements. *See* payments; checks; cash
discount date, 247, 250

discounts
  adding to invoices, 151
  applying vendor, 249–250
  early payment, 131
  enabling, 248
  posting, 189
  sorting bills by discount date, 247
  taking after discount date, 250
  taking for timely payment, 249
  timely payment, 187–189
  untimely payment, 189
  using discount items, 89–90, 96
Discounts account, 189
Discounts And Credits dialog, 186, 188
Discounts Taken account, 249
Discrepancy reports, 287
Display tab (Modify Report window), 207, 425
displaying icons without title, 19
dividing date, 399, 401–403
Doc Center, 16–17
double-entry bookkeeping, 116
downloading
  bank transactions, 293, 300–301, 302
  duplicate transactions, 302
  Intuit updates in background, 548
  latest exchange rates, 575
  W-4 forms, 345
drilling down report details, 410
.DSN file, 506
due date, sorting vendor bills by due date, 246–247
duplicate check numbers, 531
duplicate invoices, 547
duplicate names unallowed, 127
duplicate purchase order numbers, 539
duplicate purchase order warnings, 105
duplicate transaction downloading, 302
duplicating estimates, 166

• E

e-mail, 488–491
  attaching files to, 491–492
  notifications about accountant's copy, 401, 402, 403
  QuickBooks solutions for, 491
  selecting as send method, 47
  sending forms and reports by, 488, 489–490
  setting as preferred method, 547–548
  setting up, 488–489
  statements sent by, 218
  using your software for, 490–491
e-payments. *See* online payments
earned discounts, 249–250
EasySaver service, 539
EasyStep Interview
  creating Chart of Accounts in, 12–13
  launching, 9
  selecting industry in, 10
Edit Account window, 239
Edit Customer window, 67
Edit Employee window, 314
Edit Vendor dialog
  editing and updating data in, 79–81
  entering custom fields and data with, 83–84
  marking 1099 recipients in, 86
editing
  941/943 form data, 373–374
  amount of reimbursable expenses, 175
  chart of accounts, 37
  currency for customers and vendors, 577
  customer records, 55–56
  employee W-2 forms, 378
  finance charge amount, 213
  icon's appearance, 19
  information about vendors, 79–81
  invoices, 159
  jobs, 60

editing (cont.)
    multiple vendor records, 74–76
    original timesheets, 323
    paycheck data, 356
    timesheet entries on reports, 322
    transactions, 280, 536
    user information, 499
EFTPS (Employer Federal Tax Payment
    System), 335, 368
Employee Center
    about, 359–360
    customizing, 360, 362
    defined, 15
    Employees tab, 360
    illustrated, 359
    Payroll tab, 360, 361
    tabs of, 360
    Transactions tab, 360, 361
Employee Defaults window, 340
employees
    adding historical data for, 346–347
    configuring with QuickBooks Payroll
        Setup Wizard, 351–352
    creating template for, 339–341
    direct deposit services for, 332
    entering data for, 314–315
    including custom name field for, 62–64
    invoicing customers for time spent,
        324–325
    linking to time tracking, 314–315, 319
    making changes on W-2 forms, 378
    online W-2 forms for, 380
    payroll data for, 341–345
    preparing W-2 forms for, 377–380
    re-configuring to track time data for, 320
    reports about, 417
    scheduling pay checks for, 353–355
    tracking time spend for vendor, 315
    types of, 345–346

Employees & Payroll submenu, 417
Employees tab (Employee Center), 360
Employer Federal Tax Payment System
    (EFTPS), 335, 368
Employment Info tab set (New Employee
    window), 345
enabling/disabling
    account numbering, 26–27
    class tracking, 319
    compounding in P&L budgets, 447–448
    credit card protection feature, 65, 66
    direct deposits, 344
    discounts and credits, 248
    estimates, 164
    Excel macros, 381
    inventory and purchase orders, 539
    inventory tracking, 104–105
    Multicurrency feature, 125, 572–574
    multiple currency, 125, 540, 572–574
    online banking, 293
    price levels, 123, 547
    progress billing invoices, 167
    reimbursable expenses, 238
Enhanced Payroll, 359, 375
Enter Bills window
    about, 222–223
    adjusting Amount Due field, 226
    default due date in, 224
    entering data in, 224
    illustrated, 94, 223
    recording reimbursable expenses, 241–242
    recording vendor credits, 233–234
    splitting expenses among accounts, 225–226
    using foreign currency in, 580–581
Enter Credit Card Charges window, 272
Enter Payroll Information dialog, 356
Enter Vehicle Mileage dialog, 328
equity, 24
error checking. See reviewing

estimates, 164–166
  creating, 164–165
  customer send method for, 47
  duplicating, 166
  e-mailing, 488
  enabling, 164
  entering in opening trial balance, 140
  memorizing, 166
  multiple job, 166
Excel
  creating tax form worksheets in, 380–382
  exporting budgets to, 454, 455
  exporting report data to, 437
exchange rates for currency, 575
expenses. *See also* reimbursable expenses
  configuring reimbursable, 171–172
  entering in opening trial balance, 140–141
  invoicing customers for reimbursable, 170–177
  splitting among multiple accounts, 225–226
  types of, 25–26
exporting
  budgets, 454–455
  report data to Excel, 437
Express Start wizard, 8, 496
External Accountant user, 421–422
external drives. *See* removable media

• F

Favorites menu, 21
Federal Insurance Contribution Act. *See* FICA withholding
federal taxes
  paying 941/943, 367, 368
  scheduling payment of, 364–365
Federal Unemployment Tax Act. *See* FUTA payments

fees. *See also* finance charges
  calculating credit card merchant's, 200
  NSF service charges, 265, 277
  outside payroll service, 392–393
  paying outside payroll service, 188
  recovering bounced check, 266
  statement charges, 215–216
FICA withholding
  paying from outside payroll service, 390–391
  payroll accounts needed for paying, 335
  remitting payments for, 368
fields
  creating item, 92
  custom customer, 47
  forcing cursor to check's Payee, 531
  option account, 33–34
  pressing ENTER to move between, 535
  setting up custom name, 63
  using custom report, 426
file host computer, 565, 567
files. *See also* company file; PDF files
  attaching, 491–492
  deleting company, 506–507
  .DSN, 506
  exporting budgets as delimited text, 454
  .IFF, 455
  merging changes from accountant's copy, 404–405
  .ND, 506
  providing accountant's copy, 398–399
  .QBB, 515, 517
  .QBW, 506, 517
  saving when downloading Web Connect, 548
  time stamping backup filenames, 511
  .TLG, 506, 507, 517
  transaction log, 517

filtering
    A/R aging data, 206–208
    report data, 428–430
    statements by send methods, 218
    vendor information displayed, 78–79
Filters tab
    Modify Report: A/R Aging Detail
      window, 207
    Modify Report window, 429
finance charge invoices, 212, 214
Finance Charge Preferences dialog, 210–212, 534
finance charges, 210–214
    about, 210
    adding to statements, 219
    assessing, 212–213
    checking history of, 213–214
    configuring, 210–212
    date for assessing, 213
    editing amount of, 213
    including on customer invoice, 213
    printing invoices for, 214
    selecting customers to receive, 213
financial institutions
    downloading transactions from, 293,
      300–301, 302
    enabling Direct Connect access to,
      296–298
    finding online, 293–295
    selecting region for, 297
    setting up Web Connect services with,
      298–301
    transferring money between accounts,
      263–265, 309–310
Financial Institutions Directory, 294
Find & Select Items window, 113
fiscal year
    calendar vs., 460
    running reports for, 428
    setting, 11

Fix This Error Now message, 351
Fixed Asset Item list, 122–123
fixed assets
    defined, 24
    depreciating, 387–389
    running year-end report for, 461
FOB (Free On Board), 547
folders
    creating for company file, 11, 507
    setting permissions for data, 12
fonts
    check, 480
    customizing template, 553
    modifying on reports, 431–432
Fonts & Numbers tab (Modify Report
    window), 431–432
footers
    configuring A/R aging report, 208
    invoice, 147, 152–154
    making template modifications for, 556
foreign currency. See multicurrency option
forgotten Admin password, 497–498
formatting
    A/R aging reports, 209
    check fonts, 480
    designating defaults for reports, 545
    redesigning forms, 556–558
    saving desktop preferences, 532–534
    setting default for time, 317, 538
    specifying report account display, 545
forms. See also specific forms
    aligning for printing, 478, 481
    batch printing of, 486–487
    checking spelling of, 548–549
    choosing printer for, 477
    customizing templates for, 551–553
    e-mailing, 488–491
    Intuit preprinted, 478

previewing printouts of, 486

printing, 477, 485–487

redesigning, 556–558

saving as PDFs, 478

selecting paper for printing, 478

sending by e-mail, 489–490

setting e-mail as preferred method, 547–548

tax form worksheets, 380–382

W-2, 377–380

W-3, 378, 379

W-4, 345

Free On Board (FOB), 547

FUTA (Federal Unemployment Tax Act) payments

    making, 369

    paying from outside payroll service, 390–391

    preparing 940 form for, 376–377

• G

general ledger. *See also* chart of accounts; journal entries

    about, 24, 26

    making journal entries in, 384–386

General Preferences dialog, 317, 534–537

    about, 534

    beeping during transactions, 535–536

    formatting time and date from, 317, 538

    keeping custom item information when editing transactions, 538

    moving between fields, 535

    open drop-down lists while typing, 535

    prefilling account or transaction data, 537

    restoring one-time messages, 536

    running QuickBooks in background, 537

    selecting Company Preferences tab options in, 538–539

    setting default for time, 317

    setting transaction default date, 537

ToolTips for clipped text, 536

turning off pop-up messages from, 536

warning when editing or deleting transaction, 536–537

go live date, 347

graphs

    Budget vs. Actual, 454

    refreshing after editing, 544

    using class data, 418

gross pay calculations, 359

group items, 95–96

groups

    dragging reports to, 434

    memorized bill, 236–237

    memorized report, 433–436

    tax, 100–102

• H

hard drive

    backing up company file to, 509–510

    unattended backups onto, 514–515

Header/Footer tab (Modify Report window), 208, 430, 432

headers

    configuring A/R aging report, 208

    configuring Excel worksheet, 381

    customizing template, 554–555

    options for custom cash sales receipts, 193

help

    manual payroll, 333

    QuickBooks Live Community, 559

hiding

    accounts, 38–39

    detailed data on tax worksheets, 381–382

    inactive customers and jobs, 60–62

    invoice details, 174

    transactions after reconciliation period, 278–279

    vendors, 82

hiring date, 345
historical data
  batch entry of payroll, 348–349
  entering with QuickBooks Payroll Setup
    Wizard, 352
  how to enter payroll, 346–347
  reviewing customer's finance charges,
    213–214
Home page, 14–15

• I

Icon Bar, 18–20
icons
  adding current window, 20
  adding to Icon Bar, 19–20
  displaying without title, 19
  editing appearance of, 19
  online access, 295
  paperclip, 491
  removing, 19
  reordering on Icon Bar, 18–19
  separating, 19
.IFF files, 455
importing
  accountant's copy, 404–405, 406
  budgets back into QuickBooks, 455
  customer and vendor lists, 13–14
inactive accounts, 38–39
inactive customers and jobs, 60–62
inactive inventory items, 111
inactive items, 123
inactive vendors, 82
income
  defined, 25
  entering in opening trial balance, 140–141
  tracking reimbursed expenses as, 550
income accounts, 239–241
income statement. See P&L reports
independent contractors, 346

installing QuickBooks. See also Intuit
  QuickBooks Installer
  on client computers, 565–567
  on client-server network, 568–569
  for non-networked systems, 5–6
Integrated Applications Preferences dialog, 539
interest income, 277
Internal Revenue Service (IRS)
  e-paying, 368
  notification to use 944 form, 371, 377
Internet. See online banking; Direct Connect;
  Web Connect
Intuit
  downloading updates in background, 548
  E-File Service, 469
  EasySaver service, 539
  Intuit Payment Network Service, 310, 542
  preprinted forms, 478
  purchasing checks from, 479
  templates compatible with preprinted
    forms, 551
  turning off pop-up messages from, 536
Intuit QuickBooks Installer
  choosing installation types, 563
  custom and network options for, 563–564,
    566, 568
inventory. See also counting inventory;
  inventory items
  accounts required for, 106
  condensing transactions for, 522
  counting, 110–117
  creating items for, 106–108
  effects of adjustments on, 116
  enabling, 539
  establishing balances for, 141–142
  gathering information about, 5
  getting bills simultaneous with inventory
    items, 233
  making adjustments to, 112–116
  managing purchases of, 229–231
  multiple location tracking for, 104

performing physical, 460
posting of inventory receipts and bills, 221
quantity on hand warnings in, 540
receiving items without bill, 229–231
recording bills for items received, 232–233
setting up Inventory Adjustment Account, 116–117
subitems for, 108–110
tracking, 104–106
types of adjustments for, 117
Inventory Adjustment Account, 116–117
Inventory Asset account, 106
inventory assets, 24
inventory items
about, 89
creating, 106–108
defined, 104
designing parents for subitems, 108–109
getting bills simultaneous with, 233
Intuit review of, 539
receiving without bill, 229–231
recording bills for received, 232–233
using subitems, 108–110
inventory reports
about, 417
Inventory Stock Status report, 118–119
Inventory Valuation Detail report, 118
Inventory Valuation Summary report, 117–118
running, 117–119
invoice header, 147–150
invoices, 146–177. *See also* finance charges;
  packing slips
about, 146
about FOB, 547
adding discounts to, 151
applying credit memos to, 162–164
balance forward or open item systems for, 180
batch invoicing, 156–157
billable time on, 324–325
changing data on, 149, 323
creating for unpaid, 139–140
credits applied to different job, 187
customer send method for, 47
defaults for applying payments on, 180
duplicate, 547
e-mailing, 488
editing, 159
entering previous unpaid, 4
excluding reimbursable expenses on, 175
finance charge, 212, 214
footer section for, 147, 152–154
header information for, 147–150
issuing credits and refunds, 160–164
line items on, 150
marking up reimbursable expenses, 175–177
memorized, 158–159
memos at bottom, 153–154
messages on, 153
method of sending, 154
multiple numbering schemes for, 148
numbering, 148
offering credit without previous, 161
omitting details on, 174
payments applied to, 183–184
posting customer balances from, 44
price levels applied on, 150–151
printing as created, 485–486
progress billing, 167–170
recording payments on, 181–182
recovering bounced check fees, 266
redesigning form for, 556–558
reimbursable expenses on, 170–177
retaining customer credits, 162
saving, 154
subtotals for, 152
templates for, 146–147
underpayments on, 184–185
updating customer name changes on, 55
voiding and deleting, 159–160

IRS. *See* Internal Revenue Service
Issue A Refund window, 162–163
items, 88–102. *See also* inventory items; payroll
   items
      applying price levels to, 150–151
      cautions using fixed asset, 123
      changing prices for, 96–97
      creating NSF check and charge, 265
      custom fields for, 92
      defined, 88
      discount, 89–90, 96
      entering invoice, 150
      entering or changing progress billing
        invoice, 168–170
      group, 95–96
      how QuickBooks uses, 88–89
      importance in job costing, 94
      inventory subitems, 108–110
      mileage, 327
      non-inventory, 89, 93–94, 104
      other charge, 95
      over and short, 196
      payment, 96
      sales tax, 97–100
      service, 89, 90–92
      subtotal, 95
      tax groups, 100–102
      types of, 89–90
Items & Inventory Preferences dialog, 539–540

• J

Job Info tab
   New Customer window, 49–60
   New Job window, 58
Job Type list, 130
jobs. *See also* billable time; Customer:Job
   budgets; estimates
      about, 42, 56
      applying credit to different, 187
      choosing estimate for progressed billing
        invoice, 167–168
      creating, 57–60
      custom fields for, 62–64
      customizing list of, 53–54
      deleting, 60–62
      editing, 60
      entering data for, 49–50
      hiding inactive, 60–62
      items for costing, 94
      merging, 62
      providing estimates for, 164–165
      reports for, 62, 210
      using special pricing for, 123–124
Jobs & Estimates Preferences dialog, 540, 541
journal entries
      A/R account, 204
      about, 384
      beginning balances as, 137–138
      creating, 138, 384–386
      depreciation, 387–389
      entering outside payroll service
        transactions as, 389–393
      options for voiding checks, 268
      when changing accounts, 386–387
      year-end, 470

• L

launching QuickBooks, 5–7
Layout Designer, 556–558
Lead Center, 17
letterhead paper, 478
liabilities. *See also* payroll liabilities
      defined, 24
      gathering balance for, 4
      SDI, 370
Liability Payment window, 367
license requirements for networks, 562, 569
line item section, 147

lists
 about, 122
 automatically opening drop-down, 535
 building customer, 42–52
 Class, 126
 Currency, 125, 574–575
 Customer Message, 131
 Customer Type, 129
 customizing Customers & Jobs, 53–54
 customizing name fields for customer, vendors, and employees, 62–64
 deleting unused list items, 536–537
 Fixed Asset Item, 122–123
 Job Type, 130
 Memorized Transaction, 133
 Other Names, 127–128
 Payment Method, 131–132
 Price Level, 123–124
 removing unused entries in, 522–523
 Sales Rep, 129
 Ship Via, 132
 Templates, 553
 Terms, 130–131
 types of Customer & Vendor Profile, 128–133
 Vehicle, 132–133
 Vendor Type list, 129
loans, 260, 262
local taxes
 about, 254
 preparing annual returns for, 376
 remitting, 369–370
Locate Discrepancies dialog, 286
Locked Template dialog, 553
Locked Template message box, 552
login. See also passwords
 changing password for, 503
 importance of user, 494
 requiring Admin password for, 496
 settings on Icon Bar for, 18

Login dialog, 503–504
logos
 adding to template, 552
 check, 480
long term liabilities, 24

• M

macros in Excel worksheets, 381
magnifying glass pointer, 410
mail
 selecting as customer send method, 47
 sending statements by, 218
Make Deposits window
 adding items to deposit, 199–200
 calculating merchant card fees, 200
 illustrated, 199, 261
 printing deposit slips, 201
 using for noncustomer deposits, 261
Make General Journal Entries window, 138, 384–386
Manage Sales Tax feature, 255
manual checks, 252–254
manual payroll processing, 333
manufacturer's part numbers (MPNs), 227–229
markup percentages, 238, 550
matching downloaded transactions, 302–308
Medicare payments, 335, 368
Memorize Report dialog, 433
Memorize Transaction window, 158
Memorized Transaction list, 133
memorizing
 A/R aging reports, 209
 bill groups, 236–237
 creating, 236, 434
 customized reports, 432–436
 estimates, 166
 invoices, 158–159
 recurring bills, 235–236
 report groups, 433–436

memos on invoices, 153–154
merchant banks, 198, 200
merging
    accounts, 39
    customers and jobs, 62
    vendors, 82
messages. *See also* warnings
    adding on invoices, 153
    bringing back one-time, 536
    turning off pop-up, 536
Microsoft Excel. *See* Excel
Microsoft Outlook, 488–489, 490–491
mileage
    creating mileage items, 327
    entering, 328–329
    rates for, 327
    reports for, 329–330
    tracking, 312, 325–326
Mileage By Job Detail report, 330
Mileage By Job Summary report, 329
Mileage By Vehicle Detail report, 329
Mileage By Vehicle Summary report, 329
missing check numbers, 281–282
Modify Report window
    Customize Report button in, 424
    Display tab, 207, 425
    Filters tab, 207, 428, 429
    Fonts & Numbers tab, 431–432
    Header/Footer tab, 430
    opening before opening reports, 543
MPNs (manufacturer's part numbers), 227–229
Multi-user Hosting Setup Required dialog, 567
multi-user license requirements, 562, 569
Multi-user mode, 565
multicurrency option, 572–582
    backing up before using, 125, 572
    creating customers and vendors using, 576–577

editing customer and vendor currency, 577
    effect on vendor bill amount due, 222
    enabling, 125, 540, 572–574
    reports in different currencies, 582
    selecting currencies, 574–575
    setting vendor's currency, 70
    tracking exchange rates, 575
    transactions using non-USD currency, 579–582
    using, 43
multiple budgets, 441
multiple company files, 7
Multiple Currencies Preferences dialog, 540, 572–574
multiple invoice numbering schemes, 148
multiple job estimates, 166
multiple location inventory tracking, 104
multiple report processing, 435
multiple users. *See also* accountant's copy
multi-user license requirements, 562, 569
    on peer-to-peer networks, 562–567
    types of network installations for, 562
    using client-server installations, 568–569
My Preferences tab (Preferences dialog), 528

• N

names
    entering customer, 42–43, 55
    never updating when saving transactions, 538–539
    setting up custom fields for, 63
naming
    accounts, 30
    company file, 11
    memorized report groups, 434
    vendors, 71–72
navigating in QuickBooks
    centers in, 15–17
    Home page, 14–15

.ND file, 506
networks, 562–569
    backing up company file on, 508
    designating host computers, 565, 567
    importance of user logins, 494
    installing on peer-to-peer, 562–567
    installing QuickBooks on client-server,
        568–569
    QuickBooks multi-user license
        requirements for, 562, 569
    switching to Multi-user mode, 565
    types of installations for, 562
New Class dialog, 126
New Currency dialog, 575
New Customer window
    adding currency in, 576, 578
    Additional Info tab fields, 45–47
    Address Info tab fields for, 42–45
    illustrated, 43
    Job Info tab fields, 49–60
    opening, 42
    Payment Info tab fields, 48–49
New Employee window
    Employment Info tab set, 345
    Payroll Info tab, 343
    Personal Info tab set, 341–342
    tabs for, 341
    Workers Compensation tab set, 345
New Item window, 90–92, 122
New Job window, 58
New Name window, 128
New Price Level window, 124
New Sales Rep window, 129
New Terms window, 130
New Vendor window
    Account Prefill tab, 73–74
    Additional Info tab, 72–73

Address Info tab, 70–71
    illustrated, 71
    opening, 70
non-inventory items
    creating, 93–94
    defined, 89
    Intuit review of, 539
    uses for, 104
noncustomer deposits, 260–263
    assigning accounts to, 263
    entering in bank register, 260–261
    payee assignments to, 261–263
    types of, 260
    using Make Deposits window for, 261
nonposting transactions in opening trial
    balance, 140
nonsufficient funds. *See* NSF
Note field, 33
Notepad window
    keeping notes on vendor with, 79–81
    opening and dating notes, 55
NSF (nonsufficient funds), 265–267
    creating NSF check and charge items, 265
    recording bank's charges for, 267
    recovering bounced check fees, 266
numbering
    accounts, 29
    chart of accounts, 26–29
    checks, 252, 483, 484
    invoices, 148
    multiple types of invoices, 148
    subaccounts, 29, 35

• O

officer employees, 346, 471
online access icon, 295
online backups, 508–509

online banking
    available services for, 292
    avoiding duplicate bank charges for, 277
    bill paying with, 308–309
    connecting with or without password, 548
    deleting unmatched transactions, 307–308
    Direct Connect access for, 296–298
    enabling, 293
    entering downloaded deposits, 307
    matching downloaded transactions to
        bank register, 302–308
    QuickBooks methods for, 292
    receiving online customer payments, 310
    recording downloaded payment in bank
        register, 305–307
    renaming transactions, 304
    setting transaction display for, 532
    transferring money between accounts,
        309–310
    using Online Banking Center, 301
    viewing downloaded transactions, 302
    Web Connect services for, 298–301
Online Banking Center
    defined, 16
    using, 301
    working with downloaded transactions
        in, 303
online payments
    e-paying 941/943 payments, 368
    making, 293, 308–309
    receiving from customers, 310, 542
Open Balance report, 203
open item invoice system, 180
opening
    customer To Do notes, 55
    drop-down lists automatically, 535
    last company file loaded, 506
    Modify Report window before opening
        reports, 543
    previous company, 507
Opening Balance Equity account, 34, 143

opening trial balance, 136–143. See also
    beginning balances
    about, 136–137
    adjusting sales tax payments, 141
    in aging reports, 427
    cautions entering account, 34
    correcting differences in, 288
    creating accurate, 137–143
    entering beginning balances, 137–138
    entering customer's, 44
    establishing bank account balances, 139
    establishing inventory balances, 141–142
    inaccessible for foreign currencies, 577
    information needed for, 2, 3–5
    mid-year income and expenses for, 140–141
    nonposting transactions in, 140
    outstanding checks and deposits in, 139
    running Trial Balance report, 143
    unpaid payables and receivables in, 139–140
    zero out Opening Balance Equity
        account, 143
organizing QuickBooks files, 507
other charge items, 95
Other Names list, 127–128, 315
Outlook, 488–489, 490–491
outside payroll service, 389–393
    handling entries as journal entry, 390–391
    paying fee as operating expense, 188
    payroll account reconciliation, 393
    reconciling payroll outside QuickBooks, 393
    recording transactions from, 389–390
    template for payroll entry with, 392–393
    transferring money to payroll account, 391
Over/Short account, 195
overpaying 941/943 liabilities, 371
overwriting
    backups intentionally, 515
    data with restored backup or portable
        file, 518
    upgrading QuickBooks without, 564
owner employee, 346

• P

P&L budgets, 443–450
    class-based, 450
    compounding in, 447–448
    copying numbers across months, 445–446
    creating, 443–444
    creating Customer:Job budgets, 448–450
    data entry shortcuts for, 444–448
    entering amounts for, 443
    increasing or decreasing figures
        automatically, 446–447
P&L reports
    displaying, 409
    Profit & Loss Budget Overview report, 451
    Profit & Loss Budget Performances
        report, 453
    Profit & Loss By Class report, 418
Profit & Loss Detail report, 411
    Profit & Loss Prev Year Comparison
        report, 411
    Profit & Loss Standard report, 410–411
    Profit & Loss Unclassified report, 418
    Profit & Loss YTD Comparison report, 411
    running year-end, 462
    types of, 410–411
packing slips
    changing default, 155–156
    printing default, 154–155
    template for, 154
paperclip icon, 491
parent accounts
    incorrect posting to, 35
    showing only lowest subaccount, 28,
        37, 529
parent items, 108–109
Password Removed dialog, 498
passwords
    about, 494
    adding or changing Admin, 496–497
    Challenge Question for, 65, 496–497
    changing own, 503

    complex, 65, 66, 401, 495
    connecting to online banking without, 548
    designating administrator, 11
    Direct Connect, 297
    resetting Admin, 497–498
    setting closing date, 473
pausing during bank reconciliation, 284
Pay Bills window, 246
pay stubs, e-mailing, 488
paychecks. *See* checks
payees
    assigning to noncustomer deposits,
        261–263
    autofilling account number in check
        memo, 532
    forcing cursor to check's Payee field, 531
Payment Card Industry Data Security Standard
    (PCI DSS), 64
Payment Info tab (New Customer window),
    48–49
Payment Method list, 131–132
Payment Summary dialog, 251
payments. *See also* cash sales; deposits; payroll
  liabilities
    adding merchant fees for credit card, 200
    applying, 180, 183–184
    automatically applying, 541
    calculating automatically, 180, 182, 542
    cash sales, 191–194
    choosing vendor bills for, 246–248
    credit balances applied to, 185–187
    credit card, 198, 271–273
    credits applied to, 250
    date for bill, 247
    defining payment terms, 46
    depositing, 189–190, 196–198
    discounts for, 131, 187–189, 248–250
    entering downloaded expenses as, 305–307
    finance charges on overdue, 210–214
    making vendor, 244
    matching to invoice, 184

payments (*cont.*)
    method for bill, 247–248
    online customer, 293, 308–309, 310, 542
    partial or full vendor, 248
    printing receipt for, 190
    recording invoice, 181–182
    reporting 1099 vendor, 467
    reviewing amount due with A/R aging reports, 203–209
    sales tax, 99, 100, 257–258
    selecting account for, 247, 248
    sending statements about, 215–220
    sending vendor, 251–252
    separating deposits by method of, 198
    setting customer's method of, 49
    underpayments, 184–185
    using Intuit Payment Network, 542
    using payment items, 96
Payments Preferences dialog, 540–542
    about, 540
    automatically applying payments, 541
    calculating payments automatically, 542
    configuring invoice payments through Intuit Payment Network, 542
    depositing cash in Undeposited Funds account, 542
    illustrated, 541
Payments To Deposit window, 196–197
payroll. *See also* employees; payroll items; payroll liabilities
    accounts needed for, 334–335
    calculating gross pay from net entry, 359
    checking data for, 352, 353
    configuring, 334–339
    creating vendors for, 335
    data review for, 352
    Direct Deposit services for, 332
    Fix This Error Now message, 351

    gathering balance for, 5
    historical employee data for, 346–347
    outside services for, 389–393
    preparing employee W-2 forms, 377–380
    processing manually, 333
    QuickBooks Enhanced Payroll, 359, 375
    reports about, 417
    reviewing payroll checks, 357–358
    running, 355–362
    setting up employee data for, 341–345
    signing up for services, 333
    special runs for, 354–355
    types of QuickBooks's, 332
    using payroll schedules, 353–355
    using QuickBooks Payroll Setup Wizard, 349–352
    year-end procedures for, 461
Payroll & Employee Preferences dialog, 542
Payroll Checkup, 353
Payroll Expenses account, 334
Payroll Info tab (New Employee window), 343
Payroll Item List window, 337
payroll items
    custom setup of, 338–339
    defined, 336
    EZ setup of, 337–338
    types of, 336–337
payroll liabilities
    940 taxes and payments, 367, 369
    941/943 taxes and payments, 367, 368
    944 form preparations, 377
    annual FUTA returns, 376–377
    configuring employee tax data, 343–344
    confirming payment schedules for, 364–365
    handling outside payroll service remittances of, 391–392
    making FICA payments, 368
    making state and local returns, 376

other types of, 370–371
preparing annual 941/943 returns, 376
remitting, 365–370
state and local remittances for, 369–370
wizard set up for, 352
workers comp, 371
Payroll Liabilities account, 334
payroll schedules
about, 353
assigning to employees, 354–355
confirming liability payment schedules, 364–365
creating, 354
Payroll Setup Wizard, 337–338
Payroll tab (Employee Center), 360, 361
Payroll Tax Form window, 373, 378, 379
PCI DSS (Payment Card Industry Data Security Standard), 64
PDF files
e-mailing, 488
printing forms as, 478
saving accountant's copy changes as, 405
peer-to-peer QuickBooks installation, 562–567
Pending Builds report, 119
pension plans, paying from outside payroll service, 390–391
permissions. *See also* passwords
accessing credit card data, 67–68, 501
Admin privileges in QuickBooks, 495
configuring user, 499–501
editing existing transactions, 502
logins linked to, 494
reasons for using, 494
required to view payroll data, 360
restricting sensitive accounting data, 501–502
setting for company file, 12
when Login dialog appears, 503–504

personal identification number. *See* PIN
Personal Info tab set (New Employee window), 341–342
petty cash
account for, 269, 270–271
tracking, 269
Physical Inventory Worksheet, 110–111, 119
PIN (personal identification number)
about, 293
entering for Direct Connect, 297
portable company file
backups vs., 517
creating, 517–519
defined, 517
overwriting data with restored, 518
restoring, 519
posting
inventory receipts and bills, 221
inventory receipts and bills to A/P account, 231
outside payroll service in journal, 389–390
reimbursable expenses to income account, 239–241
transactions to correct subaccount, 35
Preferences dialog
about, 528
Accounting options in, 26–27, 528–534
adjusting job status descriptions, 58–60
Bills options in, 530
Calendar options in, 530
Checking options in, 530–532
Company Preferences tab for, 529
configuring reimbursement settings, 171–172
Desktop View options in, 532–534
enabling account numbering, 26–29
enabling inventory tracking, 104–105
Finance Charge options in, 210–212, 534

Preferences dialog (*cont.*)
    Integrated Applications options in, 539
    Items & Inventory options in, 539–540
    Jobs & Estimates options in, 540, 541
    making estimates available from, 164
    Multiple Currencies options in, 125, 540
    My Preferences tab for, 528
    options in General, 534–537
    paying workers comp, 371
    Payments options in, 540–542
    Payroll & Employee options for, 542
    providing 1099 forms, 85, 463–470
    Reminders options in, 542–543
    Reports & Graphs options in, 543–546
    Sales & Customers options in, 546–547
    Sales Tax options, 547
    saving transactions automatically before printing, 154
    selecting progress billing invoices, 167
    Send Forms options, 547–548
    Service Connection options in, 548
    setting default time format, 317
    setting sales tax, 97, 98
    setting up e-mail, 488–489, 490
    Spelling options, 548–549
    Tax:1099 options in, 549
    Time & Expense options for, 549–550
    time tracking options in, 313–314
    tracking classes, 319
    tracking reimbursable expenses, 238
    turning off invoice name update feature, 149
    using discounts and credits, 248
    using price levels, 123, 547
prefilling information on vendor bills, 73–74, 537
preprinted forms
    about Intuit, 478
    templates designed to work with, 551
Preview Your Company Settings window, 8

previewing
    form printouts, 486
    selected timesheets, 324
    statements, 220
Price Level list, 123–124
price levels
    applying on invoices, 150–151
    creating, 124
    customizing customer, 47
    enabling use of, 123, 547
    linking to customers, 124
prices for items, 96–97
Print Check dialog, 483
Print Invoices window, 487
Print Packing Slip window, 155
Printer Setup dialog, 476, 479
printers
    aligning forms for, 478
    checking check alignment for, 481
    choosing for forms, 477
    configuring, 476, 479
    printing partial check pages, 480–481
    reprinting checks, 485
    setting up for checks, 479
    types of settings for, 481–482
printing, 476–487
    941/943 form, 375
    1099 forms, 469–470
    account names on vouchers, 530
    aligning forms for, 478, 481
    A/R aging reports, 209
    batches of checks, 254
    batches of forms, 486–487
    cash sales receipts, 193
    changing check date when, 531
    checks, 479–485
    choosing paper for form, 478
    configuring, 476–477

default packing slips, 154–155
deposit slips, 201
displaying reconciliation report vs., 283, 284
finance charge invoices, 214
forms, 478, 485–487
partial check pages, 480–481
payment checks, 251
payment receipts, 190
Physical Inventory Worksheet, 110–111
reconciliation report, 282–284
saving transactions before, 154, 539
selecting printer for, 477
setting up form, 477
statements, 219, 220
weekly timesheets, 323–324
Process Multiple Reports dialog, 435
Profit & Loss reports. *See* P&L reports
Profit and Loss budgets. *See* P&L budgets
progress billing invoices, 167–170
choosing estimate for, 167–168
enabling, 167
entering or changing line items on, 168–170
illustrated, 169
projecting cash flow, 455–458
purchase orders
creating, 226–227
duplicate numbers for, 539
e-mailing, 488
enabling, 539
ordering inventory or parts using, 226
printing as created, 485–486
using part numbers on, 227–229
warning about duplicate, 105
Purchase Orders account, 226
Purchases reports, 417
purchasing QuickBooks checks, 479

• Q

.QBB file, 515, 517
.QBW file, 506, 517
quantity on hand (QOH) warnings, 540
Quick Launch toolbar, 6
QuickBooks. *See also* setting up QuickBooks
accounts used by, 24–26
Admin privileges in, 495
Attach Documents feature, 491–492
before you setup, 2
closing the books, 21, 472–473
creating company file, 6, 7–14
customizing for industry, 10
Direct Deposit services for payroll, 332
e-mail solutions in, 488–489, 491
Enhanced Payroll, 359, 375
getting help for, 559
Home page for, 14–15
importing budgets back into, 455
installing and launching, 5–7
items in, 88–89
keeping open after Web Connect done, 548
multi-user license requirements for, 562, 569
opening company files, 506
other information needed for setup, 5
payroll services available for, 332–333, 380
printer settings in, 481–482
purchasing checks for, 479
reconciling payroll outside, 393
requirements for client-server networks, 568
selective access permissions in, 499–500
sharing data with third-party applications, 539
starting automatically and running in background, 537
switching to Multi-user mode, 565
turning off Intuit pop-up messages, 536

QuickBooks (*cont.*)
  updating, 524–525
  upgrading, 6, 564
  uploading accountant's copy to secure
    server, 399, 400–404
  using on peer-to-peer networks, 562–567
QuickBooks 1099 Wizard, 465–468
QuickBooks Bill Pay Service, 308–309
QuickBooks Billing Solutions, 488–489, 491
QuickBooks Database Server Manager window,
  565, 566
QuickBooks Enterprise Solutions, 106
QuickBooks Live Community, 559
QuickBooks Login dialog, 497
QuickBooks Merchant Service, 200
QuickBooks Payroll Setup Wizard, 349–352
  about, 349–350
  Company Setup section, 351
  employee setup, 351–352
  entering payroll history in, 352
  illustrated, 350
  payroll tax setup, 352
  reviewing and checking data for, 352, 353
  scheduling payroll liabilities, 364–365
QuickBooks Point of Sale, 191
QuickBooks Setup Wizard, 7, 13–14
QuickBooks Time Tracker, 312
QuickBooks Transfer Funds Between Accounts
  window, 310
QuickReports
  Customer Center, 203
  Inventory, 119

• R

RA (Return Authorization) numbers, 234
rebate checks, 260, 261, 262
rebuilding company file, 519–520
recalling previous transactions, 537

receipts
  printing payment, 190
  sales, 191
Receive Payments window
  depositing payments from, 189–190
  illustrated, 181
  setting customer payment method, 49
  showing payment toolbar on, 546
reconciling bank accounts, 276–290
  adding transactions while, 279–280
  clearing transactions, 279
  configuring Begin Reconciliation window,
    277–278
  correcting opening balance differences, 288
  deleting transactions while, 280
  downloading bank statements, 293,
    300–301, 302
  editing transactions while, 280
  entering interest income and service
    charges, 277
  entering payroll check details when,
    393–394
  finding and correcting problems, 284–285
  finding differences in beginning
    balances, 286
  finishing, 282
  giving up search for errors, 290
  hiding transactions after reconciliation
    period, 278–279
  making deposits while, 280
  permitting adjusting entries, 285
  printing reconciliation report, 282–284
  resolving missing check numbers,
    281–282
  stopping while, 284
  undoing last reconciliation, 289
  using Begin Reconciliation window,
    276–277
reconciling payroll account, 393

Record An Expense window, 306
recurring vendor bills, 235–237
redesigning templates, 556–558
refunds, 162–163
regular employees, 345
reimbursable expenses
    adding taxes to, 174
    adding to sales transactions, 173–177
    applying automatic markups, 238, 550
    changing amount of, 175
    configuring preferences for, 171–172
    creating transaction for, 172, 173
    defined, 237
    excluding, 175
    invoicing for, 170–177, 546–547
    marking up, 175–177
    methods for managing, 237
    posting to income account, 239–241
    recording, 241–242
    removing from list, 175
    splitting among customers, 241–242
    tracking, 238, 241, 550
    voiding or deleting transactions having, 177
Reimbursed Expenses account, 240–241
reimbursements paid from Other Names list, 127
reminders
    backup, 511
    setting task, 542–543
remitting
    1099 and 1096 forms, 469–470
    FICA payments, 368
    liabilities through outside payroll service, 391–392
    payroll liabilities, 365–367
    sales taxes, 100, 254–258
    state and local payroll liabilities, 369–370
    SUI, 370

remote company file backups, 508–509
removable media
    backing up company file to, 508, 509–510
    copying accounting files on, 399
    creating portable company file on, 517–519
    unattended backups onto, 514–515
removing
    all transactions, 523–524
    icons from Icon Bar, 19
renaming transactions, 304
reopening 941/943 form, 374–375
reordering icons on Icon Bar, 18–19
Report Center
    defined, 16
    illustrated, 408
    using, 408–409
reports. *See also* A/R aging reports; P&L reports; *and specific reports*
    accountant and taxes, 418
    Audit Trail, 494
    banking, 417
    budget, 451–454
    Cash Flow, 413–415, 545–546
    Cash Flow Forecast, 415
    Collections Center, 203
    creating tax code, 256–257
    customer and job, 210
    customizing, 424
    data included on inactive jobs, 62
    detail, 410, 425, 521
    Discrepancy, 287
    displaying in Report Center, 408–409
    e-mailing, 488–491
    editing timesheet entries on, 322
    exporting to Excel, 437
    filtering data in, 428–430

reports (*cont.*)
 formatting defaults for, 545
 found on Employees & Payroll
  submenu, 417
 individual class, 417
 inventory, 117–119
 inventory and purchasing, 417
 memorizing customized, 432–436
 memorizing standard, 209
 mileage, 329–330
 Missing Checks, 281–282
 modifying columns in, 426
 multicurrency, 582
 open balance in aging, 427
 opening Modify Report window before
  opening, 543
 Pending Builds, 119
 Physical Inventory Worksheet, 110–111
 QuickReports, 119, 203
 reconciliation, 282–284
 refreshing after editing, 544
 reporting on all classes, 428
 restricting access to sensitive, 501–502
 running year-end financial reports,
  462–463
 Sales, 415–416
 sales taxes, 255–257
 setting calendar basis for, 428
 sharing customized, 436
 specifying accounting basis for
  summary, 544
 specifying advanced options for, 426–428
 specifying display format for accounts
  on, 545
 standard financial, 410–415
 Statement of Cash Flows, 413–414
 summary, 435, 544
 timesheet, 322
 Trial Balance, 143, 413

 using memorized report groups, 433–436
 vendor, 416–417
 viewing Client Data Review, 420–421
 Voided and Deleted Transactions, 419
 Voided and Deleted Transactions
  reports, 160
Reports & Graphs Preferences dialog, 543–546
reprinting checks, 485
Reset QuickBooks Administrator Password
 dialog, 498
resetting
 forgotten Admin password, 497–498
 passwords, 65
restoring
 company file, 6, 507, 516–517, 518
 portable company file, 519
Retained Earnings warning, 138
retained earnings, 24
Return Authorization (RA) numbers, 234
revenue. *See* income
Review And Create Paychecks window, 357
reviewing
 941/943 forms, 374
 1099s, 468
 finding reconciliation errors, 284–285, 290
 Fix This Error Now message, 351
 payroll checks, 357–358
 payroll data, 352, 353
 W-2 forms, 380
rows
 adjusting budget figures automatically
  in, 447
 clearing in new budgets, 446
 report, 427, 428
running payroll
 changing paycheck data, 356
 creating checks before, 355–356
 printing checks, 479–481

• S

Sales & Customers Preferences dialog, 546–547
sales receipts
    custom template for cash, 193
    customizing options for, 546–547
    e-mailing, 488
    handling cash sales with, 191–192
    illustrated, 192
    printing, 193
    using payment toolbar for, 546
Sales reports, 415–416
sales representatives
    adding field in New Job window for, 58
    assigning to customers, 46–47
    defined, 129
    Sales Rep list, 129
Sales tax Adjustment dialog, 258
sales tax codes
    assigning to customers, 101–102
    using, 99
sales tax items, 97–100
Sales Tax Liability report, 256
Sales Tax Preferences dialog, 547
sales taxes
    adding to reimbursable expenses, 174
    adjusting payment amounts, 258
    codes for, 99, 101–102
    collecting from customers, 47
    creating tax code reports, 256–257
    paying, 99, 100, 257–258
    payment adjustments during setup, 141
    remitting, 254–258
    reports for, 255–257
    setting preferences for, 97, 98
    using Manage Sales Tax feature, 255
    using sales tax items, 97–100
saving
    accountant's copy as PDF, 405
    accountant's copy on removable media, 399

    backups, 511–512
    budgets automatically, 440–441
    company file, 11
    finance charge invoices, 214
    invoices, 154
    memorized report in group, 435
    QuickBooks desktop when closing
        company, 533–534
    and reopening 941/943 form, 374–375
    transactions before printing, 154, 539
    when downloading Web Connect data, 548
Schedule B of 941/943 form, 372, 373
scheduling backups, 512–515
SDI liabilities, 370
Search feature, 547
security. See also passwords; permissions
    credit card security log, 68
    standards for credit card, 64
Select Employees For Form W-2/W-3 window,
    378, 379
Select Invoices To Print window, 487
Select Item Receipt dialog, 232
Select Payroll Form dialog, 378
Send Accountant's Copy window, 400
Send Forms Preferences dialog, 488–489, 490,
    547–548
send methods
    choosing invoice, 154
    e-mail as default, 547–548
    filtering statements by, 218
    setting customer, 47
separating or grouping icons, 19
server installation of QuickBooks, 569
service charges
    creating line item for NSF, 265
    reconciling, 277
Service Connection Preferences dialog, 548
service items, 89, 90–92
Set Closing Date And Password dialog, 473

Set Up Account For Online Services For
Company Checking Account dialog, 296,
297, 298
Set Up Budget window, 444–448
Set Up Custom Fields For Items dialog, 92
Set Up User Password And Access window, 500
Set Up YTD Amounts Wizard, 348–349
setting up QuickBooks, 9–13
checking opening balances with Trial
Balance, 143
choosing company's legal entity, 11
creating opening trial balance, 136–143
designating administrator password, 11
entering company information, 9–10
fiscal year setup in, 11
information needed for setup, 5
launching Easy Step Interview, 9
saving and naming company file, 11
selecting business type in, 10
steps before, 2
sharing
customized reports, 436
QuickBooks data with other applications,
37, 539
Ship Via list, 132
shipping addresses
multiple customer, 44–45
updating customer name changes on, 55
shipping method, 546
Show Estimates report, 203
shrinkage, 112
sick pay, 344
signatures on checks, 480
Single Activity form
about, 316
saving and viewing on Weekly Timesheet
form, 316
using, 317–320
Single-User mode, 399
skipping statements, 219

snapshot of company data, 419–420
social security number, entering for company, 10
sorting
chart of accounts, 26, 27, 29
order for reconciled transactions, 278
vendor bills, 246–247
Specify Invoice Amounts For Items On
Estimate window, 170
Spelling Preferences dialog, 548–549
standard financial reports, 410–415
about, 410
Balance Sheet, 411–413
Profit & Loss reports, 410–411
running year-end, 462–463
Trial Balance, 143, 413
start date
defined, 2
running Trial Balance report for, 143
selecting, 2–3
Start menu, 6
state taxes
about, 254
preparing annual returns for, 376
remitting, 369–370
scheduling liability payments, 364–365
state unemployment insurance. See SUI
statement charges, 215–216
statements, 215–220
assessing finance charges on, 219
creating, 217–219
customer send method for, 47
customizing, 220
e-mailing, 488
entering statement charges, 215–216
previewing, 220
printing, 219, 220
selecting date range for, 217
sending, 215
skipping, 219

status stamps, 553
statutory employees, 346
stopwatch, 320
strong passwords, 65, 66, 401, 495
subaccounts
    creating, 36
    multiple levels of, 36–37
    needed for payroll processing, 334–335
    sharing data with other applications, 37
    showing only lowest, 28, 37, 529
    timely payment discount, 249
    using, 26, 35
    viewing, 35–36
subclasses, 127
subitems, 108–110
subtotals
    invoice, 152
    subtotal items, 95
SUI (state unemployment insurance)
    deducting, 344
    remitting payment for, 370
    scheduling payment of, 364–365
summary reports
    about, 425
    effect of data removal on, 520–521
    specifying accounting basis for, 544
summary transactions, 520–521

• T

Tax:1099 Preferences dialog, 549
tax form worksheets, 380–382
tax groups, 100–102
tax ID, 9–10
Tax-Line Mapping field, 33
taxes. *See also* payroll liabilities; sales taxes
    configuring employee data for, 343–344
    designating form used for, 471
    electronic payroll tax deposits, 335

    including vehicle mileage on tax return, 326
    mapping in accounts, 33
    payment priority for, 244
    preparing annual 941/943 returns, 376
    remitting state and local, 369–370
    running reports for tax year, 428
    scheduling payment of, 364–365
    setting preferences for, 547
    setting up payroll with wizard, 352
    using Excel tax form worksheets, 380–382
    using TurboTax to do, 472
    year-end procedures for, 470–472
Taxes dialog, 343–344
templates, 551–558
    additional customization options for, 553–558
    basic customization of, 550, 551–553
    changing company information on, 553
    changing headers, 554–555
    column modifications for, 555–556
    compatible with Intuit preprinted forms, 551
    creating employee, 339–341
    custom colors on, 552
    customizing, 550–551
    defined, 550
    estimate, 165
    fonts customization on, 553
    invoice, 146–147
    list of, 553
    logos on, 552
    making footer modifications on, 556
    managing, 552
    modifying cash sales, 193
    packing slip, 154
    payroll entry, 392–393
    redesigning, 556–558
    status stamps on, 553
    types available, 147

Templates list, 553
termination
    entering date of, 345
    running checks for, 355
terms
    customer payment, 46
    vendor bill due date with, 224
Terms list, 130–131
text, showing ToolTips for clipped, 536
time. *See also* time tracking; timesheets
    billable, 171, 324–325, 546–547
    setting default format for, 317, 538
    time stamping backup filenames, 511
Time & Expenses Preferences window, 238,
    312–313, 549–550
Time/Enter Single Activity window, 318
time stamps in backup filenames, 511
time tracking. *See also* timesheets
    about, 312, 313
    configuring timesheet tasks, 315–316
    invoicing customers for time, 324–325
    linking employees to, 314–315, 319
    prompting for billable time, 171
    recording data on Weekly Timesheets,
        320–321
    setting default time format, 317, 538
    setting up, 312–315
    stopwatch for, 320
    Time By Item report, 322
    Time By Job Detail report, 322
    Time By Job Summary report, 322
    Time By Name report, 322
    tracking vendor time, 315
    using Other Names list for, 315
    using Single Activity form, 317–320
timesheets. *See also* Weekly Timesheet form
    changing report entries from, 322
    configuring tasks on, 315–316

copying previous, 322
editing original, 323
filling out online, 312
printing weekly, 323–324
recording data on Weekly, 320–321
running reports from, 322
Single Activity, 316–320
types of, 316
.TLG file, 506, 507, 517
To Do lists, 55–56, 81, 460
ToolTips for clipped text, 536
totals. *See* subtotals
tracking inventory. *See* inventory
Tracking Multiple Currencies dialog, 573
transaction log file, 517
transactions. *See also* journal entries;
    memorizing; *and specific transactions*
    adding during bank reconciliation, 279–280
    attaching files to, 491–492
    beeping when recording, 535–536
    calendar display for upcoming and past
        due, 530
    changing currency in open, 577–578
    clearing during reconciliation, 279
    condensing data, 520–524
    configuring Begin Reconciliation, 277–278
    correcting reconciliation, 288
    creating reimbursable expenses, 172, 173
    default date for new, 537
    deleting during reconciliation, 280
    deleting unmatched downloaded, 307–308
    downloading from bank, 293, 300–301, 302
    e-mailing, 488
    editing while reconciling accounts, 280
    enabling inventory, 539
    GJE, 384
    hiding after reconciliation period, 278–279
    keeping custom item information when
        editing, 538

list of memorized, 133
never updating names when saving,
    538–539
nonposting, 140
permission to edit existing, 502
posting to correct subaccount, 35
printing as created, 485–486
recalling previous, 537
recording outside payroll service, 389–390
removing all, 523–524
removing selected, 522
renaming rules for, 304
saving before printing, 154, 539
selecting for statements, 217
setting online banking display for, 532
sorting order for, 278
summary, 520–521
using non-USD currency, 579–582
viewing downloaded, 302
voided and deleted invoices, 159–160
voiding one with reimbursable expense, 177
warning when editing, 536
Transactions tab
    Customer Center, 52, 53
    Employee Center, 360, 361
Transfer Funds Between Accounts window,
    263, 264
Trial Balance report. *See also* opening trial
    balance
    checking opening balances with, 143
    viewing, 413
TurboTax, 472

• **U**

UNC (Universal Naming Convention), 515
Undeposited Funds account
    automatically posting payments to, 180
    depositing cash receipts into, 190
    designating default for deposits, 542

underpaying
    941/943 liabilities, 371
    invoices, 184–185
undoing last reconciliation, 289
Universal Naming Convention (UNC), 515
unmatched transactions, 303, 307–308
Unpaid Bills Detail window, 244–245
unscheduled payroll liability payments, 365
unscheduled payroll runs, 354–355
unvoided transactions, defined, 160
Update QuickBooks window, 525
updating
    names when saving transactions, 538–539
    QuickBooks, 524–525, 548
upgrading
    QuickBooks on network, 6
    without overwriting previous
        QuickBooks, 564
uploading accountant's copy, 399, 400–404
U.S. Treasury Department
    payroll accounts needed for paying, 335
    preparing 941/943 Form for, 371–374
USB drives. *See* removable media
users. *See also* Admin user; permissions
    accessing sensitive activities and reporting,
        501–502
    adding, 498–499
    changing own password, 503
    configuring preferences for, 561
    converting to External Accountant, 422
    creating External Accountant, 421–422
    deleting, 499
    editing information about, 499
    importance of logins for, 494
    managing, 494
    officer employees, 346, 471
    permissions to edit existing
        transactions, 502
    setting permissions for, 499–501

• V

vacation pay, 344
Vehicle list, 132–133
vehicle mileage. *See* mileage
vendor bills
    adding memorized bills to groups, 236–237
    applying discounts to, 248–250
    choosing A/P account for paying, 247
    creating for unpaid, 139–140
    creating memorized bill groups, 236
    default due date for, 224
    entering, 222–224, 530
    entering previous unpaid, 4
    full or partial payment of, 248
    making payments, 244
    methods for paying, 222, 247–248, 530
    paying online, 308–309
    payment date for, 247
    posting of inventory receipts and, 221
    prefilling information on, 73–74, 537
    receiving inventory items without, 229–231
    recording reimbursable expenses, 241–242
    recurring, 235–237
    reimbursable expenses on, 237–242
    selecting for payment, 246–248
    sending payments for, 251–252
    showing all, 247
    sorting by due date, 246–247
    splitting expenses among accounts, 225–226
    taking discounts after discount date, 250
    treating credit card as, 273
    viewing unpaid, 244–245
    writing checks without entering, 252

Vendor Center
    customizing, 77–79
    defined, 15, 76
    displaying currency data in, 578–579
    illustrated, 76
    using, 76–77
Vendor Type list, 129
vendors. *See also* vendor bills
    adding and editing multiple records for, 74–76
    applying discounts to payments, 249–250
    changing currency in open transactions, 577–578
    creating list of, 70–76
    creating payroll, 335
    creating state tax liability, 370
    currency settings for, 70
    custom fields for, 83–84
    customizing display in Vendor Center, 77–78
    deleting, 81–82
    editing currency for, 577
    editing data about, 79–81
    filtering data displayed for, 78–79
    gathering balance for, 4
    hiding inactive, 82
    importing lists of, 13–15
    including custom name field for, 62–64
    merging, 82
    naming, 71–72
    pre-filling accounts for, 537
    recording credits offered by, 233–234
    reports for, 416–417
    requiring 1099 forms, 72, 73, 85–86, 463–470
    sorting bills by, 247

tracking time by, 315
using multicurrency option for, 576–577
verifying
backup data, 511
company file, 519
viewing
Discrepancy report, 287
downloaded bank transactions, 302
multiple QuickBooks windows, 532–533
packing slips before printing, 155–156
reconciliation report, 283, 284, 288
reports in Report Center, 408–409
security log, 68
subaccounts, 35–36
unpaid vendor bills, 244–245
ViewMyPaycheck.com, 380
Voided and Deleted Transactions Detail History
reports, 160, 419
Voided and Deleted Transactions Summary
reports, 160, 419
voiding
bank disbursements, 267–268
invoices, 159–160
transactions with reimbursable
expenses, 177
voucher checks, 480
vouchers, printing account names on, 530

• W

W-2 forms
making available online, 380
preparing, 377–380
W-3 forms, 378, 379
W-4 forms, 345
wallet checks, 480

warnings
duplicate check number, 531
duplicate invoices, 547
duplicate purchase order numbers, 539
duplicate purchase orders, 105
insufficient inventory quantities, 105
quantity on hand, 540
when editing transactions, 536
Web Connect
defined, 292
keeping QuickBooks open after done, 548
services available with, 301
setting preferences for, 548
website for bank, 298–301
Weekly Timesheet form
about, 316
illustrated, 321
recording data on, 320–321
viewing all single activities on, 316
Windows operating system
client-server network requirements for, 568
QuickBooks requirements for peer-to-peer
network operation, 562
workers comp payments, 371
Workers Compensation tab set (New Employee
window), 345
worksheets
Physical Inventory Worksheet, 110–111
tax form, 380–382
Write Checks window
not used for sales tax payments, 257
recording petty cash payments in,
269–270
using, 253–254
Write Off Amount dialog, 184

• Y

year-end procedures, 460–473
    closing the books, 472–473
creating fixed asset report, 461
    creating To Do list for, 460
    issuing 1099 forms, 463–470
    making journal entries, 470
    payroll, 461
    performing physical inventory, 460

    preparing for taxes, 470–472
    reconciling bank, cash, and credit card
      accounts, 460
    running year-end financial reports,
      462–463
    year-end backups, 473

• Z

zero out Opening Balance Equity account, 143